Invitaciones

An Interactive Worktext for Beginning Spanish

Deana Alonso-Lyrintzis
Southwestern College

Esther Alonso
Southwestern College

Brandon Zaslow
Occidental College

Lab Activities

Beverly Burdette
Pellissippi State Community College

VISTA
HIGHER LEARNING

Boston, Massachusetts

Publisher: José A. Blanco

President: Stephen Pekich

Editorial Director: Denise St. Jean

Director of Production: Nancy Jones

Art Director: Linda Jurras

Senior Designer: Polo Barrera

Design Team: Linde Gee

Staff Editors: Sarah Kenney, Alicia Spinner

Contributing Writers and Editors: Francisco de la Rosa, Gabriela Ferland, Claudi Mimó, Lourdes Murray

Production Team: María Eugenia Castaño, Oscar Díez, Mauricio Henao, Charles Leo, Ray Levesque, Kristin Mehring

Student Text ISBN-13: 978-1-59334-219-7
          ISBN-10: 1-59334-219-5

Library of Congress Card Number: 2003108875

6 7 8 9 RRD 11 10 09 08

Dedication

At the time of his tragic death on August 15, 1996, my husband, **Costas Lyrintzis,** was a professor of Aerospace Engineering at San Diego State University. He was loved and respected by his students and colleagues because of his friendliness, his intelligence and his ability to smile and make others feel better, even in the worst of times.

Even though his death made the process of writing this book so much more difficult, he has been with us all along the way. His memory gave us strength, his faith in us and our ability to contribute to the teaching of Spanish kept us going at times when we wanted to quit. Our desire to write a book worthy of him and his memory raised our spirits.

We all love you, Costas. Our lives will never be the same without you.

Deana Alonso-Lyrintzis

Introduction

Bienvenido a INVITACIONES, your invitation to the rich language and the diverse cultures of the Spanish-speaking world! This program takes a communicative approach to developing your ability to use and understand Spanish in practical, everyday contexts. It also aims at building your cultural knowledge and competency.

▶ Unique interactive worktexts

A brand new program, **INVITACIONES** consists of two volumes, **Primera parte** and **Segunda parte**. Both are interactive worktexts, the first of their kind published for introductory college Spanish. Because you write in and otherwise "interact" with the lessons, the worktexts are spiral-bound, with paperback covers and perforated pages for easy removal.

▶ Five resources in one package

Each **INVITACIONES** worktext contains fifteen lessons, called *episodes*, and each episode is organized in exactly the same way: full-color lesson pages, immediately followed by black-and-white pages with workbook and lab activities. As a result, the worktext offers you three printed learning tools you need for learning Spanish in one self-contained volume. In addition, each new worktext comes packaged with the **INVITACIONES** Video CD-ROM and the Worktext & Lab MP3 Files Audio CD-ROM, ensuring that you have one convenient package with the multimedia ancillaries you need for success in your introductory Spanish course.

▶ Video-driven program

Specially shot for **INVITACIONES**, the video revolves around the everyday lives and relationships of a group of Spanish-speaking friends from various countries as they attend college in the United States. Photos from the video, events from the storyline, and characters from the episodes are systematically integrated into virtually every section of each lesson, including the workbook and lab activities.

▶ Personalized learning experience

Throughout the full-color pages of its lessons, **INVITACIONES** invites you to interact with the worktext by filling in information that interests you, prompting personalized reactions, and by providing ideas for use with a partner, small groups, or the entire class. As you work through each lesson, you will find that the worktext consistently gives you the support you need to carry out real-life tasks in Spanish.

To familiarize yourself with the worktext's organization and features, turn to page xiv and take the **INVITACIONES: Primera parte**-at-a-glance tour. For more information on **INVITACIONES: Segunda parte**, see page xxx.

	Escenas de la vida	**Para comunicarnos mejor**

Escenas de la vida

opens every lesson with an input-driven *and* video-based introduction to the lesson's theme, vocabulary, and grammar.

Objetivos comunicativos This brief list highlights the real-life tasks you will be able to carry out in Spanish by the end of the lesson in terms of language functions.

The INVITACIONES Video The **Escenas de la vida** sections in your worktext are designed to be used in conjunction with the corresponding **Escenas de la vida** video episode on the **INVITACIONES** video. The episodes tell the story of a group of Spanish-speaking friends attending college in the United States. To learn more about the video, turn to pages xxvi – xxvii in this at-a-glance tour.

Video Stills Images from the lesson's video episode set the scene for the video, visually support the topic and vocabulary being presented, and preview the grammatical structures of the lesson in context and in a comprehensible way.

Activities The **Escenas de la vida** activities guide you through the lesson's video episode and check your understanding of the key events and ideas. Frequently, activities are set up to let you interact hands-on with the materials by writing directly in your worktext.

Cultura a lo vivo Brief readings deepen your understanding of culture by providing an analysis of the video characters' behavior or by expanding on cultural concepts mentioned in the video.

Práctica adicional Cross-references to the **Cuaderno de tareas** part of your worktext let you know exactly which activities and technology ancillaries are available to reinforce **Escenas de la vida**.

Para comunicarnos mejor

presents the grammatical structures necessary to carry out the real-life tasks of the lesson.

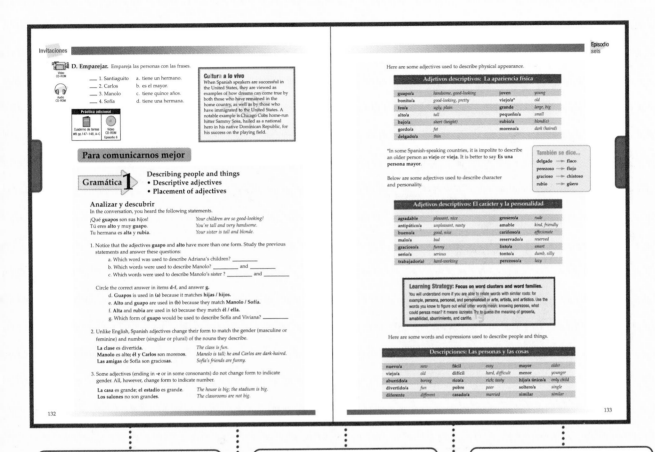

Gramática Grammatical concepts previewed in **Escenas de la vida** activities and featured in the corresponding **Escenas de la vida** video episode are presented in the grammar section of your worktext.

Analizar y descubrir This section appears, when appropriate, to guide you in analyzing and discovering grammatical structures and patterns featured in **Escenas de la vida**, before you use them in upcoming practice activities.

Examples Examples, frequently taken from the lesson's video episode, highlight the language and structures you are studying and put them in real-life contexts.

Charts Colorful, easy-to-use charts call out key grammatical structures and forms, as well as vocabulary fundamental to communicating with the structures at hand.

Learning Strategy Learning strategy boxes, related to specific language-learning tasks, present general techniques you can use to maximize your learning opportunities.

Para comunicarnos mejor
also focuses on the vocabulary necessary to carry out the real-life tasks of the lesson.

Vocabulario These sections present words and expressions taken from the lesson's video episode, as well as additional vocabulary related to the lesson's topic, using the same type of charts, examples, and other elements as in the **Gramática** sections.

Visual support New featured vocabulary is generally introduced through or supported by illustrations, photographs, or images from the lesson's **Escenas de la vida** video episode.

También se dice In recognition of the richness and diversity of the Spanish language, this feature presents alternate words and expressions used throughout the Spanish-speaking world.

Cultura a lo vivo Brief cultural notes appear, where applicable, to provide background information related to the vocabulary topic.

Para comunicarnos mejor
provides varied types of guided, yet meaningful practice.

Práctica A wide variety of guided, yet meaningful activities develop both your language skills and your ability to express yourself in Spanish. Often, cultural information is also often embedded in these activities, as an integral part of their content.

Listening comprehension Listening activities based on real-life interactions are built into your worktext to develop your listening comprehension skills.

Progression of activities To build your confidence and accurate use of Spanish, the activities generally begin with those that require only comprehension and progress to those in which you produce and use the language.

Activity types Activity types include oral exercises, written activities, exercises that recycle previously learned vocabulary, pair work, and small group work. As in **Escenas de la vida**, activities are often set up to let you interact hands-on with the materials by writing directly in your worktext.

Banco de palabras These boxes provide you with on-the-spot vocabulary support directly related to the activities they accompany, so you may readily complete the language tasks at hand.

Icons Icons allow you to quickly identify the types of activities you are dealing with: listening, video viewing, reading, writing, pair work, and group work.

Para comunicarnos mejor
also features personalized and video-related activities.

Práctica Activities in diverse formats offer opportunities for personal responses, as well as contexts that deepen the storyline of the **INVITACIONES** video. In addition, there is always one activity that asks you to carry out the same types of conversations and tasks that you saw in the video.

¡Fíjate! These boxes appear throughout the lessons, offering on-the-spot explanations, examples, reminders, and references to language structures you have already learned, to help you manipulate the language you are learning and maneuver through the tasks at hand.

Modelo Sample answers complement and clarify the instructions, providing you with a model to emulate in your own answers.

Práctica adicional Cross-references to the **Cuaderno de tareas** part of your worktext let you know exactly which activities and technology ancillaries are available to reinforce the **Gramática** and **Vocabulario** sections of **Para comunicarnos mejor**.

Actividades comunicativas

uses information gap activities to strengthen your communication skills.

Information gap activities
Information gap activities support you as you practice the vocabulary and grammar of the lesson in problem-solving or other situations. These activities are frequently culturally-oriented. You and a partner each have only half of the information you need, so you must work together to accomplish the task at hand.

Varied activity types In **Crucigrama**, you and a partner give each other hints in order to complete a crossword puzzle, while in **En imágenes**, you work together to interpret a series of pictures. **Sopa de palabras** is based on scrambled sentences, and **Diferencias** deals with different versions of an illustration. Other information gap activities involve completing stories and enacting role-plays.

Actividades comunicativas
includes other creative and interactive activities that build your communication skills.

Communicative work The activities in this section require you to use all of the Spanish you have learned to accomplish the tasks at hand, but, as with the information gap activities, you are given the support you need for successfully doing them: illustrations, models, graphs, and charts.

Activity types In **Submarino**, you and a partner ask each other questions in order to locate and sink each other's submarines, while in **Fotonovela**, you use illustrations to create or reconstruct a story.

More activity types In **La encuesta dice**, you and your teammates determine the most common answers to questions that elicit language you have studied. In **La historia va así**, you listen to a story in order to put a series of pictures in the correct order.

Other activity types Other activities involve surveying your classmates to find out certain information. Story completions and role-plays are also included.

La correspondencia

develops your reading and writing skills in the context of the lesson theme.

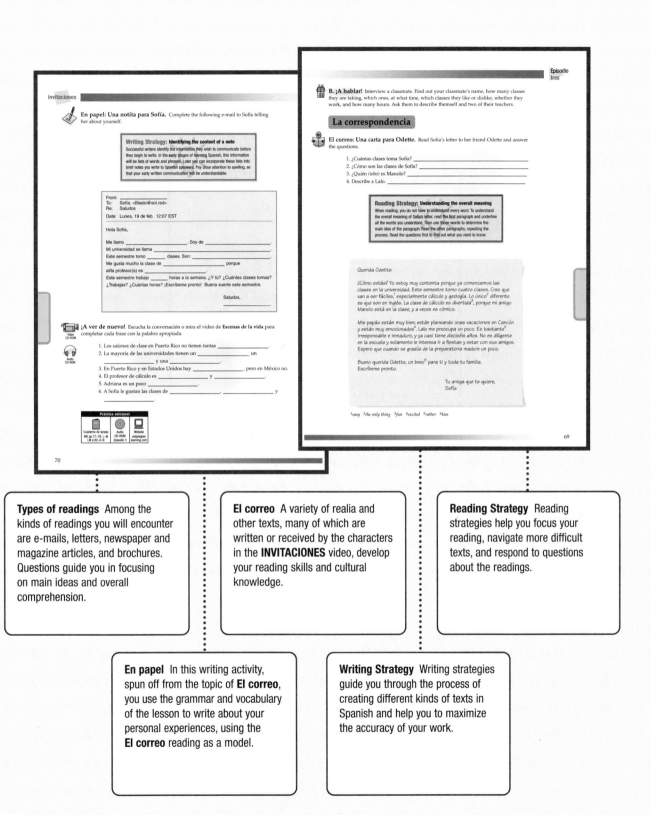

Types of readings Among the kinds of readings you will encounter are e-mails, letters, newspaper and magazine articles, and brochures. Questions guide you in focusing on main ideas and overall comprehension.

El correo A variety of realia and other texts, many of which are written or received by the characters in the **INVITACIONES** video, develop your reading skills and cultural knowledge.

Reading Strategy Reading strategies help you focus your reading, navigate more difficult texts, and respond to questions about the readings.

En papel In this writing activity, spun off from the topic of **El correo**, you use the grammar and vocabulary of the lesson to write about your personal experiences, using the **El correo** reading as a model.

Writing Strategy Writing strategies guide you through the process of creating different kinds of texts in Spanish and help you to maximize the accuracy of your work.

La correspondencia
also synthesizes the language of the lesson and spotlights culture.

¡A ver de nuevo! In this final activity, you synthesize the vocabulary and grammar of the entire lesson by reviewing and summarizing the content of the lesson's **Escenas de la vida** video episode.

Invitación a… A captioned photo from the albums of the characters in the **INVITACIONES** video introduces you to key places, customs, and artifacts from all twenty-one countries of the Spanish-speaking world, including the United States.

Vocabulario and Español al instante
serve as important vocabulary references.

Vocabulario del Episodio 10

Objetivos comunicativos
You should now be able to do the following in Spanish:
- ✓ accept and decline invitations
- ✓ extend invitations

Verbos

almorzar (o → ue)	to have lunch	pensar (e → i) en	to think about (someone)
dormir (o → ue) bien/mal	to sleep well/poorly	pensar (e → i) que	to think that (phrase)
empezar a... (e → ie)	to start...	poder (o → ue)	to be able to, can
encontrar (o → ue)	to find	(no) poder (o → ue) ir	(not) to be able to go
entender	to understand	preferir (e → ie)	
el problema (e → ie)	the problem		to prefer
invitar a	to invite	querer (e → ie)	to want; to love
jugar (u → ue) (al) tenis	to play tennis	recordar (o → ue)	to remember
manejar	to drive	venir por mí	to come for me

Las preposiciones y los pronombres preposicionales

a mí	for me	por él	for him	de ellos/as	from them
para ti	for you	de nosotros/as	from us	conmigo	with me
con ella	with her	de ustedes	from you (pl.)	contigo	with you

Vocabulario personal

Write all the words you need to know in Spanish so that you can better talk about your dates and your weekend plans.

250

Objetivos comunicativos This list restates the communicative tasks that you practiced throughout the lesson and should now be able to perform in Spanish.

Vocabulario personal This unique feature allows you to personalize your language learning by providing you with space to write down vocabulary related to the lesson's theme that is important to your own experiences and interests.

Vocabulario A list of all new words and expressions summarizes the active vocabulary of the lesson, providing an easy reference for review and study.

Español al instante The inside back cover of your worktext conveniently lists practical vocabulary key to the successful navigation of both your worktext and your classroom.

Cuaderno de tareas: ¡A escribir!
provides workbook activities that reinforce and expand on the materials in the lesson.

Cuaderno de tareas

Nombre _____ Fecha _____

Quinta etapa: *El compromiso*

Esta etapa debe considerarse el período de entrenamiento[1] antes del matrimonio. Una vez que hemos encontrado a la persona ideal para nosotros, es el momento de comprometerse. Este período es ideal para crear memorias duraderas del amor especial que sienten y comparten. Las parejas que tienen de cinco a ocho meses de compromiso están mejor preparados para la prueba del matrimonio. Es el momento de prepararse para los rigores del matrimonio, de formar una familia, de vivir juntos, de compartir una vida.

Según Grey, los marcianos deben recordar que en Venus, pedir la mano es la segunda cosa más importante (la primera es la boda) en los recuerdos personales de las venusianas. Es esencial que planeen el día o el momento cuidadosamente.

En la quinta etapa, la pareja debe practicar una de las cualidades más importantes en un matrimonio entre marcianos y venusianas: el arte de pedir perdón y el arte de perdonar.

"Cuando un hombre no reconoce sus errores, la mujer se los recordará hasta que lo haga". (pág. 114) El doctor añade que no es suficiente pedir perdón, sino saber hacerlo: no es suficiente explicar por qué llegó tarde, aunque tenga una excelente razón, sino que debe entender y validar los sentimientos de enojo de la mujer. Por otro lado, la mujer debe perdonar al hombre de manera que quede claro que lo acepta y lo quiere de todas maneras. Decir simplemente, "Te perdono", no es suficiente. Es necesario añadir algo como "Está bien, pero la próxima vez llámame, estaba preocupada por ti".

[1]*training*

Quinta etapa: El compromiso

17. ¿Para qué sirve la última etapa?

18. ¿Qué puede hacer el hombre para que la mujer tenga recuerdos inolvidables del compromiso?

19. ¿En qué consiste el arte de pedir perdón y saber perdonar?

20. ¿Te gustó la reseña? ¿Por qué?

395

Cuaderno de tareas

Nombre _____ Fecha _____

G. ¡Tú eres el experto! A friend of yours has had a history of unsuccessful dates. After reading the book review **Marte y Venus en una cita**, give them six or seven suggestions and recommendations to improve their dating techniques. Use the following pairs of expressions.

es importante que…	para que/hasta que	dudo que… cuando…
(no) te aconsejo que…	a menos que…	es necesario que… antes de que…
(no) te recomiendo que…	hasta que…	es bueno que… para que…

Primera etapa: la atracción

Modelo Es importante que sientas genuino interés en la persona para que compartan la conversación.

Segunda etapa: la duda

Tercera etapa: la exclusividad

Cuarta etapa: la intimidad

Quinta etapa: el compromiso

396

Workbook activities A series of workbook activities directly follow the color pages of each lesson in your worktext. You will know precisely when to complete these activities because they are referenced in the **Práctica adicional** boxes throughout the preceding pages of the lesson.

Lesson reinforcement A wide range of exercise types, often placed in the context of the **INVITACIONES** video and/or featuring the video characters, gives you ample written practice of the vocabulary and structures in the **Escenas de la vida**, **Gramática**, and **Vocabulario** sections of each lesson.

Cultural focus and language use The **Para terminar** section contains open-ended activities that synthesize the vocabulary and grammar of the lesson and recycle language from previous lessons. Cultural readings—realia, letters, and other formats—followed by comprehension and personal reaction questions are frequently included.

Cuaderno de tareas: ¡A escuchar!
develops listening comprehension skills while reinforcing the lesson's theme, vocabulary, and grammar.

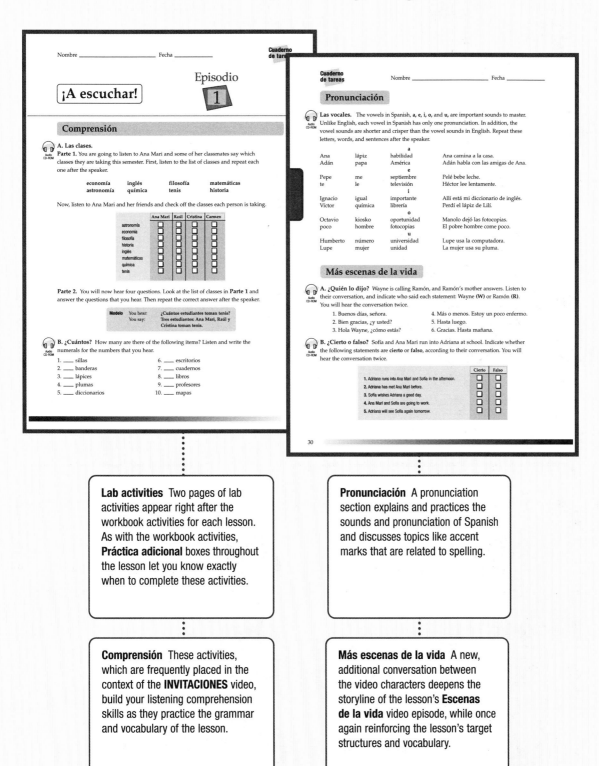

Lab activities Two pages of lab activities appear right after the workbook activities for each lesson. As with the workbook activities, **Práctica adicional** boxes throughout the lesson let you know exactly when to complete these activities.

Pronunciación A pronunciation section explains and practices the sounds and pronunciation of Spanish and discusses topics like accent marks that are related to spelling.

Comprensión These activities, which are frequently placed in the context of the **INVITACIONES** video, build your listening comprehension skills as they practice the grammar and vocabulary of the lesson.

Más escenas de la vida A new, additional conversation between the video characters deepens the storyline of the lesson's **Escenas de la vida** video episode, while once again reinforcing the lesson's target structures and vocabulary.

Video Program

Fully integrated with your worktext, the **INVITACIONES: Primera parte** video contains fifteen episodes, one for each lesson in your worktext. The episodes follow a group of Spanish-speaking students attending college in the United States as they confront the challenges and experience the joys of daily life. Several of the friends hold down part-time jobs. One is an American man who speaks good Spanish, while yet another is a Puerto Rican housewife who is returning to school and the workforce. The video, shot in southern California, follows the characters through an academic year and focuses on the Latino experience and influence in the United States.

Before you see each video episode, your instructor will use the **Escenas de la vida** section to preview the vocabulary and grammatical structures the characters will use and that you will study in the corresponding lesson. As the video progresses, the video conversations carefully combine new vocabulary and grammar with language taught in earlier lessons in your worktext. In this way, the video provides comprehensible input as it puts the language you are learning in action in real-life contexts.

The Cast

Here are the main characters you will meet when you watch the **INVITACIONES: Primera parte** video:

From Mexico,
Sofía Blasio Salas

From Cuba,
Manolo Báez Rodríguez

From the United States, of Mexican and Honduran heritage,
Ana Mari Robledo Suárez

From Puerto Rico,
Adriana Ferreira de Barrón

Ana Mari's brother,
Ramón Robledo Suárez

From the United States,
Wayne Reilly

A powerful and important learning tool, the video is integrated into every section of all the lessons in your worktext. The opening section of each lesson, **Escenas de la vida**, prepares you for the video episode and checks your comprehension. Vocabulary and grammar used by the video characters appear throughout the **Para comunicarnos mejor** explanations and activities. The **Actividades comunicativas** and **La correspondencia** sections of each lesson reference the events and characters of the corresponding video episode, and both the workbook and lab activities in each lesson's **Cuaderno de tareas** pages are often set in the context of the video episode.

Student Ancillaries

Video CD-ROM

Free-of-charge with each new copy of **INVITACIONES: Primera parte**, this easy-to-navigate CD-ROM contains the complete **INVITACIONES** video with videoscript.

Worktext & Lab MP3 Files Audio CD-ROM

Free-of-charge with each new copy of **INVITACIONES: Primera parte**, the MP3 Files Audio CD-ROM contains all of the recordings you need to complete the listening activities in both the color pages of your worktext and the lab activities in the **Cuaderno de tareas: ¡A escuchar!**

Companion Website (accessed through *www.vistahigherlearning.com*)

The **INVITACIONES** website offers Internet activities and a wide range of on-line resources for you and your instructor that directly correlate to your worktext and go beyond it.

Instructor Ancillaries

Instructor's Annotated Edition (IAE)

The **Instructor's Annotated Edition** provides a wealth of information designed to support classroom teaching and management. The same size as the student worktext, the **IAE** provides answers overprinted on the student pages, as well as resources and suggestions for implementing and extending the worktext activities.

Instructor's Resource Manual (IRM)

The **Instructor's Resource Manual** offers materials that reinforce and expand upon the lessons in the student worktext. The **Comprehensible Input** section provides guidance on what language to pre-teach before showing the video for the **Escenas de la vida** section. The **Additional Activities** section offers suggestions and materials for additional activities to accompany the worktext episodes. The **Videoscript** and **Tapescript** sections provide transcriptions of all of the conversations from the **Escenas de la vida** video and the recorded activities, respectively.

VHS Video

This VHS version of the **INVITACIONES** video is ideal for showing the episodes in class.

Worktext CD

This audio CD contains the audio tracks of the **Escenas de la vida** video episodes on the **INVITACIONES** video and the recordings for all of the listening activities on the color pages of the lessons in the worktext. The printed scripts are available in the **IRM.**

Lab Audio CDs

These audio CDs contain the recordings that are used in conjunction with the lab activities in the **Cuaderno de tareas: ¡A escuchar!** section of each worktext lesson.

Cuaderno de tareas Answer Key

The **Answer Key** provides answers to the workbook and lab activities in the **Cuaderno de tareas** section of the worktext, should instructors wish to distribute them to students for self-correction.

Overhead Transparencies

This set of overhead transparencies contains maps of the Spanish-speaking world, as well as selected images from the student worktexts, for use in presenting and reinforcing the language introduced throughout the lessons.

Testing Program

The **Testing Program** contains a quiz for every lesson in **INVITACIONES**, as well as midterm and final exams.

Test Files CD-ROM for Windows® and Macintosh®

This CD-ROM contains the complete, printed **Testing Program** as Microsoft Word® files, so instructors can readily customize the tests and exams for their courses.

INVITACIONES: Segunda parte

This companion volume completes the course, continuing the video storyline and building on the grammatical structures and vocabulary presented in INVITACIONES: Primera parte.

SEGUNDA PARTE

Invitaciones

An Interactive Worktext for Beginning Spanish

Alonso-Lyrintzis ▪ Alonso ▪ Zaslow

INVITACIONES: Segunda parte offers the same features, input-driven instructional approach, and ancillary package as **Primera parte**, as it both reviews the first volume and rounds out the entire **INVITACIONES** program with **Episodios 16–30**.

Reviewers

The authors and the publishing professionals at Vista Higher Learning express their sincere appreciation to the college instructors nationwide who reviewed portions of the **INVITACIONES** program. Their comments and suggestions were invaluable to the final product.

Beatrice L. Bongiorno
Bellevue Community College, WA

Jose A. Carmona
Daytona Beach Community College, FL

Sharon Cherry
University of South Carolina Spartanburg, SC

Maritza Chinea-Thornberry
University of South Florida, FL

Conxita Domenech
Front Range Community College, CO

Marcella Fierro
Mesa Community College, AZ

Jennifer Garson
Pasadena City College, CA

Judy Getty
California State University, Sacramento, CA

Pamela A. Gill
Gaston College, NC

Andrew S. Gordon
Mesa State College, CO

Irene B. Hodgson
Xavier College, OH

Patricia Houston
Pima Community College, East Campus, AZ

Teresa Dee Kennedy
Lenoir Community College, NC

Marta F. Loyola
Trinity College, DC

Matthew Luke
Lane Community College, OR

John Markovich
Messiah College, PA

Kathryn McConnell
Point Loma Nazarene University, CA

Lori L. McGee
Kent State University, Stark Campus, OH

Susan McMillen Villar
University of Minnesota, Twin cities, MN

Silvina Montrul
University of Illinois at Urbana Champaign, IL

Eduardo Pacheco
Judson College, AL

Mercedes Palomino
Florida Atlantic University, FL

Marcela Ruiz-Funes
East Carolina University, NC

Loreto Sánchez
Johns Hopkins University, MD

Phillip Santiago
Buffalo State College, NY

Jennifer Schaber
St. Louis Community College, MO

Nidia A. Schuhmacher
Brandeis University, MA

Theresa Ann Sears
University of North Carolina at Greensboro, NC

Wendy Woodrich
Lewis and Clark College, OR

Susan Yoder-Kreger
University of Missouri-St. Louis, MO

Student Reactions

The authors would like to thank the students at California State University San Marcos, where the program was class tested in the summer of 1999, and at Southwestern College, where the **INVITACIONES** program was class-tested from the fall of 1999 until the time of publication. Their patience and candid remarks about the activities, the characters, and the philosophy of the text were invigorating and truly useful to the completion of the project. Below are some of their reactions.

"What I liked the most is that it was not a bunch of conjugating. It actually teaches you useful conversations."

"It is a brilliant idea to have everything in one book; I feel I am getting my money's worth."

"All the side notes helped me learn things!"

"I really liked the layout of the book. The activities help to break down your inhibitions about using the language."

"I loved having the vocabulary at the end of every episode."

"I enjoy learning about the characters and their lives; it helps to personalize the material for me."

"I enjoyed being able to write all my notes directly on the book. I know that in the future, I can look back and review my Spanish."

"Everything in the episodes was relevant and related to what we were learning!"

"This book made it fun to learn, and the language is sticking to me."

"I really appreciate not carrying three books around!"

Acknowledgments

The long process of writing this textbook was challenging and full of unexpected changes. It took a lot of tenacity, endurance, and our unappeasable dream that many more students would be successful in learning Spanish, if only the materials they used were more inviting, realistic, interactive, and fun.

Our most heartfelt gratitude goes to José Blanco and Denise St. Jean, who share our dream and were willing to take the inherent risk of bringing to the market a new, "out of the box" set of books. We are delighted to have been given the opportunity to work with them and their outstanding team of professionals, who made this program a reality.

We are grateful to Beverly Burdette, of Pellissippi State Community College, for creating lab activities to accompany our text; her conscientious contributions have always been in keeping with our own intentions, and round-out our Spanish program.

We would like to thank our editors, Sarah Kenney and Gabriela Ferland, for their astute observations, unfaltering hard work and dedication, and, most of all, for their patience and cheery responses to our inquiries.

We are also indebted to our colleagues and friends, whose advice and contributions during the different stages of the manuscript helped us shape the book: Dinorah Guadiana-Costa and Concetta Calandra, of Southwestern College, for their support, constructive suggestions and enthusiasm while using our materials in their classes; Cuban poet Pedro Báez, Ana Hami, of Chapman University, and Francisco Zabaleta, of San Diego State University, for helping us create culturally and linguistically authentic Cuban, Puerto Rican, and Spanish characters, respectively; Diana Rossner and Nancy Barley, of Lake Tahoe Community College, for always offering sincere and encouraging remarks; Gary Anderson for sharing his ideas unselfishly; Virginia Young, of Grossmont College, for adding activities to our Instructor's Resource Manual; Hal Wingard, the Executive Director of the California Language Teachers Association, for embracing our materials and speaking on our behalf at the Foreign Language Conference of the California Community Colleges. We also give a special thanks to our colleagues and friends at the different institutions in San Diego, who have openly and warmly supported us, both personally and professionally.

A project of this magnitude could not be undertaken without the support of our families and close friends, who have unselfishly shared a piece of their lives by taking care of our children and pets, allowing us to use their pictures, their names, and their stories. Thank you for enduring the joys and sorrows of the past few years with us.

We would also like to thank Southwestern College, for not only class testing our program, but also for being so cooperative and accommodating when we shot our video on the campus. Last but not least, we offer our sincere thanks to our wonderful team of adjunct instructors, who have served as anonymous reviewers.

Deana Alonso-Lyrintzis, Esther Alonso, and Brandon Zaslow

¡Bienvenidos al mundo hispano!

A. How much do you know about the Spanish language? Indicate whether you believe the following statements are true or false.

	Cierto	Falso
1. After English, Spanish is the most frequently spoken language in the United States.	☐	☐
2. One out of every ten United States residents speaks Spanish.	☐	☐
3. The United States has the fifth largest population of Spanish speakers in the world.	☐	☐
4. The first Europeans to settle in the modern-day United States were Spanish speakers.	☐	☐
5. Spanish is spoken in twenty-one countries.	☐	☐
6. More than 350 million people speak Spanish.	☐	☐
7. Spanish is a modern derivative of Latin.	☐	☐

B. Let's meet each other! Listen to your instructor as they model the pronunciation of the following exchange. Then practice the conversation with three or four classmates.

Estudiante 1:	¡Hola! ¿Cómo estás?
Estudiante 2:	Bien, ¿y tú?
Estudiante 1:	Bien, gracias.
Estudiante 2:	Me llamo _____ (*your name*). Y tú, ¿cómo te llamas?
Estudiante 1:	_____ ¡Mucho gusto!
Estudiante 2:	Igualmente.

1

C. The Spanish-speaking world. Spanish speakers are a diverse group of ethnicities, religions, and cultures. Learn about exciting places and facts, using your knowledge of English and of the world, as you read the captions under the following photographs.

> **Learning Strategy: Using cognates**
>
> A cognate is a word that is similar in two or more languages because of a common origin. The English word *publication* and the Spanish word **publicación** are cognates. Cognates in Spanish and English are always pronounced differently, are often spelled differently, and sometimes differ in meaning. Most of the time, however, you can guess what a Spanish cognate means by associating it with an English word you know. Can you guess the meaning of these cognates?
>
> | colonial | falsos | indicar | contraste | fotografía | millones |
> |---|---|---|---|---|---|
> | comentarios | glaciares | moderna | construcciones | habitantes | montañas |
>
> You can use cognates to help you understand the overall meaning of Spanish sentences. To practice this strategy, read the captions under the following photographs.

En la Ciudad de México hay *(there are)* más de 20 millones de habitantes. Es la ciudad más poblada del mundo.

Chile y Argentina comparten *(share)* la Patagonia, donde hay glaciares e inmensas montañas.

En Puerto Rico, el contraste entre la arquitectura moderna y la arquitectura colonial es visible.

La Avenida 9 de Julio en Buenos Aires, Argentina, es enorme. Buenos Aires se considera el París de América.

Los mayas habitaron parte de México y de Centroamérica.

Las impresionantes murallas de Ávila fueron *(were)* construidas para proteger la ciudad después de expulsar a los árabes del territorio español.

El pueblo inca construyó Machu Picchu en las montañas de los Andes.

D. Latinoamérica. Examina las fotografías para *(in order to)* indicar si los comentarios son **ciertos** o **falsos**.

	Cierto	Falso
1. En la Ciudad de México hay más de 20 millones de personas.	☒	☐
2. Puerto Rico tiene *(has)* muchas construcciones antiguas y modernas.	☒	☐
3. Los aztecas construyeron Machu Picchu.	☐	☒
4. El clima de Chile es tropical.	☐	☒
5. La Avenida 9 de Julio es enorme.	☒	☐
6. Los incas eran *(were)* habitantes de México y Guatemala.	☐	☒
7. Los árabes fueron expulsados de España.	☒	☐

3

Learning Strategy: How to be a successful language-learner

Learning to speak another language can be fun and exciting. Many successful language-learners share certain basic characteristics. Read the following statements to determine why these particular traits are useful in language learning.

1. Students who are excited about learning Spanish do better than students who are indifferent.
   Why do you think a positive attitude is important?

2. Students who are not afraid of speaking Spanish learn more than students who are reluctant to speak.
   Why do you think being willing to speak is important?

3. Students who take risks progress more rapidly than students who are inhibited.
   Why do you think taking risks is important?

4. Students who accept that uncertainty and inconsistency are part of learning a language learn at a faster rate.
   Why do you think that tolerance of ambiguity is important?

Whether or not you possess these traits, you can learn to communicate well in Spanish. Throughout this book, you will encounter **Learning Strategy** sections designed to improve your study skills. Here are a few for starters.

Listen

Listen carefully in class. At first, you will not be able to understand everything you hear, but you will absorb a lot of Spanish without realizing it.

Speak

Speak as much Spanish as you can. Talk to your instructor and to your classmates in Spanish. Don't be afraid to make mistakes, as they will help you to identify things you need to learn.

Take Notes

Take notes in class. Your memory is going to get a workout, so write things down. Be sure to ask questions in class. Remember, there are no silly questions.

Practice

You will need to practice every day. Learning Spanish is like learning to swim or to play the guitar—the more you practice, the better you become. Cramming the night before an exam is a recipe for disaster!

Take Charge

The key element in shaping your success is you. Look for opportunities to practice Spanish outside of class: watch television in Spanish and listen to Spanish radio, talk to your neighbors, use the Internet. Take charge of your own learning!

Have Fun

You are going to learn Spanish, but it will take time. After all, you didn't learn to speak English overnight! Your worktext is designed to make your learning enjoyable. Have fun and relax. If you do, you will learn faster and more easily.

Escenas de la vida: El primer día de clases

Video CD-ROM

Audio CD-ROM

A. ¡Mira cuánto puedes entender! *(See how much you can understand!)* As you watch the video or listen to your Audio CD-ROM, fill in the blanks with the characters' names.

Cultura a lo vivo

Did you notice how, when the characters greet each other, there is always some kind of physical contact? Hispanics like to touch each other (a kiss, a pat on the back, or simply a handshake) to demonstrate openness and warmth.

Video
CD-ROM

B. ¿Te diste cuenta? *(Did you realize?)* Escucha las conversaciones otra vez para indicar si los comentarios son **ciertos** o **falsos**.

Audio
CD-ROM

	Cierto	Falso
1. Adriana es de México.	☐	☐
2. Manolo necesita estudiar más.	☐	☐
3. Ana Mari es amiga de Manolo.	☐	☐
4. Manolo toma una clase de inglés.	☐	☐
5. Ana Mari no tiene novio *(doesn't have a boyfriend).*	☐	☐

Video
CD-ROM

C. ¿Quién lo dijo? *(Who said it?)* Indica quién hace estos comentarios: Adriana (**A**), Sofía (**S**), Ana Mari (**AM**), Manolo (**M**) o el prof. López (**pL**).

Audio
CD-ROM

_____ 1. Soy de Puerto Rico.

_____ 2. Buenos días, profesor López.

_____ 3. Este semestre necesitas estudiar más.

_____ 4. Te presento a Ana Mari.

_____ 5. Encantada.

_____ 6. Tengo clase de inglés ahora.

_____ 7. Mucho gusto de conocerte.

_____ 8. ¡Que te vaya bien!

Práctica adicional
Cuaderno de tareas WB pp.21–22, A–C · Video CD-ROM Episodio 1

Para comunicarnos mejor

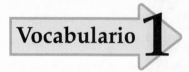
Vocabulario 1

Greeting and saying good-bye to others
• Greetings and good-byes

Use these informal expressions when speaking to someone with whom you have a close relationship, such as a family member, friend, or someone your age or younger.

Para hablar con amigos	
¿Cómo estás?	*How are you?*
¿Y tú?	*And you?*
¿Cómo te llamas?	*What's your name?*
¡Que te vaya bien!	*Have a nice day!*
Te presento a...	*I'd like you to meet...*

¡Fíjate!
Be aware that you are responsible for learning all words and structures presented in the **Vocabulario** and **Gramática** sections of your book. They will be practiced in activities that follow and will appear on tests.

When speaking to someone with whom you do not have a close relationship, someone you would address with a title and a last name, or an older or higher–ranking person, use these formal expressions to show respect:

Para hablar con respeto			
¿Cómo está?	*How are you?*	**señor (Sr.)**	*Mr., sir*
¿Y usted?	*And you?*	**señora (Sra.)**	*Mrs., ma'am*
¿Cómo se llama?	*What's your name?*	**señorita (Srta.)**	*Miss*
¡Que le vaya bien!	*Have a nice day!*	**doctor(a) (Dr(a).)**	*Doctor*
Le presento a...	*I'd like you to meet...*	**profesor(a) (Prof(a).)**	*Professor*

¡Fíjate!

When in doubt about whether you should use **tú** or **usted**, use the formal **usted** forms to show respect.

Más saludos, despedidas y expresiones de cortesía	
Hola.	*Hi.*
Buenos días.	*Good morning.* (from dawn until noon)
Buenas tardes.	*Good afternoon.* (from noon until dusk)
Buenas noches.	*Good evening/Good night.* (from dusk until dawn)
Hasta luego.	*See you later.*
Hasta mañana.	*See you tomorrow.*
Nos vemos mañana.	*See you tomorrow.* (you have arranged to meet tomorrow)
Adiós.	*Good-bye.*
Mucho gusto.	*Nice to meet you.*
Encantado.	*Pleased to meet you.* (said by a man)
Encantada.	*Pleased to meet you.* (said by a woman)
Igualmente.	*Nice to meet you, too.*
Gracias.	*Thank you.*
De nada.	*You're welcome.*
Bien.	*Fine.*
Muy bien.	*Very well.*
Más o menos.	*So-so.*

Learning Strategy: Avoid word-for-word translation

Because English and Spanish are independent languages that often express the same thought in different ways, you should avoid translating word-for-word. For example, **¡Que te vaya bien!** might be translated as *May it go well with you.* The idea Spanish speakers mean to convey, however, is *Have a nice day!* So, learn the meaning of language "chunks," and avoid word-for-word translations.

PRÁCTICA

 A. ¡A actuar! With a classmate, act out the following conversations.

Después de la clase

Manolo	**Buenos días**, profesor López. **¿Cómo está usted?**
Profesor	¿Otra vez aquí? (*(You) here again?*)
Manolo	Sí, necesito pasar esta clase.
Profesor	Este semestre necesitas estudiar más.
Manolo	Sí, ya sé. **Hasta mañana.**
Profesor	**¡Que te vaya bien!**
Manolo	**Gracias. Igualmente.**

Te presento a Ana Mari

Sofía	**Hola**, Ana Mari. **¿Cómo estás?**
Ana Mari	**Muy bien. ¿Y tú?**
Sofía	**Bien, gracias.**
Sofía	Mira, Manolo, **te presento** a Ana Mari. Es mi mejor amiga. Y no tiene novio.
Ana Mari	¡Sofía!
Manolo	**Mucho gusto.**
Ana Mari	**Encantada.** Bueno, tengo clase de inglés ahora. **Hasta luego.** Y **mucho gusto** de conocerte.
Manolo	**Gracias. Igualmente.**
Sofía	**Adiós**, Ana Mari. **¡Que te vaya bien!**

B. ¿Qué respondes? Imagina que conversas con Sofía. Responde apropiadamente.

1. Hola, ¿cómo te llamas? _____
2. Te presento a Manolo. _____
3. Hasta luego. _____
4. ¡Buenos días! _____
5. Gracias. _____
6. Adiós. _____

C. Buenos días, profesor. Imagina que conversas con el profesor López. Responde apropiadamente.

1. Buenas tardes. _____
2. ¿Cómo estás? _____
3. Mucho gusto. _____
4. Hasta mañana. _____
5. ¡Que te vaya bien! _____
6. Buenas noches. _____

Audio
CD-ROM

D. ¿Saludo o despedida? Escucha las frases para indicar si cada una *(each one)* es un **saludo** o una **despedida**.

	Saludo	Despedida
1.	☐	☐
2.	☐	☐
3.	☐	☐
4.	☐	☐
5.	☐	☐
6.	☐	☐

Audio
CD-ROM

E. ¿Cómo respondes? *(How do you answer?)* Escucha las frases para seleccionar la respuesta apropiada.

1. a. Más o menos.   b. Mucho gusto.   c. Gracias.
2. a. Igualmente.   b. ¡Que le vaya bien!   c. Buenos días.
3. a. Igualmente.   b. ¿Y usted?   c. ¡Que te vaya bien!
4. a. ¿Y tú?   b. ¿Cómo se llama?   c. Muy bien, gracias.
5. a. Sí, gracias.   b. Me llamo...   c. Hasta luego.

F. ¡A conversar! Con un(a) compañero/a, usa las expresiones necesarias para inventar una conversación para cada *(each)* situación.

1. You see your instructor at ten in the morning. Extend a greeting, ask how they are, then say good-bye.

2. A new student has just joined the class. Greet the student and find out their name.

3. Your friend wants to meet the new student. Introduce them.

4. Class is over. Say good-bye to your friend and wish them a good day.

5. Your roommate returns home at four in the afternoon. Greet each other and ask each other how you are.

Práctica adicional

Cuaderno de tareas
WB pp.22–23, D–H

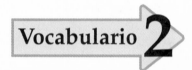

Vocabulario 2

Saying which classes you take
- **The alphabet**
- **Class subjects**

You have probably noticed that, in Spanish, there is a very close relationship between the way words are written and the way they are pronounced. This feature facilitates the learning of spelling and pronunciation. Spanish sounds, however, do not have exact equivalents in English. For this reason, do not rely on English sounds to pronounce Spanish words.

A **ABCD EFGH**	B**e** (grande)	C**e**	CH**e**	D**e**
alfabeto	bandera	cuaderno	mochila	diccionario
E	e**F**e	G**e**	**Hache**	I *adiós* good bye *au revoir ciao*
escritorio	fotocopias	geografía	hombre	inglés
Jota	**Ka**	e**L**e	e**LL**e	e**M**e
mujer	kiosko	libro	silla	mapa
e**N**e **1 2 3 4 5 6**	e**Ñ**e	O	P**e**	Q(cu)
números	baño	oficina	pluma	química
e**R**e	e**RR**e	e**S**e	T**e**	**USC** UNIVERSITY OF SOUTHERN CALIFORNIA
librería	carro	salón de clases	tenis	universidad
V**e** (chica)	W **doble u**	X **equis**	Y **(i griega)**	**Zeta**
video	Washington	examen	playa	lápiz

¡Fíjate!

Because the letters **b** and **v** have the same pronunciation in Spanish, Spanish speakers distinguish between the two by calling **b** "**Be grande**" and **v** "**Ve chica**."

¡Fíjate!

To *say uppercase* and *lowercase*, use the terms **mayúscula** and **minúscula**, respectively. To indicate that a letter takes an accent, say **con acento** after the letter.

1. As of 1994, **ch** and **ll** are no longer regarded as letters in the Spanish alphabet. Even though these letters can no longer be found in separate sections of the dictionary, people continue to use them when spelling names or difficult words. You should use them when spelling your name to Spanish speakers.

2. The letter **ñ** does not exist in English. However, the [ñ] sound does exist in words like *onion* and *canyon*.

3. The Spanish vowels **a, e, i, o,** and **u** are short and tense. Do not move your tongue, lips, or jaws when pronouncing them, to avoid the glide sound of English vowels.

PRÁCTICA

G. Pronunciación. Repeat the letters and the words in the alphabet box on page 10 after your instructor. Which words are cognates (words that are the same or almost the same in the both languages)?

_____

H. ¿Tienes buena memoria? Write the words in Spanish.

1. pen _____   4. pencil _____   7. book _____

2. bookstore _____   5. dictionary _____   8. classroom _____

3. notebook _____   6. English _____   9. office _____

Audio
CD-ROM

I. Dictado. You will hear eight famous last names. Write the names in the spaces provided.

1. _____   4. _____   7. _____

2. _____   5. _____   8. _____

3. _____   6. _____

J. ¿Quiénes son? *(Who are they?)* Match the last names from **Práctica I** with the first names below to describe eight Spanish-speaking celebrities.

| John | Jennifer | Edward | Celia |
| Sammy | Óscar | Antonio | Salma |

1. _____ es un actor colombiano.

2. _____ es una actriz de origen puertorriqueño.

3. _____ es un actor mexicoamericano.

4. _____ es una actriz mexicana.

5. _____ es un beisbolista dominicano.

6. _____ es una cantante cubana.

7. _____ es un actor español.

8. _____ es un boxeador mexicoamericano.

• Class subjects

Listen carefully as your instructor pronounces the names of following class subjects **(las materias)**. Repeat each word after them, reproducing the Spanish sounds as closely as you can.

Las materias			
antropología	economía	geografía	matemáticas
astronomía	(educación) física	historia	música
biología	español	inglés	química
drama	filosofía	literatura	sicología

K. Personas famosas. Empareja las personas famosas con las materias.

_____ 1. antropología   a. Shakespeare

_____ 2. astronomía   b. Sócrates

_____ 3. economía   c. Adam Smith

_____ 4. filosofía   d. Barbara Tuchman

_____ 5. drama   e. Galileo

_____ 6. historia   f. Jane Goodall

L. Asociaciones. ¿Qué materia(s) asocias con estas (these) personas?

1. Charles Darwin _____

2. Pitágoras (Pythagoras) _____

3. Toni Morrison _____

4. Gabriel García Márquez _____

5. Wolfgang Amadeus Mozart _____

6. Sigmund Freud _____

M. ¿Tomas una clase de...? (Are you taking a...class?) Use the list of classes from page 11 to find out which classes your partner is currently taking.

Modelo	—¿Tomas (are you taking) una clase de historia?
—Sí, ¿Y tú? —Yo también (Me too). or Yo no.	—No, ¿Y tú? —Yo tampoco (Me neither). or Yo sí.

Now write the classes your partner is taking.

Las clases de mi compañero/a son: _____

N. Mis clases. Escribe las clases que tomas (you take) este (this) semestre/trimestre y las clases que necesitas tomar (you need to take) el próximo (next) semestre/trimestre.

Este semestre/trimestre	El próximo semestre/trimestre
_____	_____
_____	_____
_____	_____
_____	_____
_____	_____

Ñ. Tus clases. Talk to a classmate to find out which classes they are currently taking and which classes they need to take next semester/trimester.

| Modelo | —¿Qué clases tomas este semestre/trimestre (*which classes are you taking this semester/trimester*)?
—Historia, matemáticas y español.
—¿Qué clases necesitas tomar el próximo semestre/trimestre (*which classes do you need to take next semester/trimester*)?
—Física, antropología y español. ¿Y tú, qué clases tomas este semestre? |

Práctica adicional

Cuaderno de tareas
WB p.23, I–J

Vocabulario **3**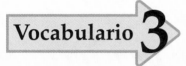

Saying how many credits/units you take and how many hours you work
• Numbers 0–40

Los números del 0 al 40

0 **cero**			
1 **uno**	11 **once**	21 **veintiuno**	31 **treinta y uno**
2 **dos**	12 **doce**	22 **veintidós**	32 **treinta y dos**
3 **tres**	13 **trece**	23 **veintitrés**	33 **treinta y tres**
4 **cuatro**	14 **catorce**	24 **veinticuatro**	34 **treinta y cuatro**
5 **cinco**	15 **quince**	25 **veinticinco**	35 **treinta y cinco**
6 **seis**	16 **dieciséis**	26 **veintiséis**	36 **treinta y seis**
7 **siete**	17 **diecisiete**	27 **veintisiete**	37 **treinta y siete**
8 **ocho**	18 **dieciocho**	28 **veintiocho**	38 **treinta y ocho**
9 **nueve**	19 **diecinueve**	29 **veintinueve**	39 **treinta y nueve**
10 **diez**	20 **veinte**	30 **treinta**	40 **cuarenta**

1. In some countries, the numbers from 16 through 19 and 21 through 29 are written as three separate words: **diez y seis, veinte y tres.**
2. The number *one* has three forms: **uno** (used when counting: **treinta y uno, treinta y dos...**), **un** (used before masculine nouns: **un libro, veintiún cuadernos**), and **una** (used before feminine nouns: **una pluma, treinta y una señoras**).
3. To ask and say how many classes you take and how many hours you work, use the following expressions.

¿Cuántas clases tomas? Tomo...	*How many classes are you taking? I take...*
¿Cuántas horas trabajas? Trabajo...	*How many hours do you work? I work...*

PRÁCTICA

O. Asociaciones. What number do you associate with...?

1. a week
2. the month of May
3. a triangle
4. all of your fingers
5. a square
6. the lives of a cat
7. an octopus
8. your eyes
9. your head

P. Sumas y restas. *(Additions and subtractions.)* Imagine you are a teacher **(maestro/a)** tutoring a first-grade student in math. Ask the student to give you the answers to the following problems.

Modelo	2 + 5 = ?	25 -12 = ?
	Maestro: **Dos más *(plus)* cinco son...**	Maestro: **Veinticinco menos *(minus)* doce son...**
	Estudiante: **Siete.**	Estudiante: **Trece.**

1. 8 + 6 = ?   5. 30 - 18 = ?   9. 47 - 14 = ?
2. 11 + 9 =?   6. 28 - 7 = ?   10. 15 + 17 = ?
3. 23 - 12 = ?   7. 18 + 4 = ?   11. 45 - 7 = ?
4. 12 + 13 = ?   8. 20 - 1 = ?   12. 26 - 16= ?

Q. Trabajas demasiado. *(You work too much.)*

Parte 1. Find out from four of your classmates how many academic units/credits they are taking and how many hours per week they work. Fill out the chart below.

Modelo	—¿Cuántos créditos tomas este semestre?	—¿Cuántas horas trabajas?
	—12. ¿Y tú?	—25. ¿Y tú?
	—18.	—No trabajo.

Nombre	Créditos este semestre	Horas de trabajo a la semana
1. _____	_____	_____
2. _____	_____	_____
3. _____	_____	_____
4. _____	_____	_____

> **¡Fíjate!**
>
> You are not responsible for learning the words in the **Banco de palabras**, although you may be responsible for learning these words and structures in later episodes. Currently, they appear to help you complete the activity at hand.

Parte 2. Now check the chart to see if your classmates follow the recommended work/study ratio. Comment on the results. You may use expressions from the **Banco de palabras**.

Si trabajas...	Debes tomar sólo...	Necesitas estudiar...
40 hrs.	6 créditos	12 horas por semana
30 hrs.	9 créditos	18 horas por semana
20 hrs.	12 créditos	24 horas por semana
10 hrs.	15 créditos	30 horas por semana
0 hrs.	18 créditos	36 horas por semana

> **Banco de palabras**
>
> **Trabajas demasiado.**
> *You work too much.*
>
> **...horas (hrs.) por semana**
> *...hours per week*
>
> **Necesitas tomar menos clases.**
> *You need to take fewer classes.*
>
> **Vas a salir bien.**
> *You're going to do well.*

Audio
CD-ROM

R. Juego de lotería. You are going to play the lottery. First write six numbers between ten and forty on the lines in your worktext. Then listen to the three sets of winning numbers, write them down, and circle the ones that match your selections.

Juego # 1 _____ _____ _____ _____ _____ _____

Juego # 2 _____ _____ _____ _____ _____ _____

Juego # 3 _____ _____ _____ _____ _____ _____

Invitación a **Estados Unidos**

Del álbum de
Sofía

La comunidad hispana más grande (*biggest*) en Estados Unidos es la mexicoamericana. Su influencia en la cultura estadounidense es obvia en la comida (*food*), la música y el arte. La fiesta del 5 de mayo se celebra en muchas ciudades y prácticamente en todos los estados del suroeste del país (*southwest of the country*). Los mariachis y grupos folclóricos son espectáculos comunes en muchos eventos norteamericanos.

Práctica adicional		
Cuaderno de tareas WB p.24, K–M LM pp.29–30, A–B, Pron.	Audio CD-ROM Episodio 1	Website vistahigher learning.com

Actividades comunicativas

In this activity, you will interact with another student. Before you begin, decide who will take the role of **Estudiante 1,** and who will take the role of **Estudiante 2. Estudiante 1** follows one set of instructions, while **Estudiante 2** follows another set found on the following page. Neither you nor your partner should look at the other's instructions or information.

¡Fíjate!

The **Actividades comunicativas** require you to use all the Spanish you have learned to accomplish the task at hand. Do not be afraid of making mistakes. The purpose of these activities is to provide practice communicating in Spanish.

 A. Las agendas.

Instrucciones para **Estudiante 1**

You took home your co-worker's list of clients and left your own list at the office. By telephone, ask your co-worker to give you the names and phone numbers of your clients. Ask your partner to spell out the names. When asked, be ready to tell your co-worker the names and numbers of their clients. Alternate asking and answering questions. Use questions like the ones below.

Banco de palabras

¿Cómo se llama el cliente número uno?
What is the first client's name?

¿Cómo se escribe su nombre?
How do you spell their name?

¿Cuál es su teléfono?
What is their phone number?

¡Fíjate!

Review **El alfabeto** on page 10 to prepare for this activity. Notice that telephone numbers are given in sets of two, except for the first number (4-21-05-25).

Mis clientes:

	Nombre	Teléfono
1.		
2.		
3.		
4.		

Los clientes de tu compañero/a:

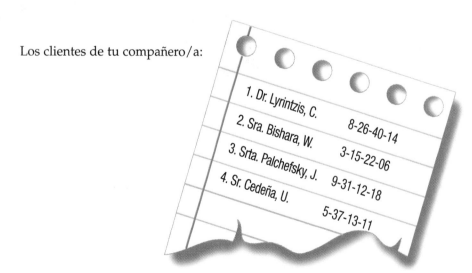

1. Dr. Lyrintzis, C.   8-26-40-14
2. Sra. Bishara, W.   3-15-22-06
3. Srta. Palchefsky, J.   9-31-12-18
4. Sr. Cedeña, U.   5-37-13-11

A. Las agendas.

Instrucciones para Estudiante 2

You took home your co-worker's list of clients and left your own list at the office. By telephone, ask your co-worker to give you the names and phone numbers of your clients. Ask your partner to spell out the names. When asked, be ready to tell your co-worker the names and numbers of their clients. Alternate asking and answering questions. Use questions like the ones below.

Banco de palabras

¿Cómo se llama el cliente número uno?
What is the first client's name?

¿Cómo se escribe su nombre?
How do you spell their name?

¿Cuál es su teléfono?
What is their phone number?

¡Fíjate!

Review **El alfabeto** on page 10 to prepare for this activity. Notice that telephone numbers are given in sets of two, except for the first number (4-21-05-25).

Mis clientes:

	Nombre	Teléfono
1.	_____	_____
2.	_____	_____
3.	_____	_____
4.	_____	_____

Los clientes de tu compañero/a:

1. Dr. Prathimano, G.   4-11-16-19
2. Sra. Vasconselos, X.   6-20-14-03
3. Prof. Babayants, Q.   7-27-12-28
4. Sra. Corrella, J.   2-10-15-23

La correspondencia

Audio
CD-ROM

El correo: La Universidad Autónoma de Guadalajara.

Parte 1. You received a brochure in the mail from the Universidad Autónoma de Guadalajara, but it has been damaged and you cannot read all of the information. Call the university and listen to their automated message to fill out the missing information.

UNIVERSIDAD AUTÓNOMA DE GUADALAJARA

ÚNICO. Universidad en la comunidad ofrece las siguientes carreras:

- Fisioterapia
- Comercialización y ventas
- _____
- _____
- Prótesis Dental
- Mercado de valores
- _____
- Fotografía
- Diseño y _____ de parques y _____
- Electromecánica industrial
- _____

VEN A FORMAR
PARTE DE UNA
UNIVERSIDAD

¡Con un estilo ÚNICO!

ÚNICO

UNIVERSIDAD EN LA COMUNIDAD

Parte 2. Read the complete brochure and answer the following questions. Answer in English.

1. Which area of study look the most interesting to you? Why?

_____

2. Which areas appeal you the least? Why?

_____

En papel: Presentación. Introduce yourself to your instructor! Fill out the card your instructor will give you with your personal information.

Video
CD-ROM

¡A ver de nuevo! Watch or listen to the **Escena** again to match the elements from the two columns.

Audio
CD-ROM

I.
- _____ 1. Adriana
- _____ 2. Sofía
- _____ 3. Manolo

a. es amiga de Ana Mari.
b. necesita pasar la clase de cálculo.
c. es de Puerto Rico.

II.
- _____ 1. El Prof. López
- _____ 2. Manolo
- _____ 3. Ana Mari

a. tiene una clase de inglés.
b. es profesor.
c. necesita estudiar más (*needs to study more*).

III.
- _____ 1. Sofía
- _____ 2. Ana Mari
- _____ 3. El Prof. López

a. no tiene novio (*doesn't have a boyfriend*).
b. es de México.
c. dice (*says*) "Manolo, ¿otra vez aquí?"

Práctica adicional		
Cuaderno de tareas WB pp.25–28, N–P LM p.30, A–B	Audio CD-ROM Episodio 1	Website vistahigher learning.com

Vocabulario del Episodio 1

Para hablar con amigos *To speak to friends*

¿Cómo estás?	*How are you?*
¿Y tú?	*And you?*
¿Cómo te llamas?	*What's your name?*
¡Que te vaya bien!	*Have a nice day!*
Te presento a...	*I'd like you to meet...*

Para hablar con respeto *To speak with respect*

¿Cómo está?	*How are you?*	**señor (Sr.)**	*Mr., sir*
¿Y usted?	*And you?*	**señora (Sra.)**	*Mrs., ma'am*
¿Cómo se llama?	*What's your name?*	**señorita (Srta.)**	*Miss*
¡Que le vaya bien!	*Have a nice day!*	**doctor(a) (Dr(a).)**	*Doctor*
Le presento a...	*I'd like you to meet...*	**profesor(a) (Prof(a).)**	*Professor*

Más saludos y despedidas *More greetings and good-byes*

Hola.	*Hi.*
Buenos días.	*Good morning.* (from dawn until noon)
Buenas tardes.	*Good afternoon.* (from noon until dusk)
Buenas noches.	*Good evening/Good night.* (from dusk until dawn)
Hasta luego.	*See you later.*
Hasta mañana.	*See you tomorrow.*
Nos vemos mañana.	*See you tomorrow.* (you have arranged to meet tomorrow)
Adiós.	*Good-bye.*
Mucho gusto.	*Nice to meet you.*
Encantado.	*Pleased to meet you.* (said by a man)
Encantada.	*Pleased to meet you.* (said by a woman)
Igualmente.	*Nice to meet you, too.*
Gracias.	*Thank you.*
De nada.	*You're welcome.*
Bien.	*Fine.*
Muy bien.	*Very well.*
Más o menos.	*So-so.*

Las materias *Class subjects*

antropología	economía	geografía	matemáticas
astronomía	(educación) física	historia	música
biología	español	inglés	química
drama	filosofía	literatura	sicología

Los números del 0 al 40

0 cero			
1 uno	11 once	21 veintiuno	31 treinta y uno
2 dos	12 doce	22 veintidós	32 treinta y dos
3 tres	13 trece	23 veintitrés	33 treinta y tres
4 cuatro	14 catorce	24 veinticuatro	34 treinta y cuatro
5 cinco	15 quince	25 veinticinco	35 treinta y cinco
6 seis	16 dieciséis	26 veintiséis	36 treinta y seis
7 siete	17 diecisiete	27 veintisiete	37 treinta y siete
8 ocho	18 dieciocho	28 veintiocho	38 treinta y ocho
9 nueve	19 diecinueve	29 veintinueve	39 treinta y nueve
10 diez	20 veinte	30 treinta	40 cuarenta

¿Cuántas clases tomas? Tomo... *How many classes are you taking? I take...*
¿Cuántas horas trabajas? Trabajo... *How many hours do you work? I work...*

¡Fíjate!

This section is the place where you can write down and easily reference the vocabulary that applies to your own life and interests.

Vocabulario personal

Write the words that you need to know to talk about yourself in Spanish.

¡A escribir!

Episodio 1

Escenas de la vida: El primer día de clases

Video CD-ROM

A. ¡Mira cuánto entendiste! See how much of the **Escena** you understood by matching the Spanish sentences with their English equivalents.

1. En la clase de cálculo

_____ 1. Mucho gusto.   a. And you?

_____ 2. ¿Hablas español?   b. Nice to meet you, too.

_____ 3. Igualmente.   c. Do you speak Spanish?

_____ 4. ¿Cómo te llamas?   d. I'm from...

_____ 5. Soy de...   e. What's your name?

_____ 6. ¿Y usted?   f. Nice to meet you.

2. Después de la clase

_____ 1. Hasta mañana.   a. I'd like you to meet...

_____ 2. ¡Que te vaya bien!   b. See you later.

_____ 3. Necesito pasar esta clase.   c. I need to pass this class.

_____ 4. Es mi mejor amiga.   d. Have a nice day!

_____ 5. Hasta luego.   e. She's my best friend.

_____ 6. Te presento a...   f. See you tomorrow.

Video CD-ROM

B. ¡Hola! Use the words from the list to complete the conversations between Adriana and Pilar, a counselor.

Adriana	**mucho**
cómo	**soy de**
español	**usted**
igualmente	**vaya**

Adriana   ¿Habla (1) _____?

Pilar   Sí, (2) _____ España.

Adriana   ¿(3) _____ se llama?

Pilar   Pilar. ¿Y (4) _____?

Adriana   Me llamo (5) _____.

Pilar   (6) _____ gusto.

Adriana   (7) _____.

Video CD-ROM

C. Te presento a Ana Mari. Order the statements in the dialogue, so that it makes sense.

_____ a. Igualmente.

__1__ b. Hola, Ana Mari. ¿Cómo estás?

_____ c. Mucho gusto.

_____ d. Pilar, te presento a Ana Mari.

_____ e. Muy bien. ¿Y tú?

_____ f. Bien, gracias.

_____ g. Adiós, Ana Mari. ¡Que te vaya bien!

_____ h. Bueno, hasta luego. Tengo clase ahora.

Vocabulario 1

Greeting and saying good-bye to others
• Greetings and good-byes

D. Saludos. Match each statement with the appropriate response.

_____ 1. Hola. ¿Cómo te llamas?

_____ 2. Te presento a Roberto.

_____ 3. Hasta luego.

_____ 4. ¿Cómo está usted?

a. Bien, ¿y usted?

b. Martha.

c. Adiós.

d. Mucho gusto.

E. ¿Formal o informal? Write the expressions that you would use when talking to Manolo and those you would use when talking to Professor López in the appropiate column.

| ¿Cómo estás? | ¿Cómo se llama? | ¿Y tú? | ¿Y usted? |
| Te presento a... | ¿Cómo está? | ¿Cómo te llamas? | ¡Que le vaya bien! |

Manolo

_____

_____

_____

_____

Profesor López

_____

_____

_____

_____

F. Para saludar. Select the appropriate greeting, according to the time of the day: **Buenos días, Buenas tardes,** or **Buenas noches.**

1. 1:45 pm _____.

2. 8:00 pm _____.

3. 6:30 am _____.

4. 10:30 pm _____.

5. 11:00 am _____.

6. 3:30 pm _____.

G. Hablas con Sofía. Complete the conversation.

Sofía   ¡Hola! ¿Cómo estás?

Tú   (1) _____

Sofía   Bien, gracias. Mira, te presento a Manolo.

Tú   (2) _____.

Manolo   Igualmente. Bueno, adiós.

Tú   (3) _____.

H. Una conversación con tu profesor(a). Complete the conversation.

Profesor(a)   Buenas tardes, (1) ¿_____?

Tú   (2) Me llamo _____.

Profesor(a)   Mucho gusto. ¿Cómo está hoy?

Tú   (3) _____

Profesor(a)   Bien, también. Hasta mañana.

Tú   (4) _____

Profesor(a)   Gracias. Igualmente.

Vocabulario 2

Saying which classes you take
• **The alphabet**
• **Class subjects**

I. Ésa me gusta. *(I like that one.)* Indicate which subjects you like **(me gusta)** and which ones you do not like **(no me gusta).**

antropología	_____	**economía**	_____
drama	_____	**filosofía**	_____
literatura	_____	**educación física**	_____
astronomía	_____	**geografía**	_____
sicología	_____	**química**	_____
biología	_____	**historia**	_____
música	_____	**español**	_____
botánica	_____	**inglés**	_____

J. El alfabeto. Write the names of the underlined letters in the following words. Then write their English equivalents.

> **Modelo**   **Mil̲l̲ones** se escribe con **elle** y significa *millions.*

1. **G̲eografía** se escribe con _____ y significa _____.

2. **Ex̲amen** se escribe con _____ y significa _____.

3. **Bañ̲o** se escribe con _____ y significa _____.

4. **Muj̲er** se escribe con _____ y significa _____.

5. **D̲iccionario** se escribe con _____ y significa _____.

6. **Car̲ro** se escribe con _____ y significa _____.

7. **Lápiz̲** se escribe con _____ y significa _____.

8. **M̲ochila** se escribe con _____ y significa _____.

9. **Fot̲ocopia** se escribe con _____ y significa _____.

10. **Univ̲ersidad** se escribe con _____ y significa _____.

Vocabulario 3

Saying how many credits/units you take and how many hours you work
• Numbers 0–40

K. Los números. Match each number with its Spanish equivalent. Draw a line to link them.

14	doce
0	veinticinco
24	veintidós
12	dieciséis
7	cero
25	trece
13	catorce
37	once
40	veinticuatro
11	siete
22	treinta y siete
16	cuarenta

L. ¿Qué sigue? *(What's next?)* Write out the numbers that precede and follow the given numbers.

1.	_____cuatro_____	cinco	_____seis_____
2.	_____	quince	_____
3.	_____	dieciocho	_____
4	_____	veintiocho	_____
5.	_____	treinta y tres	_____
6.	_____	treinta y seis	_____
7.	_____	treinta y nueve	_____

M. Preguntas personales. Answer the following questions.

1. ¿Qué *(which)* clases tomas este semestre? _____

2. ¿Cuántas unidades *(units/credits)* son? _____

3. ¿Cuántas horas trabajas? _____

4. ¿Cuántas horas estudias? _____

5. ¿Qué clases necesitas tomar *(do you need to take)* el próximo *(next)* semestre?

_____

Para terminar

N. Una invitación de boda. *(A wedding invitation)* Examine the Mexican wedding invitation below in order to answer the following questions. You will also need to read the explanation that follows.

1. What is the name of the bride's father?

_____

2. What is the name of the groom's mother?

_____

3. What will be the traditional married name of the bride?

_____

4. What is the groom's full name? (first name and last names)

_____

Minerva Guadalupe y Arturo

Ante Dios y con la bendición de nuestros padres

Jesús Moreno Olivarria	*Arturo Hauter Salazar*
Minerva Ibarra de Moreno	*Ada González de Hauter*

*Nos uniremos en matrimonio y les invitamos
a la ceremonia religiosa el sábado
veintidós de octubre a las diecinueve horas
en la Iglesia del Espíritu Santo,
Fraccionamiento Chapultepec.*

*Impartiendo la Bendición
el Reverendo Alfonso González Quevedo S. E.*

Tijuana, Baja California

Cultura a lo vivo

You may have noticed that Spanish speakers often have long names. Most Spanish speakers have two first names, both of which they may or may not use. Some double names, however, are common, such as Ana Mari and José Luis. In addition, Spanish speakers use two last names—their father's family name (which goes first), and their mother's family name (which goes second). For example, a brother and a sister, both single, might be called Ramón Robledo Suárez and Ana María Robledo Suárez (informally, they would be Ramón Robledo and Ana Mari Robledo). If Ana Mari marries, she will not change her last name; traditionally, her husband's last name will be added, using **de,** and replacing her mother's last name. So, if Ana María Robledo Suárez marries Manolo Báez Rodríguez, her name would be Ana María Robledo de Báez. Today many Hispanic women keep their maiden name; in this case, Mrs. Báez would be Ana María Robledo.

Ñ. Los personajes de Escenas de la vida. In **Escenas de la vida**, you will follow the lives of several Spanish speakers who live and study in the United States. As you learn about them, you will learn to communicate in Spanish, and you will get a glimpse into the rich and diverse culture of the Spanish-speaking world. Read the information for each character and answer the questions in **Práctica O.**

Sofía Blasio Salas

mexicana

20 años

arquitectura

extrovertida

Nombre

Nacionalidad

Edad

Carrera

Personalidad

Manolo Báez Rodríguez

cubano

25 años

no ha decidido[1]

bohemio

Wayne Andrew Reilly

norteamericano

23 años

computación

aventurero

Nombre

Nacionalidad

Edad

Carrera

Personalidad

Adriana Ferreira de Barrón

puertorriqueña

45 años

contabilidad[2]

reservada

Ana María Robledo Suárez

mexicoamericana

20 años

leyes[3]

sociable

Nombre

Nacionalidad

Edad

Carrera

Personalidad

Emilio Andrés Pradillo Salas

español

30 años

publicidad

serio

[1]*undecided* [2]*accounting* [3]*law*

O. ¡Mucho gusto! Based on the information about the characters, answer the following questions.

1. What is Sofía's mother's last name?

_____

2. Which of the female characters is married?

_____

3. Who has a double name?

_____

4. What is Manolo's father's last name?

_____

5. If Sofía married Wayne Reilly, what would be her traditional married name?

_____

6. Where is Sofía from?

_____

7. What is Manolo studying?

_____

8. What is Wayne studying?

_____

9. How old is Adriana?

_____

10. Where is Emilio from?

_____

11. How do you say *serious* in Spanish?

_____

12. What is the English equivalent of
    a. **aventurero?** _____
    b. **arquitectura?** _____

P. ¿Y tú? Now write your information.

```
┌─────────────────────────────┐
│                             │
│                             │
│    Your picture goes here!  │
│                             │
│                             │
└─────────────────────────────┘
```

Apellido: _____

Nacionalidad: _____

Edad: _____

Carrera: _____

Personalidad: _____

¡A escuchar!

Episodio **1**

Comprensión

Audio
CD-ROM

A. Las clases.

Parte 1. You are going to listen to Ana Mari and some of her classmates say which classes they are taking this semester. First, listen to the list of classes and repeat each one after the speaker.

economía	inglés	sicología	matemáticas	filosofía
astronomía	química	tenis	historia	

Now, listen to Ana Mari and her friends and check off the classes each person is taking.

	Ana Mari	Raúl	Cristina	Carmen
astronomía	☐	☐	☐	☐
economía	☐	☐	☐	☐
filosofía	☐	☐	☐	☐
historia	☐	☐	☐	☐
inglés	☐	☐	☐	☐
matemáticas	☐	☐	☐	☐
química	☐	☐	☐	☐
sicología	☐	☐	☐	☐
tenis	☐	☐	☐	☐

Parte 2. You will now hear four questions. Look at the list of classes in **Parte 1** and answer the questions that you hear. Then repeat the correct answer after the speaker.

Modelo	You hear:	¿Cuántos estudiantes toman tenis?
	You say:	Tres estudiantes: Ana Mari, Raúl y Cristina toman tenis.

Audio
CD-ROM

B. ¿Cuántos? How many are there of the following items? Listen and write the numerals for the numbers that you hear.

1. ___ sillas
2. ___ banderas
3. ___ lápices
4. ___ plumas
5. ___ diccionarios

6. ___ escritorios
7. ___ cuadernos
8. ___ libros
9. ___ profesores
10. ___ mapas

Pronunciación

Audio CD-ROM

Las vocales. The vowels in Spanish, **a, e, i, o,** and **u,** are important sounds to master. Unlike English, each vowel in Spanish has only one pronunciation. In addition, the vowel sounds are shorter and crisper than the vowel sounds in English. Repeat these letters, words, and sentences after the speaker.

a			
Ana	lápiz	habilidad	Ana camina a la casa.
Adán	papa	América	Adán habla con las amigas de Ana.
e			
Pepe	me	septiembre	Pelé bebe leche.
te	le	televisión	Héctor lee lentamente.
i			
Ignacio	igual	importante	Allí está mi diccionario de inglés.
Víctor	química	librería	Perdí el lápiz de Lilí.
o			
Octavio	kiosko	oportunidad	Manolo dejó las fotocopias.
poco	hombre	fotocopias	El pobre hombre come poco.
u			
Humberto	número	universidad	Lupe usa la computadora.
Lupe	mujer	unidad	La mujer usa su pluma.

Más escenas de la vida

Audio CD-ROM

A. ¿Quién lo dijo? Wayne is calling Ramón, and Ramón's mother answers. Listen to their conversation, and indicate who said each statement: Wayne **(W)** or Ramón **(R)**. You will hear the conversation twice.

_____ 1. Buenos días, señora.

_____ 2. Bien gracias, ¿y usted?

_____ 3. ¿Qué pasó, Wayne?

_____ 4. Más o menos. Estoy un poco enfermo.

_____ 5. Hasta luego.

_____ 6. Gracias. Hasta mañana.

B. ¿Cierto o falso? Sofía and Ana Mari run into Adriana at school. Indicate whether the following statements are **cierto** or **falso**, according to their conversation. You will hear the conversation twice.

	Cierto	Falso
1. Adriana runs into Ana Mari and Sofía in the afternoon.	☐	☐
2. Adriana has met Ana Mari before.	☐	☐
3. Sofía wishes Adriana a good day.	☐	☐
4. Ana Mari and Sofía are going to work.	☐	☐
5. Adriana will see Sofía again tomorrow.	☐	☐

Episodio

2

Escenas de la vida: En la librería

A. ¡Mira cuánto puedes entender!

Video CD-ROM

Audio CD-ROM

1. Watch or listen to the **Escena** to indicate who needs to buy the following items: Manolo (**M**), or Sofía (**S**). Place an **X** next to the items no one mentions.

___ a. ___ b. ___ c.

___ d. ___ e. ___ f.

___ g. ___ h. ___ i.

2. First, place a check next to the classes Manolo has tomorrow. Then, write the time when the classes begin.

miércoles	
7:45	Cálculo
9:20	Geología
	Física

lunes/miércoles/ viernes	
☐ Cálculo	7:45
☐ Sicología	
martes/jueves	
☐ Computación	8:45
☐ Historia	10:00
☐ Sociología	5:15

Cultura a lo vivo

In the Spanish-speaking world, a student must complete all general education requirements in high school in order to enter the university. The specifics vary from country to country, but before entering a university, a student must declare a major and frequently take an admissions exam to determine whether they qualify for admission. Upon entering the university, a student begins a specific field of study; there are no undeclared majors.

B. ¿Te diste cuenta? Listen to or watch the **Escena** again to match the following sentence fragments.

Video
CD-ROM

Audio
CD-ROM

_____ 1. Manolo gasta más de... a. dos cuadernos.

_____ 2. Sofía necesita comprar... b. al café mañana.

_____ 3. Los libros cuestan... c. es sicología.

_____ 4. La clase favorita de Manolo... d. 200 dólares en libros.

_____ 5. Manolo y Sofía van... e. mucho dinero.

C. ¿Quién lo dijo? Review the **Escena** and indicate whether the following phrases describe Sofía (**S**), Manolo (**M**), or both.

Video
CD-ROM

Audio
CD-ROM

_____ 1. Necesita novio.

_____ 2. Necesita libros.

_____ 3. Gasta mucho en libros.

_____ 4. Toma cinco clases.

_____ 5. Necesita ir a la biblioteca.

_____ 6. Va al café mañana.

Práctica adicional	
Cuaderno de tareas	Video CD-ROM
WB pp.51–52, A–C	Episodio 2

Para comunicarnos mejor

Vocabulario 1

Identifying university-related objects, places, and people
• **University-related vocabulary**

Las cosas, los lugares y las personas en la universidad

Cosas	_Things_	Lugares	_Places_
la bandera	_flag_	el auditorio	_auditorium_
la calculadora	_calculator_	el baño	_bathroom_
el cuaderno	_notebook_	la biblioteca	_library_
el diccionario	_dictionary_	la cafetería	_cafeteria_
el escritorio	_desk_ (teacher's)	la cancha de tenis	_tennis court_
el lápiz	_pencil_	de vóleibol	_volleyball court_
el libro	_book_	el edificio	_building_
el mapa	_map_	la enfermería	_health center; infirmary_
la mochila	_backpack_	el estacionamiento	_parking lot_
el papel	_paper_	el estadio	_stadium_
la papelera	_wastebasket_	el gimnasio	_gym_
el pizarrón	_chalkboard_	la librería	_bookstore_
la pluma	_pen_	la oficina	_office_
la prueba	_quiz_	la piscina	_swimming pool_
la puerta	_door_	la residencia estudiantil	_dormitory_
el pupitre	_desk_ (student's)	el salón de clase	_classroom_

el reloj	clock
la silla	chair
la tele(visión)	TV
la ventana	window
la videocasetera	VCR

Personas — *People*

el compañero	la compañera	los/las compañeros/as	classmate(s)
el consejero	la consejera	los/las consejeros/as	counselor(s)
el estudiante	la estudiante	los/las estudiantes	student(s)

También se dice...

el estudiante ⟶ el alumno
la papelera ⟶ el basurero,
el bote/cubo/latón de basura
el pizarrón ⟶ la pizarra
la pluma ⟶ el bolígrafo
el profesor ⟶ el maestro
el salón ⟶ el aula, la sala

Learning Strategy: Make your own tape

Record the words or phrases you need to learn and their English equivalents on a cassette. Listen to them as often as you can, perhaps even while you drive or jog. When preparing the tape, be sure to pause before recording the English translation in order to allow yourself time to say the word/phrase.

¡Fíjate!

You will see **También se dice** boxes throughout the text. Because Spanish is spoken in many countries, many times there are five or six different words for the same item. You do not need to learn all the variations; learn the ones your professor tells you or the ones you hear in your community.

PRÁCTICA

A. ¿Qué es? Identifica las cosas, los lugares y las personas en las ilustraciones.

a 1. _____
2. _____
3. _____
4. _____
5. _____
6. _____
7. _____
8. _____
9. _____
10. _____

b 1. _____
2. _____
3. _____
4. _____
5. _____
6. _____

B. ¿Qué compraste? *(What did you buy?)* Write down the items you bought this semester for your classes.

Este semestre compré *(I bought)...* _____

_____

_____

C. ¿Adónde vas *(Where do you go)* con más frecuencia?

Parte 1. How often do you go to the following places? Write **0** next to places you never go to, **1** next to places you almost never go to, **2** next to places you sometimes go to, **3** next to places you often go to, and **4** next to places you go to every day.

¡Fíjate!

The words in **Banco de palabras** are presented to enable you to carry out specific classroom activities. You are not expected to memorize them or use them without support. However, begin to familiarize yourself with the words, since they may become part of your active vocabulary in later episodes.

Banco de palabras	
Voy	(2) **a veces**
I go	*sometimes*
(4) **todos los días**	(1) **casi nunca**
every day	*almost never*
(3) **con frecuencia**	(0) **nunca**
often	*never*

¿Con qué frecuencia vas...?

_____ 1. al auditorio

_____ 2. al gimnasio

_____ 3. a la piscina

_____ 4. a la librería

_____ 5. al estadio

_____ 6. a la cafetería

_____ 7. a la biblioteca

_____ 8. a la oficina de los profesores

_____ 9. a la enfermería

_____ 10. a las canchas

 Parte 2. Now interview a partner to find out how often they go to these places. Use the expressions from the **Banco de palabras.**

> **Modelo** —¿Con qué frecuencia vas al auditorio?
> —Casi nunca voy. ¿Y tú?
> —Yo voy todos los días.

¡Fíjate!

Use **nunca** and **casi nunca** before the verb **voy**; use the other expressions after it.

Práctica adicional

Cuaderno de tareas
WB pp.52–53, D–G

Gramática 1

Talking about university-related objects, places, and people

- **Gender of nouns**
- **Plural of nouns**
- <u>Hay</u>

In the dialogue, Manolo mentioned **el libro de sicología** and **unos libros de historia.** They also mentioned **una mochila** and **la biblioteca. Libro, mochila,** and **biblioteca** are nouns. A noun is a word that names a person, a place, an animal, an object, or an idea. The articles **(los artículos)** *the* **(el, la)** or *a(n)* **(un, una)** usually accompany nouns.

• Gender of nouns

Every noun in Spanish has a gender (feminine or masculine) and number (singular or plural). When you learn a new word, you must also learn whether that word is feminine or masculine, since the gender of nouns is arbitrary. See if you can make some helpful generalizations.

Analizar y descubrir

1. Look at the following feminine words:

la plum**a**	una televisi**ón**	la universid**ad**
la sill**a**	una conversaci**ón**	la libert**ad**

Using these words, what observations can you make about the endings of feminine nouns? Most words that end in the letters _____ , _____, and_____ are feminine. Use **la** or **una** with feminine words.

2. Look at the following masculine words:

un libr**o**   un pupitr**e**   el pizarr**ón**   el ingl**és**   un profeso**r**   el pape**l**

Using these words, what observations can you make about the endings of masculine nouns? Most words that end in the vowels _____ and _____, or in a _____ are masculine. Use **el** or **un** with masculine nouns.

3. Although most words that end in **-e** are masculine, some words that end in **-e** are feminine. Therefore, it is best to learn the word along with its article:

(feminine)	**la clase**	**la noche**
(masculine)	**el pupitre**	**el coche** (*car*)

4. Most words that end in **-a** are feminine, but a few words (of Greek origin) that end in **-ma** are masculine. Notice that these words are cognates.

(masculine)	**el** proble**ma**	**el** progra**ma**	**el** siste**ma**

Los artículos					
	Singular		**Plural**		
Definidos	**el, la**	*the*	**los, las**	*the*	
Indefinidos	**un, una**	*a(n)*	**unos, unas**	*some*	

PRÁCTICA

D. ¿Masculino o femenino? Escribe **el** o **la**.

1. _____ estacionamiento
2. _____ pizarrón
3. _____ bandera
4. _____ drama

5. _____ oficina
6. _____ piscina
7. _____ teatro
8. _____ inglés

9. _____ cancha
10. _____ biblioteca
11. _____ computación
12. _____ pupitre

E. Artículos indefinidos. Escribe **un** o **una**.

1. _____ auditorio
2. _____ reloj
3. _____ silla
4. _____ libro

5. _____ profesor
6. _____ clase
7. _____ pluma
8. _____ ventana

9. _____ diccionario
10. _____ lápiz
11. _____ juego de béisbol
12. _____ comunidad

• Plural of nouns

Analizar y descubrir

In a conversation with Adriana, Sofía said:

Las universidades aquí son muy diferentes...	*The universities here are quite different...*
Aquí **los salones** están muy bien equipados.	*Here the classrooms are very well-equipped.*
¿En Puerto Rico hay **consejeros...?**	*Are there counselors in Puerto Rico...?*
Hablando de **profesores...**	*Speaking of professors...*

1. Examine the above examples to complete the following:

    a. What is added to the word **universidad** to make it plural? _____

    b. What is added to **salón** to make it plural? _____

    c. What is added to **consejero** to make it plural? _____

    d. What is added to **profesor** to make it plural? _____

2. Based on your answers, what observations can you make about how plural nouns are formed in Spanish?

Pluralizing rule:

    a. When a word ends in a consonant, add _____ to make it plural.

    b. When a word ends in a vowel, add _____ to make it plural.

Spelling rule: lápiz ⟶ lápices

    c. When a word ends in _____, change the **-z** to _____ in the plural form.

Accent marks: pizarrón ⟶ pizarrones

    d. When a word has an accent mark on the last syllable and it ends in a consonant, it loses _____ in the plural form.

PRÁCTICA

F. En la universidad. Escribe la forma plural de estos sustantivos.

1. el profesor _____

2. la silla _____

3. un estadio _____

4. la biblioteca _____

5. una cancha _____

6. un baño _____

G. Personas y cosas. Escribe la forma singular de estos sustantivos.

1. los consejeros _____   5. unos relojes _____

2. las compañeras _____   6. los cuadernos _____

3. unos mapas _____   7. unos lápices _____

4. los pizarrones _____   8. las bibliotecas _____

• Hay

Use **hay** + [*indefinite article*] to express the English equivalent of *there is/are* and to describe what you see. Use **unos/as** to say *some*.

Hay un diccionario en la mochila.   *There is a dictionary in the backpack.*

Hay unos estudiantes en la oficina.   *There are some students in the office.*

PRÁCTICA

H. ¿Qué hay en el escritorio? Escribe los nombres *(names)* de las cosas que hay en el escritorio.

Modelo

Hay una mochila.

1. _____

2. _____

3. _____

4. _____

5. _____

6. _____

I. ¿Qué hay en tu mochila? Escribe los nombres de cuatro cosas.

1. _____

2. _____

3. _____

4. _____

J. ¿Está bien equipado tu salón? Describe what your classroom does and doesn't have, using the vocabulary on pages 32–33. Write your answers in your notebook.

Práctica adicional

Cuaderno de tareas
WB pp.53–54, H–K

Modelo	En el salón de... hay...
	En el salón de... no hay...

Asking and telling when an event takes place
• Time of events

You heard the following statements and questions when Sofía and Manolo were discussing the times their classes meet.

¿A qué hora es tu clase de sicología?	*(At) What time is your psychology class?*
Es a la una y media.	*It's at one-thirty.*
¿Nos vemos mañana **a las doce?**	*See you tomorrow at twelve?*
...mi clase de física es **a las doce y cuarto.**	*...my physics class is at twelve-fifteen.*

Spanish, like English, depends on a few routine phrases to express clock time. One formula with **a** is used to say when events happen. Look at Ana Mari's weekly agenda to answer the following questions.

¿A qué hora?

¿A qué hora es...

la clase de horticultura?	**A la** una **de la tarde.**
la clase de inglés?	**A las** once y cuarto **de la mañana.**
la clase de biología?	**A las** siete y media **de la noche.**
el concierto?	**A las** cinco menos veinte **de la tarde.**
la fiesta?	**A las** diez menos cuarto **de la noche.**

AGOSTO/SEPTIEMBRE

semana 36

31 lunes	1 martes	2 miércoles
8	8	8
9	9	9
10	10	10
11	11 :15 inglés	11
12	12	12
1 horticultura	1	1
2	2	2
3	3	3
4	4	4
5	5	5
6	6	6
7	7 :30 biología	7
8	8	8

3 jueves	4 viernes	5 sábado
8	8	4:40 concierto
9	9	
10	10	
11	11	
12	12	6 domingo
1	1	
2	2	
3	3	
4	4	
5	5	
6	6	
7	7	
8	8	
	9:45 ¡fiesta!	

Notice that **a la** is used with *one o'clock* and that **a las** is used for the rest of the hours.

PRÁCTICA

K. ¿A qué hora...? When does Professor López teach this semester? Look at his schedule and write out when the calculus class meets. Note that the 24-hour clock (military time) is used.

Modelo	16:40
	El profesor tiene una clase a las cinco menos veinte de la tarde.

¡Fíjate!

The 24-hour clock is generally used in newspapers, and in TV, train, flight, and class schedules throughout the Spanish-speaking world. To convert between a 24-hour and a 12-hour clock, subtract twelve from times after 12:00 p.m. (15:00-12 = 3:00 p.m.).

Cálculo   a. 7:30 _____

b. 10:00 _____

c. 14:15 _____

d. 15:00 _____

e. 17:20 _____

f. 19:45 _____

L. Vamos al cine. *(Let's go to the movies.)* Tienes planes para ir al cine con un amigo. Pregúntale a qué hora son las funciones *(screenings)*. Túrnense.

Modelo	*Fresa y chocolate:* 11:30 / 18:20 / 21:55
	—¿**A qué hora es** *Fresa y chocolate*?
	—**Es a las once y media de la mañana, a las seis y veinte de la tarde y a las diez menos cinco de la noche.**

¡Fíjate!

These films are highly acclaimed and are available in most video stores. Check them out!

★	1. Frida	14:45-16:30-18:05
★	2. El crimen del padre Amaro	11:15-17:40-22:25
★	3. Como agua para chocolate	14:30-16:15-19:10
★	4. Hable con ella	10:50-12:15-21:20
★	5. Chasing papi	17:25-19:35-20:17

M. Hoy y mañana. Dile a tu compañero/a a qué hora son tus clases hoy *(today)* y mañana *(tomorrow)*.

Modelo

Hoy tengo clases a las ocho, a las nueve, a las once y media y a las cuatro. Mañana tengo clases a las ocho y a la una. ¿Y tú?

N. ¿A qué hora...? Conversa con tres compañeros para saber quién sale de casa más temprano *(leaves home earliest)* y quién llega más tarde *(gets home latest)*.

Modelo	—¿A qué hora sales de casa por la mañana?
	—A las siete y media. ¿Y tú?
	—A las seis y cuarto. ¿A qué hora llegas a casa?
	—A la una y media de la tarde. ¿Y tú?
	—A las ocho de la noche.

	nombre *(name)*	sale de casa	llega a casa
1.	_____	_____	_____
2.	_____	_____	_____
3.	_____	_____	_____

Audio
CD-ROM

Ñ. El horario. *(The schedule)* Listen to find out when the following classes are being offered. Write each time in the space provided.

1. inglés   _____   4. arte moderno   _____

2. historia de Estados Unidos   _____   5. física   _____

3. biología   _____

O. ¡A hablar! In pairs, discuss your schedules. Fill in the agenda with the times your partner has classes, which classes they are, and the times your partner works.

Estudiante					Semestre Nº 1
	lunes	martes	miércoles	jueves	viernes
AM					
PM					

Práctica adicional	
Cuaderno de tareas WB p.55, L–N LM pp.57–58, A–B, Pron.	Audio CD-ROM Episodio 2

Actividades comunicativas

 A. El horario de clases.

Instrucciones para **Estudiante 1**

It is time to plan your class schedule for next semester. The chart shows the hours you will be at work **(trabajo)**. Before you graduate, you need to complete six courses:

antropología	biología	historia
álgebra	español	sicología

You will not be able to take all these classes this semester. Call your peer advisor for information and choose the four courses that best meet your needs. Use expressions like the ones below.

Banco de palabras:
Los días de la semana

los lunes
on Mondays

los martes
on Tuesdays

los miércoles
on Wednesdays

los jueves
on Thursdays

los viernes
on Fridays

los sábados
on Saturdays

los domingos
on Sundays

¿A qué hora es la clase de...?	*When is... class?*
¿Qué día es...?	*What day is...?*
Los lunes trabajo de... a...	*On Mondays I work from... to...*
¿Hay una clase de... a las...?	*Is there a... class at...?*
A esa hora no puedo.	*I can't do that time.*
¿Hay otra clase de...?	*Is there another... class?*

	Lunes	Martes	Miércoles	Jueves	Viernes
8:00–9:00					
9:00–10:00					
10:00–11:00					
11:00–12:00		Trabajo		Trabajo	
12:00–1:00		Trabajo		Trabajo	
1:00–4:00					
4:00–6:00	Trabajo		Trabajo		
6:00–8:00	Trabajo		Trabajo		

A. El horario de clases.

Instrucciones para **Estudiante 2**

You are a peer advisor. By phone, help a student prepare a class schedule for next semester. Use expressions like the ones below.

¿Por qué no tomas...?   *Why don't you take...?*
Hay una clase de...a...   *There's a class from... to...*
¿Puedes tomar...?   *Can you take...?*
No hay clase de... a esa hora.   *There is no... class at that time.*
La clase de... es de... a...   *The class is from... to...*
Hay dos secciones de...   *There are two sections of...*

Clase/hora	Clase/hora
álgebra	**antropología**
lun. mar. miér. juev. vier. 9:00–10:00	lun. mar. miér. juev. 8:00–9:00
lun. mar. miér. juev. vier. 10:00–11:00	mar. juev. 16:00–17:30
biología	**español**
lun. mar. miér. juev. 8:00–9:00	lun. mar. miér. juev. vier. 8:00–9:00
mar. juev. 10:00–12:00	lun. mar. miér. juev. vier. 10:00–11:00
miér. 16:00–20:00	mar. juev. 12:00–14:30
historia	**sicología**
mar. juev. 11:00–12:15	lun. miér. vier. 10:00–11:00
lun. miér. vier. 17:00–19:30	lun. miér. vier. 16:00–18:15
	mar. juev. 10:00–11:15

B. Los precios.

Instrucciones para **Estudiante 1**

You and a friend are tired of spending so much for school supplies. This semester you are shopping for the best prices. The prices you found in **Papelería Las Rosas** are shown in the drawing. Your partner found different prices in **Papelería El Trópico.** Share your information to determine the best price. Circle the items you decide to buy at your store. Follow the model.

Modelo	—¿**Cuánto cuesta** *(how much is)* **una calculadora ahí** *(there)*?
	—**Aquí** *(here)* **cuesta veinte dólares y diecinueve centavos. ¿Y ahí?**
	—**Aquí cuesta veinte dólares y veintinueve centavos.**
	—**Ah, pues aquí es más barato** *(cheaper)*.

B. Los precios.

Instrucciones para Estudiante 2

You and a friend are tired of spending so much for school supplies. This semester you are shopping for the best prices. The prices you found in **Papelería El Trópico** are shown in the drawing. Your partner found different prices in **Papelería Las Rosas**. Share your information to determine the best price. Circle the items you decide to buy at your store. Follow the model.

Modelo —¿**Cuánto cuesta** (how much is) **una calculadora ahí** (there)?
—**Aquí** (here) **cuesta veinte dólares y diecinueve centavos. ¿Y ahí?**
—**Aquí cuesta veinte dólares y veintinueve centavos.**
—**Ah, pues aquí es más barato** (cheaper).

C. Diferencias.

Instrucciones para **Estudiante 1**

The picture of the classroom below differs in several ways from your partner's picture. You and your partner will take turns saying what you see until you find seven differences. Check off the seven differences. Follow the model.

Modelo	—Hay una profesora en el salón.
	—Aquí también.
	or
	—Aquí no hay una profesora. Hay un profesor.

C. Diferencias.

Instrucciones para **Estudiante 2**

The picture of the classroom below differs in several ways from your partner's picture. You and your partner will take turns saying what you see until you find seven differences. Check off the seven differences. Follow the model.

Modelo	—Hay una profesora en el salón.
	—Aquí también.
	or
	—Aquí no hay una profesora. Hay un profesor.

![Illustration of a classroom with a teacher standing by the chalkboard pointing, a television on a stand, and several students seated at desks.]

La correspondencia

El correo: El catálogo. Look over the following brochure in order to answer the questions below.

Reading Strategy: Determining the purpose for reading

Successful readers first determine a purpose for reading, which guides the way they approach a selection. You should develop this strategy as you read in Spanish, where a purpose for reading is even more important, since here, at the beginning of your study, you will not understand large amounts of the text. For this reason, limit your purpose to understanding words and phrases—those you have learned and those you can understand based on their similarity to English.

You will read an entry from the catalog of the **Universidad Autónoma de Guadalajara.** First look at the following questions (1–4) to determine your purpose for reading. Then, after you have read the selection, answer the questions.

Plan de estudios

1. What is the English equivalent of **Fisioterapia?** _____

2. How many quarters are necessary to complete a degree? _____

3. Indicate in which quarter students take the following courses:

   a. Human Anatomy _____   c. Introduction to Pathology _____

   b. Nutrition _____   d. Pharmacology _____

Mercado de trabajo

4. Where may a person with this degree work?

   a. _____   b. _____   c. _____   d. _____

COLEGIO DE CIENCIAS ASOCIADAS A LA SALUD

Fisioterapia

Perfil del esgresado

El profesional en Fisioterapia estará capacitado para distinguir, en una evaluación física, los estados de normalidad e implementar, en su caso, el tratamiento de rehabilitación indicado, así como la aplicación del mismo, manejando el material y equipo necesarios en un área de medicina física y rehabilitación. Podrá participar conjuntamente con el médico fisiatra en la rehabilitación de casos especiales y en medicina del deporte.

Mercado de trabajo

El campo de trabajo del fisioterapeuta es amplio considerando su participación en programas dirigidos a personas sanas o enfermas y en el deporte. Escuelas de Educación Física, Clubes Deportivos, Gimnasios, Hospitales y Clínicas del Sector Público y Privado, Departamentos de Medicina del Deporte y Atención a pacientes particulares.

PLAN DE ESTUDIOS

PRIMER TRIMESTRE
- Introducción a la Fisioterapia.
- Anatomía Humana.
- Fisiología General.

SEGUNDO TRIMESTRE
- Principios para el Cuidado del Paciente.
- Primeros Auxilios.
- Fisiología Especial.

TERCER TRIMESTRE
- Sicología Aplicada a la Fisioterapia.
- Física Aplicada a la Fisioterapia.
- Introducción a la Patología.

CUARTO TRIMESTRE
- Instrumentación a la Fisioterapia.
- Técnicas de Evaluación del Estado Físico Normal.
- Ejercicio Físico.

QUINTO TRIMESTRE
- Técnicas de Evaluación de Escuelas Patológicas.
- Medios en la Fisioterapia.
- Deontología.

SEXTO TRIMESTRE
- Rehabilitación Músculo-Esquelética.
- Técnicas de Rehabilitación Pediátrica.
- Técnicas de Rehabilitación Geriátrica.

SÉPTIMO TRIMESTRE
- El Deporte y la Fisioterapia.
- Nutriología.
- Terapia y Kinesiología.

OCTAVO TRIMESTRE
- Rehabilitación del Paciente Cardíaco.
- Rehabilitación del Paciente Neurológico.
- Farmacología.

En papel: ¿Qué hay en tu universidad? Write sentences describing what there is and what there is not at your school, using the vocabulary on pages 32–33. Also indicate what classes you are taking and when they meet.

| Modelo | En mi universidad hay una piscina, pero *(but)* no hay auditorios. Mi clase de matemática es a las ocho de la mañana. |

¡A ver de nuevo! Contesta las preguntas.

Video
CD-ROM

Audio
CD-ROM

1. ¿Qué necesita comprar Sofía? _____

_____

2. ¿Cuántas clases toma Manolo? _____

3. ¿Qué clases tiene Manolo mañana? _____

4. ¿Adónde va Sofía antes *(before)* de su clase de física? _____

5. ¿A qué hora es su clase de física? _____

6. ¿Adónde van mañana después de la clase de cálculo? _____

Invitación a **Honduras**

Del álbum de
Ana Marí

Honduras es un país pequeño *(small country)*; es un poco más grande que *(slightly larger than)* el estado de Tenessee. Copán es una bella ciudad maya *(beautiful Mayan city)* en Honduras. Durante más de un milenio, Copán fue *(was)* el centro cultural y educativo más importante para los Mayas.

Práctica adicional		
Cuaderno de tareas WB p.56, Ñ LM p.58, A–B	Audio CD-ROM Episodio 2	Website vistahigher learning.com

Vocabulario del Episodio 2

¿A qué hora es...?
Es a las once y cuarto de la mañana.
Es a la una y media de la tarde.
Es a las diez menos veinte de la noche.
Hay...

(At) What time is...?
It's at eleven-fifteen in the morning.
It's at one-thirty in the afternoon.
It's at twenty till ten in the evening.
There is/are...

En la universidad *At the university*

Cosas	*Things*	**Lugares**	*Places*
la bandera	*flag*	el auditorio	*auditorium*
la calculadora	*calculator*	el baño	*bathroom*
el cuaderno	*notebook*	la biblioteca	*library*
el diccionario	*dictionary*	la cafetería	*cafeteria*
el escritorio	*desk* (teacher's)	la cancha de tenis	*tennis court*
el lápiz	*pencil*	de vóleibol	*volleyball court*
el libro	*book*	el edificio	*building*
el mapa	*map*	la enfermería	*health center; infirmary*
la mochila	*backpack*	el estacionamiento	*parking lot*
el papel	*paper*	el estadio	*stadium*
la papelera	*wastebasket*	el gimnasio	*gym*
el pizarrón	*chalkboard*	la librería	*bookstore*
la pluma	*pen*	la oficina	*office*
la prueba	*the quiz*	la piscina	*swimming pool*
la puerta	*door*	la residencia estudiantil	*dormitory*
el pupitre	*desk* (student's)	el salón de clase	*classroom*
el reloj	*clock*		
la silla	*chair*		
la tele(visión)	*TV*		
la ventana	*window*		
la videocasetera	*VCR*		

Personas *People*

el compañero	la compañera	los/las compañeros/as	*classmate(s)*
el consejero	la consejera	los/las consejeros/as	*counselor(s)*
el estudiante	la estudiante	los/las estudiantes	*student(s)*

Artículos definidos *Definite articles*

el	*the* (for masculine singular nouns)
la	*the* (for feminine singular nouns)
los	*the* (for masculine plural nouns)
las	*the* (for feminine plural nouns)

Artículos indefinidos *Indefinite articles*

un	*a/an* (for masculine singular nouns)
una	*a/an* (for feminine singular nouns)
unos	*some* (for masculine plural nouns)
unas	*some* (for feminine plural nouns)

Vocabulario personal

Write the words that you need to know to talk about your class schedule and academic life in Spanish.

¡A escribir!

Episodio

2

Escenas de la vida: En la librería

Video
CD-ROM

A. ¡Mira cuánto entendiste! See how much of the **Escena** you understood by matching the Spanish sentences with their English equivalents.

1. Los libros cuestan mucho dinero.

_____ 1. Necesito cuadernos y plumas.   a. I already have my books.

_____ 2. Ya tengo los libros.   b. I need notebooks and pens.

_____ 3. ¿Qué clases tienes mañana?   c. What do you need to buy?

_____ 4. ¿Cuántas clases tomas?   d. How many classes are you taking?

_____ 5. ¿Qué necesitas comprar?   e. What classes do you have tomorrow?

2. Vamos al café.

_____ 1. Está bien.   a. Why don't we go to the café?

_____ 2. Necesito ir a la biblioteca.   b. Let's go after class.

_____ 3. Vamos después de clase.   c. Should I invite Ana Mari?

_____ 4. Nos vemos mañana.   d. That's fine.

_____ 5. ¿Invito a Ana Mari?   e. I need to go to the library.

_____ 6. ¿Por qué no vamos al café?   f. See you tomorrow.

Video
CD-ROM

B. En la librería. Use the words below to complete the conversation.

comprar	cuadernos	historia	mochila
crimen	dinero	libros	plumas

Sofía   ¿Qué necesitas (1) _____?

Manolo   Unos libros de (2) _____. ¿Y tú?

Sofía   Necesito lápices, (3) _____, (4) _____ y una

(5) _____.

Manolo   Cada semestre gasto mucho (6)_____ en libros.

Sofía   No entiendo por qué los (7) _____ cuestan tanto.

Manolo   Es un (8) _____.

Video
CD-ROM

C. Después de clase. Order the statements in the dialogue so that it makes sense.

_____ a. ¡Qué horror! Cinco clases, pobrecito. Oye, ¿qué clases tienes mañana?

_____ b. ¿A qué hora es tu clase de sicología?

_____ c. Cinco, y tres son horribles.

_____ d. ¿Cuántas clases tomas este semestre?

_____ e. Es a la una y media.

_____ f. Cálculo y sicología.

Vocabulario 1 Identifying university-related objects, places, and people
• University-related vocabulary

D. En el salón de clase. Identify the items in the illustration.

1. _____
2. _____
3. _____
4. _____
5. _____
6. _____
7. _____
8. _____
9. _____
10. _____
11. _____
12. _____

E. En la papelería. Identify the items in the illustration.

1. _____
2. _____
3. _____
4. _____
5. _____
6. _____
7. _____
8. _____

Papelería El Trópico

F. ¿Qué son? Examine the following words to determine whether they are **una cosa, un lugar,** or **una persona.** Write them in the appropriate column.

el auditorio	el consejero	la consejera
la bandera	el edificio	el reloj
el compañero	el mapa	la residencia estudiantil
la prueba	la piscina	las sillas

una cosa	un lugar	una persona
_____	_____	_____
_____	_____	_____
_____	_____	_____
_____	_____	_____
_____	_____	_____

G. ¿Adónde vas? Say where you would go in each case.

Modelo	to swim	la piscina

1. to buy a book _____

2. to exercise _____

3. to eat something while at the university _____

4. to park your car _____

5. to watch a football game _____

6. to play tennis _____

7. to study while on campus _____

8. to wash your hands _____

Gramática 1

Talking about university-related objects, places, and people
- **Gender of nouns**
- **Plural of nouns**
- **Hay**

H. ¿Qué necesitas comprar? To express what you need to buy in Spanish, use indefinite articles, just as in English (*I need to buy* a *pen*). Fill in the missing articles.

Necesito comprar...

1. _____ libro

2. _____ reloj

3. _____ mochila

4. _____ mapas de Latinoamérica

5. _____ lápices

6. _____ cuaderno

7. _____ pluma

8. _____ videocaseteras

I. ¿Masculino o femenino? Examine the following words to determine whether they are masculine or feminine. Write them in the appropriate column. Use the definite articles.

auditorio	comunidad	inglés	química	televisión
compañera	consejero	pizarrón	salón	ventana

Masculino

1. _____
2. _____
3. _____
4. _____
5. _____

Femenino

6. _____
7. _____
8. _____
9. _____
10. _____

J. El plural. Make each statement plural.

> **Modelo** Hay <u>un lápiz</u> en la mochila.
> **Hay unos lápices en la mochila.**

1. Hay <u>un estudiante</u> en el salón.

_____

2. Hay <u>una piscina</u> en el gimnasio.

_____

3. Hay <u>una calculadora</u> en el pupitre.

_____

4. Hay <u>un edificio</u> en la universidad.

_____

5. Hay <u>un compañero</u> en la cafetería.

_____

K. Las opiniones. In Spanish, when a general statement is made about something (a noun) the definite article is needed. In English, the article is not needed (i.e., *Books cost too much.* **Los libros cuestan demasiado dinero**). Provide the necessary article and state whether you agree (**estoy de acuerdo**) or disagree (**no estoy de acuerdo**).

1. _____ relojes son indispensables. _____
2. _____ clases son difíciles. _____
3. _____ universidades son instituciones importantes. _____
4. _____ profesores no ganan mucho dinero. _____
5. _____ papeles necesitan reciclarse siempre. _____
6. _____ papeleras están llenas (*full*). _____
7. _____ cafeterías en las universidades son caras (*expensive*). _____

Gramática 2

Asking and telling when an event takes place
• Time of events

L. ¡Pon la hora! Set the clocks to the correct time.

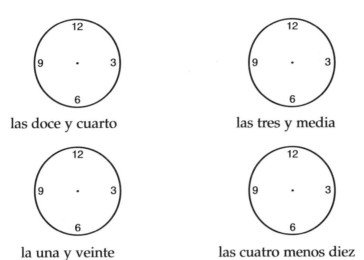

las doce y cuarto

las tres y media

la una y veinte

las cuatro menos diez

M. Los eventos universitarios. A Spanish-speaking friend has asked you to find out when the following events will take place. Write down what you would say in Spanish. Remember: **a las tres de la tarde**, but **a la una de la tarde**.

¿A qué hora es...

1. el concierto de música clásica? (9:00 pm) _____

2. el programa sobre literatura moderna? (8:15 pm) _____

3. el partido de fútbol? (5:45 pm) _____

4. la reunión del club latino? (10:30 am) _____

5. la conferencia sobre el arte prehispánico? (1:30 pm) _____

6. la excursión al Museo de Ciencia y Tecnología? (8:10 am) _____

N. Preguntas personales. Answer the following questions with the times requested; you do not need to use full sentences.

1. ¿A qué hora sales (*leave*) de casa por la mañana? _____

2. ¿A qué hora regresas (*return*)? _____

3. ¿A qué hora llegas a la universidad? _____

4. ¿A qué hora es tu primera (*first*) clase los lunes? _____

5. ¿A qué hora miras la tele (*watch TV*)? _____

Para terminar

Ñ. La Universidad en la Comunidad-Único. Read the following brochure for the **Universidad en la Comunidad** and answer the following questions.

Plan de estudios

1. What is the English word for **Nutrición**? _____

2. How many quarters are necessary to complete a degree? _____

3. Indicate in which quarter students take the following courses:

    a. Epidemology   _____

    b. Thesis Seminar   _____

    c. Human Physiology   _____

    d. Pediatric Nutrition   _____

Mercado de trabajo

4. Where may a person with this degree work?

    a. _____

    b. _____

    c. _____

    d. _____

COLEGIO DE CIENCIAS ASOCIADAS A LA SALUD

Nutrición

Perfil del esgresado

El profesional en Nutrición tendrá los conocimientos necesarios para colaborar en la solución de los problemas de nutrición y alimentación de México, ofreciendo apoyo nutricional, orientación y asesoría a todo individuo sano o enfermo.

Mercado de trabajo

El campo de trabajo del nutriólogo es amplio, ya que podrá prestar asesoría y desempeñar funciones de apoyo nutricional en hospitales y clínicas del sector público y privado, así como en otras disciplinas de interés: Salud Pública, epidemiología, saneamiento ambiental e industria del alimento.

PLAN DE ESTUDIOS

PRIMER TRIMESTRE
- Bioquímica de la Nutrición.
- Morfología Humana.
- Fisiología Humana.

SEGUNDO TRIMESTRE
- Introducción a la Fisiopatología.
- Nutrición Básica.
- Salud Pública y Nutrición.

TERCER TRIMESTRE
- Química de los alimentos.
- Epidemiología.
- Métodos de la Investigación.

CUARTO TRIMESTRE
- Bioestadística.
- Principios de Dietocálculo.
- Principios Básicos de Administración.

QUINTO TRIMESTRE
- Nutrición Clínica en Adultos.
- Saneamiento Ambiental.
- Dietoterapia en Salud y Enfermedad.

SEXTO TRIMESTRE
- Apoyo Nutricional Especial.
- Nutrición Pediátrica.
- Salud Materno Infantil.

SÉPTIMO TRIMESTRE
- Sicología y Nutrición.
- Nutrición Comunitaria.
- Seminario de Tesis.

OCTAVO TRIMESTRE
- Tecnología Educativa en Nutrición.
- Administración de los Servicios de Alimentación y Nutrición.
- Nutrición Clínica Intrahospitalaria.

¡A escuchar!

Episodio 2

Comprensión

Audio CD-ROM

A. Los planes de tres amigos.

Parte 1. Ana Mari and two classmates from her English class want to get together to study for a test. They need to compare their schedules to determine at what time all three are free. As Carmen and Ana Mari speak, fill in the schedule. You will hear the conversation twice.

	9:00	10:00	11:00	12:00	1:00	2:00
Carmen						
Ana Mari						
Cristina						

Parte 2. Now, look at the schedule you completed in **Parte 1** and, in Spanish, answer the questions that you hear. There will be six questions.

Modelo	You hear:	**¿A qué hora tiene Ana Mari la clase de sicología?**
	You say:	**A las diez.**

Audio CD-ROM

B. Asociaciones. You are going to hear nine words. For each word, select the word you associate with it from the choices provided.

Modelo	You hear:	**el tenis**		
	You see:	**la librería**	**la cancha**	**la mochila**
	You say:	**la cancha**		

1. el estadio   el edificio   el baño
2. la calculadora   el diccionario   el cuaderno
3. el auditorio   el consejero   el pupitre
4. el cálculo   la literatura   el libro
5. la piscina   la pluma   el pizarrón
6. la mochila   la bandera   la cafetería
7. la puerta   el reloj   la silla
8. la antropología   la geografía   la filosofía
9. la enfermería   el estacionamiento   la oficina

Audio
CD-ROM

Pronunciación

Los diptongos. Spanish has five vowels: **a, e, i, o,** and **u.** Every syllable has a vowel: **a-ni-mal, e-le-fan-te.** The vowels **i** and **u,** when unstressed, can combine with another vowel in the same syllable (**suel-do, sie-te**) to form a diphthong: **ai, ia, ou, ue,** and so on.

Here are possible combinations of **i** and **u** with other vowels and with each other. As you repeat these diphthongs and words after the speaker, notice that the stressed syllable of each word is in bold type.

ia	**dia**-rio	ai	Rai-**mun**-do
ie	**sie**-te	ei	**seis**
io	dic-cio-**na**-rio	oi	**oi**-go
iu	ciu-**dad**	ui	cui-**da**-do
ua	i-**gual**	au	nau-**fra**-gio
ue	**bue**-no	eu	**deu**-da
uo	**cuo**-ta	ou	**Sou**-za

Más escenas de la vida

Audio
CD-ROM

A. ¿Entendiste? Sofía and Ana Mari are looking at the newspaper. They call Manolo to make plans for a movie. Listen to their conversation and then answer the questions. You will hear the conversation twice.

1. What times is the movie showing today? _____
2. When are Sofía, Ana Mari, and Manolo going to the movies? _____
3. Where does Ana Mari have to go? _____
4. What does Ana Mari think about Manolo? _____
5. When does Manolo get off work? _____
6. Where will they meet to go to the movies? _____

Audio
CD-ROM

B. ¿Cierto o falso? Adriana is at home, talking to her children, Viviana and Santiaguito. Indicate whether the statements are **cierto** or **falso,** according to their conversation. You will hear the conversation twice.

	Cierto	Falso
1. Adriana desea comprar los materiales de la escuela para sus hijos.	☐	☐
2. Viviana necesita un escritorio.	☐	☐
3. Viviana necesita una computadora más grande.	☐	☐
4. Santiaguito necesita cuatro cuadernos.	☐	☐
5. Santiaguito necesita unas plumas y una calculadora.	☐	☐
6. Viviana necesita una mochila nueva.	☐	☐

In this episode, you will practice:

✓ expressing likes and dislikes

✓ describing yourself and others

✓ identifying Spanish-speaking countries

Episodio 3

Escenas de la vida: Los profesores y las clases

Video
CD-ROM

Audio
CD-ROM

A. ¡Mira cuánto puedes entender! As you listen to or watch the **Escena**, indicate the correct characteristic.

1. ¿Cómo es el profesor de cálculo?

☐ arrogante ☐ competente
☐ atractivo ☐ reservado
☐ estricto ☐ flexible

2. A Adriana le gusta la clase de composición porque el profesor es...

☐ extrovertido ☐ interesante
☐ paciente ☐ serio
☐ excelente ☐ flexible

> ### Cultura a lo vivo
> In the Spanish-speaking world, the concept of the nuclear family versus the extended family does not exist. The boundaries of the family extend beyond the immediate family to include grandparents, aunts and uncles, cousins, and others. Spanish speakers are widely assumed to have large families. However, Latin American families come in just as many sizes and varieties as families in the U.S. Many countries in Latin America have launched TV, radio, and billboard campaigns to promote smaller families— **"La familia pequeña vive mejor"** (*Smaller families live better*) is a popular slogan in Mexico.

Sofía   **Adriana**

3. A Adriana no le gusta la clase de contabilidad porque la profesora es...

☐ impaciente ☐ seria
☐ reservada ☐ arrogante
☐ pesimista ☐ tímida

4. Indica qué características aplican a Sofía (**S**) y cuáles a Adriana (**A**)

__ sociable   __ activa
__ tímida   __ responsable
__ madura   __ inteligente

Video
CD-ROM

Audio
CD-ROM

B. ¿Te diste cuenta? Indica si los comentarios son **ciertos** o **falsos**.

	Cierto	Falso
1. En las universidades de México hay televisiones y videocaseteras en todos los salones.	☐	☐
2. En Puerto Rico, las universidades tienen un gimnasio, un auditorio y una biblioteca.	☐	☐
3. En México no hay consejeros.	☐	☐
4. A Adriana le gusta mucho la clase de composición.	☐	☐
5. El profesor de la clase de diseño es increíble.	☐	☐
6. La clase de geología es aburrida *(boring)*.	☐	☐
7. El esposo de Adriana es impaciente.	☐	☐

Video
CD-ROM

Audio
CD-ROM

C. ¿Quién lo dijo? ¿Quién dijo las siguientes frases, Sofía (**S**) o Adriana (**A**)?

_____ 1. ¿Le gusta la clase de cálculo?

_____ 2. El cálculo es difícil.

_____ 3. A mí me gusta mucho la clase.

_____ 4. No me gusta la clase, pero la necesito porque es mi carrera.

_____ 5. ¿Cuál te gusta más?

Práctica adicional	
Cuaderno de tareas WB p.73, A–C	Video CD-ROM Episodio 3

Para comunicarnos mejor

Gramática 1

Expressing likes and dislikes
• Me gusta, te gusta, le gusta

In their conversation, Sofía and Adriana made the following statements.

La clase de composición **me gusta** mucho. *I like composition class a lot.*
¿**Le gusta** la clase de cálculo? *Do you like calculus class?*
A mí **me gusta** mucho la clase. *I like the class a lot.*
¿Cuál **te gusta** más? *Which one do you like better?*

1. Notice that you need to use the definite article after **gusta** when it is followed by a noun.

¿Le gusta **la** clase de cálculo?

2. When Sofía asks Adriana about her preferences, she does not use **¿te gusta?**; she uses **¿le gusta?** instead. Adriana is older, and Sofía just met her, so she wants to be polite. When you ask or tell a friend whether they like something, use **te gusta.** Use **le gusta** with your instructor, and **me gusta** when referring to your own preferences.

PRÁCTICA

A. ¿Qué clases te gustan? Use the list of class subjects on page 11 to interview a partner and find out your classmate's preferences. Remember, you need to use **el** or **la** before a noun.

Modelo	—¿Te gusta el drama?
	—Sí, me gusta. ¿Y a ti?
	—A mí también. or —A mí no.
	—¿Te gusta la biología?
	—No, no me gusta. ¿Y a ti?
	—A mí tampoco. or —A mí sí.

¡Fíjate!
Look at the ending of the class subjects to determine whether they are masculine or feminine.

B. Tus preferencias. Find out whether your classmate likes the activities listed below. Each activity begins with a verb. You can guess what the verbs mean from the context. For example, in **¿Te gusta jugar fútbol?** you can safely guess that **jugar** means *to play.*

Modelo	—¿Te gusta jugar fútbol?
	—No, no me gusta. ¿Y a ti?
	—A mí tampoco. or —A mí sí.
	—¿Te gusta comer ensaladas?
	—Sí, me gusta. ¿Y a ti?
	—A mí también. or —A mí no.

También se dice...
These sports are also spelled without accent marks because many Spanish speakers stress the last syllable when pronouncing them:

vóleibol ⟶ volibol

béisbol ⟶ beisbol

fútbol ⟶ futbol

fútbol americano ⟶ futbol americano

1. jugar (vóleibol, béisbol, fútbol americano, fútbol *(soccer)*, tenis)
2. comer (pizza, tacos, enchiladas, hamburguesas, frutas, ensaladas)
3. estudiar (en casa, en la biblioteca, con compañeros de clase)
4. escuchar música (clásica, alternativa, rap, latina, moderna)
5. leer (novelas, poemas, el periódico *(newspaper)*, el horóscopo)
6. mirar programas (cómicos, policíacos, de suspenso)

C. Las preferencias de tu profesor(a). As a class, find out whether your instructor likes some of the same activities.

Modelo	—Profesor(a), ¿le gusta escuchar música rap?

D. Una entrevista. Find out whether your classmate has similar preferences. Write down your own preferences before you begin the interview.

Modelo	—A mí me gusta Britney Spears. ¿Y a ti?
	—No me gusta. Christina Aguilera me gusta más. ¿Te gusta el programa *Friends*?
	—Sí, me gusta mucho.

Mis cantantes (singers) **favoritos**　　　　**Mis actores favoritos**　　　　**Mis programas favoritos**

_____　　　_____　　　_____

_____　　　_____　　　_____

_____　　　_____　　　_____

Práctica adicional

Cuaderno de tareas
WB p.74, D–E

Gramática 2

Describing yourself and others
- **Ser** + [*adjectives*] (cognates)
- **Subject pronouns**

In the dialogue, Adriana says **soy un poco tímida** when describing herself and **el profesor es muy estricto** when describing her calculus instructor. **Soy** and **es** are forms of the verb **ser** (*to be*). Use the following forms to describe yourself and others.

Ser		
yo	**Soy** un poco tímida.	*I'm a little shy.*
tú	**Eres** muy pesimista.	*You are very pessimistic.* (informal)
usted (Ud.)	**Es** creativo/a.	*You are creative.* (formal)
él	**Es** ambicioso.	*He is ambitious.*
ella	**Es** seria.	*She is serious.*
nosotros nosotras	**Somos** inteligentes.	*We are intelligent.*
ustedes (Uds.)	**Son** impacientes.	
vosotros* vosotras	**Sois** impacientes.	*You are impatient.* (plural)
ellos ellas	**Son** muy sociables.	*They are easy-going.*

*Spain is the only country that uses **vosotros/as** for *you* (plural, informal) and **ustedes** for *you* (plural, formal). All other Spanish-speaking countries use **ustedes** for both formal and informal second-person plural.

¡Fíjate!

The **vosotros** forms are provided for your reference only; you are not responsible for learning them.

1. Notice that **nosotros, vosotros,** and **ellos** may refer to a group of men or to a mixed group, whereas **nosotras, vosotras,** and **ellas** refer only to women.

2. Notice that there is no pronoun for *it*. Use **es** to convey the idea *it is*.

　　Es mi libro.　　*It is my book.*　　**Son mis libros.**　　*They are my books.*

• Subject pronouns

In their conversation, Sofía and Adriana said:

Soy de Puerto Rico.   *I'm from Puerto Rico.*
Es mi mejor amiga.   *She is my best friend.*

Notice that the characters do not say *yo* **soy** or *ella* **es**. In Spanish, the verb form itself
and/or the context indicates the person we are talking about (*I, you, he, she, we, they*).
Therefore, it is not necessary to use subject pronouns. The subject pronouns (**yo, tú, usted,
él, ella, nosotros/as, vosotros/as, ustedes, ellos/as**) are used only when:

    a. you want to establish contrast or emphasis.   **Tú no eres responsable, yo sí.**
    b. there is no verb. **Yo también, nosotros tampoco, tú no.**
    c. you are answering a "who" question. **¿Quién es romántico? Yo soy.**

Read the following descriptive adjectives. They are all cognates. Can you understand what
they mean? The spelling of these adjectives stays the same whether they describe
a man or a woman.

Para describir la personalidad I		
arrogante	increíble	pesimista
competente	interesante	(ir)responsable
excelente	materialista	sentimental
flexible	optimista	sociable
idealista	(im)paciente	terrible

The following adjectives end in **-o** when they refer to a man and in **-a** when they refer
to a woman.

Para describir la personalidad II			
activo/a	discreto/a	(des)honesto/a	romántico/a
ambicioso/a	estudioso/a	(in)maduro/a	serio/a
atractivo/a	extrovertido/a	nervioso/a	tímido/a
creativo/a	generoso/a	reservado/a	tranquilo/a

To ask what someone is like, use the expression **¿Cómo es/son...?**
¿Cómo es la profesora de composición?   *What is your composition professor like?*

PRÁCTICA

E. Los amigos de Sofía. Complete Sofía's description and answer her questions using **ser**.

1. Mi mamá _____ extrovertida y sociable. ¿Y tú mamá?
   Mi mamá _____

2. Ana Mari y Ramón _____ responsables y maduros.
   ¿Cómo son tus amigos?
   Mis amigos _____

3. Manolo y yo _____ amigos; _____ muy diferentes.

4. ¿Cómo es tu mejor amigo? _____

5. ¿Cómo eres tú? _____

6. Mi mejor amigo y yo _____

Sofía

Audio
CD-ROM

F. Características. Escucha los comentarios para indicar si las características mencionadas son **positivas** o **negativas**.

	Positiva	Negativa
1.	☐	☐
2.	☐	☐
3.	☐	☐

	Positiva	Negativa
4.	☐	☐
5.	☐	☐
6.	☐	☐

G. ¿Cómo eres? Chat with a partner about each other's characteristics. Ask questions like:

Modelo —¿Eres responsable?   —¿Eres reservado?
        —Sí, soy responsable. ¿Y tú?   —No, no soy reservado ¿Y tú?
        —Yo también.   or   —Yo no.   —Yo tampoco.   or   —Yo sí.

H. ¿Cómo es tu profesor(a)? With your partner, try to determine the three characteristics that best describe your instructor. Then ask your instructor to tell whether your guesses are correct.

Modelo   Profesor(a), ¿usted es romántico/a?

Práctica adicional

Cuaderno de tareas
WB pp.75–76, F–I

Vocabulario 1 — Identifying Spanish-speaking countries

Study the map below to learn the positions, names, and capitals of the Spanish-speaking countries.

Los países de habla hispana y sus capitales

Estados Unidos, Washington D.C.

España, Madrid

Océano Atlántico

Cuba, La Habana

República Dominicana, Santo Domingo

Puerto Rico, San Juan

México, Ciudad de México

Honduras, Tegucigalpa

Guatemala, Ciudad de Guatemala

Colombia, Bogotá

Venezuela, Caracas

El Salvador, San Salvador

Nicaragua, Managua

Costa Rica, San José

Panamá, Ciudad de Panamá

Ecuador, Quito

Perú, Lima

Paraguay, Asunción

Uruguay, Montevideo

Océano Pacífico

Bolivia, La Paz y Sucre

Chile, Santiago

Argentina, Buenos Aires

PRÁCTICA

I. El mundo hispano. Examina el mapa para completar las frases.

1. ¿En cuántos países (countries) se habla español? En _____.

2. Los países hispanos de Centroamérica son: _____, _____,
   _____, _____, _____ y _____.

3. En el Caribe, se habla español en _____,
   _____ y _____.

4. ¿Qué países de Sudamérica no tienen (do not have) acceso
   al océano? _____ y _____.

5. En Europa, un país de habla hispana es _____.

> **¡Fíjate!**
>
> Bolivia has two capitals: La Paz, the administrative capital and the center of government, and Sucre, the constitutional capital and judicial center.

J. Capitales. Escribe los países o las capitales necesarias para completar la lista.

Países	Capitales
1. Argentina	Buenos Aires
2. Chile	_____
3. _____	Bogotá
4. Cuba	_____
5. _____	Quito
6. El Salvador	_____
7. _____	Madrid
8. _____	Managua
9. _____	Montevideo
10. Perú	_____
11. _____	Caracas
12. Costa Rica	_____
13. _____	La Paz y Sucre
14. Puerto Rico	_____

Invitación a **Bolivia**

Del álbum de
Sofía

Bolivia es aproximadamente tres veces el tamaño *(size)* de Montana y su población es de 9.1 millones de habitantes. Es el país más alto y aislado *(isolated)* de América. La influencia indígena es palpable; hay estaciones de radio en Qechua (lengua inca) y Aymará (lengua pre-inca) y en la televisión se pueden escuchar las noticias en Qechua.

Práctica adicional

Cuaderno de tareas WB p.76, J–K LM pp.79–80, A–C, Pron.	Audio CD-ROM Episodio 3	Website vistahigher learning.com

Actividades comunicativas

A. Los habitantes en Latinoamérica.

Instrucciones para **Estudiante 1**

You have half of the information on populations in Latin America, and your partner has the other half. First, write the names of the countries you are missing, then ask your partner to give you the number of inhabitants for each one. Take turns and use the following model.

> **Modelo**   —**Cuántos habitantes hay en México?**
>   —**En México hay ciento uno punto ocho millones de habitantes.**

¡Fíjate!

The numbers next to each country represent the number of people in millions. They are read as follows:

El Salvador, seis punto ocho millones de habitantes.

*Sources: US Census Bureau and the Population Division, UN Secretariat.

A. Los habitantes en Latinoamérica.

Instrucciones para **Estudiante 2**

You have half of the information on populations in Latin America, and your partner has the other half. First, write the names of the countries you are missing, then ask your partner to give you the number of inhabitants for each one. Take turns and use the following model.

Modelo	—Cuántos habitantes hay en México? —En México hay ciento uno punto ocho millones de habitantes.

¡Fíjate!
The numbers next to each country represent the number of people in millions. They are read as follows:
Honduras, siete millones de habitantes.

En Estados Unidos hay más de 30 millones de hispanohablantes.

República Dominicana, 8.9

Puerto Rico, 4

Guatemala, 12.6

Honduras, 7

Nicaragua, 5.6

Venezuela, 26

Perú, 27.4

Paraguay, 6

Argentina, 38.8

Sources: US Census Bureau and the Population Division, UN Secretariat.

B. ¡A hablar! Interview a classmate. Find out your classmate's name, how many classes they are taking, which ones, at what time, which classes they like or dislike, whether they work, and how many hours. Ask them to describe themself and two of their teachers.

La correspondencia

El correo: Una carta para Odette. Read Sofia's letter to her friend Odette and answer the questions.

1. ¿Cuántas clases toma Sofía? _____

2. ¿Cómo son las clases de Sofía? _____

3. ¿Quién *(who)* es Manolo? _____

4. Describe a Lalo. _____

> **Reading Strategy: Understanding the overall meaning**
>
> When reading, you do not have to understand every word. To understand the overall meaning of Sofía's letter, read the first paragraph and underline all the words you understand. Then use those words to determine the main idea of the paragraph. Read the other paragraphs, repeating the process. Read the questions first to find out what you need to know.

Querida Odette:

¿Cómo estás? Yo estoy muy contenta porque ya comenzamos las clases en la universidad. Este semestre tomo cuatro clases. Creo que van a ser fáciles,[1] especialmente cálculo y geología. Lo único[2] diferente es que son en inglés. La clase de cálculo es divertida[3], porque mi amigo Manolo está en la clase, y a veces es cómico.

Mis papás están muy bien; están planeando unas vacaciones en Cancún y están muy emocionados[4]. Lalo me preocupa un poco. Es bastante[5] irresponsable e inmaduro, y ya casi tiene dieciséis años. No es diligente en la escuela y solamente le interesa ir a fiestas y estar con sus amigos. Espero que cuando se gradúe de la preparatoria madure un poco.

Bueno querida Odette, un beso[6] para ti y toda tu familia. Escríbeme pronto.

Tu amiga que te quiere,
Sofía

[1]*easy* [2]*the only thing* [3]*fun* [4]*excited* [5]*rather* [6]*kiss*

En papel: Una notita para Sofía. Complete the following e-mail to Sofía telling her about yourself.

> **Writing Strategy: Identifying the content of a note**
> Successful writers identify the information they wish to communicate before they begin to write. In the early stages of learning Spanish, this information will be lists of words and phrases. Later you can incorporate these lists into brief notes you write to Spanish speakers. Pay close attention to spelling, so that your early written communication will be understandable.

From: _____
To: Sofía. <Blasio@sol.red>
Re: Saludos

Date: Lunes, 19 de feb. 12:07 EST

Hola Sofía,

Me llamo _____. Soy de _____.
Mi universidad se llama _____.
Este semestre tomo _____ clases. Son: _____.
Me gusta mucho la clase de _____ porque
el/la profesor(a) es _____.
Este semestre trabajo _____ horas a la semana. ¿Y tú? ¿Cuántas clases tomas?
¿Trabajas? ¿Cuántas horas? ¡Escríbeme pronto! Buena suerte este semestre.

Saludos,

_____

¡A ver de nuevo! Escucha la conversación o mira el video de **Escenas de la vida** para completar cada frase con la palabra apropiada.

Video
CD-ROM

Audio
CD-ROM

1. Los salones de clase en Puerto Rico no tienen tantas _____.
2. La mayoría de las universidades tienen un _____, un
   _____ y una _____.
3. En Puerto Rico y en Estados Unidos hay _____, pero en México no.
4. El profesor de cálculo es _____ y _____.
5. Adriana es un poco _____.
6. A Sofía le gustan las clases de _____, _____ y
   _____.

Práctica adicional		
Cuaderno de tareas WB pp.77–78, L–M LM p.80, A–B	Audio CD-ROM Episodio 3	Website vistahigher learning.com

Vocabulario del Episodio 3

Los gustos *Likes and dislikes*

¿Te gusta...?	*Do you like... (informal)*
Sí, me gusta.	*Yes, I like it.*
No, no me gusta.	*No, I don't like it.*
¿Le gusta...?	*Do you like...? (formal)*

Los pronombres personales y el verbo <u>ser</u>

yo **soy**	*I am*
tú **eres**	*you are* (informal)
usted (Ud.) **es**	*you are* (formal)
él **es**	*he is*
ella **es**	*she is*
nosotros/as **somos**	*we are*
ustedes (Uds.) **son** }	*you are* (plural)
vosotros/as **sois**	
ellos/as **son**	*they are*

Adjetivos

activo/a	excelente	(in)maduro/a	romántico/a
ambicioso/a	extrovertido/a	materialista	sentimental
arrogante	flexible	nervioso/a	serio/a
atractivo/a	generoso/a	optimista	sociable
competente	(des)honesto/a	(im)paciente	terrible
creativo/a	idealista	pesimista	tímido/a
discreto/a	increíble	reservado/a	tranquilo/a
estudioso/a	interesante	(ir)responsable	

Los países de habla hispana y sus capitales

Argentina, Buenos Aires	Honduras, Tegucigalpa
Bolivia, La Paz y Sucre	México, Ciudad de México
Chile, Santiago	Nicaragua, Managua
Colombia, Bogotá	Panamá, Ciudad de Panamá
Costa Rica, San José	Paraguay, Asunción
Cuba, La Habana	Perú, Lima
Ecuador, Quito	Puerto Rico, San Juan
El Salvador, San Salvador	República Dominicana, Santo Domingo
España, Madrid	Uruguay, Montevideo
Guatemala, Ciudad de Guatemala	Venezuela, Caracas

Vocabulario personal

Write the words that you need to know to describe yourself and express your likes and dislikes in Spanish.

¡A escribir!

Episodio 3

Escenas de la vida: Los profesores y las clases

Video CD-ROM

A. ¡Mira cuánto entendiste! See how much of the **Escena** you understood by matching the Spanish sentences with their English equivalents.

En la universidad

_____ 1. ¿Hay consejeros?   a. It's my major.

_____ 2. ¡Qué mala suerte!   b. The professor gives good explanations.

_____ 3. El profesor explica bien.   c. Are there counselors?

_____ 4. Es mi carrera.   d. Too bad!

_____ 5. Me gusta hacer ejercicio.   e. I play tennis with my husband.

_____ 6. Juego tenis con mi esposo.   f. I like to exercise.

Video CD-ROM

B. Los profesores y las clases. Use the words in the box to complete the conversation.

atractivo	consejeros	excelentes	le gusta
difícil	diferentes	salones	auditorio

Sofía   Las universidades aquí son muy (1) _____. ¿En Puerto Rico

hay (2) _____ como en Estados Unidos?

Adriana   Sí, y los profesores son (3) _____.

Sofía   ¿(4) _____ la clase de cálculo?

Adriana   Más o menos. Es (5) _____ y el profesor es muy estricto.

Sofía   Pero es muy (6) _____.

Video CD-ROM

C. ¿Qué clase te gusta? Order the statements in the dialogue so that it makes sense.

_____ a. A mí me gusta mucho la clase. La de vóleibol también. Me gusta mucho hacer ejercicio. ¿Y a usted?

_____ b. En Puerto Rico, sí. Y los profesores son excelentes.

_____ c. Pues, más o menos. El cálculo es difícil. ¿Y a ti?

__1__ d. ¿En Puerto Rico hay consejeros como en Estados Unidos? En México no hay.

_____ e. A veces juego tenis con mi esposo, pero no me gusta.

_____ f. Hablando de profesores, ¿le gusta la clase de cálculo?

Nombre _____ Fecha _____

Gramática 1

Expressing likes and dislikes
•**Me gusta, te gusta, le gusta**

D. ¿Qué materias te gustan? Indicate which subjects you like and which ones you do not like. You may use the subjects on the list below, or any subjects you wrote in your **Vocabulario personal** section. Remember to use the definite article after **gusta**.

cálculo	geología	inglés	contabilidad
economía	español	música	drama

1. Me gusta el arte. _____   No me gusta la astronomía. _____
2. _____   _____
3. _____   _____
4. _____   _____
5. _____   _____

E. ¿Qué te gusta hacer? Indicate six activities you like to do and six activities you do not like to do.

a. jugar (vóleibol, béisbol, fútbol americano, fútbol, tenis)

b. comer (pizza, tacos, enchiladas, hamburguesas, frutas, ensaladas)

c. estudiar (en casa, en la biblioteca, con compañeros de clase)

d. escuchar música (clásica, alternativa, rap, latina, moderna)

e. leer (novelas, poemas, el periódico, el horóscopo)

f. mirar programas (cómicos, policíacos, de suspenso)

1. Me gusta estudiar en la biblioteca. _____
2. _____
3. _____
4. _____
5. _____
6. _____
7. _____
8. No me gusta escuchar música clásica. _____
9. _____
10. _____
11. _____
12. _____
13. _____
14. _____

Nombre _____ Fecha _____

Gramática 2

Describing yourself and others
- <u>Ser</u> + [*adjective*] (cognates)
- **Subject pronouns**

F. Descríbelos. Describe yourself, your family members, your friends, and your Spanish instructor. Use at least three adjectives per person.

> **Modelo** Mis hermanos son activos, irresponsables y sociables.

arrogante	idealista	optimista	sentimental
competente	increíble	(im)paciente	sociable
excelente	interesante	pesimista	terrible
flexible	materialista	(ir)responsable	tranquilo/a
activo/a	discreto/a	(des)honesto/a	romántico/a
ambicioso/a	estudioso/a	estricto/a	serio/a
atractivo/a	extrovertido/a	nervioso/a	tímido/a
creativo/a	generoso/a	reservado/a	inmaduro/a

1. (Yo) _____

2. Mi mamá _____

3. Mi papá _____

4. Mis compañeros _____

5. Mi profesor(a) de español _____

G. Mis amigos y yo: una descripción. Fill in the appropriate forms of **ser**.

(Yo) (1)_____ estudioso y ambicioso, pero no (2)_____ muy   creativo.
Y tú, ¿cómo (3)_____ ? (4) Tú _____ un poco nerviosa, ¿no?
Sofía (5)_____ muy sociable y Manolo (6)_____ tímido. Ellos
(7)_____ buenos amigos. Ramón y yo (8)_____ inteligentes, pero también
(9)_____ materialistas. Y tus amigos, ¿cómo (10)_____?

H. ¿Cómo es... ? Describe the famous people below. To ask someone to describe a person/people, you ask **¿Cómo es/son... ?**

> **Modelo** Mike Tyson
> **¿Cómo es Mike Tyson? Es irresponsable y arrogante.**

1. Christina Aguilera _____

2. La Sra. Clinton _____

3. Bill Gates _____

4. Tiger Woods _____

5. Eminem _____

I. Un poco sobre mí. *(A little about me.)* Write a paragraph with the following information: your name, the classes you take (**tomo...**), a description of your instructors (**Mi profesor de... es...**), the number of hours a week you work (**trabajo...**) and study (**estudio...**), and something you like to do.

_____

_____

_____

_____

_____

Vocabulario 1 Identifying Spanish-speaking countries

J. Capitales. Write the capitals of the following countries.

País	Capital
México	_____
Guatemala	_____
Costa Rica	_____
Panamá	_____
Chile	_____
España	_____
República Dominicana	_____
Puerto Rico	_____
Uruguay	_____

K. Los países. Look at the map in order to identify the countries.

1. _____   10. _____
2. _____   11. _____
3. _____   12. _____
4. _____   13. _____
5. _____   14. _____
6. _____   15. _____
7. _____   16. _____
8. _____   17. _____
9. _____   18. _____

Para terminar

L. La Universidad Estatal de San Marcos en California.

Parte 1. Read the description of the university and answer the questions.

La universidad está en la ciudad de San Marcos, localizada a unas cuarenta millas al norte de San Diego. Es la última universidad (la número vientiuno) construída en California por el sistema californiano de universidades estatales. California State University San Marcos es una universidad nueva y todavía es pequeña. La universidad no está totalmente terminada aún. Los salones son nuevos y modernos. Uno de los edificios es muy moderno, los salones tienen televisiones, computadoras, videocaseteras, pupitres y pizarrones nuevos, pero no hay piscinas ni gimnasios. La cafetería y la biblioteca son muy bonitas y modernas. Además hay un *Centro para el estudio de libros en español* que tiene una de las colecciones de libros infantiles y juveniles más grandes en español. Asisten aproximadamente seis mil estudiantes, pero no hay residencias estudiantiles para ellos todavía. Hay estacionamiento porque casi todos los estudiantes llegan a la universidad en coche.

1. Describe the university, its size, and its facilities.

   _____

2. Describe the classrooms. _____

   _____

3. Why is this a good place to study? _____

   _____

4. How many students are there? How many live on campus? How is parking?

   _____

   _____

Parte 2. Use the reading above as a model to write about your own university or college.

_____

_____

_____

_____

_____

_____

_____

M. Una miniprueba. Complete the following communicative tasks to test your knowledge of the content of this chapter.

1. Ask Sofía:
   a. how many classes she is taking.
   b. if she likes the calculus class.

2. Ask Adriana:
   c. when her composition class is.
   d. to describe her instructor.

3. Tell Manolo:
   e. the classes you take.
   f. which ones you like and why.

4. Describe:
   g. yourself.
   h. your favorite instructor.

a. _____

b. _____

c. _____

d. _____

e. _____

f. _____

_____

_____

_____

_____

_____

g. _____

_____

_____

_____

_____

h. _____

_____

_____

_____

_____

¡A escuchar!

Episodio
3

Comprensión

A. La clase de Ana Mari. Listen to Ana Mari talk about her classmates and one of her classes, and then fill in the missing information. **¡Atención!** Pay attention to the gender and number of the adjectives. You will hear Ana Mari's narration twice.

Audio
CD-ROM

> **La clase de _____**
>
> La clase es _____. El profesor es un hombre _____ y _____.
> Hoy los estudiantes están _____ porque hay un examen. Natalia es _____
> y _____. Pete no está _____ porque está bien _____. Él es un
> estudiante _____ y _____.

B. Descripciones. The following adjectives are listed in the masculine singular form. You will hear a cue for each one (masculine or feminine, singular or plural). Aloud, match the adjective to each cue with **es** or **son**. Repeat the correct answer after the speaker.

Audio
CD-ROM

Modelo	You see:	**generoso**	You see:	**estricto**
	You hear:	**Adriana**	You hear:	**los profesores**
	You say:	**Adriana <u>es</u> generos<u>a</u>.**	You say:	**Los profesores <u>son</u> estrict<u>os</u>.**

1. honesto	3. optimista	5. extrovertido	7. difícil	9. romántico
2. inmaduro	4. interesante	6. sentimental	8. estudioso	10. sociable

C. La mejor respuesta. You will hear ten questions or statements. Select the best response for each one. You will hear each question or statement twice.

Audio
CD-ROM

1.	a. Bien, gracias.	b. La clase de química.	c. Ana Mari.
2.	a. Igualmente.	b. Más o menos.	c. Que le vaya bien.
3.	a. Adiós.	b. A mí tampoco.	c. Mucho gusto.
4.	a. Buenos días.	b. Que te vaya bien.	c. Regular.
5.	a. Con frecuencia.	b. A las diez.	c. Hay dos clases.
6.	a. Sí, me gusta.	b. No le gusta.	c. Mucho gusto.
7.	a. Sí, señorita.	b. Hasta mañana.	c. Bien, ¿y tú?
8.	a. Es arrogante.	b. Es optimista.	c. Es paciente.
9.	a. A las nueve.	b. A veces.	c. Los martes y los jueves.
10.	a. Hay cinco.	b. Dos dólares.	c. Necesito uno.

Pronunciación

Audio CD-ROM

La h y la ch. H (hache) is completely silent in Spanish. Repeat these words and sentences after the speaker. Pay close attention to the vowels **a, e, i, o,** and **u**, as well.

hambre	humo	almohada	**Hasta ahora no tengo hambre.**
honor	hielo	alcohol	**Humberto es de Honduras.**

Ch (che) is pronounced just like the English *ch*. In Spanish, **ch** was a separate letter of the alphabet until 1994. You may still see it treated as a separate letter, following **c**, in texts published before that date. Repeat these words and sentences after the speaker.

chico	chile	muchacha	**El chico sale con la muchacha.**
hacha	concha	choca	**Me choca usar el hacha.**

Más escenas de la vida

Sofía, Ana Mari, and Manolo are coming out of the movies. Listen to their conversation, and then complete activities **A** and **B**. You will hear the conversation twice.

Audio CD-ROM

A. ¿Cierto o falso? Indicate whether the following statements are **cierto** or **falso**, according to the conversation.

	Cierto	Falso
1. Ramón es el hermano de Ana Mari.	☐	☐
2. Ramón es impaciente.	☐	☐
3. Ramón es irresponsable e inmaduro.	☐	☐
4. Ana Mari y Sofía son perfectas.	☐	☐
5. Ramón es un controlador.	☐	☐
6. A Manolo le gusta la música latina.	☐	☐
7. Ana Mari quiere ir a un concierto de música latina.	☐	☐
8. Los artistas favoritos de Ana Mari son Jennifer López y Christina Aguilera.	☐	☐

B. Responde. Write the answers to the following questions.

Audio CD-ROM

1. ¿Cómo es Ramón, según Ana Mari? _____

2. ¿Cómo es Ramón, según Sofía? _____

3. ¿Cómo es Ramón, según Sofía y Ana Mari? _____

4. ¿Qué cantantes *(singers)* le gustan a Manolo? _____

Objetivos comunicativos

In this episode, you will practice:

✓ talking about your family

✓ telling and asking for someone's age

✓ saying and asking where someone is from

✓ asking for and giving phone numbers

Episodio 4

Escenas de la vida: ¡Qué internacionales!

Video
CD-ROM

Audio
CD-ROM

A. ¡Mira cuánto puedes entender!

1. Indicate where the following people are from.

los padres de Manolo

Manolo

Adriana

Ramón

los padres de Ramón

2. Indicate who prefers to speak English and who prefers to speak Spanish.

Los papás y los hermanos de Ramón.

Cultura a lo vivo

Educational politics, where schools actively discourage the use of any language other than English, has intensified the problem of language loss within the Hispanic family. Because of educational politics, many Hispanic children have stopped speaking Spanish and so will be unable to pass it on to their children.

This trend has led many Spanish-speaking Americans to use Spanish in their homes as a way of preserving the links to their native countries. These families maintain their native language in order to enjoy the cultural and economic benefits of being bilingual and bicultural.

Video
CD-ROM

Audio
CD-ROM

B. ¿Te diste cuenta? Escucha las conversaciones otra vez para indicar si los comentarios son **ciertos** o **falsos**.

	Cierto	Falso
1. A la hija de Adriana no le gusta hablar español.	☐	☐
2. Manolo está en la clase de cálculo.	☐	☐
3. Adriana y Sofía toman geología juntas.	☐	☐
4. Ana Mari habla español muy bien.	☐	☐
5. Ramón y Sofía tienen una clase a las nueve.	☐	☐

Video
CD-ROM

Audio
CD-ROM

C. Completa las oraciones. Complete the following sentences, according to what you heard in the **Escena**.

1. _____ es la hermana de Ramón.
2. Los padres de Manolo viven en _____.
3. Adriana _____ tres hijos.
4. Los _____ menores de Ramón no hablan español, pero lo entienden.
5. Manolo escribe _____ en español.

Práctica adicional	
Cuaderno de tareas WB pp.101–102, A–D	Video CD-ROM Episodio 4

Para comunicarnos mejor

Vocabulario 1

Identifying family members and friends
- **The family**
- **Expressing possession**

When Ramón and Adriana talked about their families, they made the following statements.

Mi **mamá** es de México.	*My mom is from Mexico.*
Mi **papá** es de Honduras.	*My dad is from Honduras.*
Mis **hijos** mayores hablan español.	*My older children speak Spanish.*
Mis **hermanos** menores lo entienden todo.	*My younger brothers understand everything.*

Learning Strategy: Make associations

Think of English words that sound similar to Spanish words you are trying to learn. Then associate them with each other in some creative way. For example, the name *Sabrina* sounds a lot like the Spanish **sobrina** *(niece)*. Create a mental link: **Mi amiga Sabrina tiene una sobrina.** Recognize the relationships that exist in the two languages. For example, look at the words *apprentice (student)* and **aprender** *(to learn)*; to remember the Spanish, visualize an apprentice that must **aprender mucho.**

The following table contains the terms you use to identify the members of your family and your friends.

La familia, los familiares y más			
los abuelos	*grandparents*	el abuelo	la abuela
los amigos	*friends*	el amigo	la amiga
los chicos	*adolescents, teenagers*	el chico	la chica
los cuñados	*brother(s)-in-law and sister(s)-in-law*	el cuñado	la cuñada
los esposos	*husband and wife*	el esposo	la esposa
los familiares	*relatives*	el familiar	
los hermanos	*brother(s) and sister(s)*	el hermano	la hermana
los hijos	*children (one's own): son(s) and daughter(s)*	el hijo	la hija
los nietos	*grandchildren*	el nieto	la nieta
los niños	*children: boy(s) and girl(s)*	el niño	la niña
los novios	*boyfriend and girlfriend; bride and groom; fiancés*	el novio	la novia
los padres	*parents*	el padre	la madre
los primos	*cousins*	el primo	la prima
los sobrinos	*nephew(s) and niece(s)*	el sobrino	la sobrina
los suegros	*father-in-law and mother-in-law*	el suegro	la suegra
los tíos	*uncle(s) and aunt(s)*	el tío	la tía

Las mascotas	*pets*
el gato	*cat*
el pájaro	*bird*
el perro	*dog*
el pez	*fish*

También se dice...

los padres ⟶ los papás (el papá, la mamá)
los familiares ⟶ los parientes
los chicos ⟶ los muchachos

¡Fíjate!

Ask your instructor for other family relationships you may need to describe your family. Write them in the **Vocabulario personal** at the end of **Episodio 4**.

• Expressing possession

1. Notice how Spanish uses the construction **el esposo de Adriana** to say *Adriana's husband*. Where English uses *'s* to express possession, Spanish uses [*article*] + [*noun*] + **de** + [*noun*].

la hermana de Ramón	*Ramón's sister*
los hijos de Adriana	*Adriana's children*
el gato de Manolo	*Manolo's cat*

Ana Mari es la hermana de Ramón.

2. Another way of indicating possession or relationship is to use possessive adjectives. Read the following examples:

Mis padres son de México.	*My parents are from Mexico.*
¿De dónde son **tus** padres?	*Where are your parents from?*
Sus abuelos son de Irlanda.	*His/Her grandparents are from Ireland.*
Éstos son **nuestros** hijos.	*These are our children.*
No me gusta **su** gata. ⎫	
No me gusta **vuestra** gata. ⎬	*I don't like your cat.*
Su perro es un chihuahueño.	*Their dog is a chihuahua.*

3. Notice that the possessive adjectives agree in number with the noun possessed, not with the possessor. **Nuestro/a** and **vuestro/a** also agree in gender.

Los adjetivos posesivos

mi, mis	*my*	nuestro, nuestros	⎫
tu, tus	*your* (informal)	nuestra, nuestros	⎭ *our*
su, sus	*his, her, your* (formal)	vuestro, vuestros	⎫
	their, your (plural)	vuestra, vuestras	⎭ *your* (informal)

PRÁCTICA

A. La familia de Adriana. Indicate if the following statements are **cierto** *(true)* or **falso** *(false)*, according to Adriana's family tree. Correct the false statements by replacing the incorrect word.

> **Modelo** José Luis es el esposo de Adriana.
> **Falso. Es el hermano de Adriana.**

	Cierto	Falso
1. Doña Cristina es la esposa de don José Luis.	☐	☐
2. Beto y Esther son primos.	☐	☐
3. Roberto es el papá de Santiaguito.	☐	☐
4. Las sobrinas de José Luis son Tina, Esther y Viviana.	☐	☐
5. El abuelo de Beto se llama Roberto.	☐	☐
6. Don José Luis y doña Cristina tienen tres nietas.	☐	☐
7. Roberto es el tío de Santiaguito y Viviana.	☐	☐
8. Beto, Tina y Esther son hermanos.	☐	☐

don José Luis (73)   doña Cristina (69)

Roberto (51)   Cristina (53)   José Luis (40)   Adriana (45)   Santiago (46)

Beto (17)   Tina (16)   Esther (15)   Carlos (25)   Santiaguito (15)   Viviana (11)

B. Relaciones familiares. ¿Cuál es la relación entre estas personas en la familia de Adriana?

Modelo	Adriana y Santiago son **esposos.**

1. Santiaguito y Viviana son _____.

2. Esther y Viviana son _____.

3. Roberto y Cristina son los _____ de Esther.

4. Carlos, Santiaguito y Viviana son los _____ de Adriana.

5. Santiaguito y Beto son _____ de doña Cristina.

6. José Luis es _____ de Santiaguito.

7. Don José Luis y doña Cristina son los _____ de Tina, Esther, Viviana, Beto, Carlos y Santiaguito.

8. Doña Cristina es la _____ de Roberto y Santiago.

C. ¿Quiénes son? *(Who are they?)* Completa las frases lógicamente.

> **Modelo** La hija de mi mamá es **mi hermana**.
> Los papás de tus primas son **tus tíos**.

1. La madre de mi madre es _____.
2. Los hijos de mi hermana son _____.
3. La esposa de tu hermano es _____.
4. Las hijas de tus hijas son _____.
5. El hijo de mis tíos es _____.
6. El padre de tu esposa es _____.

D. ¿Y tus parientes? Who **(quién)** do the following questions describe? Answer them yourself, and then interview a partner.

1. ¿Con qué familiares vives *(do you live)*? _____
2. ¿Qué *(which)* familiares viven lejos *(far)*? _____
3. ¿Qué familiares ves *(do you see)* con frecuencia? _____
4. ¿Con quién celebras las fiestas del fin del año *(the holidays)*? _____

> **Práctica adicional**
>
> Cuaderno de tareas
> WB pp.102–104, E–I

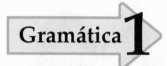

Gramática 1

Expressing age
- **The verb tener**
- **Numbers 41–100**

In the conversation, you heard the following statements.

Yo **tengo** tres hijos.	*I have three children.*
¿Y **tienes** familia en Cuba?	*And do you have family in Cuba?*
En mi casa también **tenemos** ese problema.	*We also have that problem at home.*

Tengo, tienes, and **tenemos** are forms of the verb **tener** *(to have)*. You will use these forms, and the other forms of **tener,** to talk about the members of your family and to tell how old they are. Observe the conjugation of **tener** below.

Tener	
No **tengo** hijos.	*I don't have children.*
¿**Tienes** hermanos?	*Do you have brothers and sisters?*
Sofía **tiene** un hermano.	*Sofía has a brother.*
Tenemos mucha tarea.	*We have a lot of homework.*
¿Uds. **tienen** familia en España? ¿**Tenéis** familia en España?	*Do you have family in Spain?*
Ellos no **tienen** gatos, ¿verdad?	*They don't have cats, right?*
Tener is also used to indicate age.	
¿**Cuántos años tienes?**	*How old are you?*
Tengo treinta y seis **años**.	*I'm thirty-six years old.*
¿**Cuántos años tienen** tus papás?	*How old are your parents?*
Mi papá **tiene** sesenta y tres **años** y mi mamá **tiene** cincuenta y nueve.	*My dad is sixty-three years old and my mom is fifty-nine.*

PRÁCTICA

E. ¿Cierto o falso? Completa cada frase con la forma apropiada del verbo **tener**. Después decide si la frase es **cierta** o **falsa**.

Basado en la conversación:	Cierto	Falso
1. Adriana y su esposo _____ dos hijas.	☐	☐
2. Ramón _____ una hermana.	☐	☐
3. Adriana dice *(says)*: "Yo _____ tres hijos."	☐	☐
4. Sofía no _____ novio.	☐	☐
5. Ramón y Sofía _____ clase de cálculo.	☐	☐
Basado en tu experiencia personal:		
6. Mis compañeros y yo _____ mucha tarea *(homework)*.	☐	☐
7. Yo _____ cuatro clases este semestre.	☐	☐
8. Mis papás y yo _____ un perro.	☐	☐
9. Yo _____ veinte años.	☐	☐
10. ¿Y tú, _____ mascotas?	☐	☐

• Numbers 41–100

Más números			
41	cuarenta y uno	42, 43 . . .	cuarenta y dos, cuarenta y tres…
50	cincuenta	53, 54 . . .	cincuenta y tres, cincuenta y cuatro…
60	sesenta	64, 65 . . .	sesenta y cuatro, sesenta y cinco…
70	setenta	75, 76 . . .	setenta y cinco, setenta y seis…
80	ochenta	86, 87 . . .	ochenta y seis, ochenta y siete…
90	noventa	97, 98 . . .	noventa y siete, noventa y ocho…
100	cien		

PRÁCTICA

F. El inventario. You work in the bookstore at your university. Here is this week's inventory. Inform your co-worker of how many of the following articles are in stock. When you are done, your co-worker will repeat them back to you.

> **Modelo**   48 calculadoras ⟶ **Hay cuarenta y ocho calculadoras.**

1. 86 libros de historia
2. 79 cuadernos
3. 100 mochilas
4. 65 calculadoras
5. 92 plumas
6. 43 diccionarios
7. 58 lápices
8. 74 libros de cálculo

G. ¿Cuántos años tiene...? Usa el árbol genealógico de la página 85 para contestar las preguntas.

1. ¿Quién (who) es la persona que tiene sesenta y nueve años? _____

2. ¿Quién tiene cuarenta y cinco años? _____

3. ¿Cuántos años tiene la hermana de Adriana? _____

4. ¿Cuántos años tiene el suegro de Santiago? _____

5. ¿Cuántos años tiene el menor (the youngest) de los primos? _____

H. ¿Cuál es tu teléfono? Write down the phone numbers of three of your classmates, and ask them when they are home.

¡Fíjate!
Pay attention to the way Spanish speakers give phone numbers. Look at the model.

Modelo	—¿Cuál es tu teléfono? (What is your phone number?)
	—Es el cuatro-veintitrés-sesenta y ocho-cuarenta y tres (423-6843).
	—¿A qué hora estás en casa? (What time are you home?)
	—A las seis.

Nombre	Buena hora para llamar (to call)
1. _____	_____
2. _____	_____
3. _____	_____

I. Preguntas personales. Answer the following questions about your family, your classes, and your social life. Afterwards, interview a partner.

1. **Acerca de (concerning) tu familia:** ¿Tienes una familia grande (large)? ¿Cuántos hermanos tienes? ¿Cuántos años tienen? ¿Cuántos años tienen tus papás? ¿Tienes mascotas?

   _____

   _____

   _____

2. **Acerca de tus clases:** ¿Cuántas clases tienes este semestre? ¿Cuáles (which ones) son? ¿Cómo son tus clases: interesantes o aburridas (boring)? ¿Qué clase te gusta más?

   _____

   _____

   _____

3. **Acerca de ti:** ¿Tienes novio/a o esposo/a? ¿Cómo se llama? ¿Cuántos años tiene? ¿Cómo es: romántico/a o reservado/a?

   _____

   _____

   _____

Práctica adicional

Cuaderno de tareas
WB pp.104–106, J–L

Gramática 2 **Saying where someone is from**
• Ser de

In the conversation, you heard the following statements.

¿Y tú, **de dónde eres**?	*Where are you from?*
Soy de aquí.	*I'm from here.*
Mi papá **es de** Honduras.	*My dad is from Honduras.*

When asking and telling where someone is from, use the verb **ser**, plus the preposition **de**.

–¿**De** dónde **son** tus abuelos?	*–Where are your grandparents from?*
–Mis abuelos **son de** España.	*–My grandparents are from Spain.*

Notice that when asking where someone is from, the Spanish **de** (*from*) is always at the beginning of the question.

PRÁCTICA

J. Personas famosas. With a classmate, match these famous people with their country of origin by asking each other questions. Be prepared to report to the class.

> **Modelo** —¿De dónde es Julio Iglesias?
> —Es de España.

¿De dónde es/son...

_____ 1. Nelson Mandela?	a. Colombia
_____ 2. Luciano Pavarotti y Sophia Loren?	b. Israel
_____ 3. Rigoberta Menchú?	c. Sudáfrica
_____ 4. Tony Blair?	d. Italia
_____ 5. Gabriel García Márquez?	e. España
_____ 6. Enrique Iglesias?	f. Inglaterra
_____ 7. Shimon Peres y Benjamín Netanyahu?	g. Japón
_____ 8. el emperador Akihito y su esposa?	h. Guatemala

K. ¿De dónde son? Complete each description with the appropriate form of **ser**.

1. Adriana _____ de Puerto Rico.
2. Sofía y Lalo _____ de México.
3. Manolo _____ de Cuba.
4. ¿De dónde _____ tú?
5. Yo _____ de aquí.
6. ¿De dónde _____ ustedes?
7. Nosotros _____ de Estados Unidos.
8. Emilio y su esposa _____ de España, ¿verdad?

¡Fíjate!

You may want to review the conjugation of **ser** on page 62 before completing this activity.

L. ¿De dónde es tu familia? Interview three classmates to find out where their parents and grandparents are from **(de dónde son)**. Write down their answers.

Modelo —¿De dónde eres?
—Soy de...
—¿Y tus abuelos?
—Mi abuela materna es de... Mis abuelos paternos son de...
—¿De dónde son tus padres?
—Mi papá es de..., y mi mamá es de...

Banco de palabras

Soy adoptado/a.
I'm adopted.

No sé de dónde es/son.
I don't know where they are from.

Mi abuela murió.
My grandmother died.

Mis padres murieron.
My parents died.

Lo siento.
I'm sorry.

Nombre	Padres	Abuelos
_____	_____	_____
_____	_____	_____
_____	_____	_____

Audio
CD-ROM

M. Una familia internacional. Escucha la narración de Ana Mari para completar la información.

Ana Mari

Nombre	Relación	Edad	Origen
Ramón	abuelo		
Carmen		72	Cuba
	mamá		
Alejandro		46	
Álex, Luis y Ramón			

Práctica adicional

Cuaderno de tareas
WB p.106, M
LM pp.107–108, A–C, Pron.

Audio
CD-ROM
Episodio 4

Actividades comunicativas

A. Árbol genealógico: la familia de Ramón y Ana Mari Robledo.

Instrucciones para **Estudiante 1**

Parte 1. With a partner, complete Ramón and Ana Mari's family tree. You have half of the information; your partner has the other half. Use the following expressions.

—**¿Cuántos años tiene Luis?**   —**¿Cuál es la profesión de Pilar?**

—**Tiene... años.**   —**Es...**

—**¿De dónde es?**   —**¿Cómo se llama el papá de Ana Mari?**

—**Es de...**   —**Se llama...**

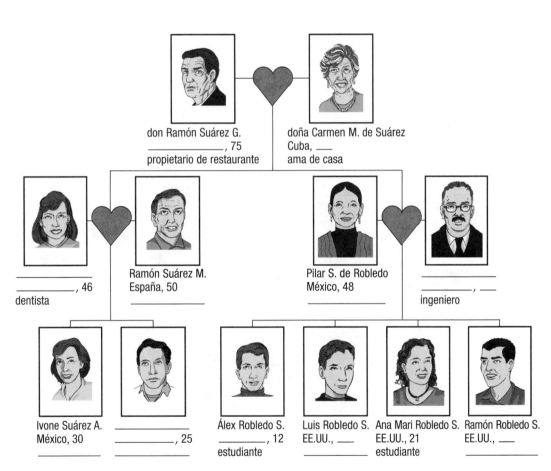

don Ramón Suárez G.
_____, 75
propietario de restaurante

doña Carmen M. de Suárez
Cuba, ___
ama de casa

_____, 46
dentista

Ramón Suárez M.
España, 50

Pilar S. de Robledo
México, 48

_____, ___
ingeniero

Ivone Suárez A.
México, 30

_____
_____, 25

Álex Robledo S.
_____, 12
estudiante

Luis Robledo S.
EE.UU., ___
_____

Ana Mari Robledo S.
EE.UU., 21
estudiante

Ramón Robledo S.
EE.UU., ___
_____

Parte 2. Now write a paragraph, describing Ramón and Ana Mari's family.

> **Modelo**   **Ramón tiene... hermanos. Sus hermanos son... Su papá se
> llama... Tiene... años.** etc.

A. Árbol genealógico: la familia de Ramón y Ana Mari Robledo.

Instrucciones para Estudiante 2

Parte 1. With a partner, complete Ramón and Ana Mari's family tree. You have half of the information; your partner has the other half. Use the following expressions.

—¿Cómo se llama la mamá de Ana Mari? —¿Cuál es la profesión de Alejandro?
—Se llama... —Es...
—¿De dónde es? —¿Cuántos años tiene Álex?
—Es de... —Tiene... años.

don Ramón Suárez G.
España, ____
propietario de restaurante

doña Carmen M. de Suárez
_____, 80
ama de casa

Lucía A. de Suárez
México, ____
_____

Ramón Suárez M.
_____, ____
doctor

_____
_____, 48
intérprete

Alejandro Robledo C.
Honduras, 46
_____

_____
México, 30
reportera

Iván Suárez A.
México, ____
maestro

Álex Robledo S.
EE.UU., ____
_____

Luis Robledo S.
_____, 13
estudiante

Ana Mari Robledo S.
EE.UU., ____
estudiante

_____
_____, 23
estudiante

Parte 2. Now write a paragraph, describing Ramón and Ana Mari's family.

Modelo	Ramón tiene... hermanos. Sus hermanos son... Su papá se llama... Tiene... años. etc.

B. Los números de emergencia.

Instrucciones para **Estudiante 1**

Imagine you are going to Guadalajara, Mexico, with Sofía and her friends. As a precaution, you want the telephone numbers of various emergency services, and other important numbers. You were able to locate only a few. Ask your partner for the numbers you need and fill them in.

Modelo   —¿Tienes el número de teléfono de los bomberos *(firefighters)*?

NOMBRE	TELÉFONO
La Cruz Roja	6-13-15-50 y 6-14-27-07
Los Ángeles Verdes (problemas mecánicos)	
La casa de Odette	
La policía federal	6-21-91-74 y 6-22-88-37
La casa de los abuelos de Ramón	5-54-13-90
Los bomberos	
La policía municipal	6-17-60-60 y 6-18-02-06
La defensa del consumidor	

B. Los números de emergencia.

Instrucciones para **Estudiante 2**

Imagine you are going to Guadalajara, Mexico, with Sofía and her friends. As a precaution, you want the telephone numbers of various emergency services, and other important numbers. You were able to locate only a few. Ask your partner for the numbers you need and fill them in.

Modelo   —¿Tienes el número de teléfono de la policía federal?

NOMBRE	TELÉFONO
La Cruz Roja	
Los Ángeles Verdes (problemas mecánicos)	5-13-26-64
La casa de Odette	5-82-99-24
La policía federal	
La casa de los abuelos de Ramón	
Los bomberos (*firefighters*)	6-19-52-41 y 6-23-08-33
La policía municipal	
La defensa del consumidor	6-14-94-16 y 6-14-94-01

C. En imágenes.

Instrucciones para **Estudiante 1**

Use the following words and the drawings to create logical sentences. When you know what your sentences are, read them to your partner, who will check the answer key to see if your sentences are correct. Take turns.

1. Necesito comprar un _____ , dos _____ y una _____ para la clase de matemáticas.

2. En esa _____ venden _____ y _____ .

3. Mis _____ paternos viven en _____ ; ellos tienen dos _____ , un _____ y muchos _____ .

4. En las mañanas, es difícil encontrar _____ en la _____ .

5. En la _____ de mi novio hay muchos _____ y _____ .

Las respuestas de tu compañero/a:
1. En nuestro **salón de clases** hay treinta y ocho **pupitres**, tres **pizarrones**, una **bandera** y un **reloj**.
2. En la **escuela** de mi prima no hay **canchas de tenis**, **piscina** ni **gimnasio**.
3. Necesito ir al **baño** antes de mi clase de **química** porque hoy tenemos un **examen** difícil.
4. Mi **profesor** de **matemáticas** tiene cuarenta **chicos/estudiantes** en su clase.
5. Tengo una **familia** pequeña: mis **padres**, una **hermana** y un **perro**.

C. En imágenes.

Instrucciones para **Estudiante 2**

Use the following words and the drawings to create logical sentences. When you know what your sentences are, read them to your partner, who will check the answer key to see if your sentences are correct. Take turns.

1. En nuestro hay treinta y ocho , tres , una y un .

2. En la escuela de mi prima no hay , ni .

3. Necesito ir al antes de mi clase de porque hoy tenemos un difícil.

4. Mi de $5x^2 + 9y^2 = 21$ tiene cuarenta en su clase.

5. Tengo una pequeña (small): mis , una y un .

Las respuestas de tu compañero/a:
1. Necesito comprar un **lápiz**, dos **plumas** y una **calculadora** para la clase de matemáticas.
2. En esa **librería** venden **escritorios** y **computadoras**.
3. Mis **abuelos** paternos viven en **México**; ellos tienen dos **gatos**, un **pájaro** y muchos **peces**.
4. En las mañanas, es difícil encontrar **estacionamiento** en la **universidad**.
5. En la **mochila** de mi novio hay muchos **libros** y **papeles**.

La correspondencia

El correo: Sofía te escribe. *(Sofía writes to you).* Read the questions and Sofía's letter to you. Then answer the questions.

1. ¿Cuántas personas hay en la familia de Sofía? _____

2. ¿Por qué la abuela de Sofía es más generosa con Lalo? _____

3. ¿Qué profesión tienen los padres de Sofía? _____

4. ¿Cómo es Lalo? ¿Conoces *(do you know)* a una persona similar? ¿Quién *(who)?*

_____

5. ¿La relación de Sofía y Lalo es buena *(good)* o mala *(bad)?* _____

Querido/a estudiante:

Tengo una familia pequeña: mis abuelos, mis padres, un hermano y un perro. Mi abuela es mexicana y mi abuelo es español. Viven seis meses en Guadalajara y seis meses en Estados Unidos con nosotros. Mi abuela es muy generosa, especialmente con Lalo porque es su nieto favorito.

Mis padres son jóvenes. Mi papá se llama Rubén. Tiene cuarenta y cuatro años. Es banquero; trabaja mucho y es muy estricto con nosotros. Mi mamá se llama Diana. Es una señora muy elegante e inteligente. Trabaja en un banco también, donde es supervisora de créditos comerciales.

Lalo, mi hermano, tiene quince años. Es estudiante. Es un poco irresponsable e inmaduro, pero es muy buen hermano. Le gustan los deportes y la música alternativa.

Con cariño,
tu amiga Sofía

En papel: Una carta para Sofía. Sofía wants to know what your family is like. Use her letter as a model to write a description of your own family.

Modelo	Tengo una familia...: mi..., mi... y...
	Mi... se llama..., tiene... años. Es de...
	Le gusta... (actividades). Etc.

¡Fíjate!

Try to express yourself simply with the language you know. Although you may be tempted, avoid writing your letter in English and translating it into Spanish. At this point, your ability to write in English far exceeds your ability to communicate in Spanish... as time goes on, this will change!

¡A ver de nuevo! Review this episode's **Escena** to complete the summary that follows.

Adriana y Manolo están en la clase de (1)_____ con Sofía. Manolo es

(2)_____ de Sofía. En este episodio, conocemos (we meet) a Ramón, el

(3)_____ de Ana Mari. Él es de (4)_____, pero su papá es

de (5)_____ y su (6)_____ es de México. Adriana no es de

México; es de (7)_____. Tiene (8)_____ hijos. Sus hijos

mayores hablan español, pero a su (9)_____ no le gusta hablarlo. En la

familia de Ramón (10)_____ el mismo problema. (11)_____

hermanos (12)_____ entienden español, pero no lo hablan.

Invitación a **Cuba**

Del álbum de
Manolo

Cuba es una isla grande; es un poco más grande que *(slightly larger than)* el estado de Pennsylvania. Hay aproximadamente 11.2 millones de habitantes. La mitad de los cubanos es de descendencia afro-española; el 11% es de descendencia africana; el 37% es blanco y un pequeño porcentaje es de origen chino.

Un restaurante famoso, La Bodeguita del Medio, está en una calle típica de la parte vieja de la ciudad de La Habana, Cuba. El escritor norteamericano Ernest Hemingway visitaba ese restaurante con frecuencia.

Práctica adicional		
Cuaderno de tareas WB p. 106, N LM p. 108, A–B	Audio CD-ROM Episodio 4	Website vistahigher learning.com

Vocabulario del Episodio 4

Objetivos comunicativos

You should now be able to do the following in Spanish:

✓ talk about your family

✓ tell and ask for someone's age

✓ say and ask where someone is from

✓ ask for and give phone numbers

La familia, los familiares y más

los abuelos	*grandparents*	el abuelo	la abuela
los amigos	*friends*	el amigo	la amiga
los chicos	*adolescents, teenagers*	el chico	la chica
los cuñados	*brother(s)-in-law and sister(s)-in-law*	el cuñado	la cuñada
los esposos	*husband and wife*	el esposo	la esposa
los familiares	*relatives*	el familiar	
los hermanos	*brother(s) and sister(s)*	el hermano	la hermana
los hijos	*children (one's own): son(s) and daughter(s)*	el hijo	la hija
los nietos	*grandchildren*	el nieto	la nieta
los niños	*children: boy(s) and girl(s)*	el niño	la niña
los novios	*boyfriend and girlfriend; bride and groom; fiancés*	el novio	la novia
los padres	*parents*	el padre	la madre
los primos	*cousins*	el primo	la prima
los sobrinos	*nephew(s) and niece(s)*	el sobrino	la sobrina
los suegros	*father-in-law and mother-in-law*	el suegro	la suegra
los tíos	*uncle(s) and aunt(s)*	el tío	la tía

Las mascotas *pets*

el gato	*cat*
el pájaro	*bird*
el perro	*dog*
el pez	*fish*

Posesivos

mi, mis	*my*
tu, tus	*your*
su, sus	*his; her; their*
nuestro/a(s)	*our*
la hija de Adriana	*Adriana's daughter*

Verbs

tener	*to have*
ser de	*to be from*
tener... años	*to be... years old*
¿Cuántos años tienes? Tengo... años.	*How old are you? I'm... years old.*
¿De dónde eres? Soy de...	*Where are you from? I'm from...*

Más números

41	cuarenta y uno	42, 43...	cuarenta y dos, cuarenta y tres...
50	cincuenta	53, 54...	cincuenta y tres, cincuenta y cuatro...
60	sesenta	64, 65...	sesenta y cuatro, sesenta y cinco...
70	setenta	75, 76...	setenta y cinco, setenta y seis...
80	ochenta	86, 87...	ochenta y seis, ochenta y siete...
90	noventa	97, 98...	noventa y siete, noventa y ocho...
100	cien		

Vocabulario personal

Write the words that you need to know to talk about yourself and your family in Spanish.

¡A escribir!

Episodio

4

Escenas de la vida: ¡Qué internacionales!

A. ¡A ver cuánto entendiste! See how much of the **Escena** you understood by matching the Spanish sentences with their English equivalents.

_____ 1. ¡Qué bueno que hablas español!

_____ 2. Los dos mayores hablan español muy bien.

_____ 3. A mi hija no le gusta hablar español.

_____ 4. También tenemos ese problema.

_____ 5. Mis hermanos menores lo entienden todo, pero no lo hablan.

a. The two older ones speak Spanish well.

b. We also have that problem.

c. That's great that you speak Spanish!

d. My daughter doesn't like to speak Spanish.

e. My younger brothers understand everything, but they do not speak it.

B. ¿Quién lo dijo? Write the initial of the person who made each statement: Adriana **(A)**, Ramón **(R)**, or Sofía **(S)**.

_____ 1. Manolo es escritor; escribe poemas.

_____ 2. Vamos a llegar tarde.

_____ 3. Yo tengo tres hijos.

_____ 4. Ya son las nueve menos cinco.

_____ 5. Tomamos geología juntos.

C. ¡Qué internacionales! Complete the conversation, based on what you saw in the video.

Manolo	Ramón, ¿tú, de dónde (1)_____?
Ramón	Soy de (2) _____. Mi mamá (3) _____ México y (4) _____ es de Honduras. ¿Y tú?
Manolo	(5) _____ Cuba. Tengo algunos parientes en Cuba, pero (6) _____ viven en la Florida.
Ramón	Señora, ¿usted también es de Cuba?
Adriana	No. Soy de (7) _____.
Ramón	¡Qué (8) _____!

Video
CD-ROM

D. ¿Quién habla español? Use the following words to complete the conversation.

entienden	hija	menos cinco
tener	hijos	mis hermanos menores
habla	mayores	tarde

Adriana   Tengo tres (1) _____. Los dos (2) _____ hablan español, pero

a mi (3) _____ no le gusta hablarlo.

Ramón   (4) _____ lo (5) _____ todo, pero no lo hablan.

Sofía   Ana Mari (6) _____ español perfectamente.

Ramón   ¡Ya son las nueve (7) _____! Vamos a llegar (8) _____ a clase.

Vocabulario 1

Identifying family members and friends
- **The family**
- **Expressing possession**

E. ¿De quién son las cosas? Tell Adriana to whom the following objects belong.

Modelo	calculadoras/Manolo
	Son las calculadoras de Manolo.

1. mochila/Sofía _____

2. lápices/Santiaguito _____

3. reloj/Santiago _____

4. cuadernos/Viviana _____

5. diccionario/Manolo _____

6. plumas/Ana Mari _____

F. La familia de Manolo.

Parte 1. Read Manolo's description of his family. Then answer the questions.

> Hola, soy Manolo Báez Rodríguez. Soy estudiante y me gusta mucho tocar la guitarra. Tengo una familia relativamente pequeña. Solamente somos mi hermana y yo. Mi hermana es dos años menor que yo. Se llama Nancy. Mis papás son cubanos y ahora viven en Miami. Mi papá es doctor y mi mamá es profesora. Mi papá se llama Manuel Báez y mi mamá es Isabel Rodríguez de Báez. Los padres de mi papá son Arturo y Carlota. Ellos todavía viven en La Habana. Tengo un tío y una tía. Son los hermanos de mi papá. Mi tío Francisco es soltero, tiene 50 años; mi tía Perla es viuda[1] y tiene tres hijos: dos hombres y una mujer. Mi prima tiene 25 años, como yo; por eso, somos muy buenos amigos. Ahora ella tiene novio, y creo que van a casarse[2] pronto. Mis dos primos son menores que[3] nosotros. Yo no tengo novia, pero hay una chica que me gusta.

[1]widowed   [2]get married   [3]younger than

1. ¿Cuántos hermanos tiene Manolo? _____

2. ¿Dónde viven sus padres? ¿Como se llaman? _____

_____

3. ¿Qué profesión tiene su papá? ¿Y su mamá? _____

4. ¿Cómo se llaman los abuelos de Manolo? ¿Dónde viven?

_____

5. ¿De quién (*whose*) son hermanos los tíos de Manolo? _____

6. ¿Cuántos años tiene Manolo? _____

7. ¿Cuántos primos tiene? _____

Parte 2. Use Manolo's letter as a model to write about your own family. Be as thorough as you can with the Spanish you have. Remember: keep it simple!

_____

_____

_____

_____

_____

G. Crucigrama. You've been asked to create the clues for the crossword puzzle (**crucigrama**) in this week's school newspaper. Write a description or definition of the words in the puzzle.

horizontales

1. _____

4. _____

6. _____la hija de tus papás es tu...___

7. _____

8. _____

9. _____

10. _____

14. _____

15. _____

verticales

1. _____

2. _____

3. _____

5. _____

11. _____un animal como Pluto_____

12. _____

13. _____

Crossword grid across:
- 1 horizontal: C U Ñ A D A
- 4 horizontal: H I J O
- 6 horizontal: H E R M A N A
- 7 horizontal: P R I M O S
- 8 horizontal: N O V I A
- 9 horizontal: G A T O
- 10 horizontal: E S P O S O
- 14 horizontal: M A D R E
- 15 horizontal: A M I G O S

Crossword grid down:
- 1 vertical: C H I C O
- 2 vertical: A B U E L O S
- 3 vertical: P Á J A R O
- 5 vertical: N E S (NÉS)
- 11 vertical: P E R R O
- 12 vertical: S O B R I N O
- 13 vertical: P A D R E

H. El primo Emilio. Lalo and Sofía talk about their cousin Emilio. Complete their description with the appropriate forms of the possessive adjectives.

Él es (1) _____ (nuestro/tu) primo. Se llama Emilio
y tiene treinta años. (2) _____ (su/mi) esposa está
en España. (3) _____ (Su/Sus) padres viven (live) en
Madrid. (4) _____ (nuestro/nuestros) tíos, los padres
de Emilio, se llaman Laura y Emilio. Son muy buenos.
Emilio es (5) _____ (mis/mi) primo favorito.
¿Quién es (6) _____ (tu/tus) primo favorito?

Emilio

I. Tu familia. You are showing a family picture to a friend. Answer their questions using the appropriate forms of the possessive adjectives.

> **Modelo** ¿Ella es la hermana de tu mamá?
> Sí, es **su** hermana.

1. ¿Éste es tu hermano?

   No, es _____ primo.

2. ¿Él es tu papá?

   Sí, es _____ papá.

3. Ah, y ellos son los papás de tus primos.

   Sí, son (their) _____ papás.

4. ¿Ellos son tus abuelos?

   Sí, son _____ abuelos paternos.

5. ¿De quién son estos perritos?

   Son (our) _____ mascotas.

6. ¿Los chicos son tus hermanos?

   No, él es _____ amigo y ella es (his) _____ novia._____

   hermanos no están en la foto.

Gramática 1

Expressing age
- **The verb tener**
- **Numbers 41–100**

J. ¿Cuántos años tienen tus familiares? Complete the followig information with the ages of different people in your own family, or an imaginary family.

1. Mi papá _____ años.

2. Mi mamá _____ años.

3. Mi hermano/a menor _____ años.

4. Mi _____ tiene _____ años.

5. Yo _____ años.

K. ¿Qué tiene? Create true statements or questions using an element from each column.

Manolo		mucha tarea
Sofía		cinco clases este semestre
Las universidades		novio/a
Mis amigos y yo	(no) tener	veintitrés años
Mis compañeros		una clase de español
Tú		coche
Ana Mari		un hermano
Yo		biblioteca y gimnasio

1. _____.
2. _____.
3. _____.
4. _____.
5. _____.
6. _____.
7. _____.
8. _____.

L. ¡Cuánto dinero! *(So much money!)* As the bookkeeper at your university bookstore, you have to pay the distributor of foreign books and movies. Complete the checks according to the invoices. Remember to make note of the items you are paying for (under *Memo*).

Libro/Video	Cantidad	Total
Relato de un náufrago	23 libros	$98.35
Pedro Páramo	15 libros	$64.73
Fresa y chocolate	1 video	$51.69
¡Ay, Carmela!	1 video	$42.80

Tienda Universitaria 5322

Fecha _____

Páguese a la orden de ___*Distribuidora Internacional*___ $ _____

La cantidad de _____ dólares

Memo _____   _____

|00231334: 232443 ||2343243434

Tienda Universitaria 5323

Fecha _____

Páguese a la orden de ___*Distribuidora Internacional*___ $ _____

La cantidad de _____ dólares

Memo _____ _____

|00231334: 232443 ||2343243434

Tienda Universitaria 5324

Fecha _____

Páguese a la orden de ___*Distribuidora Internacional*___ $ _____

La cantidad de _____ dólares

Memo _____ _____

|00231334: 232443 ||2343243434

Tienda Universitaria 5325

Fecha _____

Páguese a la orden de ___*Distribuidora Internacional*___ $ _____

La cantidad de _____ dólares

Memo _____ _____

|00231334: 232443 ||2343243434

 Gramática 2

Saying where someone is from
- **Ser de**

M. ¿De dónde son? Complete the sentences based on what you know about the characters.

1. Sofía _____ mexicana. _____ la Ciudad de México.
2. Ramón y Ana Mari _____ mexicoamericanos. _____ Estados Unidos.
3. El papá de Ramón _____ Honduras. Su mamá es mexicana; es de _____.
4. Adriana y su familia _____ Puerto Rico.
5. Manolo es cubano. Él _____ Cuba.

Para terminar

N. Mi árbol genealógico. To preserve your heritage, you have decided to record the name, place of origin, and age of as many relatives as you can. Create your family tree. If you prefer not to do your own, you may want to interview a friend.

¡A escuchar!

Episodio

4

Comprensión

Audio
CD-ROM

A. Los familiares. You will hear six statements about family. Listen and say whether each statement is true **(cierto)** or false **(falso)**. If it is false, change the last word in the statement to make it true. Repeat the correct answer after the speaker.

Modelo	You hear:	**El esposo de mi tía es mi hermano.**
	You say:	**Falso. El esposo de mi tía es mi tío.**

Audio
CD-ROM

B. Los nuevos estudiantes internacionales. You have a telephone message from the president of the Club Latino. She needs you to go to the airport to pick up four students who are arriving on various flights **(vuelos)**. Listen to her message and fill in the form with the necessary information. You will hear the message twice.

Nombre	Hora	Aerolínea	Vuelo	De

Audio
CD-ROM

C. La nueva compañera de cuarto. Listen as Mónica describes her new roommate. Then select the best completion for each sentence. You will hear the description twice.

1. Mónica y su compañera de cuarto viven en...
   a. un apartamento.   b. una casa.   c. una residencia estudiantil.

2. La compañera se llama...
   a. Mariquita.   b. Silvia.   c. Miguela.

3. La compañera es de...
   a. Costa Rica.   b. Perú.   c. México.

4. Aquí en la universidad, ella...
   a. no tiene familia.   b. tiene una prima.   c. tiene un hermano.

5. La nueva compañera no tiene...
   a. novio.   b. dinero.   c. amigos.

Pronunciación

La *n* y la *ñ*. The **n (ene)** is pronounced much like the English pronunciation of the same letter. Repeat these words and sentences after the speaker.

nuevo	moreno	Nicaragua	Gana el número nueve.
nieto	interesante	Norteamérica	Buenas noches, Nena.
nombre	grande	Noruega	Nicolás no necesita nada.

The **ñ (eñe)** is pronounced as English *ny*, as in the words *canyon* and *onion*.

año	señora	compañero	Son niños de nueve años.
mañana	señor	cuñado	Es una señorita española.

Más escenas de la vida

Ramón and Wayne run into Manolo in the cafeteria. Listen to their conversation, and then complete activities **A** and **B**. You will hear the conversation twice.

A. ¿Entendiste? Rearrange the following statements in the order they occur in the conversation.

_____ a. No. ¡Yo estoy muy contento!

_____ b. Hola, Manolo. Te presento a Wayne.

_____ c. ¿No quieres vivir allá con tu familia?

_____ d. Igualmente.

_____ e. Mucho gusto.

B. ¿Cierto o falso? Indicate whether the following statements are **cierto** or **falso,** according to the conversation.

	Cierto	Falso
1. Wayne no tiene familia aquí.	☐	☐
2. Su familia es de Wisconsin.	☐	☐
3. Sus padres son de Manhattan.	☐	☐
4. Wayne quiere vivir con su familia.	☐	☐
5. Wayne tiene veinticuatro años.	☐	☐
6. Manolo necesita su independencia.	☐	☐
7. Manolo no habla muy bien español.	☐	☐
8. Wayne vivió en Chile.	☐	☐

Episodio

5

Escenas de la vida: ¿Estudiamos el sábado?

Video
CD-ROM

Audio
CD-ROM

A. ¡Mira cuánto puedes entender! Listen to the conversation or watch the **Escena** to complete the tasks below.

1. ¿Qué días están libres *(are free)* Manolo y Adriana para estudiar?

	lunes	martes	miércoles	jueves	viernes	sábado	domingo
Manolo							
Adriana							

2. Adriana dice que nunca descansa; ¿por qué? ¿Qué hace Adriana los martes y jueves?

Compra la comida.

Trabaja en una oficina.

Llega tarde a casa.

3. ¿Qué hace la hija de Adriana los lunes?

Baila en un grupo.

Lava su ropa.

Limpia su cuarto.

4. ¿Qué hacen su hijo y sus amigos?

Miran **la tele.**

Visitan **a los abuelos.**

Tocan **la guitarra.**

Video
CD-ROM

B. ¿Te diste cuenta? Escucha la conversación o mira la **Escena** otra vez para indicar a quién se refieren los siguientes comentarios: Manolo **(M)**, Adriana **(A)**, Sofía **(S)** o todos **(T)** (*everybody*).

Audio
CD-ROM

_____ 1. No es pesimista.

_____ 2. Está libre los sábados por la tarde.

_____ 3. Necesitan estudiar para el examen.

_____ 4. Nunca tiene tiempo para descansar.

_____ 5. Está muy preocupada.

Cultura a lo vivo

In Spanish-speaking countries, most young adults do not move out to become "independent." It is common for them to stay home until they get married, or relocate to another city to work or pursue their studies.

Video
CD-ROM

C. Responde. Contesta las siguientes preguntas.

Audio
CD-ROM

1. ¿Qué día toca la guitarra el hijo de Adriana?

_____

2. ¿A qué hora trabaja Adriana?

_____

3. ¿Dónde tocan la guitarra el hijo de Adriana y sus amigos?

_____

4. ¿Por qué Adriana nunca descansa?

_____

5. ¿Dónde y cuándo van a estudiar?

_____

Práctica adicional

Cuaderno de tareas
WB pp.123–124, A–C

Video
CD-ROM
Episodio 5

Para comunicarnos mejor

Gramática

Talking about activities at school and at home
- **-ar verbs**
- **Days of the week**
- **Infinitive constructions**

In their conversation, you heard the following statements:

Trabajo en una oficina.	*I work in an office.*
Mi hija **baila** en un grupo folclórico.	*My daughter dances in a folk group.*
Mi hijo **toca** la guitarra.	*My son plays the guitar.*
Estudiamos el sábado a las dos, ¿de acuerdo?	*We'll study on Saturday at two, okay?*

To talk about the activities of her friends and family, Adriana uses different verb endings, which change depending on whom she is describing. In Spanish, verb forms consist of two parts: the stem **(la raíz)**, and the ending **(la terminación)**. For example, the verb form **trabajo** *(I work)* is made up of the stem **trabaj-** and the ending **-o**. Different endings are attached to the stem to indicate who does the action *(I, you, he, she, it, we, they)*, when the action occurs *(today, yesterday, tomorrow)*, and how the action is carried out *(right now, only once, all the time)*. Attaching different endings to verb stems is called *conjugating the verb* **(conjugar el verbo)**. Study the following conjugation and use it to conjugate regular **-ar** verbs.

El presente de los verbos del grupo **-ar**		
yo	**Trabajo** en una oficina.	*I work in an office.*
tú	**Trabajas** mucho.	*You work a lot.* (informal)
usted	**Trabaja** por la mañana.	*You work in the morning.* (formal)
él/ella	**Trabaja** en un hospital.	*He/She works in a hospital.*
nosotros/as	**Trabajamos** juntos/as.	*We work together.*
ustedes	**Trabajan** de noche, ¿no?	*You work at night, right?* (plural)
vosotros/as	**Trabajáis** de noche, ¿no?	
ellos/as	**Trabajan** en un banco.	*They work in a bank.*

1. When the ending of the verb is **-ar** (as in **trabajar**), **-er**, or **-ir**, the verb has not been conjugated; that is, we do not know who is doing the action. This verb form is called the *infinitive* **(el infinitivo)**. In English, the infinitive is indicated by the word *to*, as in *to work*.

2. As a form of the present tense, **trabajo** may mean *I work* or *I am working*.

Trabajo en una oficina en Nueva York.	*I work in an office in New York.*
Trabajo en una oficina este semestre.	*I'm working in an office this semester.*

3. Every Spanish verb belongs to one of three groups, according to its infinitive ending.

• Verbs that end in **-ar**	**trabajar**	*to work*
• Verbs that end in **-er**	**comer**	*to eat*
• Verbs that end in **-ir**	**vivir**	*to live*

4. Remember that the **vosotros** form is used only in Spain.

5. The following verbs use the same endings as **trabajar**.

Actividades frecuentes	
En la escuela	
buscar información en Internet	*to look for information on the Internet*
estudiar mucho/poco	*to study a lot/a little*
llegar a tiempo	*to arrive (get somewhere) on time*
necesitar libros	*to need books*
sacar buenas notas	*to get good grades*
tomar clases	*to take classes*
café	*to drink coffee*
usar la computadora	*to use the computer*
Los fines de semana	
bailar (bien)	*to dance (well)*
comprar cosas	*to buy things*
comida	*food*
ropa	*clothes*
descansar	*to rest*
llegar tarde/temprano/a tiempo a casa	*to get home late/early/on time*
trabajar en una tienda	*to work at a store*
visitar a los abuelos	*to visit one's grandparents*
En la casa	
escuchar música	*to listen to music*
hablar por teléfono	*to talk on the phone*
lavar el coche	*to wash the car*
la ropa	*to do the laundry*
limpiar la casa	*to clean the house*
el cuarto	*the (one's) room*
mirar la tele	*to watch TV*
tocar la guitarra	*to play the guitar*

También se dice...

el coche ⟶ el carro, el auto

mirar la tele ⟶ ver la tele

las notas ⟶ las calificaciones

Learning Strategy: Create flash cards

On one side, write the word in Spanish; on the other, write its English equivalent. If possible, draw a picture of the item and write a sentence where you use the word in a meaningful way. Study the words in both directions: from English to Spanish, and vice versa.

PRÁCTICA

A. ¿Qué hacen? Empareja las ilustraciones de la página siguiente con las oraciones apropiadas.

___ 1. Trabajo en una oficina.

___ 2. Los chicos siempre buscan información en Internet.

___ 3. Sofía escucha música alternativa.

___ 4. A veces tomamos el autobús a la escuela.

___ 5. Me gusta mucho comprar ropa.

___ 6. Los chicos sacan buenas notas.

B. ¿Cuáles son tus actividades? Indica si las frases son ciertas o falsas para ti.

	Cierto	Falso
1. Mis amigos y yo necesitamos dinero.	☐	☐
2. Nunca lavo mi coche.	☐	☐
3. Mi mamá usa la computadora en casa.	☐	☐
4. Mi papá descansa por la noche.	☐	☐
5. Siempre llego a tiempo a la clase de español.	☐	☐
6. No trabajo este semestre.	☐	☐
7. Mis compañeros de clase estudian mucho.	☐	☐
8. Mi novio/a busca mucha información en Internet.	☐	☐

C. Las actividades de la familia de Adriana.

Parte 1. Adriana habla de sus actividades y de las actividades de su familia los sábados.
Usa estos verbos para completar sus comentarios.

llegar	escuchar	trabajar	hablar	estudiar
lavar	mirar	descansar	necesitar	tomar

Los sábados por la mañana, mi esposo (1) _____ su coche. Yo (2) _____
preparar la comida para toda la semana. Mis hijos (3) _____ de la escuela a las
tres de la tarde. Por la tarde, mi hija (4) _____ lecciones de baile.
Mi hijo (5) _____ con sus amigos por teléfono. Yo (6) _____ para mis
clases por lo menos (*at least*) dos horas todos los días. Por la noche, nosotros no
(7) _____ la televisión; hablamos y (8) _____ música.

Parte 2. Usa las oraciones como modelo para escribir sobre tu familia. Haz los cambios necesarios.

> **Modelo** Los sábados por la mañana mi **papá** lava su coche.

• Days of the week

Los días de la semana y más			
los lunes	*on Mondays*	**entre semana**	*on weekdays*
los martes	*on Tuesdays*	**los fines de semana**	*on weekends*
los miércoles	*on Wednesdays*	**por la mañana**	*in the morning*
los jueves	*on Thursdays*	**por la tarde**	*in the afternoon*
los viernes	*on Fridays*	**por la noche**	*in the evening*
los sábados	*on Saturdays*	**todos los días**	*every day*
los domingos	*on Sundays*		

Note: In Spanish, the days of the week are not capitalized. **Los lunes** means on *Mondays*, but **el lunes** means *on Monday*.

PRÁCTICA

D. Mis actividades. Escribe en tu cuaderno una de tus actividades para cada día de la semana.

> **Modelo**   Los lunes lavo la ropa. Los martes trabajo cinco horas. Los miércoles…

E. Lotería. Find out who does the following things. Write the name of a different classmate who responds **sí** to your question in each box. Ask appropriate questions, according to the model. The first student to form three straight lines wins the game.

> **Modelo**   _____ visita a sus abuelos los domingos
> —José, ¿visitas a tus abuelos los domingos?
> —Sí, visito a mis abuelos los domingos.
> **(Write "José" on the corresponding line)**

_____ lava la ropa los viernes.	_____ saca buenas notas en la clase de español.	_____ no trabaja.	_____ necesita comprar una computadora.
_____ escucha música alternativa.	_____ habla otro idioma *(another language)* con sus padres.	_____ toma cuatro clases este semestre.	_____ siempre llega tarde a clase.
_____ toca bien el piano.	_____ no es de aquí.	_____ no estudia en la biblioteca.	_____ visita a sus abuelos los domingos.
_____ le gusta bailar los fines de semana.	_____ descansa los lunes por la tarde.	_____ busca información para las clases en Internet.	_____ no tiene hermanos.

• Infinitive constructions

In the conversation, Adriana said:

Necesito repasar todo.   *I need to review everything.*
Necesito estar presente, porque si no...   *I need to be there, otherwise...*

1. In both English and Spanish, some verbs may be used in combination with other verbs in the infinitive. Notice that Adriana uses a combination of two verbs: the main verb, which is conjugated, and a second verb, which is in the infinitive form (the **-r** form). These combined verbs are called *infinitive constructions*, as in the following examples.

No **me gusta llegar** tarde a clase.   *I don't like to be late for class.*
Necesitamos buscar información en Internet.   *We need to look for information on the Internet.*
No **quiero sacar** F.   *I don't want to get an F.*

PRÁCTICA

F. Las actividades de Sofía. Sofía nos habla de sus actividades y las de *(those of)* su familia. Completa las frases.

1. Los sábados me gusta _____; por eso *(because of that)*, no trabajo por las tardes.
2. Los domingos necesito _____ la ropa y _____ para mis clases.
3. Mi hermano nunca _____; por eso, no _____ buenas notas.
4. Mis papás _____ trabajar mucho para vivir *(to live)* bien.
5. Hoy no quiero lavar ropa porque necesito_____ para el examen.

G. Los fines de semana. Escribe cuatro cosas que **necesitas, te gusta** o **no te gusta** hacer *(to do)* durante los fines de semana. Comparte tus comentarios con un(a) compañero/a.

> **Modelo**   Los viernes por la noche no me gusta estudiar.

¡Fíjate!
Remember to use **los viernes** for *on Fridays* and **el viernes** for *on Friday.*

1. _____
2. _____
3. _____
4. _____

H. Personas importantes. Describe las actividades de cuatro personas importantes en tu vida. Comparte tus respuestas con un(a) compañero/a.

> **Modelo**   Mi novio no baila bien.

1. _____
2. _____
3. _____
4. _____

Práctica adicional

Cuaderno de tareas
WB pp.124–125, D–F

Gramática 2

Asking yes/no questions
• Tag questions

Adding **¿no?** at the end of a statement is one of two ways of asking a yes/no question in Spanish. When asking a question that requires a yes/no answer, use the following two patterns.

1. **Tag questions.** Add **¿no?** or **¿verdad?** *(right?)* at the end.

Sus hijos podrían hacernos un show, **¿no?**	*Your kids could put on a show for us, right?*
Tus padres trabajan en un banco, **¿verdad?**	*Your parents work at a bank, right?*

2. **Intonation.** Raise your voice in a questioning tone at the end.

Me gusta bailar *La macarena.*	*I like dancing La Macarena.*
¿Te gusta bailar *La macarena?*	*Do you like dancing La Macarena?*
Este semestre no trabajo.	*I don't work this semester.*
¿Este semestre no trabajas?	*You don't work this semester?*

PRÁCTICA

I. Una entrevista. Convierte las frases de la **Práctica B** (página 113) a preguntas. Después entrevista a un(a) compañero/a.

Modelo	Mis amigos y yo necesitamos dinero.
	—¿Tus amigos y tú necesitan dinero?
	or
	Tus amigos y tú necesitan dinero, ¿no?/¿verdad?

J. ¡A hablar! In groups of four, try to set a date and time to study Spanish together **(juntos)**. Indicate which days and times you can't meet, and why **(no puedo porque...)**. Use expressions like **Estoy libre los..., Ese día no puedo..., ¿Estudiamos el...?, ¿Quién puede a las...?,** etc.

Actividades comunicativas

Práctica adicional

Cuaderno de tareas
WB pp.126–127, G–H
LM pp.129–130, A–B, Pron.

Audio
CD-ROM
Episodio 5

A. Las actividades de mis compañeros.

Parte 1. First, answer the questions by writing **yo** in column **B** after any question to which you can respond *yes*. Then, ask these questions to your classmates and fill in the empty spaces in both columns with the names of those who answer *yes*.

	A	B
1. ¿Limpias la casa los sábados?	_____	_____
2. ¿Usas una computadora Macintosh?	_____	_____
3. ¿Trabajas en un restaurante?	_____	_____
4. ¿Miras mucho la tele?	_____	_____
5. ¿Necesitas dinero?	_____	_____
6. ¿Hablas mucho por teléfono?	_____	_____

Parte 2. Now, write a brief report using the information you have uncovered. Include at least six sentences in your report. Be prepared to share your findings with the class.

Modelo	Akiko y Jenny usan una computadora Macintosh.
	Nadie (*nobody*) trabaja en un restaurante.

 B. Submarino. The object of this game, played like Battleship, is to find the location of your classmate's submarines. First, draw submarines in any five of the boxes on your grid. Do not let your partner see your grid. Then take turns asking each other yes/no questions, matching an action pictured at the top of the grid with one of the subjects on the side. If you have a submarine in the box that corresponds to your partner's question, give an affirmative answer, and vice-versa; if there is no submarine in the box that corresponds to the question, give a negative answer.

Modelo	—¿Trabajas en una oficina?
	—**Sí, trabajo en una oficina.** (*If there is a submarine in that box.*)
	or
	—**No, no trabajo en una oficina.** (*If there is no submarine in that box.*)

Depending on your classmate's answer, write **sí** or **no** in that box. If you answer **sí** to your classmate's question, put an **X** through your submarine. It's been found! The first player to find all five submarines wins.

Tú				
Tus primos				
Adriana				
Ustedes				

C. La fotonovela.

Audio CD-ROM

Parte 1. As you listen to Sofía's weekend routine, indicate which pictures were used to tell her story.

Parte 2. In groups, use five of the drawings to write a short paragraph describing what Sofía does on weekends. Your pictures do not have to reflect what you heard on the recording. Use connectors like **primero,** *(first),* **luego...** *(then),* **después...** *(later, afterward),* **por la tarde...,** **por la noche....** Begin with **Por la mañana, Sofía....** When you have finished, be prepared to read your story to the class. Your classmates will guess which pictures you used.

_____

_____

_____

_____

_____

_____

La correspondencia

 El correo: Los problemas de Manolo. Lee las siguientes preguntas. Después lee la carta que Manolo le escribe a un amigo. Contesta las preguntas.

1. ¿Cuál es el peor *(what is the worst)* defecto del compañero de cuarto de Manolo?

   _____

2. ¿Qué cualidades tiene su compañero?

   _____

3. ¿Qué cosas tienen en común?

   _____

4. ¿Cuál es la rutina de Manolo?

   _____

From: mbaez@casa.mía.red
To: Amigo@dayton.fla.red
Re: ¡Hola!

En cuanto a mi nuevo compañero de cuarto, tenemos algunos problemas. Es muy desordenado. Casi nunca lava la ropa y no limpia su cuarto; siempre está sucio[1]. Le gustan mucho las fiestas; con frecuencia invita a sus amigos y bailan y cantan toda la noche... ¡La música es horrible! Bueno, no todo es malo; él es muy generoso, compra todo para la casa y cocina muy rico. También tenemos varias cosas en común: los dos somos cubanos y tenemos conversaciones muy interesantes porque él es súper inteligente. A veces pasamos toda la noche conversando.

Yo sigo con la misma rutina; estudio por las mañanas y luego trabajo varias horas. Por la noche, lavo mi ropa, y los fines de semana estudio y limpio la casa. Nada nuevo.

[1]*dirty*

Invitación a **Estados Unidos**

Del álbum de
Manolo

De los 35 millones de hispanos en Estados Unidos, casi 2 millones son cubanos. La mayor concentración de cubanos está en Miami y el condado de Dade, en la Florida, pero hay comunidades cubanas en todos los estados. La Pequeña Habana, en Miami, es el centro cultural de los cubanoamericanos. Muchas personalidades de la música y el cine son de origen cubano, como Gloria y Emilio Estefan, Andy García, Celia Cruz, Daisy Fuentes, Jon Secada y Cameron Díaz, entre otros.

En papel: Mi vida diaria. *(My daily life)* In his e-mail, Manolo described his living situation. Use his letter as a model to write about your own situation. Write about your weekly activities and the activities of the people you live with.

 ¡A ver de nuevo!

Video
CD-ROM

Parte 1. Escucha la conversación de **Escenas de la vida** o mira el video para escribir un resumen del episodio.

Audio
CD-ROM

¡Fíjate!
Express yourself simply with the Spanish you know. Do not write your summary in English.

Adriana está preocupada porque tiene un examen de cálculo y quiere sacar A...

 Parte 2. Now, compare your summary with a classmate's and add any information you might have left out.

Práctica adicional		
Cuaderno de tareas WB pp.127–128, I–J LM p.130, A–B	Audio CD-ROM Episodio 5	Website vistahigher learning.com

Vocabulario del Episodio 5

Verbos

bailar (bien)	*to dance (well)*
buscar información en Internet	*to look for information on the Internet*
comprar cosas	*to buy things*
comida	*food*
ropa	*clothes*
descansar	*to rest*
escuchar música	*to listen to music*
estudiar mucho/poco	*to study a lot/a little*
hablar por teléfono	*to talk on the phone*
lavar el coche	*to wash the car*
la ropa	*to do the laundry*
limpiar la casa	*to clean the house*
el cuarto	*the (one's) room*
llegar a tiempo a casa	*to get home on time*
tarde	*late*
temprano	*early*
mirar la tele	*to watch TV*
necesitar libros	*to need books*
sacar buenas notas	*to get good grades*
tocar la guitarra	*to play the guitar*
tomar clases	*to take classes*
café	*to drink coffee*
el autobús	*to take the bus*
trabajar en casa	*to work at home*
usar la computadora	*to use the computer*
visitar a los abuelos	*to visit one's grandparents*

Los días de la semana y más

los lunes	*on Mondays*	**todos los días**	*every day*
los martes	*on Tuesdays*	**entre semana**	*on weekdays*
los miércoles	*on Wednesdays*	**los fines de semana**	*on weekends*
los jueves	*on Thursdays*	**por la mañana**	*in the morning*
los viernes	*on Fridays*	**por la tarde**	*in the afternoon*
los sábados	*on Saturdays*	**por la noche**	*in the evening*
los domingos	*on Sundays*		

Vocabulario personal

In this section write all the words that you want to know in Spanish so that you can better talk about your activities and the activities of those you know.

¡A escribir!

Episodio

5

Escenas de la vida: ¿Estudiamos el sábado?

Video CD-ROM

A. ¡A ver cuánto entendiste! See how much of the **Escena** you understood by matching the Spanish sentences with their English equivalents.

¿Dónde estudiamos?

_____ 1. ¿Está libre algún otro día?

_____ 2. ¿A qué hora descansa?

_____ 3. Estudiamos el sábado.

_____ 4. ¿En casa de quién?

_____ 5. ¿Cuándo estudiamos?

_____ 6. ¿Qué hace los sábados y domingos?

_____ 7. Estoy muy preocupada.

_____ 8. Sus hijos podrían cantar y bailar para nosotros.

a. Let's study on Saturday.

b. What do you do on Saturdays and Sundays?

c. Your kids could sing and dance for us.

d. Are you free any other day?

e. When are we going to study?

f. At whose house?

g. When do you rest?

h. I'm very worried.

Video CD-ROM

B. ¿Estudiamos el sábado? Use the expressions to complete the activities below, according to the **Escena**.

descansar	preocupada	por la mañana
estoy libre	los lunes	necesito
qué	los martes y los jueves	estudiamos
vieja	cuándo	por la tarde

Adriana   ¿(1) _____ estudiamos para el examen?

(2) _____ repasar (*to review*) todo. Estoy muy

(3) _____.

Sofía   ¡No se preocupe! No es tan complicado.

Adriana   Ay, chica, pero yo ya soy (4) _____. Bueno,

(5) _____ solamente los sábados (6) _____.

Sofía   ¿(7) _____ hace los otros días?

Adriana   (8) _____ trabajo en una oficina y los otros días estoy muy

ocupada con las actividades de mis hijos. Bueno, ¿a qué hora

(9) _____ el sábado?

Video
CD-ROM

C. La vida de Adriana. Use what you know about Adriana to answer Sofia's question.

¿Qué hace Adriana los otros días? (de lunes a viernes)

_____

_____

_____

_____

Gramática 1

Talking about activities at school and home
- **-ar verbs**
- **Days of the week**
- **Infinitive constructions**

D. ¿Qué hacen? Say what these people do at the places mentioned. Fill in the blanks with the appropriate forms of the verbs.

1. En la universidad

tomar	hablar	llegar	sacar	estudiar

Los lunes yo (1) _____ a la universidad a las 8:00 de la mañana.
(2) _____ una clase de español. Normalmente (3) _____ buenas notas cuando (4) _____ el vocabulario. Después de clase, me gusta
(5) _____ con mis amigos. A veces, tomamos café y nos quedamos *(stay)* hablando en la cafetería.

2. En un café

escuchar	bailar	tocar	cantar *(to sing)*

Los viernes mi amigo y yo (6) _____ la guitarra y la flauta en un grupo de jazz. También (7) _____ karaoke cuando sabemos *(we know)* la letra de las canciones. A veces (8) _____ y otras veces solamente *(only)* nos gusta
(9) _____ la música.

3. En mi casa

visitar	usar	lavar	mirar	necesitar	limpiar	trabajar

Los domingos mis hermanitos (10) _____ mi coche cuando ellos
(11) _____ dinero. Mi papá (12) _____ el garaje, mientras *(while)* mi mamá (13) _____ en su jardín *(garden)*. Yo normalmente necesito
(14) _____ la computadora por la mañana. Por la tarde, mis papás y mis hermanos (15) _____ a mis abuelos y yo visito a mis amigos. Por la noche, todos (16) _____ una película.

E. Las actividades de los estudiantes. Describe what the characters are doing in the illustrations. Use the verbs from **Episodio 5** page 112 of your textbook. Use **porque** to justify the first part of your sentence. Keep the statements simple (e.g., *They study a lot **because** they have an exam*).

Modelo

Sofía toma el autobús porque no tiene coche.

1.

2.

3.

4.

5.

6.

1. _____

2. _____

3. _____

4. _____

5. _____

6. _____

F. Los días de la semana. Complete the following statements with the appropriate word.

1. En español, el primer día de la semana es el _____.

2. Si hoy es miércoles, mañana es _____.

3. Hay siete días en una _____.

4. Mi día favorito es el _____.

5. El Día de la Madre es el segundo *(second)* _____ de mayo.

6. Un día de mala suerte *(bad luck)* en Estados Unidos es el _____ trece.

7. El día preferido para hacer *(throw)* fiestas es el _____.

Gramática **2** Asking yes/no questions
  • Tag questions

G. ¡Preguntas! Imagine you and a classmate are talking about the characters in the video. Use the elements below to form questions. Then answer each question.

> **Modelo**   la hija de Adriana / tocar la guitarra / ¿no? (bailar)
> —La hija de Adriana toca la guitarra, ¿no?
> —No, ella baila en un grupo folclórico puertorriqueño.

1. tú / estudiar italiano / ¿no? (español)

   Q. _____   A. _____

2. Adriana / trabajar en un restaurante (oficina)

   Q. _____   A. _____

3. los hermanos de Ramón / hablar español / ¿verdad? (inglés)

   Q. _____   A. _____

4. Manolo / ser de Puerto Rico / ¿no? (Cuba)

   Q. _____   A. _____

5. Sofía y Ana Mari / tener hermanas / ¿verdad? (no)

   Q. _____   A. _____

6. Ana Mari / tomar la clase de cálculo con Sofía y Manolo (Adriana)

   Q. _____   A. _____

H. Sofía y Adriana. You want to know more about Sofía and Adriana. Ask them questions using the cues. In each case, write an answer according to the drawing.

> **Modelo**
>
> if they study geology
> —¿Ustedes estudian geología?
> —No, estudiamos cálculo.

1. if they speak English

   _____
   _____

2. if she uses the computer Friday nights

   _____
   _____

3. if she always gets home late

_____

_____

4. if her mother does the laundry

_____

_____

Para terminar

I. Preguntas personales. Answer the following questions.

1. ¿Qué clases tomas? ¿Estudias todos los días?

_____

_____

2. ¿Te gusta bailar? ¿Dónde?

_____

_____

3. ¿Qué te gusta hacer *(do)* los domingos?

_____

_____

4. ¿Cuántos años tienes? ¿Cuántos años tienen tus padres? ¿Cuántos años tiene tu novio/a /esposo/a? _____

_____

5. ¿Qué programas miras en la tele?

_____

6. ¿Trabajas? ¿Dónde? ¿Qué días trabajas?

_____

_____

7. ¿Qué días de la semana descansas?

_____

8. ¿A qué hora llegas a tu casa los sábados?

_____

_____

9. ¿A qué hora llegas a la universidad los lunes?

_____

_____

10. ¿Sacas buenas notas en todas tus clases? ¿En qué clases sacas A y B? ¿Por qué?

_____

_____

J. La vida de Lorena. First read the questions, then read the following description of Lorena's activities, and then answer the questions.

1. ¿De dónde es Lorena?

_____

2. ¿Qué estudia? ¿Qué quiere estudiar en el futuro?

_____

3. ¿Cuáles son sus actividades favoritas?

_____

4. ¿Qué días tiene clase por la noche? ¿Qué clase es?

_____

5. ¿Qué hace (does) los fines de semana? ¿Con quién?

_____

Hola, me llamo Lorena; tengo 16 años. Soy de Tijuana, Baja California. Tengo un hermano mayor; se llama Iván y tiene 24 años. También tengo una gata y un hámster; ¡adoro a los animales! Estudio en una preparatoria que tiene un programa internacional; con ese programa puedo estudiar en cualquier universidad del mundo[1]. Quiero estudiar biología en San Diego. Algunas de mis clases me gustan mucho, otras no me gustan, pero tengo que tomarlas. Aquí no tenemos muchas clases opcionales.

Durante las vacaciones trabajé en una tienda de helados[2]. Ahora no trabajo, pero siempre tengo actividades. Por ejemplo, por las tardes, estudio o preparo mi tarea. Los martes por la noche, tomo una clase de actuación. Me gusta mucho la clase, pero llego a las 10 de la noche a mi casa, y el miércoles por la mañana no me puedo levantar[3]. Los jueves tengo mi clase de baile. Me gusta el jazz y el tap. Me gusta mirar películas y escuchar música, especialmente el rock mexicano y la música alternativa. La música pop no me gusta mucho. Los viernes o los sábados voy a bailar con mis amigas (y amigos). Nos gusta bailar en una discoteca donde no hay bebidas alcohólicas. Tengo muchas amigas, algunas son amigas de la escuela y otras son amigas del barrio[4]. También estudio piano con mi mamá porque ella es maestra de música en una escuela primaria y en la Normal[5].

Todavía no tengo licencia de manejar[6]. Mi papá dice que soy muy joven; ¡yo no opino lo mismo! Los domingos normalmente es día de descanso, pero a veces visito a mi abuela o a mis tías.

[1]world [2]ice cream [3]I can't get up [4]neighborhood [5]school that prepares teachers [6]driving license

Episodio 5

¡A escuchar!

Comprensión

A. Los sábados en casa de Ana Mari. Listen as Ana Mari describes what she and her family normally do on Saturdays, and indicate who does each activity. **¡Atención!** Some of the activities may be done by more than one person. The people are: Ana Mari **(AM)**, Ramón **(R)**, her mother **(M)**, her father **(P)**, and Ana Mari's younger brothers, Alex and Luis **(AL)**. You will hear Ana Mari's description twice.

_____ 1. Descansa y escucha música.   _____ 5. Compran la comida.

_____ 2. Miran la tele.   _____ 6. Limpian sus cuartos.

_____ 3. Trabaja en la oficina.   _____ 7. Miran el fútbol en la tele.

_____ 4. Lavan el coche.   _____ 8. Visitan a unos amigos.

B. El calendario de Wayne. You will hear Wayne tell Carlos what he does in a normal week. Listen and fill in the calendar with the words and phrases provided to indicate what Wayne does each day. Then answer the question at the end of this activity. You will hear the conversation twice.

Wayne

trabaja   toma clases   estudia   sale con sus amigos   descansa

	lunes	martes	miércoles	jueves	viernes	sábado	domingo
mañana							
noche							

Wayne necesita lavar la ropa y limpiar su cuarto. ¿Cuándo hay tiempo? Escríbelo en el calendario.

Pronunciación

La *r* y la *rr*. R (ere) and **rr (erre)** are two separate letters of the Spanish alphabet; they are not interchangeable. For example, **pero** means *but*, and **perro** means *dog*. The most similar sound to the Spanish **r** in English is the double *tt* or double *dd*, as in *butter* and *ladder*. The tip of the tongue taps once on the ridge behind the upper front teeth. Repeat these words and sentences after the speaker.

| cero | serio | cafetería | Ana Mari es cariñosa. |

When the single **r** is combined with a consonant, you may hear a slight trill.

| tres | drama | puerta | Mi madre es agradable. |

When **r** occurs at the beginning of a word, it becomes a trill. To produce a trill, the tip of the tongue taps in rapid succession on the ridge behind the upper front teeth. If you find it difficult to produce the sound, try imitating a motor sound, or the purr of a cat.

| Ramón | rubio | romántico | Ricardo corre rápido. |

The letter **rr** is always trilled. Repeat these words and sentence after the speaker.

| arrogante | aburrido | irregular | los verbos irregulares. |

Más escenas de la vida

Sofía arrives at Manolo's apartment. Listen to their conversation and then complete activities **A** and **B**. You will hear the conversation twice.

A. ¿Quién? Indicate to whom the following descriptions refer: Manolo's roommate Jorge **(J)**, Manolo **(M)**, Lalo **(L)** or Sofía **(S)**.

_____ 1. Es un desordenado.

_____ 2. Necesita buscar otro compañero de cuarto.

_____ 3. No limpia nada.

_____ 4. Es desordenado como Jorge.

_____ 5. Cree que nadie es perfecto.

_____ 6. Es generoso e inteligente.

_____ 7. Van a casa de Adriana.

B. ¿Entendiste? Write the answers to the following questions.

1. ¿Qué hace Jorge cuando está en casa? _____

2. ¿Cómo es Lalo? _____

3. ¿Por qué en perspectiva, la situación de Manolo no es mala?

_____

4. ¿Qué necesitan a hacer a casa de Adriana? _____

Episodio 6

Escenas de la vida: ¡Qué guapos!

 A. ¡Mira cuánto puedes entender! Use the spaces provided to describe Adriana and Sofía: what classes they take, what their families are like, where they are from, etc. Then select the statements that apply to the characters.

Adriana _____

Sofía _____

1. ¿Cómo es Adriana?

☐ Es baja.   ☐ Es alta.
☐ Es morena.   ☐ Es rubia.
☐ Es casada.   ☐ Es soltera.
☐ Es agradable.   ☐ Es antipática.
☐ Es perezosa.   ☐ Es trabajadora.

2. ¿Cómo es Sofía?

☐ Es delgada. .   ☐ Es gorda.
☐ Es antipática.   ☐ Es agradable.
☐ Es joven.   ☐ Es vieja.
☐ Es bonita.   ☐ Es fea.
☐ Es graciosa.   ☐ Es seria.

3. ¿Qué le gusta a Adriana?

☐ Preparar comida puertorriqueña.
☐ Comer comida mexicana.

4. ¿Quién le gusta a Sofía?

☐ Le gusta Manolo.
☐ Le gusta Carlos.

 B. ¿Te diste cuenta? Contesta las siguientes preguntas.

1. ¿En cuánto tiempo prepara Adriana el flan? _____
2. ¿Cómo se llaman los hijos de Adriana? _____
3. ¿Cuántos años tienen? _____
4. ¿Cómo se llama el hermano de Sofía? ¿Cuántos años tiene? _____
5. ¿Cuántas personas hay en la familia de Manolo? _____

 C. ¿Cómo son? Selecciona las características de cada uno.

1. **Carlos**	alto	guapo	moreno	casado	joven	soltero
2. **La hermana de Manolo**	rubia	vieja	casada	alta	bonita	gorda
3. **Manolo**	bajo	feo	moreno	bueno	amable	guapo

Video
CD-ROM

Audio
CD-ROM

D. Emparejar. Empareja las personas con las frases.

___ 1. Santiaguito a. tiene un hermano.
___ 2. Carlos b. es el mayor.
___ 3. Manolo c. tiene quince años.
___ 4. Sofía d. tiene una hermana.

Práctica adicional

Cuaderno de tareas
WB pp.147–148, A–C

Video
CD-ROM
Episodio 6

Cultura a lo vivo
When Spanish speakers are successful in the United States, they are viewed as examples of how dreams can come true by both those who have remained in the home country, as well as by those who have immigrated to the United States. A notable example is Chicago Cubs home-run hitter Sammy Sosa, hailed as a national hero in his native Dominican Republic, for his success on the playing field.

Para comunicarnos mejor

Gramática 1

Describing people and things
• **Descriptive adjectives**
• **Placement of adjectives**

Analizar y descubrir

In the conversation, you heard the following statements.

¡Qué **guapos** son sus hijos! *Your children are so good-looking!*
Tú eres **alto** y muy **guapo**. *You're tall and very handsome.*
Tu hermana es **alta** y **rubia**. *Your sister is tall and blonde.*

1. Notice that the adjectives **guapo** and **alto** have more than one form. Study the previous statements and answer these questions:

   a. Which word was used to describe Adriana's children? _____
   b. Which words were used to describe Manolo? _____ and _____
   c. Which words were used to describe Manolo's sister ? _____ and _____

   Circle the correct answer in items **d-f**, and answer **g**.

   d. **Guapos** is used in **(a)** because it matches **hijas / hijos.**
   e. **Alto** and **guapo** are used in **(b)** because they match **Manolo / Sofía.**
   f. **Alta** and **rubia** are used in **(c)** because they match **él / ella.**
   g. Which form of **guapo** would be used to describe Sofía and Viviana? _____

2. Unlike English, Spanish adjectives change their form to match the gender (masculine or feminine) and number (singular or plural) of the nouns they describe.

   La clase es divertid**a**. *The class is fun.*
   Manolo es alt**o**; **él y Carlos** son moren**os**. *Manolo is tall; he and Carlos are dark-haired.*
   Las amigas de Sofía son gracios**as**. *Sofía's friends are funny.*

3. Some adjectives (ending in **-e** or in some consonants) do not change form to indicate gender. All, however, change form to indicate number.

   La casa es grand**e**; **el estadio** es grand**e**. *The house is big; the stadium is big.*
   Los salones no son grand**es**. *The classrooms are not big.*

Here are some adjectives used to describe physical appearance.

Adjetivos descriptivos: La apariencia física			
guapo/a	*handsome, good-looking*	**joven**	*young*
bonito/a	*good-looking, pretty*	**viejo/a***	*old*
feo/a	*ugly, plain*	**grande**	*large, big*
alto/a	*tall*	**pequeño/a**	*small*
bajo/a	*short (height)*	**rubio/a**	*blond(e)*
gordo/a	*fat*	**moreno/a**	*dark*
delgado/a	*thin*		

*In some Spanish-speaking countries, it is impolite to describe an older person as **viejo** or **vieja**. It is better to say **Es una persona mayor**.

Below are some adjectives used to describe character and personality.

También se dice...

delgado → **flaco**

perezoso → **flojo**

gracioso → **chistoso**

rubio → **güero**

Adjetivos descriptivos: El carácter y la personalidad			
agradable	*pleasant, nice*	**grosero/a**	*rude*
antipático/a	*unpleasant, nasty*	**amable**	*kind, friendly*
bueno/a	*good, nice*	**cariñoso/a**	*affecionate*
malo/a	*bad*	**reservado/a**	*reserved*
gracioso/a	*funny*	**listo/a**	*smart*
serio/a	*serious*	**tonto/a**	*dumb, silly*
trabajador(a)	*hard-working*	**perezoso/a**	*lazy*

Learning Strategy: Focus on word clusters and word families
You will understand more if you are able to relate words with similar roots: for example, **persona, personal,** and **personalidad** or **arte, artista,** and **artístico**. Use the words you know to figure out what other words mean: knowing **perezoso**, what could **pereza** mean? It means *laziness*. Try to guess the meaning of **grosería, amabilidad, aburrimiento,** and **cariño**.

Here are some words and expressions used to describe people and things.

Descripciones: Las personas y las cosas					
nuevo/a	*new*	**fácil**	*easy*	**mayor**	*older*
viejo/a	*old*	**difícil**	*hard, difficult*	**menor**	*younger*
aburrido/a	*boring*	**rico/a**	*rich; tasty*	**hijo/a único/a**	*only child*
divertido/a	*fun*	**pobre**	*poor*	**soltero/a**	*single*
diferente	*different*	**casado/a**	*married*	**similar**	*similar*

PRÁCTICA

A. ¿Cómo son? Selecciona la característica que mejor describe a los personajes.

Sofía

Adriana

Manolo

¡Fíjate!
Be sure to look at the ending of the adjectives to select the one that matches the character in gender and in number.

1. Manolo es (bajas / gordos / moreno / rubia).
2. Sofía es (vieja / joven / feo / bonitas).
3. Los hijos de Adriana son (soltera / diferente / guapos / cariñosas).
4. Adriana es (rubios / moreno / mexicanas / trabajadora).
5. Manolo y su compañero de cuarto son (argentinas / cubano / jóvenes / casado).

B. Los opuestos. Completa cada frase con el adjetivo contrario.

> **Modelo**   Sofía no es seria: es **graciosa.**

1. La abuela de Sofía no es joven: es _____.
2. Lalo no es responsable: es _____.
3. Sofía no es tonta: es _____.
4. Los hijos de Adriana no son gordos: son _____.
5. Manolo no es serio: es _____.
6. Sofía no es casada: es _____.
7. Ramón no es grosero: es _____.

C. Tu familia. Usa adjetivos para describir a tu familia.

> **Modelo**
>
> **Mis hermanas son cariñosas y graciosas.**

1. Mis padres _____.
2. Mi mamá _____.
3. Mi papá _____.
4. Mi hermano/a _____.
5. Mis hermanos/as _____.
6. Mis abuelos _____.
7. Mi novio/a/esposo/a _____.
8. Mi mejor amigo/a _____.

• Placement of adjectives

An important difference between English and Spanish is the order of adjectives and nouns in a sentence. In English, the adjective comes *before* the noun *(I have a boring class)*, whereas in Spanish, most adjectives go *after* the noun (**Tengo una clase** *aburrida*).

A few adjectives in Spanish do precede the noun.

1. Adjectives of quantity (**mucho, poco,** etc.) always come before the noun.

Hay **pocos** estudiantes en la clase.	*There are few students in class.*
Hoy tengo **mucha** tarea.	*I have a lot of homework today.*

2. Demonstrative adjectives also precede nouns.

Necesito **este** libro.	*I need this book.*
Sofía desea comprar **esa** mochila.	*Sofía wants to buy that backpack.*

Los adjetivos demostrativos

este, esta	*this*	**ese, esa**	*that*
estos, estas	*these*	**esos, esas**	*those*

3. The adjectives **bueno** and **malo** may be used before the noun for emphasis. In this case, you must drop the **-o** from the masculine singular form.

Tengo un **buen** coche.	*I have a good car.*
¿Tienes **buenos** profesores?	*Do you have good teachers?*
No es un **mal** estudiante.	*He isn't a bad student.*

PRÁCTICA

D. ¿Qué tienen? Termina las frases usando adjetivos para describir cómo son las cosas que tienen las siguientes personas.

> **Modelo**   Este semestre Adriana tiene compañeros **agradables.**

1. Sofía tiene un coche _____.
2. Adriana tiene una casa _____.
3. Carlos, Santiaguito y Viviana tienen dos perros _____.
4. Manolo tiene un compañero de cuarto _____.
5. Este semestre tengo una clase _____.

E. La tarea de Johnny. Imagine you are helping Johnny, your eight year-old neighbor, with his Spanish homework. He wants to write the following things about his family. Teach him how to do it in Spanish.

1. The blonde girl is my sister.

_____

2. She has a pretty friend, Lulú.

_____

3. Lulú is very funny.

_____

4. I have a married brother.

_____

5. He buys a lot of cars and all of them **(todos)** are ugly.

_____

6. I also have three pets: a big dog, a fat cat, and a dumb bird!

_____

7. This year I have a very good math teacher.

_____

F. Anuncios. Read the ads, which appeared in the Spanish-language newspaper *Diario del Club Latino*, in order to answer the questions that follow. First, read the questions so you can determine the purpose of the reading.

> **Reading Strategy: Using cognates and content to determine meaning**
> You can read Spanish with far greater ease if you guess at the meaning of cognates—words that look similar to English words. Before you read the personal ads below, consider these cognates: **americano, ingeniero, económicamente estable, español, inteligente, ejercicio, computadoras, atractiva, matrimonio, tel., bilingüe, sensual, educada, elegante, cine, responder**, and **electrónico**. The content of a text will provide clues to the meaning as well. Think about what you would expect to find in a personal ad and use this knowledge to help you understand the reading.

1. ¿Cómo es la persona del anuncio?

_____

2. ¿Qué le gusta a esta persona?

_____

3. ¿Qué tipo de persona busca?

_____

AMERICANO

Ingeniero económicamente estable, hablo español. Soy inteligente, cariñoso y trabajador. Me gusta hacer ejercicio, cocinar y trabajar con computadoras. Busco mujer atractiva, flaca. 20-30 años. ¿Amistad? ¿Matrimonio? Niño ok. Tel. 434-4444

4. ¿Cómo es la persona de este anuncio?

_____

5. ¿Cuántos años tiene?

_____

6. ¿Qué le gusta hacer?

_____

ATRACTIVA

Bilingüe, 30 años, sensual, educada, elegante y simpática. Me gusta viajar, bailar e ir al cine. Busco amigo para diversiones sanas.[1] Favor de responder vía correo electrónico. Atractiva@homemail.loc

[1]*healthy fun*

G. ¡Un anuncio gratis! A local Spanish newspaper is offering free personal ads as a promotion for their weekend edition. Write an ad that will appeal to your ideal mate. Use the ads from **Práctica F** as models.

> **Writing Strategy: Using a text as a model for writing**
>
> To write successfully in Spanish, you will need to examine samples so you can identify the information you need to include when you write your own texts. Prepare to write your own personal ad. First, reread the personal ads from the previous section and identify the information they provide, such as physical characteristics, personality traits, and hobbies. Then, list the information you want to communicate in each of these categories in the space provided. Finally, write your ad.

Características físicas	Personalidad	Actividades
_____	_____	_____
_____	_____	_____
_____	_____	_____
_____	_____	_____
_____	_____	_____
_____	_____	_____

H. Las personas importantes en mi vida. Bring three or four photos of family members or friends to class. In groups of three, introduce the people in your photos and tell as much as you can about them, such as their age, their personality, and your relationship to them. Make sure you ask each classmate at least three questions about their family.

Modelo ¿Dónde trabaja tu hermano mayor?
¿Cuántos años tiene?
¿Es casado?

Práctica adicional

Cuaderno de tareas
WB pp.148–150, D–H

Asking for information
• Interrogative words

Spanish, like English, uses inversion (placing the verb before the subject) to ask information questions. To change a statement into a *wh*-question *(who, what, where, when, why)*, place the conjugated verb in front of the subject, and add the appropriate interrogative word.

Statement	Question
subject verb	verb subject
Adriana trabaja en una oficina. →	¿Dónde trabaja Adriana?
subject verb	verb subject
Manolo es alto y moreno. →	¿Cómo es Manolo?
subject verb	verb subject
Sofía toma cálculo y vóleibol. →	¿Qué clases toma Sofía?

> **¡Fíjate!**
> **Cuál** and **Qué** may be confusing. Do not use **Cuál** + [*noun*]; use **Cuál** + [*verb to be*].
> **¿Cuál es tu mochila?**
> Use **Qué** + [*nouns*].
> **¿Qué libro lees? ¿Qué coche te gusta?**

Here is a summary of all the interrogative words you have been using.

Palabras interrogativas	
¿Cómo es Manolo?	*What is Manolo like?*
¿Cuál es tu clase favorita?	*Which class is your favorite?*
¿Cuándo descansa Adriana?	*When does Adriana rest?*
¿Cuántos hijos tiene?	*How many children does she have?*
¿Cuántas clases toma Manolo?	*How many clases does Manolo take?*
¿Dónde trabaja Adriana?	*Where does Adriana work?*
¿Por qué te gusta la clase?	*Why do you like the class?*
¿Qué clases toma Manolo?	*What/which classes is Manolo taking?*
¿Quién es Carlos?	*Who is Carlos?*

PRÁCTICA

I. Las respuestas. Empareja las preguntas de arriba *(above)* con las respuestas.

1. ¿_____? Es el hijo de Adriana.

2. ¿_____? La clase de español.

3. ¿_____? Tiene tres hijos.

4. ¿_____? Es alto y moreno.

5. ¿_____? Toma cuatro clases.

6. ¿_____? Porque es muy divertida.

7. ¿_____? En una oficina.

8. ¿_____? Nunca.

9. ¿_____? Cálculo, sicología e historia.

J. Preguntas. Completa las preguntas sobre Adriana.

1. ¿_____ estudia Adriana? En la biblioteca.

2. ¿_____ días a la semana trabaja? Dos días.

3. ¿_____ días? Martes y jueves.

4. ¿_____ descansa? Nunca.

5. ¿_____ es el profesor? Es agradable.

6. ¿_____ es Santiago? Es su esposo.

K. Preguntas personales. Responde apropiadamente a las preguntas. Después entrevista a un(a) compañero/a.

1. ¿Qué clases tomas este semestre?

2. ¿Cuál es tu clase favorita? ¿Por qué?

3. ¿Qué clase no te gusta? ¿Por qué?

4. ¿Cómo es tu profesor/a de español? ¿Es divertida la clase?

5. ¿Dónde trabajas? ¿Cuántas horas a la semana trabajas? ¿Cuándo descansas?

6. ¿Cuándo estudias? ¿Dónde? ¿Con quién?

7. ¿A qué hora regresas a casa generalmente? ¿Qué haces (do you do) cuando llegas?

8. ¿Qué haces los fines de semana? ¿Lavas la ropa? ¿Limpias la casa? ¿Estudias? ¿Trabajas?

Audio
CD-ROM

L. La pareja perfecta. The individuals below are participants on a radio program called **"La pareja perfecta."** Listen to determine why the participants feel they are the ideal partner. After sharing your opinion about their comments, write a brief description of your ideal partner on a separate sheet of paper.

	características	mi opinión
participante 1		
participante 2		
participante 3		

M. La entrevista. Imagine you can meet with anyone in the world: your favorite actor, musician, or politician. Use the **Palabras interrogativas** box on the previous page to write five questions. Keep it simple!

Modelo	Preguntas para Gabriel García Márquez
	¿De dónde es usted?
	¿Cuál es su novela favorita?
	¿Cuántas novelas tiene?

Práctica adicional

Cuaderno de tareas
WB pp.150–151, I–J
LM pp.153–154, A–B, Pron.

Audio
CD-ROM
Episodio 6

Actividades comunicativas

 A. Crucigrama.

Instrucciones para **Estudiante 1**

You and your partner have a copy of the same partially completed crossword puzzle. The words missing on your copy of the puzzle are filled in on your partner's copy. Give each other clues to complete the puzzle. Do not say the word your partner needs; instead, use definitions, examples, and incomplete sentences that provide a context for the missing word. Here are some examples:

Modelo   *17 vertical:* La hija de mi hija es mi...
             15 horizontal: Un niño no es viejo; es...

¡Fíjate!

Find simple but creative ways of communicating the meaning of the words to your partner.

				¹D									
²G			³	E									
U				L									
A				G					4	⁵L		⁶A	
⁷P				A						I		G	
O				D				⁸G		S		R	
				A		⁹T		R		T		A	
	10	¹¹R	S		O		12	A		O		D	
		U			N		N				A		
		B			T		D				B		
		I		13	O		E		14		L		
	15	O	¹⁶E					¹⁷N		E			
		S			¹⁸C		I		S				
		¹⁹P			U		E						
20		O			Ñ		²¹T						
	²²S			A		A							
	O			D									
		23		A									

A. Crucigrama.

Instrucciones para **Estudiante 2**

You and your partner have a copy of the same partially completed crossword puzzle. The words missing on your copy of the puzzle are filled in on your partner's copy. Give each other clues to complete the puzzle. Do not say the word your partner needs; instead, use definitions, examples, and incomplete sentences that provide a context for the missing word. Here are some examples:

| **Modelo** | *17 vertical:* **La hija de mi hija es mi...** |
| | *15 horizontal:* **Un niño no es viejo; es...** |

¡Fíjate!

Find simple but creative ways of communicating the meaning of the words to your partner.

B. Actividades en común. First answer the questions in the column labeled **Yo**. Then look for classmates whose answers are the same as yours and write their names in the column labeled **Compañero/a**. Be prepared to share your findings with the class.

> **Modelo** —¿Dónde trabajas?
> —Trabajo en un banco. ¿Y tú?
> —Yo también. *or* Yo trabajo en una tienda.
> —Mary y yo trabajamos en un supermercado.

	Compañero/a	Yo
1. ¿Dónde trabajas?	_____	_____
2. ¿Cuántas clases tomas este semestre?	_____	_____
3. ¿Qué programa miras en la televisión?	_____	_____
4. ¿A qué hora llegas a casa los lunes?	_____	_____
5. ¿Cuántos idiomas hablas bien?	_____	_____
6. ¿Qué computadora usas?	_____	_____
7. ¿Dónde compras tu ropa?	_____	_____
8. ¿Qué estación de radio escuchas?	_____	_____
9. ¿Dónde estudias para los exámenes?	_____	_____
10. ¿Cuántas hermanas tienes?	_____	_____

C. Veinte preguntas. Think of three famous people, but do not reveal their names to your partner. Your partner will ask you yes/no questions as they try to guess the names of each person. You get a point for every question your partner has to ask you before they find out who you are thinking of. Take turns.

> **Modelo** ¿Es hombre? ¿Es actor? ¿Es alto?

Invitación a **Estados Unidos**

Del álbum de
Adriana

Después de los mexicanos, los puertorriqueños son la comunidad de hispanos más grande del país. Cada verano *(each summer)* se celebra en Nueva York el desfile *(parade)* puertorriqueño al que asisten *(attend)* más de un millón de personas. Muchas personalidades famosas son de origen puertorriqueño, como Jennifer López, John Leguizamo, Ricky Martin y Marc Anthony, entre otros.

Práctica adicional

Website
vistahigher
learning.com

La correspondencia

 El correo: Otra carta para Odette. Lee la carta que Sofía le escribe a su amiga Odette en Guadalajara, México. Primero lee las preguntas para después contestarlas.

1. ¿Cómo es el hijo de Adriana, según *(according to)* Sofía? _____

2. ¿Cómo es Lalo? _____

3. ¿Cómo es el ex novio de Odette? _____

4. ¿Cuándo van a Guadalajara? _____

Querida Odette:

Me da tanta alegría[1] recibir tus cartas. Estoy bien. Mis clases me gustan mucho. En mi clase de cálculo, tengo una compañera puertorriqueña. Se llama Adriana y es una señora muy agradable. Aunque ya es mayor, somos buenas amigas. Además, ¡tiene un hijo guapísimo! Bueno, no lo conozco[2] en persona, pero en las fotos es superatractivo. Es piloto y ahora está en Chicago. ¿Te imaginas, poder visitar todo el mundo gratis?[3] Lalo, como siempre, regresa tardísimo a casa, escucha una música horrorosa, nunca saca buenas notas en sus clases y siempre necesita dinero.

¡Qué bueno que terminaste con tu ex novio! Era grosero y flojo. Tú mereces[4] una persona buena y cariñosa como tú. No te preocupes, hay muchos muchachos. Yo no tengo novio, pero tengo muchos amigos.

Bueno, querida amiga, sí voy a visitarte en diciembre. Ramón y Ana Mari van a visitar a sus abuelos en Guadalajara. ¡Tal vez vamos juntos! Escríbeme pronto.

Tu amiga que te quiere,
Sofía

[1]*It makes me so happy*   [2]*know*   [3]*free*   [4]*deserve*

En papel: Una notita para Odette. Write a letter to Odette telling her about your family, friends, instructors, classmates, and other important people in your life. Include their name, their relationship to you, their physical description, their personality, and one or two interesting things about them.

¡Fíjate!

Create a simple outline, in Spanish, of the information you want to include in your letter before you begin to write.

¡A ver de nuevo!

Parte 1. Listen to or watch the **Escena** again and write as much as you can about Manolo, Sofía, and Adriana: age, description, family, activities, etc.

Parte 2. Now compare your summary with a classmate's, and add any information you may have left out.

Práctica adicional		
Cuaderno de tareas WB pp.151–152, K–M LM p.154, A-B	Audio CD-ROM Episodio 6	Website vistahigher learning.com

Vocabulario del Episodio 6

Objetivos comunicativos

You should now be able to do the following in Spanish:

✓ describe people and things

✓ ask for information

Para describir a las personas y las cosas

aburrido/a	*boring*		hijo/a único/a	*only child*
agradable	*pleasant, nice*		joven	*young*
alto/a	*tall*		listo/a	*smart*
amable	*kind, friendly*		malo/a	*bad*
antipático/a	*unpleasant, nasty*		mayor	*older*
bajo/a	*short (height)*		menor	*younger*
bonito/a	*good-looking, pretty*		moreno/a	*dark*
bueno/a	*good , nice*		nuevo/a	*new*
cariñoso/a	*affectionate*		pequeño/a	*small*
casado/a	*married*		perezoso/a	*lazy*
delgado/a	*thin*		pobre	*poor*
diferente	*different*		reservado/a	*reserved*
difícil	*hard, difficult*		rico/a	*rich; tasty*
divertido/a	*fun*		rubio/a	*blond(e)*
fácil	*easy*		serio/a	*serious*
feo/a	*ugly, plain*		similar	*similar*
gordo/a	*fat*		soltero/a	*single*
gracioso/a	*funny*		tonto/a	*dumb, silly*
grande	*large, big*		trabajador(a)	*hard-working*
grosero/a	*rude*		viejo/a	*old*
guapo/a	*handsome, good-looking*			

Los adjetivos demostrativos

este, esta	*this*		ese, esa	*that*
estos, estas	*these*		esos, esas	*those*

Palabras interrogativas

¿Cómo...?	*How...?*
¿Cuál...?	*Which...?*
¿Cuándo...?	*When...?*
¿Cuántos/as..?	*How many...?*
¿Dónde...?	*Where...?*
¿Por qué...?	*Why...?*
¿Qué...?	*What...?*
¿Quién...?	*Who...?*

Vocabulario personal

In this section, write all the words that you want to know how to say in Spanish so that you can better talk about yourself, family, friends, and, your activities.

¡A escribir!

Episodio

6

Escenas de la vida: ¡Qué guapos!

Video
CD-ROM

A. ¡A ver cuánto entendiste! See how much of the **Escena** you understood by matching the Spanish sentences with their English equivalents.

1. El flan de queso

_____ 1. ¿Es difícil prepararlo?   a. It's easy to make.

_____ 2. ¡Qué rico!   b. Is it hard to make?

_____ 3. Lo preparo en media hora.   c. I like to cook a lot.

_____ 4. Es fácil prepararlo.   d. How delicious!

_____ 5. Me gusta mucho cocinar.   e. I make it in half an hour.

2. Los hermanos

_____ 1. Tu hermana es alta y rubia.   a. You're tall and very good-looking.

_____ 2. ¿Cuántos años tiene?   b. You're so different!

_____ 3. ¡Qué diferentes son!   c. I have her picture.

_____ 4. Tú eres alto y muy guapo.   d. How old is she?

_____ 5. Soy moreno y feo.   e. I have dark hair and I'm ugly.

_____ 6. Tengo su foto.   f. Your sister is tall and blonde.

Video
CD-ROM

B. El flan de queso. Use the expressions below to complete the following conversation.

fácil	seria	similar	rico	difícil
está	me encanta	media hora	joven	preparar comida

Manolo   ¡Qué (1) _____! (2) _____ el flan de queso.

Sofía   Es muy (3) _____ al flan mexicano. ¿Es (4) _____ prepararlo?

Adriana   No, es muy (5) _____. Lo preparo en (6) _____. Me gusta (7) _____ puertorriqueña.

Sofía   ¡ (8) _____ delicioso!

Video
CD-ROM

Cuaderno de tareas

Nombre _____ Fecha _____

C. ¡Qué guapos! Answer the questions based on what you know about the **Escena**.

1. ¿Cuántos hijos tiene Adriana?   _____

2. ¿Quién es el mayor? ¿Es casado?   _____

3. ¿Cuántos hermanos tiene Manolo?   _____

4. ¿Cómo es la hermana de Manolo?   _____

5. ¿Y cómo es Manolo?   _____

Gramática 1

Describing people and things
• **Descriptive adjectives**
• **Placement of adjectives**

D. ¿Cómo son? Describe the characters of the book. Mention their physical appearance and their personality.

1. Sofía es _____   2. Manolo es _____

_____   _____

_____   _____

3. Ana Mari es _____   4. Adriana es _____

_____   _____

_____   _____

148

E. Las descripciones. Write sentences using all the elements.

> **Modelo** Hay / poco / **coches** / bueno / bonito / barato (*inexpensive*)
> Hay pocos coches buenos, bonitos y baratos.

1. Ramón / tener / un / **trabajo** / fácil / bueno

_____

2. El **compañero** de cuarto de Manolo / ser / antipático / grosero

_____

3. La / **universidades** públicas en Latinoamérica / ser / muy / grande

_____

4. Este semestre / yo / tener / bueno / **profesores**

_____

5. La **gata** de Manolo / ser / viejo / malo

_____

6. Sofía / tener / mucho / **amigas** / joven / soltero / guapo

_____

F. Mi familia. Adriana's adolescent daughter likes to talk about her own family. Use her family tree and the adjectives provided to describe her family.

> **Modelo** Mi hermano menor es tímido.

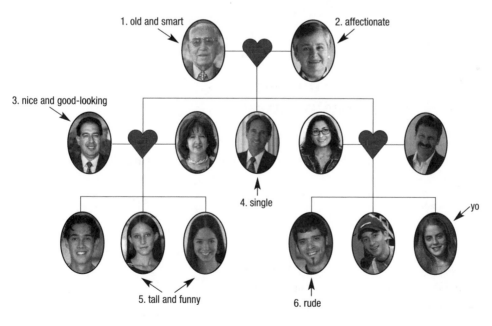

1. old and smart
2. affectionate
3. nice and good-looking
4. single
5. tall and funny
6. rude
yo

1. _____
2. _____
3. _____
4. _____
5. _____
6. _____

G. ¡Qué caro! *(How expensive!)* Sofía and Ana Mari are at the bookstore gathering supplies for Sofía's design class. Complete the conversation with the appropriate forms of the demonstrative adjectives.

este	ese	estos	esos
esta	esa	estas	esas

Sofía   ¡Mira cuánto cuestan (1) _____ *(these)* lápices de grafito!

Ana Mari   ¡Qué horror! (2) _____ *(Those)* lápices son más caros *(expensive)* que los libros. Bueno, (3) _____ *(this)* libro de diseño es carísimo también.

Sofía   A ver… ¡Ah! Por suerte ya tengo (4) _____ *(that)* libro.

Ana Mari   ¿Y (5) _____ *(these)* plumas de colores?

Sofía   Ay, de (6) _____ *(those)* plumas necesito dos paquetes.

H. Voy a comprar… Sofía is shopping for school supplies. Fill in her list with the appropriate forms of the demonstrative adjectives for each column.

Voy a comprar…

1. ___*este*___ libro de dibujo
2. _____ lápices
3. _____ plumas
4. _____ mochila
5. _____ diccionario

No necesito…

6. ___*esos*___ papeles
7. _____ mapa
8. _____ banderitas
9. _____ calculadora
10. _____ cuadernos

 Gramática 2

Asking for information
• Interrogative words

I. Preguntas y respuestas. Provide the appropriate interrogative expressions and answer the questions.

1. ¿ _____ te llamas?   Me llamo _____.
2. ¿ _____ eres?   Soy de _____.
3. ¿ _____ estudias?   En la universidad de _____.
4. ¿ _____ estudias?   Español y _____.
5. ¿ _____ hermanos tienes?   Tengo _____.
6. ¿ _____ es tu profesor(a)?   Es muy _____.
7. ¿ _____ son tus amigos?   Mis amigos son _____.
8. ¿ _____ es tu teléfono?   Es el _____.
9. ¿ _____ estudias español?   Porque _____.
10. ¿ _____ es tu clase de español?   Es a las _____ de la _____.

J. Una entrevista. You would like to know more about one of your classmates. Write four questions you might ask if you were to interview them.

1. _____
2. _____
3. _____
4. _____

Para terminar

K. Mi persona favorita. On a separate piece of paper, write a diary entry describing the person you like/admire the most. Explain why he/she is your favorite person: **Es mi persona favorita porque** *(because)*…. Include the following information.

- name
- age
- favorite activities
- where he/she is from
- physical appearance and personality
- occupation

Start like this: **Querido diario: Mi persona favorita se llama…**

L. El talento latino. Read the questions, then read the following articles and answer the questions.

Jennifer López: Una estrella puertorriqueña

1. ¿De dónde son los padres de Jennifer? _____
2. ¿Cuántas hermanas tiene? ¿Qué profesiones tienen sus hermanas? _____
_____
3. ¿Cómo es Jennifer? _____
4. ¿En qué idioma canta? _____

Jennifer López nació en el Bronx, Nueva York. Sus padres son puertorriqueños, originarios de la ciudad de Ponce. Jennifer tiene una hermana menor, que es D. J. en una radiodifusora en Nueva York, y una hermana mayor, que es maestra de música, es casada y tiene un hijo. Jennifer tomó clases de baile desde los seis años. Ella y sus hermanas hacían presentaciones "artísticas" para la familia en su apartamento de Nueva York. La carrera artística de Jennifer se establece cuando hace la película *Selena*. Su belleza física, típicamente latina, su talento artístico y su ritmo musical latino la hacen famosa. Poco tiempo después graba un disco que llega a tener ventas de más de un millón. Ella ahora canta en español y en inglés. Por el momento, es la actriz y cantante latina más conocida y mejor pagada *(highest–paid)* en Estados Unidos. Dos de sus películas son *Enough* y *Maid in Manhattan*.

Salma Hayek: Una estrella mexicana

1. ¿De dónde es Salma? _____

2. ¿Cómo es? _____

3. ¿De dónde son sus abuelos? _____

4. Según Salma, ¿qué es lo más importante para estar guapa? _____

5. ¿Cuál es su mejor película? _____

Lo más importante en una relación es aceptar a la gente como es.
–Salma Hayek

Esta bella actriz mexicana tiene 33 años, es morena, tiene unos grandes ojos cafés y mide solamente 5' 2". Sus abuelos paternos son del Líbano y su mamá es mexicana. Sus más recientes películas en Estados Unidos incluyen *The Hunchback of Notre Dame* para la televisión, *Fools Rush In* con Matthew Perry, *54*, de la famosa discoteca neoyorquina, *Studio 54* y *Dogma*. En una entrevista reciente, Hayek dijo: "Uno de los ingredientes imprescindibles para estar guapa es la felicidad." La mejor actuación de Salma es en la película *Frida*. La actriz trabajó siete años para lograr[1] que filmaran la película.

---

[1]*to achieve*

M. Una miniprueba para terminar. Complete the following communicative tasks to test your knowledge of the content of the chapter.

1. Ask Sofía:
   a. to describe her family.
   b. how old her brother is.
   c. where her grandparents are from.

2. Ask Adriana:
   d. when she works.
   e. if her children clean their rooms.
   f. when she usually gets home.

3. Ask Wayne and Ramón:
   g. if they get goods grades.
   h. who does the laundry in their house.
   i. if they use the computer.

4. Tell the characters:
   j. what your typical day is like.
   k. something you do on the weekends.
   l. something about your family.

a. _____   g. _____

b. _____   h. _____

c. _____   i. _____

d. _____   j. _____

e. _____   k. _____

f. _____   l. _____

¡A escuchar!

Episodio 6

Comprensión

Audio
CD-ROM

A. Perrolandia.

Parte 1. You will hear a radio ad. Listen and mark the statements as **cierto** or **falso**.

Banco de palabras			
blanco *white*	negro *black*	peludo *furry*	raza *breed*

	Cierto	Falso
1. Perrolandia tiene una gran selección de perros, gatos y pájaros para toda la familia.	☐	☐
2. Para las madres, se sugiere *(they suggest)* un perro pequeño, cariñoso y obediente.	☐	☐
3. Para los padres, se sugiere un perro tonto, perezoso, gordo y grande.	☐	☐
4. Para los niños, se sugiere un perro pequeño, bonito y blanco.	☐	☐

Parte 2. All of the adjectives in the list can be used to describe dogs. First, repeat the adjectives after the speaker to practice their pronunciation. You will then hear the radio ad from **Parte 1** again. As you listen, check off the adjectives you hear in the ad.

_____ adorables   _____ gordos   _____ peludos

_____ blancos   _____ grandes   _____ pequeños

_____ bonitos   _____ listos   _____ perezosos

_____ cariñosos   _____ negros   _____ trabajadores

_____ divertidos   _____ obedientes   _____ tontos

B. Una respuesta lógica. You will hear six questions. Look over the possible answers provided, and select the most logical response for each question. You will hear each question twice.

1. a. Soy inteligente.   b. Estoy en mi casa.   c. Muy bien, gracias.
2. a. Soy de Los Ángeles.   b. Estoy en la clase.   c. Soy estudiante.
3. a. Es bajo y chistoso.   b. Está muy bien.   c. Está en su oficina.
4. a. Tengo muchos amigos.   b. Tengo veinte años.   c. No tengo dinero.
5. a. Es un cuaderno.   b. Es casado.   c. Es mi tío.
6. a. Me gusta más la biología. b. Tomo cinco clases. c. Son muy difíciles.

Pronunciación

Audio
CD-ROM

La *l*, la *ll* y la *y*. The Spanish **l** (ele) is generally a lighter sound than the English *l*. Repeat these words and sentences after the speaker.

lunes	biología	biblioteca	papel	Luis lee el libro.

The Spanish **ll** (elle) sounds very much like an English *y* in most dialects.

llevar	silla	pollo	llegar	ella

The Spanish **y** (i griega) has the same sound as *i* when it stands alone or at the end of a word.

y	hoy	hay	soy	estoy

When preceding a vowel, the Spanish **y** sounds like English *y*.

yo	ya	yerno	yoga

In some areas, **y** and **ll** are pronounced like the *s* in *measure*.

yo	ya	llover	llegar

In many Latin American regions, when **y** and **ll** begin a word, they have the sound of the English *j* in *jam* and *jelly*.

yo	ya	llover	llegar

Más escenas de la vida

You will hear a conversation among Sofía, Manolo, and Carlos. Listen and then complete activities **A** and **B**. You will hear the conversation twice.

Audio
CD-ROM

A. ¿Quién? Indicate who the following statements describe: Carlos **(C),** Manolo **(M),** or Sofía **(S).**

_____ 1. Son compañeros de Adriana.

_____ 2. Es moreno y guapo.

_____ 3. Cree que Carlos es serio y reservado.

_____ 4. No quiere hablar con Sofía.

_____ 5. Es grosero y antipático.

_____ 6. Hace muchas preguntas.

Audio
CD-ROM

B. Responde. Write the answers to the following questions.

1. ¿Cómo es Carlos? _____

2. ¿Qué clase toman con Adriana? _____

3. ¿Qué trabajo tiene Carlos? _____

4. ¿Qué le gusta a Sofía? _____

5. ¿Por qué Carlos no habla con Sofía? _____

Episodio

7

Escenas de la vida: ¿Qué van a hacer el sábado?

Video
CD-ROM

Audio
CD-ROM

A. ¡Mira cuánto puedes entender! Listen to the conversation or watch the video to complete the tasks that correspond to each picture.

1. Indica qué nota creen que van a sacar en el primer examen de cálculo.

2. Indica qué tiene ganas de hacer Ramón el sábado y por qué Sofía no puede hacer nada el sábado con Ramón. ¿Qué tiene que hacer Sofía?

☐ **Tiene ganas de hacer un picnic.**

☐ **Tiene que trabajar.**
☐ **Tiene que limpiar su cuarto.**
☐ **Tiene que hacer una presentación.**
☐ **Tiene que estudiar.**

☐ **Tiene ganas de ir a la biblioteca.**

155

3. Mira los planes de Manolo; completa la hora o la actividad necesaria.

sábado	domingo
____ aeropuerto	¡nada!
después _____	
_____	
en la tarde _____	

4. ¿Qué va a hacer Adriana el domingo?

Cultura a lo vivo

Throughout the Spanish-speaking world, Sunday is considered a day to be spent with the family. Some families attend religious services and then go to a restaurant; other families visit parents and/or grandparents; still others go on outings—a picnic, a visit to a nearby town, a day at a swimming pool, a trip to the mountains, to a river, or to a park. These gatherings include family members of all ages, as well as close friends whose families may live elsewhere. Some parents feel so strongly about reserving Sunday for the family that teenage children are not allowed to go out with friends that day.

B. ¿Te diste cuenta? Escucha la conversación o mira el video otra vez para indicar quién hace estos comentarios: Sofía **(S),** Adriana **(A),** Ramón **(R)** o Manolo **(M).**

Video
CD-ROM

Audio
CD-ROM

_____ 1. El examen fue muy fácil.

_____ 2. Para mí fue muy difícil.

_____ 3. Tenemos que hacer algo divertido.

_____ 4. No tengo nada que hacer el domingo.

_____ 5. Los domingos paso el día con la familia.

_____ 6. Todos están invitados.

C. ¡A responder! Contesta las preguntas.

Video
CD-ROM

Audio
CD-ROM

1. ¿Quién tiene ganas de celebrar? ¿Por qué? _____

_____

2. ¿Qué quiere organizar Ramón? ¿Por qué? _____

_____

3. ¿Qué tiene que hacer Sofía el sábado por la tarde? _____

_____

4. ¿Qué hace Adriana los domingos? _____

_____

Práctica adicional

Cuaderno de tareas
WB pp.171–172, A–C

Video
CD-ROM
Episodio 7

Para comunicarnos mejor

Talking about weekend plans
• **Ir a** + [*infinitive*]
• **The personal a**

In the conversation, you heard Sofía, Ramón, and Adriana say the following:

Creo que **voy a sacar** A.   *I think I'm going to get an A.*
¿Qué **van a hacer** el sábado?   *What are you (all) going to do on Saturday?*
Vamos a visitar a los abuelos.   *We're going to visit our grandparents.*

Voy, van, and **vamos** are forms of the verb **ir** *(to go)*. To talk about things and activities that are going to happen in the future, Spanish uses a form of **ir** followed by **a** and the infinitive (**-r** form) of a verb. In another conversation, the characters said the following about the things they are *going to do.*

Ir a + [*infinitive*]	
Hoy **voy a llevar** a Viviana a su clase de baile.	*Today I'm going to take Viviana to her dance class.*
¿**Vas a trabajar** el domingo?	*Are you going to work on Sunday?*
Sofía **va a comprar** un regalo.	*Sofía is going to buy a present.*
El próximo domingo **vamos a celebrar** el cumpleaños de Wayne.	*Next Sunday we're going to celebrate Wayne's birthday.*
¿Qué **van a hacer** mañana? ¿Qué **vais a hacer** mañana?	*What are you going to do tomorrow? (pl.)*
Todos **van a ir** al parque.	*They are all going to go to the park.*

1. Notice that the verb **llevar** *(to take something or someone somewhere)* is followed by **a** (**llevar a Viviana**). This is called the personal **a** (la *a* **personal),** and it has no English equivalent. You need to include **a** after verbs that have a person or a pet as direct object.

> La familia de Adriana siempre visita **a** los abuelos los domingos.
> Los lunes Adriana **lleva a** su hija a la clase de baile folclórico.
> El sábado Manolo **lleva a** la gata al veterinario, ¿verdad?
> Escucho **a** mis padres.

2. To talk about your plans, use these expressions:

Expresiones de tiempo			
esta noche	*tonight*	**el próximo sábado**	*next Saturday*
hoy	*today*	**la próxima semana**	*next week*
mañana	*tomorrow*	**el año que viene**	*next year*

PRÁCTICA

A. ¿Qué vas a hacer el próximo fin de semana?

Parte 1. Indica si vas a hacer *(to do)* las siguientes actividades.

	Sí	No
1. El sábado por la mañana voy a estudiar.	☐	☐
2. Voy a trabajar todo el fin de semana.	☐	☐
3. Voy a lavar mi coche.	☐	☐
4. Voy a visitar a mi abuela.	☐	☐
5. Mi papá y yo vamos a jugar golf.	☐	☐
6. Mi compañero/a y yo vamos a ir al supermercado.	☐	☐
7. El domingo voy a mirar la televisión todo el día.	☐	☐
8. Voy a escribir *(to write)* una composición.	☐	☐

> **Learning Strategy: Getting the most out of class time**
>
> Class time is invaluable. To maximize your learning, you must actively participate during class sessions. Try to speak only Spanish during class activities.

Parte 2. Convierte las frases de la **Parte 1** en preguntas. Después entrevista a tu compañero/a.

Modelo	El sábado por la mañana voy a estudiar.
	¿Vas a estudiar el sábado por la mañana?

B. ¿Qué van a hacer? Usa las fotos para escribir lo que *(what)* van a hacer los personajes la próxima semana.

1. Sofía y Manolo...

_____

2. Adriana...

_____

3. Nosotros...

_____

4. Manolo...

_____

5. Sofía...

_____

6. Ellos...

_____

C. Una entrevista. ¿Qué van a hacer tus compañeros esta noche, mañana por la mañana y el fin de semana? Escribe los nombres y las actividades.

| Modelo | —¿Qué vas a hacer esta noche?
—Voy a estudiar. |

Práctica adicional

Cuaderno de tareas
WB pp.172–174, D–G

Gramática 2

Expressing obligations and desires
• <u>Tener que</u>, <u>tener ganas de</u>

You have used the verb **tener** to express ownership and possession.

Tenemos muy poco dinero.	*We have very little money.*
Tengo cuatro perros.	*I have four dogs.*
¿Tienes coche?	*Do you have a car?*

In every language, many common verb phrases have meanings independent of the verbs that comprise them. In English, these combinations are called *verb constructions*; in Spanish, they are called **construcciones verbales.** For example, when you use *have* as an independent verb, as in *I have a new car, have* means *to own* or *to possess*. When you use *have* in combination with an infinitive, as in *I have to buy a new car, have* does not mean *to possess*. The combination *have* + [*infinitive*] expresses an obligation, something you must do.

1. In Spanish, obligation is expressed by the verb construction **tener que** + [*infinitive*]. In this episode, you heard these statements containing **tener que:**

Tengo que trabajar por la mañana.	*I have to work in the morning.*
Tenemos que hacer algo divertido.	*We have to do something fun.*

2. Another verb construction you heard is **tener ganas de** + [*infinitive*]. Use this construction to express what you feel or don't feel like doing.

Tengo ganas de celebrar.	*I feel like celebrating.*
No tenemos ganas de estudiar.	*We don't feel like studying.*

¡Fíjate!

Tener que + [*infinitive*] expresses an obligation or duty.
Tener ganas de + [*infinitive*] expresses a desire to do something.

PRÁCTICA

Audio
CD-ROM

D. ¿Obligación, deseo o acción? Escucha los comentarios para indicar si son obligaciones, deseos o acciones futuras.

	Obligación	Deseo	Acción
1.	☐	☐	☐
2.	☐	☐	☐
3.	☐	☐	☐

	Obligación	Deseo	Acción
4.	☐	☐	☐
5.	☐	☐	☐
6.	☐	☐	☐

E. ¿Y ustedes, qué tienen que hacer? Completa las frases lógicamente.

> **Modelo**   Los jueves mi hermana tiene que **lavar la ropa.**

1. Los lunes tengo que _____

2. En la clase de español todos tenemos que _____

3. Los sábados mis amigos y yo tenemos ganas de _____

4. Los domingos no tengo ganas de _____

5. Yo (no) _____ hacer la tarea.

6. Mi mejor amigo _____

F. Las actividades de nuestros amigos. Escribe la expresión necesaria para completar los comentarios. Después indica si son **ciertos** o **falsos.** Usa **tener que, tener ganas (de)** o **tener.**

	Cierto	Falso
1. Sofía dice: "Yo _____ hacer una presentación en el Club Latino."	☐	☐
2. Adriana _____ mucho trabajo en casa.	☐	☐
3. Manolo _____ llevar a Jorge al aeropuerto.	☐	☐
4. Los chicos _____ de ir al parque después de la clase.	☐	☐
5. Y tú, ¿_____ de ir a una fiesta este fin de semana?	☐	☐
6. Sí, pero (yo) _____ trabajar el domingo.	☐	☐

G. ¿Por qué no quieres ir? Explícale a un(a) compañero/a por qué no quieres ir *(want to go)* a esos lugares. Usa **no tengo ganas de** con los siguientes verbos.

nadar   hacer ejercicio   estudiar   comprar nada
correr   jugar tenis   leer libros   escribir correo electrónico *(e-mail)*

> **Modelo**   a las canchas de tenis
> —¿Quieres ir a las canchas de tenis?
> —No, porque hoy no tengo ganas de jugar tenis.

1. al gimnasio
2. a la biblioteca
3. al laboratorio de computadoras

4. al centro comercial
5. al parque
6. a la piscina

Banco de palabras

Quiero...	nadar
I want...	*to swim*
Quieres...	**correr**
You want...	*to run*

H. Lo siento, pero no puedo. Imagina que un(a) amigo/a te invita a salir, pero tú no tienes ganas de salir. ¡Inventa excusas!

> **Modelo** ir al cine/trabajar
> —¿Quieres ir al cine el próximo sábado?
> —Lo siento, pero no puedo porque tengo que trabajar el próximo sábado.

1. ir al parque/hacer la tarea
2. ir al centro comercial/lavar la ropa
3. ir al concierto de Maná/estudiar para un examen
4. ir a la cafetería/regresar a casa temprano
5. ir a un restaurante a comer/llevar a mi hermano al doctor
6. mirar una película en mi casa/leer un libro para mi clase de historia

> **Banco de palabras**
> **No puedo**
> *I can't*
>
> **¿Puedes...**
> *Can you...?*
>
> **Lo siento**
> *I'm sorry*

I. Preguntas personales. Contesta las preguntas. Después entrevista a un(a) compañero/a.

1. ¿Qué tienes que hacer después de las clases?
2. ¿Qué tienes que hacer los fines de semana?
3. ¿Cuándo tienes ganas de estudiar? ¿Vas a estudiar esta noche? ¿Vas a mirar la tele?
4. ¿Qué tienes ganas de hacer este fin de semana?

Práctica adicional		
Cuaderno de tareas WB pp.174–175, H–J LM pp.177–178, A–B, Pron.	Audio CD-ROM Episodio 7	Website vistahigher learning.com

Invitación a **Colombia**

> Del álbum de
> *Sofía*

Colombia tiene casi tres veces el tamaño de California y tiene aproximadamente 41 millones de habitantes. Es un bello país que ha dado *(has given)* al mundo renombradas personalidades de fama mundial, como Gabriel García Márquez (Premio Nobel de Literatura) y Francisco Botero (pintor, escultor). Además de artistas e intelectuales, produce el mejor café del mundo, y por supuesto, a la cantautora *(singer-songwriter)* Shakira.

Actividades comunicativas

A. Los planes para el fin de semana.

Instrucciones para **Estudiante 1**

First, fill in the column marked **Yo** to indicate what you are going to do the days and times indicated on the grid. Then talk to your partner in order to fill in the column marked **Mi compañero/a.** Finally, interview each other in order to fill in the empty boxes in the last two columns; you each have the information that the other needs.

Modelo   ¿Qué va a hacer Sofía el sábado por la tarde?

¡Fíjate!

Remember not to conjugate the verbs that follow **ir a**. Always use the infinitive **(-r)** form.

	Yo	Mi compañero/a	Sofía	Ramón y su familia
El viernes por la noche				
El sábado por la mañana				
El sábado por la tarde				
El domingo				

A. Los planes para el fin de semana.

Instrucciones para **Estudiante 2**

First, fill in the column marked **Yo** to indicate what you are going to do the days and times indicated on the grid. Then talk to your partner in order to fill in the column marked **Mi compañero/a.** Finally, interview each other in order to fill in the empty boxes in the last two columns; you each have the information that the other needs.

Modelo	¿Qué va a hacer Sofía el sábado por la tarde?

¡Fíjate!

Remember not to conjugate the verbs that follow **ir a**. Always use the infinitive **(-r)** form.

	Yo	Mi compañero/a	Sofía	Ramón y su familia
El viernes por la noche				
El sábado por la mañana				
El sábado por la tarde				
El domingo				

B. En imágenes.

Instrucciones para **Estudiante 1**

Use the first letter of the verb and the drawings to create logical sentences stating what you and the characters are going to do, have to do, or feel like doing during the weekend. Concentrate on the actions in the drawings. When you know what your sentences are, read them to your partner, who will check the answer key to see if your sentences are correct. Take turns.

¡Fíjate!

Try to interpret the whole sentence before attempting to give your partner the answer.

1. Mañana Sofía v _____ con sus amigas.

2. Adriana y Sofía t _____ para la clase de cálculo.

3. Wayne no t _____ de .

4. Manolo t _____ a la gata al veterinario.

5. ¿Este fin de semana tú v _____ en Internet?

Las respuestas de tu compañero/a:

1. Adriana **tiene que trabajar** todo el día.
2. Los hermanos de Ramón **tienen ganas de** ir a la **piscina** con sus amigos.
3. Sofía **va a tomar el autobús** porque su coche no funciona.
4. Ana Mari y yo **vamos a mirar** un programa de terror.
5. ¿Tú **tienes que comprar** muchos libros para tus clases como Manolo y Sofía?

B. En imágenes.

Instrucciones para Estudiante 2

Use the first letter of the verb and the drawings to create logical sentences stating what you and the characters are going to do, have to do, or feel like doing during the weekend. Concentrate on the actions in the drawings. When you know what your sentences are, read them to your partner, who will check the answer key to see if your sentences are correct. Take turns.

¡Fíjate!
Try to interpret the whole sentence before attempting to give your partner the answer.

1. Adriana t_____ todo el día.

2. Los hermanos de Ramón t_____ ir a la _____ con sus amigos.

3. Sofía v_____ porque su coche no funciona.

4. Ana Mari y yo v_____ un programa de terror.

5. ¿Tú t_____ muchos libros para tus clases como Manolo y Sofía?

Las respuestas de tu compañero/a:

1. Mañana Sofía **va a bailar** con sus amigas.
2. Adriana y Sofía **tienen que estudiar** para la clase de cálculo.
3. Wayne no **tiene ganas de lavar el coche.**
4. Manolo **tiene que llevar** a la gata al veterinario.
5. ¿Este fin de semana tú **vas a buscar información** en Internet?

C. ¡Mucho gusto!

Instrucciones para **Estudiante 1**

Interview a classmate that you have not had the opportunity to get to know. Find out:

- your partner's name
- if your partner has brothers and sisters; their names, ages, and physical descriptions
- if they work; where, what days
- if they use a computer; what type **(tipo)**
- if they like to watch TV; what programs
- what your partner usually feels like doing on weekends

You will need to report some of the information you learned about your partner to the rest of the class. Take notes.

C. ¡Mucho gusto!

Instrucciones para **Estudiante 2**

Interview a classmate that you have not had the opportunity to get to know. Find out:

- your partner's name
- if your partner has a special friend; their name, age, physical description
- how many classes they take, which ones, what days
- if your partner likes to listen to music; what kind
- what they have to do after school
- what they are going to do this weekend

You will need to report some of the information you learned about your partner to the rest of the class. Take notes.

La correspondencia

El correo: Una invitación para Wayne. Lee las preguntas, luego lee el correo electrónico que recibe Wayne y después contesta las preguntas.

1. ¿Quién invita a Wayne? _____
2. ¿Qué va a hacer Wayne el sábado por la mañana? _____
3. ¿Adónde va a llevar a su sobrino? _____
4. ¿Qué planes tiene Wayne para el próximo sábado? _____

From: Wayne Reilly <wreilly@micorreo.com>
To: "Guadalupe Amaré" <gamare@micorreo.com>
Re: Invitación para el sábado

Hola Lupita,

Gracias por la invitación. Me gustaría ir pero no puedo. ¡Tengo muchísimas cosas que hacer! Por la mañana tengo que reparar el coche de un amigo, porque no puede ir a trabajar sin[1] coche. Por la tarde necesito estudiar, porque el lunes tengo un examen de física que va a ser muy difícil y tengo que sacar A. A las siete de la tarde, voy a llevar a mi sobrino a un juego de hockey. Así que muchas gracias de todas maneras[2].

No tengo planes para el próximo fin de semana. ¿Podemos organizar algo[3]? ¡Que te diviertas mucho!

Wayne

[1]*without* [2]**de todas...** *anyway* [3]*something*

En papel: Lo siento, pero no puedo. A friend sends you an e-mail message inviting you to a crafts fair (**una feria**) this weekend. You have a lot to do and cannot go. Write a reply explaining your weekend plans. Use Wayne's letter as a model, paying special attention to the way that Wayne politely declines the invitation.

¡A ver de nuevo!

Video
CD-ROM

Audio
CD-ROM

Parte 1. Escribe de lo que se trató este episodio en tus propias palabras.

¡Fíjate!

Your summary must include everybody's plans for the weekend. Be as specific as you can.

Ramón quiere organizar un picnic para Wayne porque...

Parte 2. Now compare your summary with a classmate's and add any information you may have left out.

Práctica adicional		
Cuaderno de tareas WB pp.175–176, K–L LM p.178, A–B	Audio CD-ROM Episodio 7	Website vistahigher learning.com

Vocabulario del Episodio 7

Ir a + [*infinitive*]	*to be going to* + [*infinitive*]
Tener ganas de + [*infinitive*]	*to feel like...*
Tener que + [*infinitive*]	*to have to...*
Llevar a + [*person*]	*to bring* (someone or an animal)
Llevar + [*object*]	*to bring* (something inanimate)

Expresiones de tiempo

esta noche	*tonight*	**el próximo sábado**	*next Saturday*
hoy	*today*	**la próxima semana**	*next week*
mañana	*tomorrow*	**el año que viene**	*next year*

Vocabulario personal

Write all the words that you need to know in Spanish so that you can better talk about your own obligations and weekend plans.

170

¡A escribir!

Episodio 7

Escenas de la vida: ¿Qué van a hacer el sábado?

Video
CD-ROM

A. ¡A ver cuánto entendiste! See how much of the **Escena** you understood by matching the Spanish sentences with their English equivalents.

Después del examen

_____ 1. ¿Qué les parece a las dos?

_____ 2. Está solo y es su cumpleaños.

_____ 3. ¡Todos están invitados!

_____ 4. Paso el día con la familia.

_____ 5. Y usted, ¿puede ir?

_____ 6. Tenemos que hacer algo divertido
este fin de semana, ¿no?

_____ 7. Quiero organizar un picnic en el parque.

_____ 8. No tengo nada que hacer el domingo.

a. I spend the day with my family.

b. I don't have to do anything
on Sunday.

c. How does two o'clock sound
to you?

d. We have to do something fun
this weekend, ok?

e. I want to organize a picnic in
the park.

f. He's alone and it's his birthday.

g. Can you go?

h. Everyone is invited!

Video
CD-ROM

B. ¿Qué van a hacer el sábado? Use the expressions to complete the conversation.

van a	vamos	picnic
divertido	fácil	cumpleaños
tengo ganas	voy a	difícil

Sofía   ¡El examen fue muy (1) _____, ¿verdad? Creo que
(2) _____ sacar A. (3)_____ de celebrar.

Adriana   Para mí fue muy (4) _____. Tengo que estudiar mucho más.

Manolo   No hay que ser pesimistas. Tenemos que hacer algo (5) _____
este fin de semana, ¿no?

Ramón   ¿Qué (6)_____ hacer el sábado? Quiero organizar un
(7)_____ en el parque para Wayne. Es su
(8) _____.

C. ¿A quién se refieren? Indicate whether the statements refer to Manolo (**M**), Sofía (**S**), Adriana (**A**), or Ramón (**R**).

_____ 1. Tiene que llevar a Jorge al aeropuerto.

_____ 2. Pasa el domingo con la familia.

_____ 3. Quiere organizar un picnic para Wayne.

_____ 4. Tiene que llevar a la gata al veterinario.

_____ 5. Tienen que trabajar el sábado.

_____ 6. Invita a todos al parque.

_____ 7. Tiene ganas de celebrar.

_____ 8. Tiene que estudiar más.

Gramática 1

Talking about weekend plans
- **ir a** + [*infinitive*]
- **The personal a**

D. Las actividades de la próxima semana. Describe what Sofía, her friends, and you are going to do next week.

> **Modelo**   Mis hijos y yo
>
> **Mis hijos y yo vamos a visitar a los abuelos el domingo.**

1.

2.

3.

4.

5.

6.

1. Viviana _____.

2. Ramón y su amiga _____.

3. Adriana y su familia _____.

4. Manolo y Ana Mari _____.

5. Nosotros _____.

6. Y tú, ¿ _____?

Cuaderno de tareas

Nombre _____ Fecha _____

E. Los planes de Sofía y Manolo. Sofía and Manolo are making plans for the weekend. Look at the illustrations and describe what they are going to do on Saturday and Sunday. Sequence their activities in a cohesive paragraph. Use phrases like **por la mañana/tarde/noche, después, más tarde, también,** etc.

_____
_____
_____
_____
_____
_____
_____
_____
_____

F. ¿Y tus planes? Now describe your own weekend plans. Be specific and thorough.

_____
_____
_____
_____
_____
_____
_____
_____
_____

173

G. ¡En español! How would you say the following in Spanish?

1. Are you going to work next weekend?

_____

2. No, I am going to study for (**para**) a test.

_____

3. I am going to visit my grandmother in Utah next week, so (**entonces**) I am not going to be (**estar**) in class.

_____

4. But (**pero**) you are going to get an F.

_____

5. No, I am going to talk to the teacher tonight.

_____

Gramática 2   **Expressing obligations and desires**
• **Tener que, tener ganas de**

H. Las obligaciones. Describe the activities that you and the people you know usually have to do during the weekend.

> **Modelo**   Mi hijo **tiene que lavar su ropa**.

1. Yo _____.
2. Mi papá _____.
3. Mi mamá _____.
4. Mis hermanos/as _____.
5. Mi mejor amigo/a _____.

I. ¿Qué (no) tienen ganas de hacer? Indicate what the people feel like or don't feel like doing, according to the place or activity indicated.

> **Modelo**   Mi novia va a ir a la biblioteca.   **Tiene ganas de estudiar.**
> Yo voy a quedarme (*stay*) en casa.   **No tengo ganas de visitar a mis amigos.**

1. Voy a ir al centro comercial (*mall*). _____
2. Mis amigos y yo vamos a poner (*turn on*) el radio. _____
3. Tú no vas a salir (*go out*) esta noche. _____
4. Mis padres van a ir a la tienda de videos. _____
5. Sofía y Ana Mari van a ir a una discoteca. _____
6. Ramón va a usar la computadora. _____

J. ¿Por qué no pueden salir? *(Why can't they go out?)* Explain why Ana Mari's brothers cannot go out to play on the days and at the times indicated.

> **Modelo** lunes
> **El lunes a las doce tienen que ir a la biblioteca.**

semana 36

AGOSTO/SEPTIEMBRE

31 lunes
8
9
10
11
12 biblioteca
1
2
3
4
5
6 lavar el coche
7 de Ramón
8

1 martes
8
9
10
11
12
1
2
3
4
5
6
7 estudiar
8

2 miércoles
8
9
10
11
12
1
2
3
4
5
6
7
8

3 jueves
8
9
10
11
12
1
2
3
4
5
6
7 limpiar el cuarto
8

4 viernes
8
9
10
11
12
1
2 comprar
3 libros
4
5
6
7
8

5 sábado
lavar la ropa

6 domingo
visitar a los
abuelos

1. _____
_____

2. _____
_____

3. _____
_____

4. _____
_____

5. _____
_____

6. _____
_____

Para terminar

K. Una invitación. Read the e-mail message Sofía's mother sent to her friend Liz. Then answer the questions.

> From: Diana Blasio
> To: Liz Margolis
> Re: Invitación al teatro
>
> Hola, Liz:
>
> Gracias por tu invitación al teatro esta noche, pero no voy a poder acompañarte. Tengo que trabajar hasta las cinco de la tarde y después voy a llevar a Lalo al doctor. No está bien. No tiene ganas de comer nada desde hace varios días y también tiene un poco de fiebre. Vamos a ver qué dice el doctor.
>
> Tengo muchas ganas de hablar contigo. ¿Tienes planes mañana por la noche? Llámame.
>
> Diana

1. Who is inviting Diana? _____

2. Where is she invited? _____

3. Why can't she go? _____

4. What is wrong with Lalo? _____

L. Para resumir la historia. Answer the questions about the **Escena**, based on the images.

1. ¿Quién va a sacar A en el examen?

_____

2. ¿Quién tiene que estudiar mucho más?

_____

3. ¿Qué tiene ganas de hacer Ramón? ¿Por qué?

_____

4. ¿Por qué Adriana no puede *(can't)* ir al parque?

_____

5. ¿Qué tiene que hacer Manolo el sábado?

_____

6. ¿Quiénes van a ir al picnic?

_____

¡A escuchar!

Episodio

7

Comprensión

Audio
CD-ROM

A. ¿Qué van a hacer?

Parte 1. Repeat the activities in the list after the speaker to practice their pronunciation and to familiarize yourself with them.

bailar	**escuchar música**	**limpiar la casa**	**sacar malas notas**
comprar comida	**estudiar**	**llegar tarde**	**visitar a...**
descansar	**hablar por teléfono**	**mirar la tele**	

Parte 2. You will now hear ten statements. React to them by saying or asking what the people are going to do, using the cues provided and activities from the list in **Parte 1.** Repeat the correct answers after the speaker.

> **Modelo**   You hear: **Ramón tiene un examen de geología mañana.**
> You say: **Ramón va a estudiar.**

1. Adriana...	4. (Nosotras)...	7. (Nosotros)...	10. Sofía y su mamá...
2. Sofía y sus amigos...	5. Manolo...	8. ¿(Tú)...?	
3. Yo...	6. ¿(Tú)...?	9. Lalo...	

Audio
CD-ROM

B. ¡Vamos al aeropuerto! You will hear a conversation between Manolo and his roommate Jorge as they prepare to leave for the airport. Listen and choose the best options to summarize the conversation. **¡Atención!** Items 2 and 5 have multiple responses. You will hear the conversation twice.

1. Jorge va a visitar a su familia en…

   a. Miami   b. Los Ángeles   c. Nueva York

Banco de palabras			
llamar	maletas	poner	escribir
to call	*suitcases*	*to put, place*	*to write*
el vuelo sale	pesado	regalos	
the flight leaves	*heavy*	*gifts*	

2. Jorge tiene mucha familia allí. Los parientes que menciona son sus…

   a. hermanas   b. nietos   c. padres   d. primos   e. sobrinos   f. tíos

3. El vuelo sale…

   a. temprano   b. tarde   c. a tiempo

4. Jorge tiene que…

   a. empacar las maletas   b. llamar por teléfono a sus padres   c. comprar un boleto

5. En la maleta, Jorge lleva…

   a. computadora   b. libros   c. guitarra   d. regalos   e. ropa

Pronunciación

Audio
CD-ROM

La _t_ y la _d_. To pronounce the Spanish **t (te),** touch the tip of the tongue to the back of your upper front teeth and do not emit a puff of air. Repeat these words and sentences after the speaker.

Tito	treinta	patata	Tomás te prestó el motor a ti.
total	tomar	motor	Hay treinta y tres técnicos en total.

When **d (de)** occurs as an initial sound, or after **n (ene)** or l **(ele),** it is similar to English _d_, except that the tip of the tongue rests against the back of the upper front teeth. Repeat these words after the speaker.

Donaldo	doce	Andrés	el dinero
Daniel	dos	donde	falda

When **d** follows a sound that is not **n** or **l,** in other words most of the time, it sounds similar to the _th_ sound in English _father_. Repeat these words and sentences after the speaker.

padre	mi doctor	Los sábados y domingos no estudio.
cuaderno	su dinero	Si me das tu cuaderno, te doy dos dólares.

Más escenas de la vida

Ramón first chats with Ana Mari and then phones Manolo. Listen and then complete activities **A** and **B**. You will hear the conversation twice.

Audio
CD-ROM

A. ¿Quién? Match the people to the activity they have to or (don't) want to do.

_____ 1. Manolo   a. Tiene que lavar ropa.

_____ 2. Ana Mari   b. Tiene ganas de jugar vóleibol.

_____ 3. Ramón   c. Tienen ganas de comer y hablar.

_____ 4. Ana Mari y Manolo   d. No tiene ganas de hacer ejercicio.

Audio
CD-ROM

B. Responde. Write the answers to the following questions.

1. ¿Qué quiere llevar Ramón al parque?

_____

2. ¿Qué tiene Ana Mari de todas sus clases?

_____

3. ¿Quién tiene ganas de ver una película? (_see a movie?_)

_____

4. ¿Qué van a hacer en el picnic?

_____

Objetivos comunicativos

In this episode, you will practice:

✔ talking about common daily activities

✔ identifying places to go

✔ saying where you are

Escenas de la vida: Vamos al parque

Video
CD-ROM

A. ¡Mira cuánto puedes entender! Check the activities that you hear mentioned in the **Escena.**

Audio
CD-ROM

Sofía y mi hermana corren **en el parque.**

Hace la tarea.

Después comemos **en El Huarache Veloz.**

No recibe **regalos el día de su cumpleaños.**

Lee el periódico y su correo electrónico.

Hacen ejercicio.

Salen a cenar.

Ve películas en la computadora.

Ana Mari quiere salir **con Wayne.**

B. ¿Te diste cuenta? Indica si los comentarios son **ciertos** o **falsos**.

Video
CD-ROM

Audio
CD-ROM

	Cierto	Falso
1. Wayne y Ramón van a jugar vóleibol mañana.	☐	☐
2. Wayne quiere comer en El Huarache Veloz con las chicas.	☐	☐
3. Ramón y Wayne van al parque a las 9 para correr.	☐	☐
4. Wayne lee el periódico en su computadora.	☐	☐
5. A Wayne le gusta Sofía.	☐	☐
6. Wayne tiene clases por la mañana.	☐	☐

C. Responde. Contesta las preguntas.

Video
CD-ROM

1. ¿Qué van a hacer Wayne y Ramón el domingo?
   a. Van a estudiar.   b. Van a hacer la tarea.   c. Van a correr.

2. ¿Qué actividad hace Wayne por la mañana?
   a. Mira la tele.   b. Hace su tarea.   c. Limpia su cuarto.

Audio
CD-ROM

3. ¿Qué quiere hacer Wayne después de correr?
   a. Comer.   b. Jugar tenis.   c. Escribir un trabajo.

4. ¿Quién es adicto a su computadora?
   a. Ramón.   b. Wayne.   c. Sofía.

5. ¿Qué actividades hace Wayne en su computadora?
   a. Lee su correo.   b. Escribe poemas.   c. Habla con sus amigos.

El Retiro

Práctica adicional

Cuaderno de tareas
WB p.197, A–B

Video
CD-ROM
Episodio 8

Cultura a lo vivo

Large public parks in major Hispanic cities provide an important place for inexpensive recreational activities. For example, in Mexico City, **El Parque de Chapultepec** is the oldest, most important, and largest park in the city. There are museums, a lake, rides, an area for picnics, a zoo, restaurants, outdoor cafés, and other activities. In Madrid, Spain, **El Retiro** has just as much variety. From spectacles like street performers, puppet shows, jugglers, mimes, and musical performances, to quick acupuncture sessions or yoga classes, this park offers much more than just a simple stroll or boat ride along its central lake. In Caracas, Venezuela, **Los Caobos** is one of the oldest parks in the city. People go to the park to relax, walk among the beautiful mahogany trees, go bird watching, and enjoy children's activities on weekends. These parks serve an important social function, since families may celebrate birthdays, anniversaries, or any family event at the park.

Para comunicarnos mejor

Gramática 1

Talking about common daily activities
• Regular -er and -ir verbs

You have used many regular **-ar** verbs, such as **trabajar** and **descansar**, to talk about some of your activities. When Ramón and Wayne talked, they used verbs ending in **-er** and **-ir** to talk about their activities. You will discover that the endings of these verbs are similar to the verbs you already know.

Analizar y descubrir

1. Complete these statements.

-ar verbs

a. invitar   Yo _____ a mis amigos al picnic.

b. descansar   ¿Tú _____ los fines de semana?

c. trabajar   Sofía _____ los sábados; por eso, no estudia.

d. celebrar   Nosotros _____ el cumpleaños de Wayne el domingo.

e. hablar   Los papás de Wayne _____ con él por teléfono.

2. Compare the verb endings you provided with the endings of the verb **comer** *(to eat)*.

Comer	
Yo **como** hamburguesas con frecuencia.	*I often eat hamburgers.*
¿Tú, qué **comes**?	*What do you eat?*
Sofía no **come** grasa.	*Sofía doesn't eat fat.*
Mi papá y yo no **comemos** carne.	*My dad and I don't eat meat.*
¿Ustedes también **comen** tortillas? ¿Vosotros también **coméis** tortillas?	*Do you also eat tortillas?*
En Cuba no **comen** tacos.	*They don't eat tacos in Cuba.*

3. Now examine the endings of the verb **vivir** *(to live)*.

Vivir	
Yo **vivo** en San Diego.	*I live in San Diego.*
¿Tú, dónde **vives**?	*Where do you live?*
Sofía **vive** cerca de la universidad.	*Sofía lives near the university.*
Mis hermanas y yo **vivimos** con mis papás.	*My sisters and I live with my parents.*
¿Dónde **viven** ustedes? ¿Dónde **vivís** vosotros?	*Where do you live?*
Los abuelos de Ramón **viven** en México.	*Ramón's grandparents live in Mexico.*

4. In the following chart, fill in the endings of the **-ar (trabajar)**, **-er (comer)**, and **-ir (vivir)** verbs.

	-ar verbs	-er verbs	-ir verbs
yo	trabaj _____	com _____	viv _____
tú	trabaj _____	com _____	viv _____
usted/él/ella	trabaj _____	com _____	viv _____
nosotros/as	trabaj _____	com _____	viv _____
ustedes/ellos/as	trabaj _____	com _____	viv _____

5. Compare the endings of the **-ar** and **-er** verbs in the present tense. Where the **-ar** verbs have an **a**, the **-er** verbs have an _____ .

6. Compare the endings of the **-er** and **-ir** verbs. All endings of the **-er** and **-ir** verbs are the same except for the _____ and the _____ forms.

Here are some common **-er** and **-ir** verbs you may use to talk about your activities.

Más actividades: verbos -er e -ir			
abrir	*to open*	**leer el periódico**	*to read the newspaper*
beber	*to drink*	**recibir correo electrónico**	*to receive (get) e-mail*
comer hamburguesas	*to eat hamburgers*	**regalos**	*gifts*
correr	*to run, jog*	**salir a cenar***	*to go out to dinner*
discutir (de/con)	*to discuss, argue (about/with)*	**con los amigos***	*with friends*
		vender comida	*to sell food*
escribir cartas	*to write letters*	**ver una película en casa**	*to watch a movie at home*
un trabajo	*a paper*	**vivir en/con**	*to live in/with*
hacer la tarea*	*to do homework*		
ejercicio*	*to excercise*		

*hacer and salir have a g in the yo person — **Yo hago** la tarea y **salgo** con mi novio.

7. Use these expressions to tell how often you do something.

¿Con qué frecuencia…?	
todos los días	*every day*
con frecuencia	*often*
a veces	*sometimes*
una vez a la semana	*once a week*
dos veces al mes	*twice a month*
tres (cuatro…) veces al año	*three (four…) times a year*
siempre	*always*
(casi) nunca	*(almost) never*

PRÁCTICA

A. ¿Con qué frecuencia?

Parte 1. Indica con qué frecuencia tú o los miembros de tu familia hacen las siguientes cosas.

1. Leo el periódico. _____
2. Mi papá bebe café. _____
3. Mi hermana/o va a correr al parque. _____
4. Mis abuelos comen en mi casa. _____
5. Discuto con mi papá. _____

6. Vendo mis libros viejos. _____
7. Abro mi libro de español. _____
8. Escribo mis trabajos en la computadora. _____
9. Vemos películas en casa. _____

Parte 2. Convierte las oraciones de **Parte 1** en preguntas para entrevistar a tu compañero/a.

> **¡Fíjate!**
> Remember that **nunca** and **casi nunca** go before the verb. The other expressions of frequency may go before or after the verb.

| Modelo | Leo el periódico.
—¿Con qué frecuencia lees el periódico?
—Casi nunca. ¿Y tú?
—Yo leo la sección deportiva todos los días. |

B. En casa de Ramón. Termina la descripción usando las ilustraciones.

1.

2.

3.

En la casa de Ramón tienen la misma rutina casi todos los sábados. Por la mañana, el papá de Ramón (1) _____, mientras que su mamá (2) _____ los cheques para pagar las cuentas *(pay the bills)*. Los hermanos menores siempre (3) _____ el refrigerador para buscar bebidas; generalmente (4) _____ Coca-Cola. A las dos de la tarde, toda la familia (5) _____ en su restaurante favorito: El Huarache Veloz. Después de comer, con frecuencia van a una tienda donde (6)_____ todo a muy buen precio. Los niños siempre quieren comprar juguetes *(toys)*.

4.

5.

6.

C. Manolo y su compañero de cuarto.

Parte 1. Escribe los verbos necesarios de la página 182 para completar el texto acerca de la
vida de Manolo y su compañero de cuarto.

Manolo, el amigo cubano de Sofía, no (1) _____ con su familia.
Sus padres (2) _____ en Miami, y él (3) _____
en California con un amigo. Manolo les (4) _____ correos
electrónicos a sus padres con frecuencia, pues es más barato[1] que llamarlos por
teléfono. Él también (5) _____ muchos correos electrónicos de
sus padres y de sus familiares de Cuba.

Manolo y Jorge, su compañero de cuarto, a veces (6) _____ de
política cubana. Pero en general, ellos tienen muchas cosas en común; por ejemplo,
la comida y el gusto por los libros.

A Jorge le gusta estar siempre en buena condición física[2]; por eso, él
(7) _____ dos millas todos los días. A Manolo no le gusta
(8) _____, pero le gusta jugar fútbol. Tanto Manolo como Jorge
desean estar saludables[3]; por eso, ellos siempre (9) _____
comida nutritiva y (10) _____ mucha agua[4].

[1]*cheaper* [2]**en...** *in good shape* [3]*healthy* [4]*water*

Parte 2. Ahora contesta las preguntas.

1. ¿Por qué Manolo escribe y recibe muchas cartas?
   _____

2. ¿Qué es importante para Manolo y Jorge?
   _____

3. ¿Qué hacen para estar en buena condición física?
   _____

Práctica adicional

Cuaderno de tareas
WB pp.198–200, C–G

Gramática 2

Identifying places to go and places to be
• <u>Ir a</u> + [*place*] and <u>estar en</u> + [*place*]

You have used the verbs **ir** and **estar** already. We praticed **ir a** to express the future (**Mañana voy a bailar con mis amigos**). **Ir** is also used to indicate where someone is going: **Siempre voy al Museo de Historia los jueves.** We used **estar** to find out how someone is, as in **¿Cómo estás? Estar** is also used to indicate where someone or something is located, as in **¿Dónde estás? Estoy en la escuela.** Notice that you need the preposition **en**.

Read the following examples to examine the present tense forms of **estar**.

Estar en	
Estoy en el Museo del Oro.	*I'm at the Museo del Oro.*
Estás en casa, ¿verdad?	*You're at home, right?*
El lago **está en** el centro del parque.	*The lake is in the center of the park.*
¿En qué museo **estamos**?	*What museum are we at?*
Uds. **están en** el Museo del Prado. Vosotros **estáis en** el Museo del Prado. }	*You are at the Prado Museum.*
Algunos cuadros de Picasso **están** **en** el Museo Nacional Reina Sofía.	*Some of Picasso's paintings are at the* *Reina Sofía National Museum.*

The verb **ir** usually requires the preposition **a.** Read the following examples.

Las personas van...	*People go...*
al parque	*to the park*
a los museos	*to the museums*
a la discoteca	*to the nightclub (disco)*
a las exhibiciones de arte	*to art exhibitions*

¡Fíjate!

Notice that **al** *(to the)* is used instead of **"a el"** before a masculine singular noun.

There are two contractions in Spanish: **al** and **del** (*from/of the*), both used before masculine singular nouns.

Wayne

a + el = al
Voy **al** cine con Sofía.

de + el = del
Voy a la oficina **del** profesor López.

Manolo

You have already learned the names of many places at the university or college. Here are some places where people can go in the city.

Más lugares en la ciudad	
(No) Voy...	*I (don't) go...*
al aeropuerto	*to the airport*
al boliche	*to the bowling alley*
al café	*to the café*
a la casa de mi novio/a	*to my boyfriend's/girlfriend's house*
a la casa de mis amigos /padres	*to my friends'/parents' house*
al centro comercial	*to the mall*
al cine	*to the movie theater*
a la discoteca	*to the nightclub (disco)*
al/a la doctor(a)	*to the doctor*
a la escuela	*to school*
a la exhibición de arte	*to the art exhibition*
a la iglesia /a misa	*to church/Mass*
al museo	*to the museum*
a ninguna parte	*nowhere*
al partido de fútbol	*to the soccer game*
a la playa	*to the beach*
a un restaurante	*to a restaurant*
al supermercado	*to the supermarket*
a la tienda	*to the store*
al trabajo	*to work*

¡Fíjate!

Do you remember the present tense of **ir**?
Voy a la escuela.
Vas a la cafetería.
Va al baño.
Vamos al salón.
Van al trabajo.

PRÁCTICA

D. Una llamada telefónica. Llama por teléfono a tu compañero/a para saber *(to find out)* dónde está y qué va a hacer allí. Empareja los lugares con las actividades.

Modelo   parque ⟶ correr dos millas
—¿**Dónde estás ahora?**
—**Estoy en el parque.**
—¿**Qué vas a hacer allí?**
—**Voy a correr dos millas.**

1. librería
2. casa de mi novio/a
3. supermercado
4. biblioteca
5. casa
6. cine
7. restaurante

a. mirar una película española
b. estudiar para un examen
c. comer con una amiga
d. comprar unos libros
e. leer el periódico
f. mirar la tele y descansar un rato
g. comprar la comida para la fiesta

E. ¿Es fácil localizarte? Indica dónde estás en los días y a las horas mencionadas. Después compara tus respuestas con las de tu compañero/a.

¿Dónde estás...   _____ Estoy en mi casa. _____

1. los lunes a las siete de la mañana?   _____

2. los miércoles a las diez de la mañana?   _____

3. los jueves a las dos de la tarde?   _____

4. los viernes por la noche?   _____

5. los sábados por la mañana?   _____

6. los domingos al mediodía?   _____

F. ¿Cuántas veces? *(How often?)*

Parte 1. En grupos de tres personas, contesten las preguntas para decidir quién es la persona **más activa** o **más tranquila**.

Nombres   _____   _____   _____

En el transcurso *(course)* de un mes, ¿con qué frecuencia...

1. vas al cine?   _____   _____   _____

2. comes en un restaurante?   _____   _____   _____

3. vas a las discotecas?   _____   _____   _____

4. vas al centro comercial?   _____   _____   _____

5. vas al parque?   _____   _____   _____

6. vas a casa de tus amigos? _____   _____   _____

7. vas al boliche?   _____   _____   _____

Parte 2. Ahora comparte la información con el resto de la clase. Usa expresiones como:

| **Modelo** | Nancy es la más activa porque va a las discotecas tres veces al mes. Larry es el más tranquilo porque nunca va al cine ni a las discotecas. |

G. ¿Adónde vas? Indica adónde vas en cada situación. Usa **voy**.

¡Fíjate!

When using **a ninguna parte** *(nowhere)*, place **no** before the verb. **Los domigos no voy a ninguna parte**.

¿Adónde vas...

1. cuando tienes ganas de beber algo? _____

2. cuando tienes que estudiar? _____

3. cuando tienes ganas de comer comida italiana? _____

4. cuando estás enfermo/a *(sick)*? _____

5. después de tus clases? _____

6. cuando no tienes ganas de hablar con nadie *(anybody)*? _____

7. cuando estás aburrido/a? _____

H. ¿Dónde estás ahora y adónde vas después? Usa las ilustraciones para indicar a tu compañero/a dónde están las personas ahora, adónde van después y por qué. Usa **tener ganas de, tener que** u otros verbos.

Mis hermanos pero después porque...

Modelo	Mis hermanos están en casa ahora, pero después van al aeropuerto porque tienen ganas de ver a sus abuelos de México.

1. Adriana pero después porque...

¡Fíjate!

Remember to use **en** after **estar** and **a** after **ir.**

2. Mi mamá pero después porque...

3. Yo pero después porque...

4. Mis amigas y yo pero después porque...

5. Mis compañeros de clase pero después porque...

Práctica adicional

Cuaderno de tareas
WB pp.201–204, H–N
LM pp.205–206, A–B, Pron.

Audio
CD-ROM
Episodio 8

Actividades comunicativas

Audio
CD-ROM

A. La historia va así.

Parte 1. Look carefully at each of the eight drawings. Then, as you listen to Wayne's plans for Saturday, identify the sequence of events by placing the numbers one through eight next to the appropriate image. Check your answers when you listen to Wayne's plans the second time.

Parte 2. En grupos de tres escriban la historia en diferente orden.

B. Submarino. First draw a submarine in five of the boxes on your grid. Then take turns asking your partner yes/no questions, matching an action pictured at the top of the grid with one of the subjects on the side.

Modelo　—¿Adriana lee el periódico todos los días?
　　　　—Sí, lee el periódico. *(If there is a submarine in that box.)*
　　　　　　　　　　or
　　　　—No, no lee el periódico. *(If there is not a submarine in that box.)*

Depending on your partner's answer, write **sí** or **no** in that box. If you answer **sí** to you partner's question, put an **X** through your submarine. It's been located! The first player to locate all five submarines wins.

¡Fíjate!

Be as creative as you can in your questions, using the frequency expressions on page 182. Don't just ask *do you drink?*, try *do you drink coffee frequently?* Put all the Spanish you know to use!!

Tú				
Tus primos				
Adriana				
Ustedes				

C. Cosas en común.

Parte 1. First answer the questions in the column labeled **Yo**. Then look for classmates whose answers are the same as yours and write their names in the column labeled **Compañero/a**.

Modelo	—¿Qué bebes en las fiestas?
	—Coca–Cola. ¿Y tú?
	—Yo también. or —Yo bebo agua.

	Compañero/a	Yo
1. Generalmente, ¿qué bebes en las fiestas?	_____	_____
2. ¿Con quién discutes más?	_____	_____
3. ¿Dónde vives?	_____	_____
4. ¿A qué hora comes los sábados?	_____	_____
5. ¿Qué vas a hacer hoy después de clase?	_____	_____
6. ¿A qué hora llegas a la escuela los martes?	_____	_____
7. ¿Recibes regalos el día de San Valentín?	_____	_____
8. ¿Dónde estás los lunes a las 8:00 de la mañana?	_____	_____
9. ¿Con quién sales los fines de semana?	_____	_____
10. ¿Con qué frecuencia haces ejercicio?	_____	_____

Parte 2. Be prepared to share your findings with the class.

| Modelo | —Lupe y yo bebemos Coca–Cola en las fiestas. |

D. ¡A hablar! In groups of four, find out who does the following activites at least three times a week: exercise, use the computer, read novels, sing or dance in a group, go out at night. Write the activity and the name(s) of the person/people in the appropriate columns.

Actividad	Persona(s)
_____	_____
_____	_____
_____	_____
_____	_____
_____	_____
_____	_____

La correspondencia

El correo: El regreso a la escuela. Lee las preguntas, luego lee la carta que Adriana le escribe a su hermana en Puerto Rico. Después contesta las preguntas.

1. ¿Cómo está Adriana?

_____

2. ¿Cómo son los compañeros según (*according to*) Adriana?

_____

3. ¿Por qué Adriana no tiene tiempo para cocinar ni limpiar?

_____

4. ¿Ahora quién tiene que lavar y cocinar?

_____

5. ¿Quién apoya y ayuda a Adriana?

_____

Querida hermana,   15 de octubre

¿Cómo estás? Yo estoy muy bien. Estudiar en la universidad es una experiencia fabulosa.

Éste es el segundo mes de clases y todavía[1] estoy muy nerviosa. Tengo clases muy interesantes, pero tengo que dedicar mucho tiempo a leer y estudiar.

Por suerte tengo unos compañeros de clase muy buenos y siempre me invitan a estudiar con ellos. Aunque[2] son muy jóvenes (tienen la edad de Carlos, ¿te imaginas?), son responsables e inteligentes, y siempre me incluyen en sus actividades.

Desafortunadamente para Santiago, ahora él tiene que cocinar y lavar, pues yo no tengo tiempo (ni ganas) para cocinar, limpiar y lavar. No le gusta mucho la situación. También creo que está un poco celoso[3] de mis actividades y mis nuevos amigos. Por suerte, a Viviana, Santiaguito y Carlos les gusta mucho que yo estudie, y por eso me apoyan y me ayudan[4] en la casa. Escríbeme pronto.

Tu hermana que te quiere,
Adriana

[1]*still* [2]*although* [3]*jealous* [4]***me...*** *support me and help me*

En papel: Los fines de semana. Write to Adriana about how you and your family and friends spend your weekends. Describe where you go, what you do at home, and how you prepare for school.

Invitación a **México**

Del álbum de
Sofía

Con más de 20 millones de habitantes, la Ciudad de México tiene muchos lugares que visitar los fines de semana. Puedes ir al Bosque de Chapultepec; también puedes visitar el Museo de Antropología, ver exposiciones o ir a la feria. Aquí se ve el Castillo de Chapultepec, la residencia presidencial hasta 1939. Ahora es el Museo Nacional de Historia.

Práctica adicional

Website
vistahigher
learning.com

Video
CD-ROM

Audio
CD-ROM

¡A ver de nuevo!

Parte 1. In your own words, write a description of what Ramón wants to do with Wayne at the park. Explain why he wants Wayne to go.

Ramón llama a Wayne por teléfono...

Parte 2. Now work with a partner to add any information you may have left out.

Práctica adicional		
Cuaderno de tareas WB p. 204, Ñ LM p. 206, A–B	Audio CD-ROM Episodio 8	Website vistahigher learning.com

Vocabulario del Episodio 8

Expresiones verbales

estar en	*to be (at)*
ir a + [*place*]	*to go to*
al	*to the*
a la (los, las)	*to the*

Más actividades: verbos **-er** e **-ir**

abrir	*to open*
beber	*to drink*
comer hamburguesas	*to eat hamburgers*
correr	*to run, jog*
discutir (de/con)	*to discuss, argue (about/with)*
escribir un trabajo	*to write a paper*
cartas	*letters*
hacer ejercicio	*to excercise*
la tarea	*to do homework*
leer el periódico	*to read the newspaper*
recibir correo electrónico	*to receive (get) e-mail*
regalos	*gifts*
salir a cenar	*to go out to dinner*
con los amigos	*with friends*
vender comida	*to sell food*
ver una película en casa	*to watch a movie at home*
vivir en/con	*to live in/with*

¿Con qué frecuencia...? *How often...?*

todos los días	*every day*
con frecuencia	*often*
a veces	*sometimes*
una vez a la semana	*once a week*
dos veces al mes	*twice a month*
tres (cuatro...) veces al año	*three (four...) times a year*
siempre	*always*
(casi) nunca	*(almost) never*

Los lugares en la ciudad *Places in the city*

el aeropuerto	*airport*
el boliche	*bowling alley*
el café	*café*
la casa de mi novio/a	*my boyfriend's/girlfriend's house*
la casa de mis amigos/padres	*my friends'/parents' house*

el centro comercial	*mall*
el cine	*movie theater*
la discoteca	*nightclub (disco)*
el/la doctor(a)	*doctor*
la escuela	*school*
la exhibición de arte	*art exhibition*
la iglesia/misa	*church/Mass*
el museo	*museum*
ninguna parte, (a)	*nowhere*
el parque	*park*
el partido de fútbol	*soccer game*
la playa	*beach*
el restaurante	*restaurant*
el supermercado	*supermarket*
la tienda	*store*
el trabajo	*work*

Vocabulario personal

Write the words you need to know to talk about the places you like to go to and the activities you like to do.

¡A escribir!

Episodio

8

Escenas de la vida: Vamos al parque

Video
CD-ROM

A. ¡A ver cuánto entendiste! See how much of the **Escena** you understood by matching the Spanish sentences with their English equivalents.

_____ 1. Hace mucho que no hacemos ejercicio juntos.

_____ 2. Además, ¿no quieres ver a Sofía?

_____ 3. Todo listo. Ya convencí a Wayne de ir al parque mañana.

_____ 4. ¿Qué, la usa mucho?

_____ 5. Bueno, ¿y cómo lo convenciste?

_____ 6. Le dije que Sofía muere por salir con él.

a. What, does he use it a lot?

b. I told him that Sofía is dying to go out with him.

c. Besides, don't you want to see Sofía?

d. We haven't exercised together for a while.

e. All done! I convinced Wayne to come to the park tomorrow.

f. Good, and how did you convince him?

Video
CD-ROM

B. Para el domingo. Use the expressions to complete Ramón and Wayne's conversation.

hago	comemos	corremos	vamos a
leo	corren	hacemos	ver

Wayne   Hello?

Ramón   Hey, Wayne. ¿ (1) _____ correr un par de millas al parque mañana? Hace mucho que no (2) _____ ejercicio juntos.

Wayne   No gracias. Por la mañana siempre (3) _____ mi tarea y (4) _____ mis correos tranquilamente, porque tengo clases toda la tarde y por la noche trabajo.

Ramón   Wayne, ¡mañana es domingo! Además…¿no quieres (5) _____ a Sofía? Ella y mi hermana (6) _____ todos los domingos.

Wayne   Hummm, ella es muy bonita.

Ramón   Sí, y no tiene novio.

Wayne   Está bien, pero con una condición…después, (7) _____ con las chicas en El Huarache Veloz.

Ramón   Perfecto.

> **Gramática 1**

Taking about common daily activities
• **Regular -er and ir verbs**

C. Actividades para todos. Use the expressions to complete the description of the park.

venden	restaurantes	leer	familias	celebrar
ejercicio	comer	museos	correr	discutir

Muchas personas van al parque de Chapultepec en la Ciudad de México a hacer

(1) _____ o van a (2) _____ alrededor del lago. Otros simplemente

van a descansar, estudiar, (3) _____, escribir o conversar bajo los árboles. Los

domingos muchas (4) _____ hacen picnics para (5) _____ cumpleaños

y aniversarios. Alrededor del lago (*lake*) hay bares, cafés y (6) _____ donde la

gente va a (7) _____, a beber y a escuchar música. Hay centros culturales

donde (8) _____ artesanía mexicana y recuerdos. Hay conciertos de música al

aire libre, exhibiciones en los (9) _____ y clases de pintura y teatro.

D. Más actividades. Sofía habla de las actividades de los fines de semana.
Escribe frases lógicas.

1. mis padres / leer / periódico / la mañana

_____

2. mi mamá / escribir / cartas

_____

Sofía

> **¡Fíjate!**
> Remember to conjugate the verbs appropriately!

3. yo / ver / películas / con Ana Mari / viernes

_____

4. Lalo nunca / abrir / libros / fines de semana

_____

5. Lalo y mi papá / discutir / porque / Lalo / ser / irresponsable

_____

6. por la noche nosotros / hacer / ejercicio / o escuchar / música

_____

E. Actividades frecuentes. Write a complete sentence describing each illustration. Include how often the activity takes place.

Modelo

Adriana a veces habla por teléfono con los clientes.

1.
2.
3.

1. Y tú, ¿ _____ ?
2. Adriana y su esposo _____
3. Wayne _____
4. Mis amigos y yo _____
5. Yo siempre _____
6. Los sobrinos de Ana Mari _____

4.
5.
6.

F. ¿Qué hacen? Write five true statements about your family, friends, or instructors using elements from the columns. If you like, add additional information.

Modelo   Mi amiga Angie come hamburguesas una vez a la semana.

	comer		
siempre	hacer la tarea	en la casa	una vez a la semana
a veces	salir con	hamburguesas	con frecuencia
casi nunca	leer novelas	amigos	todos los días
nunca	vivir con	novio/a	por la noche

1. _____
2. _____
3. _____
4. _____
5. _____

G. Las obligaciones y los deseos. Explain what the characters and you feel like doing but can't and why.

| Modelo | Adriana tiene ganas de descansar, pero no puede porque tiene que trabajar. |

1. Wayne _____

_____

_____

_____

2. Ana Mari y Ramón _____

_____

_____

_____

3. Manolo y yo _____

_____

_____

_____

Nombre _____ Fecha _____

Gramática 2

Identifying places to go and places to be
- **ir a** + [*place*] and **estar en** + [*place*]

H. ¿Adónde vas? Indicate where you go when you want to do the following things.

> **Modelo**   Voy **a la biblioteca** cuando tengo ganas de estudiar.

1. Voy _____ cuando tengo ganas de correr.

2. Voy _____ cuando tengo ganas de escuchar música.

3. Voy _____ cuando necesito hablar con un profesor.

4. Voy _____ cuando necesito comprar un regalo.

5. Voy _____ cuando llegan por avión mis familiares.

6. Voy _____ cuando necesito comprar la comida para toda la semana.

7. Voy _____ cuando tengo que trabajar.

8. Voy _____ cuando no tengo ganas de comer en mi casa.

I. ¿Cuándo vas? Write how often you go to the following places and explain why.

cine	casa de mis abuelos	iglesia (a misa)
trabajo	centro comercial	tienda de videos

> **Modelo**   aeropuerto
> **Nunca voy al aeropuerto porque toda mi familia vive aquí.**

1. _____

_____

2. _____

_____

3. _____

_____

4. _____

_____

5. _____

_____

6. _____

_____

J. ¿De quién son las cosas? Say to whom the following things belong. Use an element from each column.

	Modelo	Estos pacientes son del Dr. Pérez.	

gato
mochilas   del
oficina   es   de la
novela   son   de los
video   de las

profesor
estudiante de literatura
jugadores/as (*players*)
Sr. López
niño

> **¡Fíjate!**
> de + el = del
> **Del** is used to express *to whom* something belongs, often with the expression **ser de.**
> ¿Este coche nuevo es *del* hijo de Adriana?

1. _____
2. _____
3. _____
4. _____
5. _____

K. ¿Y a qué hora, Sofía? Sofía's mother always wants to know where her daughter is going and when she will come back. Complete the mother's questions and Sofía's answers, using contractions where necessary.

	Modelo	—¿A dónde vas Sofía? —Voy **al** cine. —¿Y a qué hora llegas **del** cine?

Sofía   **Mamá**

1. —Voy _____ casa de Ana Mari.
   —¿Y a qué hora llegas _____ ?

2. —Voy _____ biblioteca.
   —¿Y a qué hora llegas _____ ?

3. —Voy _____ trabajo.
   —¿Y a qué hora llegas _____ ?

4. —Voy _____ museo.
   —¿Y a qué hora llegas _____ ?

5. —Voy _____ exhibición de arte.
   —¿Y a qué hora llegas _____ ?

> **¡Fíjate!**
> **Del** indicates *where you arrive or return from*, with the expression **llegar de.**
> Vamos a llegar *del* aeropuerto a las dos.

L. ¿Dónde están? Sofía reveals where she and her friends are on different days and at different times. Complete her statements with the appropriate forms of **estar**.

1. Los lunes por la mañana, mis amigos y yo _____ en la clase de cálculo.

2. Los martes a las seis, la Sra. Barrón _____ en el trabajo.

3. Los miércoles por la tarde, generalmente Ramón y Wayne _____ en casa.

4. Los jueves a las doce, (yo) _____ en la clase de geología.

5. Y tú, ¿dónde _____ a esa hora?

M. ¡Adivina! (*guess*) Look at the images and write where the characters are now.

> **Modelo**
>
> Manolo va a hablar con el doctor.
> **Está en la clínica veterinaria.**

1. Sofía va a lavar su ropa.

_____

2. Ramón y yo vamos a mirar una película.

_____

3. Yo voy a hacer un poco de ejercicio.

_____

4. ¿Tú vas a ver a tus amigos?

_____

5. Adriana va a comprar la comida.

_____

6. Ana Mari va comprar ropa nueva.

_____

7. Adriana va a comprar libros para sus hijos.

_____

8. Wayne y Ramón van a tomar el sol.

_____

N. ¿Qué tienes que hacer? Explain what you have to do at each place using **tengo ganas de** or **tengo que**.

> **Modelo**   ¿Estás en el aeropuerto?
> **Sí porque tengo que llevar a Jorge; va a Miami.**

1. ¿Estás en la discoteca? _____

_____

2. ¿Estás en el parque? _____

_____

3. ¿Estás en la librería? _____

_____

4. ¿Estás en el supermercado? _____

_____

5. ¿Estás en la casa de tus padres? _____

_____

6. ¿Estás en un restaurante? _____

_____

Para terminar

Ñ. Una miniprueba para terminar. Complete the following communicative tasks to test your knowledge of the content of the episode.

1. Ask Sofía and Ana Mari:
    a. if they watch TVprograms in Spanish.
    b. how many times a week they run.
    c. if they argue with their parents.
    d. where they live.

2. Ask Adriana:
    e. if she sells her books at the end of the (**al final del**) semester.
    f. what she feels like doing this weekend.
    g. what her kids have to do on Sundays.

1.
  a. _____
  b. _____
  c. _____
  d. _____
2.
  e. _____
  f. _____
  g. _____

Episodio

¡A escuchar!

8

Comprensión

Audio
CD-ROM

A. Una sorpresa para Wayne. You are going to hear a phone conversation between Wayne and his former host family in Chile, where he went to study Spanish. Listen and select the best completion for each sentence. You will hear the conversation twice.

Wayne

1. Los Señores Iturbe llaman de Chile para…

    a. desearle a Wayne un feliz cumpleaños. b. invitar a Wayne a regresar a Chile.

2. El Señor Iturbe le pregunta a Wayne…

    a. ¿qué hacen sus padres?   b. ¿cómo están sus padres?

3. Ahora, Wayne tiene…

    a. 21 años.   b. 24 años.

4. La Sra. Iturbe desea…

    a. recibir una carta de Wayne.   b. ir a Estados Unidos a estudiar.

5. Wayne no escribe cartas porque…

    a. trabaja y estudia mucho.   b. no le gusta escribir cartas.

6. Si es posible, Wayne promete que…

    a. va a escribirles muchas cartas.   b. va a visitar Chile el año que viene.

Audio
CD-ROM

B. ¿Dónde están? You will hear cues indicating the locations of these people and things. Say where they are and then repeat each correct response after the speaker.

Modelo	You see:	**libros**
	You hear:	**librería**
	You say:	**Los libros están en la librería.**

    1. computadora   5. Manolo

    2. niños   6. Mis amigos y yo

    3. Sofía y Ana Mari   7. Yo

    4. Wayne y su amiga   8. Tú

Pronunciación

Audio CD-ROM

La p, la b y la v. The letters **p (pe)**, **b (be grande)**, and **v (ve chica)** are produced with both lips. The Spanish **p** sounds like English *p*, except that the lips are tighter and no puff of air is released. Hold your hand in front of your lips and say the English words *pat* and *puff*. You can feel the puff of air on your hand. Now, repeat these words and sentences after the speaker, being careful to hold your lips more tensely and not to release a puff of air.

Pablo	lápiz	Pablo pone el lápiz en el pupitre.
Perú	pluma	Paco Pérez practica el polo en Panamá.

The letters **b** and **v** in the Spanish alphabet have the same pronunciation. When they are the initial sound in a word, they sound like the English *b*. The lips touch and then release the sound.

boca	vestido
blusa	Venezuela
bikini	visitar

When Spanish **b** and **v** are not the initial sound in a word or phrase, they are pronounced with the lips touching lightly, allowing air to escape through.

abuelo	huevos	Vamos a visitar a la abuela.
rubio	avión	Su novia, Verónica, es rubia y bonita.

Más escenas de la vida

Adriana and her husband are arguing again. Listen to their conversation, then complete activities **A** and **B**. You will hear the conversation twice.

Audio CD-ROM

A. ¿Cómo ocurre? Organize these statements in chronological order, according to what you heard in the conversation.

____ 1. Van a la tienda de videos y ya está.
____ 2. No tengo ganas de ir a correr.
____ 3. Necesitas hacer ejercicio.
____ 4. ¿Adriana, vamos a correr?
____ 5. Vamos a salir a comer con papá.
____ 6. Tengo que escribir una composición.

Audio CD-ROM

B. Responde. Write the answers to the following questions.

1. ¿Adónde quiere ir Santiago? _____
2. ¿Por qué Adriana no puede? _____
3. ¿Adónde ya no va Adriana? _____
4. ¿Qué tiene ganas de hacer Adriana por la noche? _____
5. ¿Qué tienen que comprar en el supermercado? _____

Video
CD-ROM

Audio
CD-ROM

Objetivos comunicativos

In this episode, you will practice:

✓ talking about food

✓ discussing healthy eating habits

✓ ordering a meal

Escenas de la vida: ¡Qué rica comida!

A. ¡Mira cuánto puedes entender! Mira el video o escucha la **Escena** para contestar las preguntas.

1. ¿Qué comida llevan los chicos al parque?

sándwiches	carne para asar
salsa	pasteles puertorriqueños
refrescos	pastel
helado	flan
frutas	tortillas
verduras	arroz
guacamole	papas

2. ¿Cómo se prepara la carne en casa de Ramón? Selecciona los ingredientes.

Cultura a lo vivo

In the Spanish-speaking world, meals are important social events. **La comida,** the principal meal, usually begins at one and lasts until three in the afternoon. People generally go home to eat with family members and rest before returning to work for a few more hours. In Spain, for example, most small stores are closed between one and three so people can return home.

Since Spanish speakers like to relax and to enjoy the food and conversation, a meal in a restaurant may last as long as three hours. For this reason, it would be extremely rude for the server to bring the check after the meal has been served. Servers wait until the customer asks for the check.

3. ¿Qué comida pide Wayne cuando sale a comer?

4. ¿Qué comida sirven en El Rincón Caribeño?

a. mexicana   c. china

b. cubana   d. puertorriqueña

B. ¿Te diste cuenta? Indica si los comentarios son **ciertos** o **falsos**.

	Cierto	Falso
1. No es necesario ser puntual para las fiestas.	☐	☐
2. A Wayne le gusta mucho la comida puertorriqueña.	☐	☐
3. En México no hay chili.	☐	☐
4. Los pasteles puertorriqueños tienen plátano verde y carne.	☐	☐
5. El plato favorito de Manolo es arroz con carne de cerdo.	☐	☐
6. Los chicos están en el café.	☐	☐

C. El picnic. Contesta las preguntas.

1. ¿Por qué llegan tarde Ana Mari y Sofía? _____

2. ¿Quién sabe (knows) el secreto para preparar carne? _____

3. ¿Qué llevó Manolo al picnic? _____

4. ¿Qué pide Manolo en El Rincón Caribeño? _____

5. ¿Pica la salsa? _____

Práctica adicional
Cuaderno de tareas — WB p.227, A–B	Video CD-ROM Episodio 9

Para comunicarnos mejor

Vocabulario 1 | Talking about food • Food and meals

El desayuno

la leche
las peras
los plátanos
las uvas
las manzanas
el yogurt
el cereal
el café   los huevos   el pan tostado

El almuerzo

- los refrescos
- la sopa
- la limonada
- el jamón
- los sándwiches de atún
- la ensalada de lechuga y tomate
- las papas fritas
- el espagueti
- el pavo
- el pollo
- la sal y la pimienta
- las hamburguesas

También se dice...

refrescos ⟶ gaseosas

papas ⟶ patatas

plátanos ⟶ bananas, guineos

Cultura a lo vivo

In the Spanish-speaking world, table manners are important. It is disrespectful to start eating before everyone has been served, to put your elbows on the table, to speak with your mouth full, or to leave the table before everyone has finished eating. When leaving the table, Spanish speakers usually say **Con permiso, buen provecho** (*Excuse me*, and *bon appétit*).

Although the morning and evening meals vary from country to country, breakfast **(el desayuno)** and dinner **(la cena)** are generally light and less formal. Dinner or supper takes place between eight and ten in the evening, and often consists of leftovers from **la comida**, or coffee and bread.

Para hablar de las comidas en un restaurante

desayunar	*to have breakfast*	el plato/platillo	*dish*
comer	*to eat; to have lunch*	el/la mesero/a	*waiter/waitress*
cenar	*to have dinner/supper*	la cuenta	*bill*
tener hambre	*to be hungry*		
tener sed	*to be thirsty*		

La cena

el vino tinto

la cerveza

el agua

los dulces

el pastel

el helado

las galletas

la carne de cerdo

los camarones

las zanahorias

el brócoli

el arroz

las papas al horno

el bistec de res

la langosta

los frijoles

el pescado

Otro vocabulario

la bebida	*drink*	la fruta	*fruit*
la carne	*meat*	el jugo de naranja	*orange juice*
la carne de res	*beef*	los mariscos	*seafood*
la dona	*donut*	el postre	*dessert*
la ensalada de	*lettuce and tomato*	el queso	*cheese*
lechuga y tomate	*salad*	el té	*tea*
el flan	*flan*	la verdura	*vegetable*

PRÁCTICA

A. Asociaciones. ¿Qué platos y bebidas asocias con las siguientes comidas?

1. la comida china
2. la comida italiana
3. la comida mexicana
4. la comida norteamericana
5. la comida japonesa
6. la comida vegetariana

B. ¿Tienes una dieta saludable (*healthy*)? Marca con un círculo la mejor (*best*) respuesta según tus hábitos de comida.

Un "test" de nutrición

1. Generalmente, desayuno...
   a. leche y cereal.
   b. café y pan tostado.
   c. huevos con frijoles.
   d. nada.

2. Generalmente, ceno...
   a. pescado y verduras.
   b. pollo con arroz.
   c. espagueti, o arroz y frijoles.
   d. carne con papas.

3. En una fiesta prefiero beber...
   a. jugo.
   b. refresco.
   c. vino.
   d. cerveza.

4. Me gusta comer sándwiches de...
   a. atún.
   b. pavo.
   c. jamón y queso.
   d. mantequilla de cachuate[1] con mermelada.

5. Generalmente, para el almuerzo como...
   a. sopa y ensalada.
   b. un yogurt con fruta.
   c. un sándwich de jamón y queso.
   d. una hamburguesa con papas fritas.

6. Cuando tengo sed, bebo...
   a. agua.
   b. limonada.
   c. jugo de fruta.
   d. refrescos.

7. Mi postre favorito es...
   a. frutas.
   b. galletas.
   c. dulces.
   d. helado con pastel.

Convierte las letras en números
(1 por cada a, 2-b, 3-c, 4-d) y suma
tus preguntas.

marcador[2] _____

Interpreta tus resultados

De 7 a 14. ¡Bravo! Seguramente eres una persona consciente de la salud[3]. Tienes buenos hábitos de comida. Probablemente eres muy organizado/a y haces ejercicio regularmente.

De 15 a 22. ¡Muy bien! Probablemente eres una persona consciente de la salud, pero a veces sucumbes a la tentación de comer cosas con muchas calorías o grasas. Seguramente haces ejercicio para compensar.

De 23 a 28. ¡Qué barbaridad! Seguramente no tienes tiempo de preparar comidas saludables. Tienes que incluir en tu dieta más frutas y verduras. Debes evitar las cosas dulces y grasosas.

[1]*peanut butter* [2]*score* [3]*health*

C. Una entrevista. Entrevista a tu compañero/a para saber qué le gusta comer y beber. Usa el vocabulario de las páginas anteriores.

Modelo	—¿Te gusta comer verduras?	—¿Te gusta beber leche?
	—Sí, me gusta. Y, ¿a ti?	—No, no me gusta. Y, ¿a ti?
	—A mí también. *or* —A mí no.	—A mí tampoco. *or* —A mí sí.

D. La pirámide de la salud. Primero indica cuántas porciones comes de las siguientes categorías. Luego lee *La pirámide de la salud* para completar la información y determinar si llevas una dieta saludable.

Generalmente como...

1. _____ porciones de frutas.

2. _____ porciones de carnes.

3. _____ porciones de verduras.

4. _____ porciones de panes y cereales.

5. _____ porciones de productos lácteos.

6. _____ porciones de dulces y grasas.

La pirámide de la salud

Aceites[1], dulces y grasas[2]
moderadamente

Productos lácteos
- leche y yogurt
- queso
- crema
- queso crema

de 2 a 3 porciones

Carnes blancas y rojas, pescado, huevos y frijoles
- carne o pollo
- pescado asado
- 1 taza de frijoles o chícharos

de 2 a 3 porciones

Verduras
- verduras cocidas o frescas
- ensaladas

de 3 a 5 porciones

Frutas
- jugos de frutas
- ensaladas de frutas

de 2 a 4 porciones

Panes y cereales
- arroz
- pastas
- galletas
- tortillas
- 1 rebanada de pan integral
- cereal

de 6 a 11 porciones

[1]oil [2]fat

En un día, tienes que comer...

1. de 2 a 3 porciones de _____ .

2. de 2 a 3 porciones de _____ .

3. de 2 a 4 porciones de _____ .

4. de 6 a 11 porciones de _____ .

5. de 3 a 5 porciones de _____ .

Ahora compara lo que tienes que comer con lo que generalmente comes para completar la información.

6. Necesito comer más _____ .

7. Necesito comer menos _____ .

8. En general, tengo una dieta balanceada/deficiente.

E. Un menú saludable. You have realized that you are not eating a balanced diet. Using the food pyramid on page 212, write out a balanced menu that includes breakfast, lunch, dinner, and beverages.

Banco de palabras

un vaso de
a glass of

un taza de
a cup of

un pedazo de
a piece of

una rebanada de
a slice of

¡Fíjate!

Write your menu on card stock so your instructor can share it with the class.

F. Los hábitos alimenticios del grupo. En grupos de tres, contesten las preguntas para hacer un resumen de los hábitos alimenticios de sus compañeros.

1. ¿Qué desayunan generalmente? _____

2. ¿Qué cenan? _____

3. ¿Qué beben cuando tienen sed? _____

4. ¿Qué comen cuando tienen mucha hambre? _____

5. ¿Con qué frecuencia comen comida chatarra *(junk food)*? _____

6. ¿Cuáles son sus frutas y verduras favoritas? _____

7. ¿Qué tipo de comida prefieren? ¿Cuál es su plato favorito? _____

_____

G. Una madre preocupada. The mother of a six-year-old boy is concerned that her son may not have a balanced diet. Listen to the conversation between the doctor and the mother. As you listen, use the food pyramid to place a check next to the food group the mother mentions as part of her son's diet. Then decide whether her son's diet is healthy or not; formulate recommendations for them. Discuss your opinion with a classmate.

¿Come/bebe suficiente(s)...	Sí	No
1. frutas?	☐	☐
2. verduras?	☐	☐
3. carnes?	☐	☐
4. productos lácteos?	☐	☐
5. agua?	☐	☐
6. pan y cereales?	☐	☐

Recomendaciones para la madre:

_____

_____

_____

Práctica adicional

Cuaderno de tareas
WB pp.228–230, C–F

Gramática 1 ▷ Ordering a meal
• <u>Pedir</u> and <u>servir</u>

Analizar y descubrir

In the conversation, you heard the following:

¿Por qué siempre **pides** chili?	*Why do you always order chili?*
Ahí siempre **pido** arroz con pollo.	*I always order chicken with rice there.*
También **sirven** comida cubana.	*They also serve Cuban food.*

Pides, pido, and **sirven** are forms of the stem-changing verbs **pedir** *(to ask for, order a meal)* and **servir** *(to serve).*

1. Read the following examples to complete the conjugation of the verb **pedir.**

Pedir	
¿Desea **pedir** algo más?	*Do you want to order something else?*
Nunca **pido** el plato más caro del menú.	*I never order the most expensive dish on the menu.*
¿Qué **pides** cuando cenas aquí?	*What do you order when you eat dinner here?*
Ana Mari a veces **pide** postre.	*Ana Mari sometimes orders dessert.*
¿**Pedimos** vino para todos?	*Should we order wine for everyone?*
Ustedes siempre **piden** lo mismo. Vosotros siempre **pedís** lo mismo. }	*You always order the same thing.*
Ellos siempre **piden** la cuenta primero.	*They always ask for the bill first.*

2. Read the following examples to complete the conjugation of the verb **servir.**

Servir	
¿Qué van a **servir?**	*What are you going to serve?*
Casi nunca **sirvo** nada tan tarde.	*I almost never serve anything so late.*
Y tú, ¿qué **sirves?**	*And what do you serve?*
Mi mamá siempre nos **sirve** un desayuno grande.	*My mom always serves us a big breakfast.*
En casa **servimos** tamales para las fiestas.	*At home we serve tamales for parties.*
Y ustedes, ¿qué **sirven?** Y vosotros, ¿qué **servís?** }	*And what do you serve?*
¿Con qué **sirven** el bistec aquí?	*What do they serve the steak with here?*

3. Now complete the conjugations of **pedir** and **servir**.

	Pedir	Servir
yo	_____	_____
tú	_____	_____
usted/él/ella	_____	_____
nosotros/as	_____	_____
vosotros/as	pedís	servís
ustedes/ellos/as	_____	_____

4. In which forms of **pedir** and **servir** does the **-e-** of the infinitive change to an **-i-**?

_____

5. In which forms does the **-e-** remain unchanged? _____

PRÁCTICA

H. Recomendaciones. En grupos de tres personas, hagan (make) recomendaciones sobre los mejores lugares de la ciudad para comer. Incluye muchos detalles. Después comparte tu opinión con tus compañeros.

> **Modelo** comida italiana
> **Si tienes ganas de comer comida italiana, tienes que ir al Mamma Lucia. El restaurante está en la calle/avenida…. Generalmente pido la pizza vegetariana. También sirven un espagueti delicioso.**

1. comida mexicana (cubana, china, japonesa, etc.)
2. hamburguesas
3. espagueti
4. pastel de chocolate
5. desayunos
6. café
7. helados
8. ensaladas

I. Adriana y Santiago van a cenar. Usa las siguientes palabras para completar el diálogo entre el mesero, Adriana y Santiago.

ensalada	mariscos	pides	cerveza	pido
servir	vino	pedir	pescado	sirven

Mesero   Buenas tardes, señores. ¿Están listos para (1) _____?

Adriana   Pues más o menos. ¿Qué nos recomienda?

Mesero   Bueno, la especialidad de la casa es el pescado y los (2) _____.

Santiago   ¿Con qué (3) _____ el filete de pescado?

Mesero   Lo servimos con arroz y verduras. Tenemos un pescado excelente.

Adriana   Yo no tengo ganas de comer (4) _____ hoy. Voy a pedir carne.

Santiago   ¿Por qué no pedimos una (5) _____ César para los dos? Tú (6) _____ un filete miñón y yo (7) _____ el filete de pescado.

Adriana   También queremos una botella de (8) _____ tinto. Gracias.

J. ¿Qué te gusta hacer? En grupos de tres personas, hablen de las cosas que comen en algunas ocasiones especiales (cumpleaños, aniversarios, graduaciones, etc.). Incluyan en su conversación:

- qué hacen, adónde van, con quién, qué sirven en casa
- cuando van a restaurantes, qué piden, cuál es su plato favorito
- si van al parque, a qué parque van, qué hacen allí

K. En el restaurante. En grupos de tres personas, escriban las conversaciones entre las personas; inventen todos los detalles. Después actúen los diálogos para el resto de la clase.

Primera conversación

_____

_____

_____

_____

Segunda conversación

_____

_____

_____

_____

Invitación a **Argentina**

Del álbum de
Sofía

Argentina tiene aproximadamente 38 millones de habitantes y es famosa por su carne, el mate y el tango. La carne de res es uno de los platos principales de la comida argentina. El mate (un té verde) es la bebida argentina por excelencia, aunque se bebe en Uruguay y otros países también. Para beber mate, se necesita una taza (cup) especial y un popote (straw) metálico.

Práctica adicional		
Cuaderno de tareas WB p.230, G–H LM pp.233–234, A–B, Pron.	Audio CD-ROM Episodio 9	Website vistahigher learning.com

Actividades comunicativas

A. Crucigrama.

Instrucciones para Estudiante 1

Complete the crossword puzzle by testing your partner's knowledge of foods and drinks. You each have a different half of the puzzle. Read the definitions so that your partner can guess the missing words. Take turns until the puzzle is complete.

The crossword grid contains the following filled-in letters:

- 1 (vertical, starting top): J, U, G, O
- 2 (vertical): F, R, I, J, O, L, E, S
- 3 (vertical): H, U, E, V, O, S
- 4 (vertical): J, A, M, Ó, N
- 5 (vertical): A, L, M, U, E, R, Z, O
- 7 (vertical): C, O, M, I, D, A
- 8 (vertical): L
- 9 (vertical): C, E, R, E, A, L
- 10 (vertical): P, O, L, L, O
- 11: A
- 12 (vertical): C, A, F, É
- 13 (vertical): D, E, S, A, Y, U, N, O
- 14 (vertical): C, A, R, N, E
- 15 (vertical): R, E, F, R, E, S, C, O, S
- 16: E
- 17: Y
- 19: (horizontal row)

Definiciones

Verticales:

1. Una bebida de fruta común para el desayuno.
2. Se sirven con la comida mexicana; son pequeños y negros o cafés.
3. Se comen fritos o en omelet; son ricos en colesterol.
4. Es común hacer sándwiches de _____ y queso.
5. La comida del mediodía.
7. Todo lo que comemos; los alimentos.
9. Se come en el desayuno con leche; tiene fibra.
10. Lo que se come en KFC.
12. Una bebida similar al té.
13. La primera comida del día.
14. Los vegetarianos nunca comen _____ .
15. La Coca-Cola y el 7-UP son _____ .

A. Crucigrama.

Instrucciones para **Estudiante 2**

Complete the crossword puzzle by testing your partner's knowledge of foods and drinks. You each have a different half of the puzzle. Read the definitions so that your partner can guess the missing words. Take turns until the puzzle is complete.

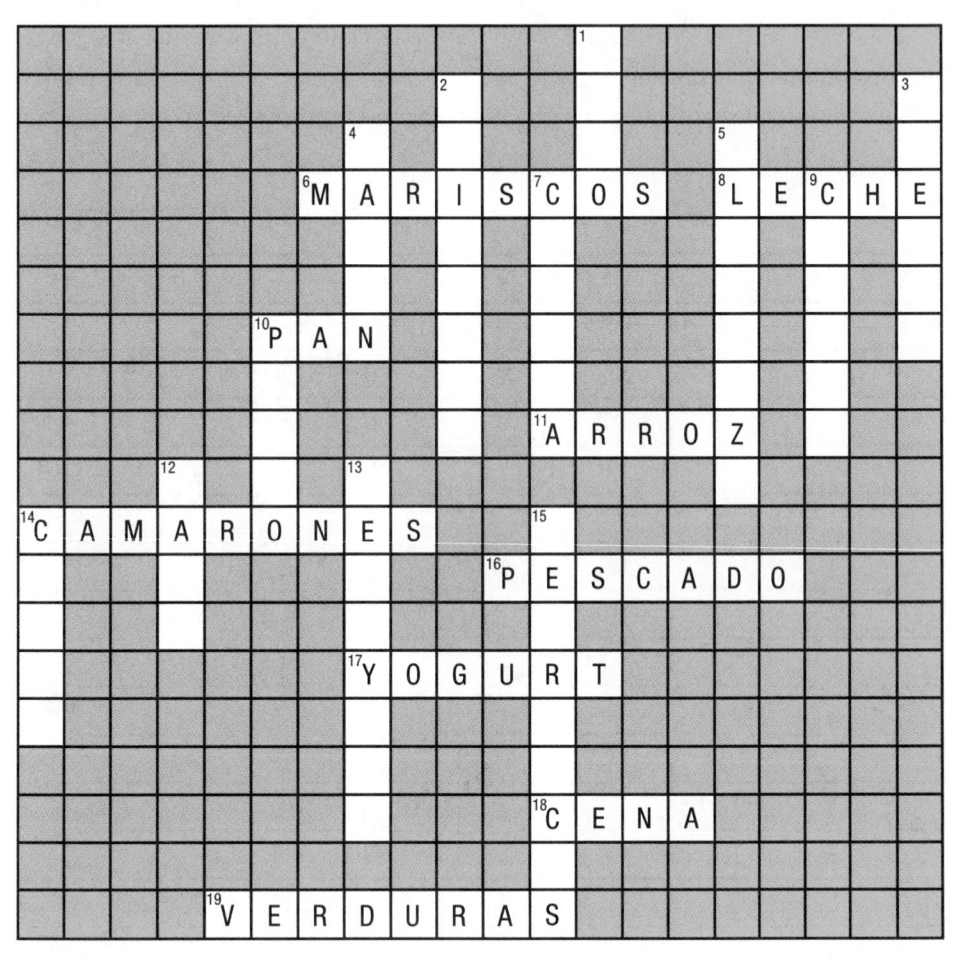

Definiciones

Horizontales:

6. Los camarones y la langosta son _____ .

8. Una bebida blanca; tiene calcio.

10. Se necesita para hacer un sándwich.

11. Se usa mucho en la comida china; es blanco.

14. Un marisco pequeño y caro (en la forma plural).

16. Vive en el agua; se come en filetes.

17. Un producto lácteo; se come con o sin frutas.

18. La última comida del día.

19. Tienen vitaminas; no son dulces; generalmente son verdes.

B. Diferencias.

Instrucciones para **Estudiante 1**

Hay varias diferencias entre tu restaurante y el restaurante de tu compañero/a. Para encontrar las diferencias, necesitas describir qué hay en el restaurante, qué comen o beben las personas, qué piden o qué sirven los meseros; anota siete diferencias.

Modelo	Hoy hay helado de chocolate en las especiales del día.

B. Diferencias.

Instrucciones para **Estudiante 2**

Hay varias diferencias entre tu restaurante y el restaurante de tu compañero/a. Para encontrar las diferencias, necesitas describir qué hay en el restaurante, qué comen o beben las personas, qué piden o qué sirven los meseros; anota siete diferencias.

Modelo Hoy hay helado de chocolate en las especiales del día.

Especiales
del día
Camarones
a la diabla $19.45
Langosta
termidor $41.95
Helado de
chocolate $2.45

C. Un programa de intercambio.

Instrucciones para **Estudiante 1**

You are considering becoming a host family for an international student. Interview the student applying to stay at your home for a summer immersion program. Based on their responses, decide if you wish to accept this student.

Find out about the student's:

- activities
- eating habits and dietary requirements
- family and hometown or country
- personality traits

¡Fíjate!

You may take time to prepare written questions for your partner before you begin this activity, i.e. ¿Te gusta bailar? ¿Qué te gusta comer? ¿Haces ejercicio?, etc.

C. Un programa de intercambio.

Instrucciones para **Estudiante 2**

You are applying for an exchange program and are being interviewed by a prospective host. Based on this interview, you will decide if you will stay with this family or look for another one. Answer all the questions you are asked, and ask a few of your own.

Ask about:

- the members of the host family
- their activities
- their eating habits
- anything else you think may be important

¡Fíjate!

You may take time to prepare written questions for your partner before you begin this activity, i.e. ¿Cuántas personas viven en la casa? ¿Cuántos años tienen? ¿Salen con frecuencia?, etc.

La correspondencia

 El correo: La Estancia Santa Gertrudis. A friend of yours wants to go to a place to relax, eat a healthy diet, and relieve stress. She found this brochure in Spanish. First, read the questions. Then read the brochure for her and answer the questions in English.

1. Where is the resort? _____

2. What is the spa like? _____

3. What is the food like? _____

4. What are the daily activities? Describe them. _____

_____

5. What do you think are some special features of this spa? Would it be a place for relaxation and meditation? Why? _____

Reading Strategy: Scanning for specific information

When reading a Spanish text for specific information, you can disregard information that does not correspond to your purpose for reading. Be content with understanding the overall meaning. *Scan* the text—that is, locate and read carefully only the information you are looking for. For example, in the following article, you need to know where **la Estancia Santa Gertrudis** is. *Scan* the first paragraph to locate the country or state. Be sure to read the questions first so you know what specific information you are looking for. Remember to look for cognates to help you understand the text.

Lo último en salud y descanso:

Un fin de semana en la Estancia Santa Gertrudis

La Estancia Santa Gertrudis es un spa ecológico de 1.660 hectáreas, con enormes arboledas,[1] un lago de 200 hectáreas y actividades para todos los gustos. Está localizada en el partido[2] de Chascomús, a 165 kilómetros de la capital, en Argentina. La estancia recibe un máximo de diez personas cada fin de semana: seis en la casa principal y cuatro en la casa de huéspedes.[3]

En un oasis de tranquilidad, comida saludable, ejercicio diario, safaris fotográficos, observación de varias clases de animales silvestres, la Estancia Santa Gertrudis es una "opción ideal para un fin de semana saludable y activo".

Las actividades del día incluyen caminatas alrededor del lago, fútbol, natación, caballos, bicicletas y, la especialidad de la casa, clases de yoga (método Iyengar).

La comida es natural y casera, elaborada con harinas integrales, verduras cultivadas en la estancia y, para quienes lo deseen, carne ecológica de producción propia. Por la tarde, usted puede descansar en la vieja arboleda que rodea la casa, leer, conversar con los otros huéspedes, remar[4] en el lago o simplemente relajarse.

Un fin de semana de dieta saludable, ejercicio diario, descanso total y cuidados especiales hacen que usted se sienta[5] extraordinariamente bien y feliz.

Para recibir más información, llame a Darío Sarachaga, teléfono (0242) 3-21-33, fax 8-06-14.

[1]forests [2]state or province [3]guests [4]row [5]you feel

En papel: Una visita por la ciudad. A good friend of yours from high school is coming to visit you for a week next month. Write a letter telling your friend what you have planned during their stay—places you will visit, activities you have planned, new restaurants you will go to, and so on.

> **Writing Strategy: Recombining learned material**
>
> As your ability to communicate in Spanish increases, you will be able to link the words and phrases you know to express more complex messages. When responding to a writing task—in this case, a letter to a friend, you should devise an appropriate plan to organize your ideas effectively. First, determine the information that needs to be included in the letter. Then identify the places you want to go. Organize your letter by linking those places with activities you plan to do. Finally, write your letter.

¡A ver de nuevo!

Parte 1. Escribe un resumen del episodio. Incluye la comida que llevan al parque y las cosas que les gusta comer.

En este episodio Sofía y sus amigos van al parque porque...

Parte 2. Después trabaja con un(a) compañero/a para añadir más información.

Práctica adicional		
Cuaderno de tareas WB pp.231–232, I–J LM p.234, A–B	Audio CD-ROM Episodio 9	Website vistahigher learning.com

Vocabulario del Episodio 9

Para hablar de las comidas

desayunar	*to have breakfast*	el almuerzo	*lunch*
comer	*to eat; to have lunch*	la cuenta	*bill, check*
cenar	*to have dinner/supper*	el/la mesero/a	*waiter/waitress*
pedir (e → i)	*to ask (for), order* (a meal)	el plato/platillo	*dish*
servir (e → i)	*to serve*		
tener hambre	*to be hungry*		
tener sed	*to be thirsty*		

La comida

Un desayuno internacional *An international breakfast*

el cereal	*cereal*	la fruta	*fruit*
la dona	*donut*	la manzana	*apple*
el huevo	*egg*	la pera	*pear*
el pan tostado	*toast*	el plátano	*banana*
el yogurt	*yogurt*	la uva	*grape*

Un almuerzo norteamericano *An American lunch*

la ensalada de lechuga y tomate	*lettuce and tomato salad*
el espagueti	*spaghetti*
la hamburguesa	*hamburger*
el jamón	*ham*
las papas fritas	*French fries*
el pavo	*turkey*
la pimienta	*pepper*
el pollo	*chicken*
el queso	*cheese*
la sal	*salt*
el sándwich de atún	*tuna sandwich*
la sopa	*soup*

La cena *Dinner*

el arroz	*rice*	la carne de res	*beef*
el bistec de res	*roast beef*	la langosta	*lobster*
los camarones	*shrimp*	los mariscos	*seafood*
la carne de cerdo	*pork*	el pescado	*fish*

225

Las verduras *Vegetables*

el brócoli	*broccoli*
los frijoles	*beans*
la papa al horno	*baked potato*
la zanahoria	*carrot*

Postres *Desserts*

los dulces	*candy, sweets*
el flan	*flan*
las galletas	*cookies*
el helado	*ice cream*
el pastel	*cake*

Las bebidas *Drinks*

el agua	*water*
el café	*coffee*
la cerveza	*beer*
el jugo de naranja	*orange juice*
la leche	*milk*
la limonada	*lemonade*
los refrescos	*sodas*
el té	*tea*
el vino tinto	*red wine*

Vocabulario personal

Write all the words you need to know in Spanish so that you can better talk about your eating habits and the foods you like/dislike.

Episodio

¡A escribir!

9

Escenas de la vida: ¡Qué rica comida!

Video
CD-ROM

A. ¡A ver cuánto entendiste! See how much of the **Escena** you understood by matching the Spanish sentences with their English equivalents.

_____ 1. Es hora latina.

_____ 2. La carne está muy buena.

_____ 3. Para fiestas no es necesario ser puntual.

_____ 4. El secreto es prepararla la noche anterior.

_____ 5. Si no es el trabajo.

_____ 6. ¡Ya era hora!

_____ 7. Eso dice mi papá.

_____ 8. La salsa no pica nada.

a. For parties, it's not necessary to be punctual.

b. The secret is to prepare it the night before.

c. It's about time!

d. But it's not work.

e. The meat is very good.

f. The sauce isn't at all hot.

g. It's Latin time.

h. That's what my dad says.

Video
CD-ROM

B. Todos en el parque. Order the statements so that the dialogue makes sense.

_____ a. El secreto para que la carne esté perfecta es prepararla la noche anterior con cerveza, sal y limón. Bueno, eso dice mi papá.

_____ b. Ana Mari, ¿pica la salsa?

__1__ c. La carne está muy buena.

_____ d. Tu papá tiene razón. Me gusta mucho la comida mexicana.

_____ e. No, no pica nada.

_____ f. ¿Entonces por qué siempre pides chili? En México no hay chili.

_____ g. *No way!*

Vocabulario 1 ➤ **Talking about food**
• **Food and meals**

C. Las categorías. Your ten-year-old niece has asked you to help her with her school project on food groups in Spanish. Fill in each of the categories with the names of foods in Spanish.

Frutas

_____

_____

_____

_____

_____

_____

Productos lácteos

_____

_____

_____

_____

_____

_____

Postres

_____

_____

_____

_____

_____

_____

Verduras

_____

_____

_____

_____

_____

_____

D. Cuerpo sano, mente sana. *(Healthy body, healthy mind.)* Look at the foods in the illustrations. Then write the foods you consider healthy under **Saludable** and write the reason why each is considered good: vitamins **(vitaminas)**, proteins **(proteínas)**, calcium **(calcio)**, or low in fat **(poca grasa)**. Under **No muy saludable,** list the foods and beverages that are high in fat **(grasa),** sugar **(azúcar),** salt **(sal),** or cholesterol **(colesterol)**.

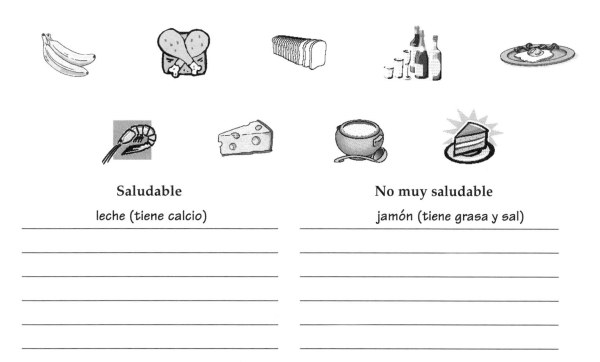

Saludable	No muy saludable
leche (tiene calcio)	jamón (tiene grasa y sal)
_____	_____
_____	_____
_____	_____
_____	_____
_____	_____

E. Tres menús. You are planning three different breakfasts for the restaurant where you work. Write down the appropriate foods and beverages.

Un desayuno norteamericano
_____
_____
_____
_____
_____

Un desayuno dominguero (Sunday brunch)
_____
_____
_____

Un desayuno ligero
_____
_____
_____
_____

F. Las definiciones. Write the food item that best fits the description.

> **Modelo**   La comida favorita de los chimpancés.   **Los plátanos.**

1. Una bebida anaranjada *(orange)*, no tiene alcohol. _____
2. Son unas verduras anaranjadas. A Bugs Bunny le gustan. _____
3. Es un marisco rojo muy caro. _____
4. Un pescado que se usa para hacer sándwiches. _____
5. Tienes que beber ocho vasos de este líquido al día. _____
6. A los niños les gusta mucho; es frío, de chocolate o vainilla. _____
7. Escribe dos ejemplos de carne. _____
8. Es la comida más popular para *Thanksgiving*. _____
9. Un plato de verduras frescas. _____
10. De esta bebida, hay tinto, blanco y rosado. _____

Gramática 1

Ordering a meal
• Pedir and servir

G. ¡Qué desastre! Lalo and Santiaguito are working at a cafeteria during their vacation. Since they are both easily distracted, they bring the wrong things to Sofía and her friends. Describe this disaster by completing the sentences with the appropriate forms of **pedir** and **servir**. (Note: **me** means *[to] me*, **te** means *[to] you*, **le** means *[to] him/her*, and **les** means *[to] them*.).

> **Modelo**   Los niños **piden** una pizza de queso, pero Lalo les **sirve** una pizza vegetariana.

1. Sofía _____ un café, pero Santiaguito le _____ un té.
2. Adriana y Ana Mari _____ frutas, pero los chicos les
   _____ pastel.
3. Yo _____ pastel, pero ellos me _____ yogurt.
4. Nosotras _____ limonadas para todas, pero Lalo nos
   _____ refrescos.
5. ¿Tú _____ helado de fresa? ¡De seguro *(for sure)*, Lalo y Santiaguito
   te van a _____ helado de vainilla!

H. ¡Vamos a cenar! Imagine you are at an Argentinian restaurant. Answer the waiter's questions.

1. Buenas noches, ¿está listo para pedir? _____
2. ¿Y quiere pedir algo *(something)* antes del plato principal? _____
3. ¿Quiere beber un café o un refresco? _____
4. ¿Va a pedir postre? _____

Para terminar

I. ¡ Vivir bien con poca grasa[1]! Lee las preguntas, después lee el anuncio de libro *Vivir bien con poca grasa* y responde a las preguntas.

1. ¿Qué beneficios puede tener el comer con poca grasa? _____
_____

2. ¿Qué ayuda a que la grasa se queme más rápidamente? _____

3. ¿Qué actividad hace que engordemos *(makes us get fat)*? _____

¡Disfrute[2] de la mejor salud de toda su vida!
Una vez que usted viva con poca grasa, su calidad de vida
va a mejorar inmediatamente. Va a tener mejor humor y más
energía. Va a dejar de[3] preocuparse por su peso y va a
comenzar a disfrutar de los beneficios de un cuerpo más delgado
y sano, sin los peligros propios[4] de las dietas. ¡No se tarde más!
Envíe el **Certificado de Inspección GRATUITA ¡hoy mismo!**

INSPECCIÓN GRATUITA DE 21 DÍAS

Secreto
para
controlar la
GRASA
automáticamente

Nº 1

Tomar agua puede ayudar a reducir los depósitos de
grasa. Cuando usted está totalmente hidratada su
cuerpo transporta más rápidamente la grasa a los
músculos para ser quemada[5] allí. En la PÁGINA 107
de VIVIR BIEN CON POCA GRASA, descubra cómo
el AGUA HELADA puede servir durante todo el día
como ¡SÚPER estimulante de la combustión de grasa!

Secreto
para
controlar la
GRASA
automáticamente

Nº 2

La TV hace aumentar de peso: Increíble, pero es ¡la
pura verdad! Estar sentada[6] delante del televisor la
hace engordar más que el estar solamente sentada.
Además, si usted mira TV por 4 horas o más, es DOS
VECES más probable que sufra[7] de sobrepeso. Antes
de prender[8] el "control de producción de grasa" de su
televisor, lea la PÁGINA 71 para saber cuántas horas
de televisión puede usted mirar.

---

[1]*fat* [2]*enjoy* [3]**dejar**... *stop* [4]**peligros**... *inherent risks* [5]*burned* [6]*sitting* [7]*suffer* [8]*turn on*

J. Una miniprueba para terminar. Give Ramón the following information about yourself. Write it in the form of a paragraph. Then write how you would ask him for the information in **2.** Remember that you have to create the questions that would ellicit the information you need.

1. Tell Ramón: a. about your eating habits.

                    b. the places you usually go after school.

                    c. who you live with.

                    d. everything you are going to do tomorrow.

2. Ask Ramón: e. what they serve at his home for dinner.

                    f. what his favorite dish is.

                    g. what he usually eats between meals (**entre comidas**).

                    h. where he goes when he feels like eating his favorite food.

                    i. if he has to work on Sundays.

1. _____

_____

_____

_____

_____

_____

_____

_____

_____

2. e. _____

f. _____

g. _____

h. _____

i. _____

Episodio

| ¡A escuchar! |

9

Comprensión

Audio
CD-ROM

A. Categorías. You will hear a list of food and drinks. As you hear each item, write its name in the appropriate category. You will hear the list twice.

Bebidas	Desayuno	Almuerzo o cena	Postres
_____	_____	_____	_____
_____	_____	_____	_____
_____	_____	_____	_____
_____	_____	_____	_____
_____	**Frutas**	_____	
_____	_____	_____	
_____	_____		
_____	_____		

Audio
CD-ROM

B. ¡A comer! Sofía and Manolo are going out to eat. You are going to hear them place their orders. As they speak to the server, write down their orders. You will hear the conversation twice.

Sofía

Manolo

Sofía

Plato principal: _____ con _____ y _____

Bebida: _____ Postre: _____

Manolo

Plato principal: _____ con _____ y _____

Bebida: _____ Postre: _____

Pronunciación

La *c*, la *z*, *que* y *qui*. The letter **c (ce)** has three sounds. **C** followed by **a, o, u,** or any consonant is pronounced as *k*. When **c** is followed by **e** or **i,** it is pronounced as *s* in Latin America and *th* in most parts of Spain. Listen and repeat these words, phrases, and sentences after the speaker as a Latin American would.

Cuba	**calculadora**	**ciencia**	**a veces**
Compro cinco cuadernos para la clase.		**Carmen come cereal con calcio.**	

The letter **z (zeta)** always has the sound of *s* in Latin American Spanish, and always has the sound of *th* in Spanish from Spain.

zanahorias	**almorzar**	**Venezuela**	**lápiz**	**perezoso**
No como zanahorias.			**Almorzamos y tomamos una cerveza.**	

Now, listen to the same words and sentences spoken by a speaker from Spain.

In Spanish, the sounds **ke** and **ki** are represented in writing by **que** and **qui** respectively.

¿qué?	**química**	**máquina**	**aquí**	**chaqueta**
¿Por qué quiere esquiar aquí?			**¿De quién es la chaqueta?**	

Más escenas de la vida

Sofía, Ana Mari, Manolo, and Wayne are eating at a Caribbean restaurant. Listen to their conversation, and complete activities **A** and **B**. You will hear the conversation twice.

A. Definiciones. Describe the following dishes based on the conversation.

1. El lechón es... _____

2. El congrí es... _____

3. La ropa vieja es... _____

4. Un postre cubano es... _____

B. Responde. Write the answers to the following questions.

1. ¿Qué plato sirven que es espectacular?

_____

2. ¿Qué va a pedir Sofía? _____

3. ¿Qué va a pedir Ana Mari?

_____

4. ¿Qué plato es similar a la machaca mexicana?

_____

5. ¿Qué va a pedir Wayne? _____

Episodio 10

Escenas de la vida: Una invitación confusa

Video
CD-ROM

Audio
CD-ROM

A. ¡Mira cuánto puedes entender! As you listen, indicate who makes the following statements: Wayne (**W**), Sofía (**S**), or Ana Mari (**AM**).

La película empieza a las 8:30. _____

Podemos **tomar café antes de la película**. _____

¿Ana Mari, puedes venir conmigo al cine? _____

Bueno, voy contigo, pero mi coche no funciona. _____

Wayne no viene por mí a **mi casa.** _____

Es difícil encontrar **estacionamiento.** _____

Prefiero no manejar de noche. _____

Cultura a lo vivo

In many Latin American countries, when a young man invites a girl out on a date, he is expected to pick her up at home. This custom provides an opportunity for the parents of the girl to meet the young man.

B. ¿Te diste cuenta? Escucha las conversaciones o mira el video otra vez para indicar el orden cronológico, del uno al seis, de las siguientes acciones.

_____ a. Wayne invita a Sofía al cine.

_____ b. Sofía habla con Ana Mari.

_____ c. Wayne llama a Sofía por teléfono.

_____ d. Ana Mari acepta ir con Sofía al cine.

_____ e. Sofía acepta la invitación de Wayne.

_____ f. Wayne y Sofía deciden encontrarse en el café.

C. Los hechos. Selecciona la respuesta correcta.

Sofía

Wayne

Ana Mari

1. Wayne dice *(says)*...

   a. Voy por ti.

   b. ¿Dónde dan la película?

   c. ¿Quieres ir al cine el sábado?

2. Wayne dice...

   a. ¿Quieres visitar el Centro Cultural de la universidad?

   b. ¿Puedes llegar a las 7:30?

   c. Mi coche no funciona.

3. Ana Mari...

   a. no entiende a Sofía.

   b. cree que Sofía es muy moderna.

   c. puede ir en su coche.

4. Sofía...

   a. sale sola por la noche con frecuencia.

   b. va al cine en el coche de Ramón.

   c. no cree que Wayne la invite a salir otra vez.

Learning Strategy: Making an educated guess

To understand the general meaning of a message, you do not have to understand every word you hear or read. In most situations, you can use the context, your knowledge of the world and of how people communicate, and also visual cues such as facial expressions, gestures, and body language to make an educated guess about meaning. Use the context to derive meaning. More often than not, you can guess correctly at the meaning of a word by focusing on the words that precede and follow it. For example, when Wayne said to Sofía, "**quiero llegar temprano porque es difícil encontrar estacionamiento,**" you had not seen **encontrar** before, but you know that **quiero llegar temprano** means *I want to arrive early* and that **estacionamiento** means *parking*. Therefore, using the context, you can easily guess that **encontrar** means *to find*.

Práctica adicional

Cuaderno de tareas
WB pp.251–252, A–C

Video
CD-ROM
Episodio 10

Gramática 1

Accepting and declining invitations
• Stem-changing verbs (e → ie) and (o → ue)

In the conversation, Wayne said **¿Quieres ir al cine el sábado?** to ask Sofía if she wanted to go to the movies. Sofía responded **Sí, puedo. Quieres** and **puedo** are forms of the verbs **querer** and **poder**.

Analizar y descubrir

1. Study the following exchanges:

Querer y poder	
—¿**Quieres** tomar un café?	*Do you want some coffee?*
—Sí, **quiero**, pero no **puedo** tomar cafeína.	*Yes, I want some, but I can't have any caffeine.*
—¿Ana Mari **quiere** llevar su coche?	*Does Ana Mari want to take her car?*
—No **puede**, porque no funciona.	*She can't, because it doesn't work.*
—¿Sofía y Ana Mari **quieren** ir al cine?	*Do Sofía and Ana Mari want to go to the movies?*
—Sí, **quieren**, pero no **pueden**.	*Yes, they want to, but they can't.*
—¿**Quieren** ustedes ir al cine? —¿**Queréis** ir al cine?	*Do you want to go to the movies?*
—**Queremos** ir pero no **podemos**, porque tenemos que trabajar.	*We want to go but we can't, because we have to work.*

2. Write the forms of **querer** and **poder**.

	Querer	Poder
yo	_____	puedo
tú	_____	_____
usted/él/ella	quiere	_____
nosotros/as	_____	_____
vosotros/as	queréis	podéis
ustedes/ellos/as	_____	_____

3. Look at the endings of **querer** and **poder**. Are they the same as other **-er** verbs you know, such as **comer** and **beber?** _____

4. Look at the stems of the two verbs **(quer-, pod-)** and answer the questions.

    a. What happens to the **-e-** of **querer**? It becomes _____.

    b. What happens to the **-o-** of **poder**? It becomes _____.

    c. Does the **-e-** of **querer** change in all the verb forms? _____.

    d. Does the **-o-** of **poder** change in all the verb forms? _____.

5. Complete these rules for stem-changing verbs.

    a. In stem-changing verbs like **querer,** -e- changes to _____ in all forms except the _____ and _____ forms.

    b. In stem-changing verbs like **poder,** -o- changes to _____ in all forms except the _____ and _____ forms.

6. The following expressions contain other common stem-changing verbs:

Para hacer planes con los amigos			
e → ie		**o/u → ue**	
empezar a...	to start . . .	almorzar	to have lunch
entender el problema	to understand the problem	dormir bien/mal	to sleep well/poorly
pensar en	to think about (someone)	encontrar	to find
pensar que	to think that (phrase)	jugar (al) tenis	to play tennis
preferir no manejar	to prefer not to drive	(no) poder ir	(not) to be able to go
querer	to want; to love	recordar	to remember
venir por mí	to pick me up		

*venir has a g in the yo person—yo vengo.

Note that jugar is the only verb that has the u → ue stem change.

PRÁCTICA

A. Hombres y mujeres.

Parte 1. Indica si estás de acuerdo *(if you agree)* con los siguientes estereotipos sobre los hombres y las mujeres.

Los hombres. . .	Sí	No	Depende
1. nunca encuentran las cosas.	☐	☐	☐
2. no pueden vivir solos.	☐	☐	☐
3. no entienden a las mujeres.	☐	☐	☐
4. prefieren no casarse *(to get married)*.	☐	☐	☐
5. no pueden aceptar sus errores.	☐	☐	☐
Las mujeres. . .			
6. siempre piensan que están gordas.	☐	☐	☐
7. no entienden a los hombres.	☐	☐	☐
8. quieren tener hijos.	☐	☐	☐
9. no pueden hacer mucho ejercicio.	☐	☐	☐
10. no juegan deportes *(sports)*.	☐	☐	☐

Parte 2. En grupos de tres personas, compartan sus respuestas y discutan sus ideas.

Modelo	No estoy de acuerdo con el comentario número dos. Mis amigos y yo vivimos solos y estamos muy bien. No necesitamos a las mujeres.

B. Lotería. Find a classmate who fits the following descriptions. Write their name in the space provided; the first student with two lines of four in a row wins.

> **Modelo** —¿Haces ejercicios tres veces a la semana?
> —Sí, hago ejercicios tres veces a la semana. ¿Y tú?
> —Yo no.

casi nunca almuerza en la cafetería.	juega vóleibol una vez a la semana.	prefiere no manejar por la noche.	empieza a estudiar tres días antes del examen.
hace ejercicio tres veces a la semana.	a veces no entiende la tarea.	quiere ir al cine este fin de semana.	no tiene ganas de hacer la tarea hoy.
ve videos en casa de su novio/a.	no duerme ocho horas por noche.	recuerda a su primer(a) maestro/a.	vive en casa de sus abuelos.
encuentra estacionamiento cuando llega.	sirve tamales en Navidad.	no puede tomar clases por las noches.	piensa que esta clase es muy fácil.

Invitación a **España**

Del álbum de
Sofía

España tiene aproximadamente 40 millones de habitantes y es dos veces el tamaño del estado de Oregon. Salamanca, en España, es una ciudad con una larga tradición intelectual y cultural. La Universidad de Salamanca se fundó en 1218 y es la más antigua del país. Hoy en día, la ciudad tiene innumerables academias, institutos, escuelas, colegios y universidades, por lo que estudian ahí miles de estudiantes nacionales e internacionales.

Práctica adicional

Website
vistahigher
learning.com

C. Problemas de familia. Completa la conversación entre Adriana y su esposo con los verbos de la lista. Después contesta las preguntas.

empiezas	almuerzas	quieres
puedes	duermes	prefiero
encontrar	jugar	vienes

Santiago	Adriana, no entiendo por qué (1) _____ trabajar y estudiar. Si quieres estudiar para contadora, es mejor que no trabajes hasta que termines.
Adriana	Si no tengo experiencia, no voy a poder (2) _____ trabajo cuando termine.
Santiago	Es cierto, pero tú (3) _____ adquirir *(acquire)* experiencia más adelante. Recuerda que tienes esposo, casa e hijos. No tienes tiempo para nada. La casa es un desastre.
Adriana	Ay, Santiago, limpiar la casa es muy aburrido. (4) _____ trabajar y estudiar. Con el dinero que gano le puedo pagar a una empleada.
Santiago	No es sólo la casa; últimamente tú no (5) _____ suficiente, a veces sólo cinco o seis horas por noche. Además (6) _____ mal, porque no tienes tiempo ni para ir al supermercado. Casi nunca hay comida en el refrigerador.
Adriana	Santiago, (7) _____ a hablar como esos hombres que no quieren que sus esposas progresen.
Santiago	No es verdad. Quiero que tú progreses, pero...

1. ¿Por qué quiere trabajar Adriana?

   _____

   _____

2. ¿Qué piensa Santiago que Adriana debe *(should)* hacer?

   _____

   _____

3. En tu opinión, ¿quién tiene razón *(is right)*?

   _____

   _____

D. Un anuncio de periódico.

Parte 1. Adriana siempre lee el periódico para estar bien informada. Hoy encuentra este anuncio de un restaurante nuevo cerca de su casa. Completa el anuncio con las formas apropiadas de los verbos.

Restaurante El Huarache Veloz

Calle Rancho del Rey 345   Tel. 2-A-COMER

Si usted (1) _____ (querer) almorzar bien y sin trabajo, venga a nuestro restaurante, El Huarache Veloz. Nosotros (2) _____ (entender) las necesidades de la mujer moderna que trabaja y que no (3) _____ (tener) tiempo para cocinar. Ud. y sus compañeros de trabajo (4) _____ (poder) comunicarse con nosotros por teléfono al número 2-A-COMER. Es muy fácil (5) _____ (recordar) nuestro número. Si usted (6) _____ (preferir), comuníquese por correo electrónico al hv@acomer.com. Nuestro restaurante se (7) _____ (encontrar) en las calles de Rancho del Rey y Paseo Ladera. Nosotros (8) _____ (empezar) a tomar órdenes desde las ocho de la mañana.

Parte 2. Encuentra un restaurante en Internet que acepte las órdenes por correo electrónico para compartir con la clase. Después hablen de la comida que sirven y los precios.

E. Preguntas personales. Contesta las preguntas en tu cuaderno y después entrevista a tu compañero/a y escribe sus respuestas aquí.

En la universidad

1. ¿Qué quieres estudiar? ¿Por qué?

_____

2. ¿Vas bien en tus clases? ¿Cuáles son más difíciles?

_____

3. ¿Empiezas a estudiar con tiempo para un examen? ¿Qué cosas haces para prepararte?

_____

4. ¿Dónde prefieres estudiar? ¿Por qué te gusta estudiar ahí?

_____

Los fines de semana

5. ¿En qué ocasiones prefieres estar con tus amigos? ¿Y con tu familia?

_____

6. ¿Puedes hacer todas las cosas que quieres? Si no, ¿por qué no?

_____

7. ¿Cuántas horas duermes? ¿Piensas que es importante dormir suficiente? ¿Por qué o por qué no?

_____

8. ¿Almuerzas en casa? ¿Qué almuerzas generalmente? ¿Con quién?

_____

9. ¿Qué deportes (*sports*) practicas? ¿Juegas béisbol?, ¿tenis?, ¿fútbol americano?

_____

10. ¿Sales mucho? ¿Con quién? ¿Qué hacen?

_____

11. Cuando sales con alguien por primera vez, ¿piensas que el chico tiene que ir por la chica a su casa? ¿En qué casos sí y en qué casos no? Explica.

_____

_____

Banco de palabras:
Para hablar del trabajo

el horario flexible/fijo
flexible/fixed schedule

el sueldo alto/bajo
high/low salary

tiempo completo/parcial
full-time/part-time

el tiempo libre
spare time

el turno de la mañana /tarde/noche
morning/afternoon/evening (night) shift

¡Fíjate!

You will need these words to answer the questions. Familiarize yourself with them, since they will become active in the next episode.

En el trabajo

12. ¿Es fácil encontrar trabajo en tu ciudad? ¿Qué tipo de trabajos hay? ¿Te gusta tu trabajo? ¿Por qué?

_____

_____

13. ¿Trabajas tiempo completo o tiempo parcial? ¿Recibes buen sueldo o quieres ganar más (*earn more*)?

_____

_____

14. ¿Cuántas horas a la semana puedes trabajar? ¿Qué días no puedes trabajar?

_____

15. ¿Prefieres trabajar el turno de la tarde o el de la mañana? ¿Tienes un horario flexible?

_____

_____

16. ¿Quieres encontrar otro trabajo este semestre? ¿Por qué?

_____

_____

Práctica adicional

Cuaderno de tareas
WB pp.252–253, D–G

Gramática 2

Extending invitations
• Prepositional pronouns

In other conversations, the characters said the following statements.

Pronombres preposicionales	
¿Quieres ir **conmigo** al cine?	*Do you want to go to the movies with me?*
Bueno, voy **contigo** si vienes **por mí**.	*Fine, I'll go with you if you pick me up.*
Wayne siempre habla **de ti**.	*Wayne always talks about you.*
¿Y Sofía? ¿Piensa **en él**?	*And Sofía? Does she think about him?*
Ramón va a jugar **con nosotros**.	*Ramón is going to play with us.*
¿Wayne vive **con ustedes**? ¿Wayne vive **con vosotros**? }	*Does Wayne live with you?*
No, él vive **con ellos**.	*No, he lives with them.*

1. Notice that the subject pronouns (**yo, tú, usted, él, ella, nosotros/as, ustedes, vosotros/as,** and **ellos/as**) and pronouns that follow prepositions (**a, de, con, para, por**) are the same, with two exceptions: **yo/mí** (**Vienes** *por mí*) and **tú/ti** (**Lo siento, no puedo ir** *por ti*.)
2. Notice that **conmigo** means *with me* and **contigo** means *with you*.
3. Some verbs you already know may be followed by prepositions: **hablar de, discutir con, vivir con, jugar con, ir por,** and **venir por**.

PRÁCTICA

F. ¿De quién habla? Sofía hizo *(made)* los siguientes comentarios. ¿A quién(es) se refiere(n) los pronombres preposicionales? Empareja las dos columnas.

_____ 1. Necesito hablar *con ella*.　　　　　a. amigos

_____ 2. Lalo va a jugar fútbol *con ellos*.　　　b. Lalo

_____ 3. Mi abuela vive *con nosotros*.　　　　c. Ana Mari y Sofía

_____ 4. Quiero hablar *contigo*.　　　　　　 d. Mis padres y yo

_____ 5. No comparte *(share)* sus cosas *con ellas*.　　e. la profesora

_____ 6. Es un irresponsable; por eso, discuto 　　f. tú
　　　　　　mucho *con él*.

G. Un poco de lógica. Empareja cada pregunta o declaración con la respuesta lógica.

_____ 1. ¿Está Sofía en casa?　　　　　　a. Lo siento, pero no puedo.

_____ 2. ¿Quieres ir conmigo al cine?　　　b. Claro que puedes venir conmigo.

_____ 3. Su hijo es muy considerado, ¿no?　c. Sí. ¿Quieres hablar con ella?

_____ 4. ¿Puedo ir contigo?　　　　　　d. Sí. Siempre piensa en

_____ 5. Estas flores son para ti.　　　　　　nosotros primero.

　　　　　　　　　　　　　　　　　　e. Gracias. Siempre piensas en mí.

243

H. Traducción. Escribe las siguientes frases en español.

1. I have tickets for the game tonight—do you want to go? Manolo and Jorge are also coming with us. We can go in Jorge's car.

_____

_____

_____

2. Sure I want to go, but I'd rather take my own car. I don't understand why you always invite Jorge—he's silly!

_____

_____

_____

¡Fíjate!

Remember not to translate word-for-word; translate ideas.

I. Escribe sobre las personas queridas. Contesta todas las preguntas en forma de párrafo. Después comparte tus respuestas con un(a) compañero/a.

Modelo Tu hermano/a: ¿Ves a tu hermano/a? ¿Qué haces con él/ella? ¿Vives con él/ella?
**Veo a mi hermana casi todos los días. Tomo café con ella por las mañanas.
A veces salgo con ella a cenar. Nunca discuto con ella. Y tampoco voy por ella
con frecuencia. Prefiere manejar su coche. No vivo con ella, vivo con mi hija.**

1. Tus abuelos: ¿Ves a tus abuelos? ¿Sales con ellos? ¿Qué actividades haces con ellos?

_____

_____

2. Tu novio/a/mejor amigo/a: ¿Hablas mucho con él/ella? ¿Discutes con él/ella?

_____

_____

_____

3. Tus compañeros de clase: ¿Qué actividades haces con ellos? ¿Estudias con ellos? ¿Dónde y cuándo?

_____

_____

_____

4. Tu mamá o tu papá: ¿Vives con él/ella? ¿Discuten con frecuencia? ¿Por qué? ¿Qué actividades hacen juntos (together)?

_____

_____

_____

_____

Práctica adicional	
Cuaderno de tareas WB pp.254–255, H–L LM pp.257–258, A–B, Pron.	Audio CD-ROM Episodio 10

Actividades comunicativas

Audio
CD-ROM

A. La historia va así.

Parte 1. Mira las ilustraciones y escucha los comentarios de Manolo con respecto a su trabajo. Indica el orden cronológico en el que menciona las actividades. Después escucha los comentarios otra vez para verificar tus respuestas.

Parte 2. En grupos de tres, escriban la historia en diferente orden.

B. ¿Qué hace Manolo los sábados?

Instrucciones para **Estudiante 1**

Parte 1. Tú tienes la mitad *(half)* de las ilustraciones, y tu compañero/a tiene la otra mitad. Juntos tienen que descubrir *(find out)* cómo es la rutina de Manolo los sábados. Describe tus ilustraciones y haz preguntas para completar el cuadro. Tu compañero/a empieza.

> **Modelo** Manolo limpia su cuarto por la mañana.
> ¿Qué hace después?

Parte 2. Ahora escribe un párrafo con los eventos. Inventa los detalles.

> **Modelo** Los sábados por la mañana Manolo generalmente…

_____

_____

_____

_____

_____

_____

_____

_____

_____

B. ¿Qué hace Manolo los sábados?

Instrucciones para Estudiante 2

Parte 1. Tú tienes la mitad *(half)* de las ilustraciones, y tu compañero/a tiene la otra mitad. Juntos tienen que descubrir *(find out)* cómo es la rutina de Manolo los sábados. Describe tus ilustraciones y haz preguntas para completar el cuadro. Tú empiezas.

Modelo	¿Qué hace Manolo primero?

Parte 2. Ahora escribe un párrafo con los eventos. Inventa los detalles.

Modelo	Los sábados por la mañana Manolo generalmente...

_____

_____

_____

_____

_____

_____

_____

_____

_____

C. Te invito a salir. Vas a salir con tu compañero/a. Selecciona una cartera *(wallet)* para saber cuánto dinero pueden gastar. Inventen una conversación que incluya (1) adónde van a ir, (2) cuándo y a qué hora van y (3) cómo van a gastar todo el dinero. Estén listos para actuar su diálogo en clase.

La correspondencia

El correo: ¡Los hombres! Primero, lee las siguientes preguntas. Después, lee la página del diario de Sofía y contesta las preguntas.

1. ¿Por qué invita Sofía a sus amigos al cine?

_____

2. ¿Por qué cree Sofía que Wayne va a pensar que está loca?

_____

3. ¿Crees que es interesante salir con una persona de otra cultura? ¿Por qué?

_____

_____

_____

Querido diario,   9 de octubre

Hoy me llamó Wayne para invitarme al cine, pero pienso que acabo de[1] tener un malentendido cultural con él. Creo que Wayne quiere salir conmigo, y yo quiero salir con él, pero como no conoce[2] mis costumbres, no se ofreció a venir a la casa por mí. Creo que él no entiende que tiene que venir por mí a mi casa; así mis papás pueden conocerlo. Wayne va a pensar que no quiero salir con él, o que estoy loca. ¡Llegar con Ana Mari y Ramón a nuestra primera cita! ¡Qué problema! Bueno, los dos tenemos que recordar que tenemos culturas y costumbres diferentes. ¡Así es más interesante. ¡A ver qué pasa el sábado!

[1]*I have just* [2]*he doesn't know*

En papel: ¡Un viaje a Salamanca! Vas a ir a Salamanca a estudiar el próximo verano *(next summer)*. Escríbele una carta a la familia con quien vas a vivir para presentarte *(introduce yourself)*. Incluye la siguiente información:

- tu nombre, tu edad y una descripción de tu familia
- tu rutina diaria y cosas que quieres hacer en Salamanca
- los platos que te gusta comer y los que no puedes comer
- las actividades que te gusta hacer después de las clases y los fines de semana

Video
CD-ROM

¡A ver de nuevo!

Parte 1. Escucha **Escenas de la vida** otra vez para escribir un resumen del episodio.

Audio
CD-ROM

En este episodio Wayne habla con Sofía para invitarla al cine...

Parte 2. Ahora trabaja con un(a) compañero/a para comparar la información y añadir lo que te haya faltado.

Práctica adicional		
Cuaderno de tareas WB p.256, M LM p.258, A–B	Audio CD-ROM Episodio 10	Website vistahigher learning.com

Verbos

almorzar (o → ue)	*to have lunch*	**pensar (e → i) en**	*to think about* (someone)
dormir (o → ue) bien/mal	*to sleep well/poorly*	**pensar (e → i) que**	*to think that* (phrase)
empezar a... (e → ie)	*to start...*	**poder (o → ue)**	*to be able to, can*
encontrar (o → ue)	*to find*	**(no) poder (o → ue) ir**	*(not) to be able to go*
entender	*to understand*	**preferir (e → ie)**	*to prefer*
el problema (e → ie)	the problem	**querer (e → ie)**	*to want; to love*
invitar a	*to invite*	**recordar (o → ue)**	*to remember*
jugar (u → ue) (al) tenis	*to play tennis*	**venir por mí**	*to pick me up*
manejar	*to drive*		

Las preposiciones y los pronombres preposicionales

a mí	*for me*	**por él**	*for him*	**de ellos/as**	*from them*
para ti	*for you*	**de nosotros/as**	*from us*	**conmigo**	*with me*
con ella	*with her*	**de ustedes**	*from you* (pl.)	**contigo**	*with you*

Vocabulario personal

Write all the words you need to know in Spanish so that you can better talk about your dates and your weekend plans.

¡A escribir!

Escenas de la vida: Una invitación confusa

Video
CD-ROM

A. ¡A ver cuánto entendiste! See how much of the **Escena** you understood by matching the Spanish sentences with their English equivalents.

Sofía   **Wayne**   **Ana Mari**

_____ 1. No viene por mí.

_____ 2. Es normal hacer eso en una cita.

_____ 3. Vamos a encontrarnos ahí.

_____ 4. La película empieza temprano.

_____ 5. Voy contigo.

_____ 6. ¿Puedes ir conmigo?

_____ 7. La próxima vez te apuesto que viene
por mí.

a. The movie starts early.

b. Next time I bet you he comes
to pick me up.

c. Can you go with me?

d. He's not going to pick me up.

e. It's normal to do that on a date.

f. We're going to meet there.

g. I'll go with you.

Video
CD-ROM

B. ¡Vamos al cine! Match the questions or statements in column **A** with the appropriate responses in column **B**. Then identify the speakers.

A

_____ 1. ¿Quieres ir al cine el sábado?

_____ 2. ¿A qué hora?

_____ 3. ¿Puedes llegar a las siete y media?

_____ 4. Bueno, entonces nos vemos el sábado
a las siete y media.

_____ 5. ¿Dónde dan la película?

B

a. Pues... sí puedo.

b. En el Centro Cultural de la
universidad.

c. Sí, claro.

d. Está bien.

e. La película empieza a las ocho y
media.

¿Quiénes conversan?

_____ y _____

Cuaderno de tareas

Nombre _____ Fecha _____

C. La conversación de Sofía con Ana Mari. Put the following statements in chronological order.

_____ a. ¿Podemos ir en tu coche? Prefiero no manejar de noche.

__1__ b. ¿Puedes ir conmigo al cine el sábado? No quiero ir sola con Wayne.

_____ c. Es normal aquí hacer eso en una cita.

_____ d. No entiendo. ¿Por qué?

_____ e. ¿Puedes creer que Wayne me invita al cine, pero no viene por mí a la casa? Eso no es una cita.

_____ f. Pues, a mí no me gusta.

_____ g. Bueno voy contigo, pero necesitas modernizarte.

_____ h. Mi coche no funciona.

Gramática 1

Accepting and declining invitations
• **Stem-changing verbs (e → ie) and (o → ue)**

D. Una invitación a jugar. Ramón wants Wayne to play soccer with him this evening. Use the verbs to complete the conversation.

quieres	puedo	empieza	encuentro
venir	prefiero	preferir	puedes

Ramón   Hola, Wayne, ¿(1) _____ ir a jugar fútbol esta tarde?

Wayne   Me gustaría, pero no (2) _____ porque no (3) _____ mis tenis *(sneakers)* de fútbol.

Ramón   ¡Qué raro! Tengo dos pares de tenis. Si quieres, (4) _____ usar los míos.

Wayne   Gracias, pero (5) _____ buscar bien mis tenis o ir a comprar otros.

Ramón   ¡Como quieras *(As you wish)!* El juego (6) _____ a las seis. Si decides ir conmigo, puedes (7) _____ a mi casa.

E. ¿Qué hacen? Write a complete sentence with each illustration.

1. Wayne y su amiga/almorzar _____

2. Adriana/(no) entender _____

3. Manolo/encontrar trabajo _____

4. ¿Tú?/venir por mí _____

F. ¡Ay, Lalo!

Parte 1. Use the verbs to complete the description. Fill in the appropriate forms.

tener	entender	llegar	preferir
recordar	querer	empezar	jugar

¡Lalo es tremendo! Sus clases (1) _____ a las siete y media de la mañana; por eso, (2) _____ que salir de casa a las seis y cuarto a más tardar *(at the latest)*. Pues nunca lo hace. Siempre (3) _____ tarde a sus clases. No (4) _____ que es muy importante ser puntual y responsable. Pero cuando (5) _____ salir con una chica, entonces sí (6) _____ que ser puntual es importante. Le dice a mi mamá: "Mami, (7) _____ salir temprano de casa porque a las chicas no les gusta que llegue tarde." ¡Vaya inconsistencia!

Parte 2. What is the inconsistency in Lalo's behavior? Explain in your own words.

_____

_____

_____

_____

G. Las actividades. Make up six true statements using an element from each column.

Modelo

Mi amigo Roberto piensa que su trabajo es aburrido.

Yo	dormir	los libros
Mi novio/a	entender	los problemas de matemáticas
Mis profesores	jugar	(a) los estudiantes
Mi hermano/a...	encontrar	la tarea
Mi amigo/a...	pensar en/que	en comer
		bien
		hasta tarde los domingos

1. _____

2. _____

3. _____

4. _____

5. _____

6. _____

Gramática 2

Extending invitations
• Prepositional pronouns

H. ¡Ramón está celoso *(jealous)*! Use five of these words to complete the conversation.

ti	usted	conmigo	mí	contigo	ella	él	nosotros

Laura   Ramón, ¿quién va a ir (1) _____ a la fiesta?

Ramón   Nadie. ¿Quieres ir (2) _____?

Laura   Lo siento, pero voy a ir con Jorge.

Ramón   ¿¡Con quién!? ¿Por qué vas con (3) _____? Es un antipático.

Laura   Pues sí, un poco, pero viene por (4) _____ a mi casa, me paga todo y me lleva a lugares elegantes.

Ramón   A (5) _____ sólo te interesa lo material y eso no está bien.

I. Hablando de Wayne. Choose the appropriate words to complete the conversation.

contigo	ella	nosotros	ustedes
ti	ellos	él	mí

Ramón   Sofía, Wayne habla mucho de (1) _____.

Sofía   ¿Ah sí? ¿Y qué cosas dice de (2) _____?

Ramón   Pues… que quiere salir (3) _____.

Sofía   Él es muy agradable. ¿Por qué no lo invitas a salir con (4) _____ con más frecuencia? Así puedo conocerlo mejor.

Ramón   Creo que tú debes salir sola con (5) _____.

J. Preguntas personales. Answer the questions using prepositional pronouns.

> **Modelo**   ¿Discutes mucho con tus hermanos?
> **Sí, a veces discuto con ellos.**

1. ¿Vives con tus padres?

_____

2. ¿Piensas mucho en tu novio/a?

_____

3. ¿Qué deporte juegas con tus amigos?

_____

4. ¿Hablas con tus profesores con frecuencia?

_____

5. ¿Vas por tu mejor amigo/a a su casa cuando salen?

_____

K. Traducción. Write the following sentences in Spanish.

1. —Do you want to go out with me on Friday or Saturday?
   —I prefer Saturday, because Friday I can't.

   _____

   _____

2. —I am going to have lunch with him, and then watch a movie.
   —Is he going to pick you up?

   _____

   _____

3. —Are you going to start going out with him?
   —Yes, I think he is a nice guy.

   _____

   _____

L. ¿Quieres salir? Manolo finally calls Ana Mari to go out. However, they have very different ideas about what kind of date it is. Write their conversation using the illustrations; take either Manolo's or Ana Mari's role. Make sure you use **poder, preferir,** and **querer** to express your preferences and desires. Finish up by agreeing to meet at a time and place.

LA MOMIA II

Manolo	Hola, Ana Mari. ¿Cómo estás? Habla Manolo.
Ana Mari	¡Hola, qué milagro!
Manolo	_____
Ana Mari	_____
Manolo	_____
Ana Mari	_____
Manolo	_____
Ana Mari	_____
Manolo	_____
Ana Mari	_____

Para terminar

M. Los problemas de Laura y Alfredo.

Parte 1. Read the description of Laura and Alfredo's marital problems.

> Laura y Alfredo son diferentes en casi todo. Alfredo tiene 48 años y es muy conservador; Laura tiene 30 y es bastante liberal. Laura piensa que la mujer puede trabajar y desenvolverse[1] profesionalmente, pero Alfredo piensa que una esposa tiene que quedarse en casa, cuidar a los hijos y atender a su esposo. Ella quiere tener sólo dos hijos y él quiere seis. Ella no entiende por qué.
>
> En cuanto a sus actividades, tampoco tienen muchas cosas en común. A Laura le gusta salir con sus amigas a los centros comerciales y al cine. Es muy activa; juega tenis con frecuencia y toma una clase de yoga. Alfredo nunca quiere salir; prefiere estar en casa, ver la televisión, trabajar en el jardín o dormir. Con frecuencia duerme doce horas, porque dice que trabaja mucho entre semana. No le gusta hacer ejercicio; de hecho[2], se pone celoso[3] porque piensa que Laura quiere estar delgada y guapa para coquetear[4] con otros hombres. Lo único que hace es jugar cartas toda la noche cuando sus amigos vienen a visitarlo una vez al mes.
>
> En fin, Laura está aburrida; por eso, va a empezar a trabajar la próxima semana. Ella cree que si no empieza a trabajar pronto se va a volver loca. Él no sabe que va a empezar a trabajar y seguramente no le va a gustar nada.

[1]develop [2]in fact [3]gets jealous [4]to flirt

Parte 2. Indicate whether the following statements are **cierto** or **falso**.

	Cierto	Falso
1. Alfredo tiene 48 años.	☐	☐
2. Laura tiene dos hijos.	☐	☐
3. Alfredo duerme mucho.	☐	☐
4. Alfredo no es muy moderno.	☐	☐
5. A Laura no le gustan los niños.	☐	☐
6. Alfredo juega a las cartas con sus amigos.	☐	☐

Parte 3. Answer the following questions.

1. ¿Cómo es Laura? ¿Cómo es Alfredo? _____

2. ¿En qué cosas son diferentes? _____

3. ¿Qué no entiende Laura? _____

4. ¿Qué va a hacer Laura pronto? _____

5. ¿Por qué va a hacer eso? _____

6. ¿Crees que ellos van a divorciarse? _____

7. ¿Cómo piensas tú que Laura tiene que solucionar su problema? _____

¡A escuchar!

Comprensión

Audio
CD-ROM

A. En el café.

Parte 1. Listen to Ramón and a classmate, Rosalía, as they have a cup of coffee in the cafeteria. Then, select the best answer to the question.

What is the main topic of Ramón's and Rosalía's conversation?

a. Rosalía's literature class   b. plans for the weekend

c. the cafeteria menu   d. a tennis match

Parte 2. You will hear the conversation between Ramón and Rosalía again, followed by four questions. Select the answers to the questions. **¡Atención!** There may be more than one answer to each question.

1. a. viernes   b. sábado   c. domingo

2. a. trabajar   c. leer una novela   e. escribir una composición
      b. dormir todo el día   d. descansar   f. estudiar para un examen

3. a. ir al cine   c. ir al parque   e. comer en un restaurante
      b. jugar al tenis   d. mirar la televisión   f. estudiar

4. a. Rosalía va por Ramón a las ocho.   c. Ramón va por Rosalía a las nueve.
      b. Los dos van a encontrarse en las canchas de tenis a las diez.

Audio
CD-ROM

B. ¿Estudias conmigo? You are going to hear eight questions. Answer each one aloud in the affirmative, using a prepositional pronoun and the written cues provided, and write the appropriate prepositional pronoun in the space provided. Repeat the correct answer after the speaker.

mí (conmigo)	él	nosotros	ellos	usted
ti (contigo)	ella	vosotros	ellas	ustedes

> **Modelo**   You hear: **¿Estudias conmigo?**
> You say/write: **Sí, estudio contigo.**

1. Sí, paso _____.   5. Sí, vivo _____.

2. Sí, voy _____.   6. Sí, hablamos _____.

3. Sí, pienso _____.   7. Sí, Ana Mari va _____.

4. Sí, Wayne viene _____.   8. Sí, discuto _____.

Pronunciación

Audio
CD-ROM

La *j* y la *g*. The Spanish letter **j (jota)** sounds similar to the English *h*. Repeat these words and sentences after the speaker.

Juan	**Jalisco**	**reloj**	**Juan es de Jalisco.**
José	**junio**	**consejero**	**El hijo de José lleva un traje.**

The letter **g (ge)** has a sound similar to the English *g* in *gap* before consonants and **a, o, u** and **a** sound similar to the English *h* or the Spanish **j** before **e** and **i**.

g + consonant, ga, go, gu		**ge, gi**	
gracias	**yogurt**	**general**	**geografía**
galletas	**langosta**	**gimnasio**	**biología**
El general Gustavo Gutiérrez es generoso.		**Mis amigos juegan en el gimnasio.**	

In order to retain the sound of *g* in *gap* before the vowels **e** and **i**, a silent **u** is placed after the **g**: **gue, gui.** Repeat these words after the speaker.

pague	**espagueti**	**guisado**

Más escenas de la vida

Holding a tennis racket, Santiago enters the room where Adriana is studying. Listen and then complete activities **A** and **B**. You will hear the conversation twice.

Audio
CD-ROM

A. ¿Quién lo dijo? Indicate who made the following statements in the conversation: Adriana **(A)**, or Santiago **(S)**.

_____ 1. ¿Quieres ir con nosotros?

_____ 2. ¿Por qué no me ayudan a limpiar?

_____ 3. Te ayudamos a limpiar si vienes con nosotros.

_____ 4. Y esta noche te dedicas a tus hijos y a tu esposo.

_____ 5. Ya vas a empezar con eso.

Audio
CD-ROM

B. Responde. Write the answers to the following questions.

1. ¿Adónde va Santiago con sus hijos? _____

2. ¿Por qué Adriana no puede ir con ellos? _____

3. ¿Por qué no tiene tiempo libre entre semana? _____

4. ¿Cuándo juegan tenis? _____

5. Si ayudan a Adriana a limpiar, ¿qué cosas no puede hacer Adriana esta noche?

_____

Episodio 11

Escenas de la vida: ¡A ganarse la vida!¹

Video
CD-ROM

Audio
CD-ROM

A. ¡Mira cuánto puedes entender! Indica qué dicen *(what they say)* sobre sus trabajos.

Wayne:

☐ Me pagan bien. ☐ Me pagan mal.
☐ Salgo tarde. ☐ Salgo temprano.
☐ Mi jefe es agradable. ☐ Mi jefe es antipático.
☐ No me gusta mi trabajo. ☐ Me gusta mucho.
☐ Me dan propinas. ☐ No me dan propinas.
☐ No busco otro trabajo. ☐ Necesito encontrar otro trabajo.

Sofía: "_____
_____
_____
_____
_____ "

Ana Mari: "_____
_____
_____
_____ "

Ramón: "_____
_____
_____
_____ "

¹*Making a living*

259

Video
CD-ROM

B. ¿Te diste cuenta? Indica quién hace los siguientes comentarios: Sofía **(S)**, Ramón **(R)**, Ana Mari **(AM)** o Wayne **(W)**.

Audio
CD-ROM

_____ 1. Mis compañeros me invitan a salir.

_____ 2. ¿Quién te da problemas?

_____ 3. Por suerte, mi trabajo es bueno.

_____ 4. A ti te dan propinas; a mí me dan problemas.

_____ 5. Sabemos que son trabajos de tiempo parcial.

_____ 6. Ramón y Ana Mari, adiós, que les vaya bien.

_____ 7. Ellos van al cine con nosotros.

> **Cultura a lo vivo**
> Traditionally in the Spanish-speaking world, students don't always work while going to school. However, depending on the family's economic situation, many students help out in the family business and/or work during the summer.

Video
CD-ROM

C. ¿En qué trabajan? Completa las frases.

Audio
CD-ROM

1. Los compañeros de Ana Mari son _____.

2. Sofía trabaja con _____.

3. Ramón es _____ de limusinas, sus clientes son _____ con él.

4. Ana Mari y Ramón van _____ con Sofía y Wayne.

5. Wayne le dice a Sofía: "Ya vámonos. Vamos a _____ al cine."

Práctica adicional	
Cuaderno de tareas WB pp.277–278, A–C	Video CD-ROM Episodio 11

Para comunicarnos mejor

Gramática **1**

Talking about your job
• <u>Saber</u>, <u>salir</u>, <u>poner</u>, and job-related vocabulary

Para hablar del trabajo	
el ama de casa (m, f)	_homemaker_
atender (e→ie) a los clientes	_to attend the customers/clients_
el/la chofer	_driver_
el/la empleado/a	_clerk, employee_
el horario flexible/fijo	_flexible/fixed schedule_
el/la jefe/a	_boss_
el/la mesero/a	_waiter/waitress_
el/la niñero/a	_baby-sitter_
poner las cosas en su lugar	_to put/place things in their place_
las prestaciones	_fringe benefits_
el puesto	_position_
saber + [verb]	_to know how (to do something)_
salir temprano/tarde	_to get off, to leave early/late_
el sueldo alto/bajo	_high/low salary_
el tiempo completo/parcial/libre	_full-time/part-time/free time_
el turno de la mañana/tarde/noche	_morning/afternoon/night shift_
las vacaciones	_vacation_
la ventaja/desventaja	_advantage/disadvantage_

Read the following examples:

¿**Saben** usar la computadora?	*Do they know how to use a computer?*
No **sé** si **saben** usarla.	*I don't know if they know how to use it.*
Mi jefe **pone** los documentos en el archivador.	*My boss puts the documents in the file cabinet.*
Yo **pongo** las cosas en su lugar.	*I put everything in its place.*
No **salgo** con mis amigos entre semana.	*I don't go out with my friends during the week.*

1. Note that *only* the **yo** forms of the verbs have a spelling change. The rest of the forms are conjugated as regular **-er** or **-ir** verbs.

Verbos con irregularidades en la primera persona (yo)			
saber	Yo **sé**...	usar la computadora.	*I know how to use the computer.*
	¿Tú **sabes**...	cocinar?	*Do you know how to cook?*
	Sofía **sabe**...	cuidar niños.	*Sofía knows how to take care of children.*
poner	Yo **pongo**...	las cosas en su lugar.	*I put things in their place.*
	Tú no **pones**...	la mesa.	*You don't set the table.*
salir	Yo **salgo**...	temprano/tarde.	*I get off (leave) early/late.*
	Él **sale**...	bien/mal en sus clases.	*He does well/badly in class.*

Learning Strategy: Advanced organizers

To maximize your learning before class, take a few minutes to look at the material that will be presented that day. Read the titles of the sections in the episode and look at the illustrations, to get an idea of the story and to find out what vocabulary and grammatical structures you will encounter. When you organize in advance, you will understand better and retain more information.

PRÁCTICA

A. Las personas y sus trabajos. Empareja la(s) persona(s) con el trabajo que sabe(n) hacer.

_____ 1. Una secretaria		a. hacer experimentos.
_____ 2. Una doctora		b. entender los problemas de las personas.
_____ 3. Los sicólogos		c. reparar coches.
_____ 4. Un mecánico		d. usar la computadora.
_____ 5. Una veterinaria	sé	e. diseñar casas y edificios.
_____ 6. Los arquitectos	sabe	f. combinar colores y formas.
_____ 7. Los científicos	saben	g. hacer operaciones médicas.
_____ 8. Un diseñador		h. crear literatura.
_____ 9. Los poetas		i. trabajar con animales.
_____ 10. Yo		j. hablar inglés.
		k. cocinar *(to cook)*.

B. ¡Cuánto sabes de Latinoamérica! En grupos de tres personas, contesten las preguntas. Decidan quién sabe más de Latinoamérica.

1. ¿Sabes dónde están las pirámides mayas?
_____

2. ¿Sabes quién es el presidente de México?
_____

3. ¿Sabes cuál es la capital de Argentina?
_____

4. ¿Sabes cuándo se celebra el Día de los Muertos *(The Day of the Dead)*?
_____

5. ¿Sabes a qué hora se comen las uvas el 31 de diciembre?
_____

6. ¿Sabes cómo se dice *"I love you"* en español?
_____

7. ¿Sabes cuántos países hay en Centroamérica?
_____

8. ¿Sabes en cuántos países se habla español?
_____

C. Ana Mari y Sofía hablan de sus trabajos. Completa las descripciones.

Ana Mari:

1. Me gusta mi trabajo porque me pagan bien. Tengo un _____ alto.
2. Trabajo tiempo _____, sólo 24 horas a la semana.
3. Tengo el _____ de la tarde: empiezo a las 2:30 y termino a las 7:30 de la tarde.
4. No me dan _____; tengo que trabajar todo el año.
5. Desafortunadamente, no tengo _____: no tengo seguro médico, pensión ni vacaciones.

Sofía:

6. Soy _____; por las tardes y los fines de semana cuido niñas y niños.
   Me gusta mi trabajo porque tiene muchas _____: es flexible, trabajo
   las horas que yo quiero y es divertido estar con los niños pequeños.
   Con frecuencia los padres me dan regalos.
7. Las _____ son que no me pagan muy bien, tengo que poner
   todas las cosas en su lugar y a veces los niños son groseros conmigo.

Práctica adicional

Cuaderno de tareas
WB pp.278–279, D–G

Gramática 2

Saying what people do for you
• The object pronouns <u>me</u> and <u>te</u>

Analizar y descubrir

In the conversation, you heard the following statements. Study the examples and answer the questions below.

Me pagan bien.	*They pay me well.*
Mis compañeros **me invitan** a salir y **me ayudan.**	*My co-workers invite me out and help me.*
Por lo menos a ti **te dan** propinas; a mí sólo **me dan** problemas.	*At least they give you tips; they only give me problems.*

1. Where are **me** and **te** placed in relation to the verb **(pagan, invitan, ayudan, dan)** in Spanish? _____
   Where are *me* and *you* placed in relation to the verb in English? _____

2. Notice the phrases **a ti** and **a mí** in the third example. Use them for emphasis or contrast.

A mí me pagan mal, pero **a ti te pagan** una fortuna. ¡No es justo!	*They pay me poorly, but they pay you a fortune. It's not fair!*

Here are some common verbs used with **me** and **te.**

Las cosas que mi familia y amigos hacen

ayudar	*to help*	Mi mamá **me ayuda** mucho.
contar (o ➝ ue) los problemas	*to tell your problems*	Mis hermanos no **me cuentan** sus problemas.
dar consejos	*to give advice*	Mi abuela **me da** buenos consejos.
dejar usar su coche	*to let someone use one's car*	Mi novio **me deja** usar su coche.
invitar a salir	*to ask someone out*	Tus compañeros, ¿**te invitan** a salir?
llamar	*to call*	Mi profesora no **me llama** a la casa.
mandar un regalo	*to send a present*	Mis abuelos siempre **me mandan** regalos.
pagar	*to pay*	¿**Te pagan** bien en el trabajo?
pedir (e ➝ i) cosas prestadas	*to borrow things*	Mi sobrina **me pide** ropa *(clothes)* prestada.
prestar dinero	*to lend money*	¿Quién **te presta** dinero cuando necesitas?

3. Now observe where **me** (or **te**) is placed in expressions with multiple verbs.

Me tienes que ayudar. ⎫ Tienes que ayudar**me.** ⎭	*You have to help me.*
No va a invitar**me** a salir otra vez. ⎫ No **me** va a invitar a salir otra vez. ⎭	*He's not going to ask me out again.*

4. In an expression with a conjugated verb and an unconjugated verb, you may place **me** and **te** _____ the first verb or attach it to the _____.

¡Fíjate!

The verb **contar** is conjugated like **recordar**. ¿Recuerdas? ¿Me cuentas ese problema?

PRÁCTICA

D. Otra cita. Después de dos semanas, Wayne llama a Sofía para invitarla a salir otra vez. Lee la conversación y escribe la forma apropiada de los verbos de la lista. Después contesta las preguntas con un(a) compañero/a.

saber	salir	estar	querer
ver	invitar	poder	hablar

> **¡Fíjate!**
> Remember that some verbs have irregular **yo** forms.

Sofía	¿Bueno?
Wayne	¿Sofía? Habla Wayne.
Sofía	¡Hola, Wayne! ¿Cómo (1) _____?
Wayne	Bien, gracias. Oye, te (2) _____ al cine mañana por la noche.
Sofía	Gracias, pero por la noche no (3) _____. Voy a (4)_____ a mis abuelos porque mañana es su aniversario. Pero si quieres, podemos (5) _____ a almorzar.
Wayne	Bueno, ¿a qué hora voy por ti?
Sofía	A las doce, ¿te parece? Esta vez (tú) no (6) _____ que invite a todos mis amigos, ¿verdad?
Wayne	¡No, por favor! Ya (7) _____ cuál fue *(was)* mi error.
Sofía	No te preocupes. Fue un malentendido. Yo tampoco quiero ir con ellos esta vez.

1. ¿Adónde quiere ir Wayne mañana?

   _____

2. ¿Qué tiene que hacer Sofía por la noche?

   _____

3. ¿Adónde van a ir Sofía y Wayne?

   _____

4. ¿Sabes cuál fue el error de Wayne?

   _____

E. ¡Tengo buenos amigos! Escribe el nombre de la(s) persona(s) que hace(n) estas cosas por ti.

> **Modelo**   **Mis primos** me hablan por teléfono el día de mi cumpleaños *(birthday)*.

1. _____ me sirve la comida.

2. _____ me habla(n) por teléfono el día de mi cumpleaños.

3. _____ me escribe(n) cartas.

4. _____ me invita(n) a salir los fines de semana.

5. _____ me ayuda(n) con la tarea.

6. _____ me lleva a la doctora cuando estoy enfermo/a *(sick)*.

F. ¡Qué consentido! (*How spoiled!*) Indica si los siguientes comentarios son **ciertos** o **falsos**.

	Cierto	Falso
1. Mi mamá me prepara el desayuno, el almuerzo y la cena.	☐	☐
2. Mi compañero/a de cuarto me ayuda en todo.	☐	☐
3. Mi familia siempre me escucha cuando tengo problemas.	☐	☐
4. Mis profesores no me dan mucha tarea.	☐	☐
5. Todos me quieren mucho.	☐	☐
6. Mis amigas siempre me prestan dinero.	☐	☐
7. Mi jefe me deja salir temprano.	☐	☐
8. Mis abuelos me dan muchos regalos.	☐	☐
9. Mis amigos vienen por mí cuando vamos a las fiestas.	☐	☐

G. ¿Quién? Contesta las siguientes preguntas. Después entrevista a tu compañero/a para ver (*see*) si tienen algo en común.

> **Modelo** ¿Quién te manda correos electrónicos con frecuencia?
> **Mi amiga Irene me manda correos electrónicos casi todos los días.**

1. ¿Quién te presta dinero? _____

2. ¿Quién te escribe cartas de amor? _____

3. ¿Quién te da buenos consejos? _____

4. ¿Quién te manda regalos? _____

5. ¿Quién te visita cuando estás enfermo/a? _____

6. ¿Quién te lava la ropa? _____

7. ¿Quién te necesita más? _____

8. ¿Quién te escucha cuando tienes problemas? _____

¡Fíjate!

Remember to place **me** before the conjugated verb.

H. Una entrevista. Convierte a preguntas las oraciones de la **Práctica F** para entrevistar a tu compañero/a. Haz los cambios necesarios. Después decide si tu compañero/a es un(a) consentido/a (*spoiled*) o no.

> **Modelo** Mi mamá me prepara el desayuno, el almuerzo y la cena.
> **¿Tu mamá te prepara el desayuno, el almuerzo y la cena?**

I. Una persona especial. Habla con un(a) compañero/a de una persona importante en tu vida. Explica las cosas que esta persona hace por ti.

> **Modelo** **Mi hermana es muy importante para mí. Siempre me ayuda cuando tengo problemas. Hablo mucho con ella porque siempre me da buenos consejos. Nunca me presta dinero; no tiene porque compra mucha ropa. Pero me deja usar su coche y su computadora.**

J. El trabajo de Adriana.

Audio CD-ROM

Parte 1. Escucha la narración de Adriana para completar el párrafo.

Adriana

(1) _____ que tengo algunos problemas con mi esposo porque trabajo y también (2) _____, pero para mí es importante adquirir experiencia y aprender cosas relacionadas con mi carrera. Mi jefe es muy bueno. (3) _____ mucho y me explica (4) _____ no sé hacer algo que él desea. (5) _____ muchas cosas interesantes en la oficina. Llamo por teléfono a (6) _____ clientes para saber si todo está bien con nuestros productos. Analizo muchos expedientes *(files)* y (7) _____ los documentos importantes en orden. Mi jefe también (8) _____ su computadora cuando necesito (9) _____ mis trabajos de la universidad. Además, (10) _____ salir temprano cuando termino todo el trabajo a tiempo.

Parte 2. Ahora escribe una descripción de tu trabajo para tu profesor(a).

_____

_____

_____

_____

_____

_____

K. El trabajo. Primero contesta las preguntas. Después entrevista a tu compañero/a para determinar quién tiene el mejor *(the best)* trabajo.

1. ¿Qué días trabajas? ¿Trabajas tiempo parcial o completo?

_____

2. ¿Tienes buen sueldo?

_____

3. ¿Qué prestaciones tienes? ¿Cuándo te dan vacaciones? ¿Cuántos días?

_____

4. ¿Cómo es tu jefe/a?

_____

5. ¿Por qué trabajas ahí? ¿Qué ventajas/desventajas tienes?

_____

6. ¿Te dejan hablar por teléfono? ¿Qué cosas no te dejan hacer?

_____

L. Preguntas indiscretas. Usa las siguientes preguntas para conversar con tu compañero/a.

> **Modelo** ¿Hace ejercicios ¿Dónde? ¿Con qué frecuencia?
> **Hago ejercicio tres veces a la semana.**
> **Voy con mi amigo Mark al gimnasio. ¿Y tú?**

1. ¿Haces ejercicio? ¿Dónde? ¿Con qué frecuencia?

   _____

   _____

2. ¿Sabes cocinar? ¿Qué platos sabes hacer? ¿Con qué frecuencia cocinas?
   ¿Te gusta cocinar?

   _____

   _____

3. ¿Sales temprano del trabajo? ¿A qué hora? ¿Qué días sales tarde?

   _____

   _____

4. ¿Ves a tus familiares con frecuencia? ¿Cuándo ves a tus tíos y primos? ¿Qué actividades
   haces con ellos?

   _____

   _____

5. ¿Pones tu ropa en el clóset o en el suelo *(floor)* cuando llegas tarde a casa? ¿Dónde pones
   tu mochila? ¿Y tus libros?

   _____

   _____

6. Generalmente, ¿sales bien en todas tus clases? ¿A veces sales mal en algunas clases? ¿En
   qué clase? ¿Por qué?

   _____

   _____

   _____

Práctica adicional	
Cuaderno de tareas WB pp.280–281, H–K LM pp.285–286, A–B, Pron.	Audio CD-ROM Episodio 11

Actividades comunicativas

A. La fotonovela. En grupos de cuatro personas, seleccionen cinco de las siguientes actividades para escribir una descripción de lo que hace Adriana entre semana. Después tu grupo va a leer la descripción a la clase y tus compañeros deben adivinar (*guess*) las letras de las actividades que usaron en la descripción. Usen expresiones como **generalmente, con frecuencia, casi siempre** y **muchas veces.**

> **Modelo** Hay semanas que son terribles para mí. A veces...

B. Sopa de palabras.

Instrucciones para **Estudiante 1**

First, create logical sentences out of the scrambled words (the first and last words of each sentence are already in place). Then read your sentences to your partner, who will tell you whether they are correct. You have your partner's unscrambled sentences. Do not tell your partner the right word order immediately; let them try to correct any mistakes.

> **Modelo**
>
> **Mis** a compañeros invitan me **salir**.
> **Mis** compañeros me invitan a salir.

En mi trabajo.

1. **Mi** hace horas a la supervisora me trabajar veinte más de **semana**.

_____

_____

¡Fíjate!
Remember to place **me** and **te** before the conjugated verb.

2. **Mis** salen me cuando amigos escriben de no **vacaciones**.

_____

_____

3. **Mis** cuando soy clientes me dan buenas con propinas amable **ellos**.

_____

_____

4. ¿**Tu** cuando ayuda problemas jefe te tienes **económicos**?

_____

_____

5. **Mis** con agradables; compañeros con son muy ellos salgo **frecuencia**.

_____

_____

Las respuestas de mi compañero/a

1. Mis papás no me dan suficiente dinero; por eso, trabajo.
2. Mis abuelos siempre me mandan chocolates el día de mi cumpleaños.
3. Mi hermano me llama por teléfono cuando necesita algo.
4. ¿Tus amigos te visitan cuando estás enfermo?
5. Mi prima estudia conmigo; por eso, voy por ella todos los días.

B. Sopa de palabras.

Instrucciones para **Estudiante 2**

First, create logical sentences out of the scrambled words (the first and last words of each sentence are already in place). Then read your sentences to your partner, who will tell you whether they are correct. You have your partner's unscrambled sentences. Do not tell your partner the right word order immediately; let them try to correct any mistakes.

> **Modelo**
>
> **Mi** ayuda primo me a la limpiar **casa.**
> **Mi primo me ayuda a limpiar la casa.**

En mi casa.

1. **Mis** dinero; no me por suficiente eso, papás dan **trabajo**.

   _____

   _____

2. **Mis** chocolates el día me siempre abuelos mi mandan de **cumpleaños**.

   _____

   _____

3. **Mi** teléfono necesita me por hermano llama cuando **algo**.

   _____

   _____

4. ¿**Tus** te cuando amigos visitan estás **enfermo**?

   _____

   _____

5. **Mi** conmigo; los por eso, estudia por ella todos prima voy **días**.

   _____

   _____

> **¡Fíjate!**
> Remember to place **me** and **te** before the conjugated verb.

Las respuestas de mi compañero/a

1. Mi supervisora me hace trabajar más de veinte horas a la semana.
2. Mis amigos no me escriben cuando salen de vacaciones.
3. Mis clientes me dan buenas propinas cuando soy amable con ellos.
4. ¿Tu jefe te ayuda cuando tienes problemas económicos?
5. Mis compañeros son muy agradables; salgo con ellos con frecuencia.

C. Dos familias diferentes.

Instrucciones para Estudiante 1

You and a friend are spending the summer in Ecuador as exchange students. Call your friend to find out how things are going with their Ecuadorian family. You will start by finding out if:

- they take them to school
- they prepare good food for them
- they let them use the computer
- they help them with homework
- your friend's parents call them often

¡Fíjate!

Review the verbs in **Las cosas que mi familia y amigos hacen** on page 263.

| **Modelo** | ¿Te preparan buena comida? ¿Te llevan a...? |

Then, read about your own situation at home, so you can answer your partner's questions.

> This is your situation at home:
>
> Your host family is nice, but they are all very busy. They do not have time to cook for you, so you prepare your own meals. About three times a week, they take you out to dinner and do not let you pay for anything. They are generous, and buy you many small presents. They do not take you to school, nor do they pick you up from school; you have to take the bus. They are very busy people, and they have little time to help you with your Spanish homework. You do your own laundry and clean your own room.

Decide who is the luckiest! Be ready to explain your reasoning to the class; take notes in the space provided.

_____

_____

_____

_____

_____

_____

_____

_____

C. Dos familias diferentes.

Instrucciones para **Estudiante 2**

You and a friend are spending the summer in Ecuador as exchange students. Your friend calls you to find out how things are going with your Ecuadorian family. Read about your own situation at home so you can answer your partner's questions:

> This is your situation at home:
>
> Your host family is nice. They take you to school every morning and they pick you up. Your Ecuadorian mother prepares all your meals for you, does your laundry, and makes your bed. Your sister helps you with your homework and lets you use her computer. Your host family does not take you out much, nor do they give you gifts. Your parents back home do not call you, but they write e-mails to you every day.

Now find out how your friend is doing.

Find out if:

- they take them out to dinner
- they do your friend's laundry and clean their room
- they pick your friend up from school
- they help them with homework
- they buy things for your friend

¡Fíjate!

Review the verbs in **Las cosas que mi familia y amigos hacen** on page 263.

| **Modelo** | ¿Te invitan a cenar? ¿Te llevan a... ? |

Decide who is the luckiest! Be ready to explain your reasoning to the class; take notes in the space provided.

_____

_____

_____

_____

_____

_____

_____

_____

_____

La correspondencia

El correo: El club de corazones solitarios. *(Lonely Hearts Club.)* Acabas de recibir esta carta. Lee las preguntas y luego la carta; contesta las preguntas.

1. ¿Qué hace **El club de corazones solitarios**? _____
2. ¿Qué ofrece el club para ayudarte? _____
3. ¿Cómo te preparan para la primera cita? _____

Querido corazón solitario:

¿No tienes pareja[1]? No te preocupes: nosotros te encontramos la pareja perfecta. No es necesario ir a bares de solteros para encontrar la pareja ideal. Nosotros te encontramos pareja sin ningún peligro[2]. Te hacemos un video donde puedes hablar de tus gustos, tus preferencias, tus actividades, tu personalidad y las características que deseas encontrar en tu pareja ideal. También te preparamos para la primera cita: te damos consejos prácticos en cuanto a la ropa, los temas[3] de conversación, los mejores restaurantes y las actividades culturales de la ciudad ese día. Solamente tienes que contestar las preguntas del cuestionario, y nosotros hacemos el resto.

[1]*partner* [2]**sin...** *safely* [3]*topics*

Invitación a **Ecuador**

Del álbum de
Sofía

Ecuador tiene unos 14 millones de habitantes y es un poco más pequeño que Nevada. En la pequeña ciudad de Otavalo, a unas horas de Quito, vemos un excelente ejemplo de cómo los indígenas ecuatorianos han logrado una prosperidad inigualable (*unequaled*). Esta industriosa comunidad de indígenas otavalenses ha logrado establecer contactos comerciales en Europa para la venta de sus productos artesanales y textiles, sin necesidad de intermediarios.

Práctica adicional

Website
vistahigher
learning.com

En papel: El club de corazones solitarios. Completa el cuestionario.

Club de corazones solitarios

1. Nombre _____ 2. Edad _____ 3. Sexo: ☐ hombre ☐ mujer

4. Estatura (en pies)
- ☐ entre 4' y 5'
- ☐ entre 5' y 5'6"
- ☐ entre 5'7" y 6'
- ☐ entre 6' y 6'6"
- ☐ entre 6'7" y 7'
- ☐ más de 7'

5. Peso (en libras)
- ☐ 100–125
- ☐ 126–140
- ☐ 141–165
- ☐ 166–190
- ☐ 190–205
- ☐ 206–225
- ☐ 225+

6. Color de pelo
- ☐ negro
- ☐ castaño
- ☐ rubio
- ☐ pelirrojo

7. Profesión u ocupación _____

8. Sueldo (en dólares):
- ☐ 5,000–15,000
- ☐ 16,000–25,000
- ☐ 25,000–35,000
- ☐ 35,000–45,000
- ☐ 45,000–55,000
- ☐ 55,000+

9. Marca **sí** o **no** según tus preferencias.

Sí No
- ☐ ☐ ¿Fumas?
- ☐ ☐ ¿Haces ejercicio?
- ☐ ☐ ¿Cocinas?
- ☐ ☐ ¿Lees?

Sí No
- ☐ ☐ ¿Viajas?
- ☐ ☐ ¿Te interesa el matrimonio?
- ☐ ☐ ¿Prefieres sólo una amistad?
- ☐ ☐ ¿Quieres tener hijos?

10. ¿Qué deportes haces/practicas? _____

11. ¿Tienes mascotas? ¿Cuáles? _____

12. ¿Cómo es tu personalidad? _____

13. ¿Cuáles son tus actividades favoritas? _____

14. ¿Qué características de la personalidad son importantes en tu pareja? _____

15. ¿Qué características físicas prefieres en tu pareja? _____

¡Fíjate!

To convert meters to feet (**pies**):
meters x 3.2808

To convert kilos to pounds (**libras**):
kilos x 2.2046

 ¡A ver de nuevo! Escribe un resumen del episodio. Incluye detalles que describen los trabajos de los amigos. Después, trabaja con un(a) compañero/a para añadir más información.

Práctica adicional
| Cuaderno de tareas WB pp.281–284, L–M LM p.286, A–B | Audio CD-ROM Episodio 11 | Website vistahigher learning.com |

Vocabulario del Episodio 11

Objetivos comunicativos

You should now be able to do the following in Spanish:

✓ talk about your job

✓ say what people do for you

✓ share your talents

Las cosas que mi familia y amigos hacen

ayudar	*to help*
contar (o ⟶ ue) los problemas	*to tell your problems*
dar consejos	*to give advice*
dejar usar su coche	*to let someone use one's car*
invitar a salir	*to ask someone out*
llamar	*to call*
mandar un regalo	*to send a present*
pagar	*to pay*
pedir (e ⟶ i) cosas prestadas	*to borrow things*
prestar dinero	*to lend money*

Para hablar del trabajo

el ama de casa (m, f)	*homemaker*
atender (e ⟶ ie) a los clientes	*to attend the customers/clients*
el/la chofer	*driver*
el/la empleado/a	*clerk, employee*
el horario flexible/fijo	*flexible/fixed schedule*
el/la jefe/a	*boss*
el/la mesero/a	*waiter/waitress*
el/la niñero/a	*baby-sitter*
poner las cosas en su lugar	*to put/place things in their place*
las prestaciones	*fringe benefits*
el puesto	*position*
saber + [*verb*]	*to know how (to do something)*
salir temprano/tarde	*to get off, to leave early/late*
el sueldo alto/bajo	*high/low salary*
el tiempo completo/parcial/libre	*full-time/part-time/free time*
el turno de la mañana/tarde/noche	*morning/afternoon/night shift*
las vacaciones	*vacation*
la ventaja/desventaja	*advantage/disadvantage*

Vocabulario personal

In this section, write all the words you want to know in Spanish so you can talk about your own job.

¡A escribir!

Episodio

11

Escenas de la vida: ¡A ganarse la vida!

Video
CD-ROM

A. ¡A ver cuánto entendiste! See how much of the **Escena** you understood by matching the Spanish sentences with their English equivalents.

_____ 1. Cuido niños por la tarde.

_____ 2. A ti te dan propinas.

_____ 3. Me invitan a salir.

_____ 4. ¿Qué tal el trabajo?

_____ 5. La verdad es que no sé qué hacer.

_____ 6. ¿Te pagan bien?

_____ 7. Sabemos que son trabajos de tiempo parcial.

a. They invite me out.

b. How's your job?

c. I baby-sit children in the afternoons.

d. Do they pay you well?

e. They give you tips.

f. The truth is, I don't know what to do.

g. We know that they're part-time jobs

Video
CD-ROM

B. ¡Tenemos que trabajar! Complete each phrase in column **A** with the appropriate element from column **B**. Then identify the speaker.

1. ¿Quién lo dijo? *(Who said it?)*

A

_____ 1. Soy mesero…

_____ 2. Tengo que trabajar de…

_____ 3. Me pagan…

_____ 4. Salgo…

B

a. mal.

b. en un restaurante.

c. tarde.

d. noche.

_____ lo dijo.

2. ¿Quién lo dijo?

A

_____ 1. Sabemos que son…

_____ 2. Me ayudan…

_____ 3. Mis compañeros…

_____ 4. Me invitan…

B

a. a salir.

b. son muy buenos.

c. trabajos de tiempo parcial.

d. cuando necesito algo.

_____ lo dijo.

Video
CD-ROM

C. Los trabajos de Ramón y Sofía. Indicate whether the statements are **cierto** or **falso**.

	Cierto	Falso
1. Sofía trabaja durante las tardes y los fines de semana.	☐	☐
2. A Sofía le dan buenas propinas.	☐	☐
3. Ramón es chofer de autobuses.	☐	☐
4. A Ramón le dan buenas propinas.	☐	☐
5. Ramón practica el español en su trabajo.	☐	☐
6. A Sofía le gustan los niños, pero le dan problemas.	☐	☐

Gramática 1

Talking about your job
• <u>Saber, salir, poner,</u> and job-related vocabulary

D. Manolo va a una agencia de colocación *(employment agency)*. Use the expressions to complete Manolo's conversation with his counselor.

ventajas	tiempo parcial	sueldo	el puesto	el turno de la tarde
tiempo libre	vacaciones	desventajas	horario fijo	el empleado

Consejero   Bueno, Manolo, ¿qué tipo de trabajo deseas encontrar?

Manolo   Pues, no sé. Quiero un trabajo que me permita tener un poco de
(1) _____ para poder continuar con mi poesía y mi música.

Consejero   ¿Cuántas horas quieres trabajar y qué días?

Manolo   Pues, unas veinte o veinticinco horas a la semana. Puedo trabajar
cualquier día de la semana.

Consejero   Creo que tengo (2) _____ perfecto para ti: asistente de maestro.
Este trabajo tiene muchas (3) _____: sólo son veinte horas de
trabajo a la semana, por las mañanas; tienes (4) _____ con
frecuencia. Además *(besides)*, te da la oportunidad de ver si te gustaría ser
maestro en el futuro. Y el (5) _____ es bastante bueno, diez
dólares la hora.

Manolo   ¡Qué lástima! *(what a pity!)*, pero por las mañanas no puedo. Sólo puedo
trabajar (6) _____. Definitivamente no puedo trabajar el turno
de la mañana.

Consejero   Bueno, hay muchos trabajos de (7) _____ en restaurantes. El
sueldo no es malo, pero una de las (8) _____ es que no te dan
muchas vacaciones.

Manolo   ¿Y el horario?

Consejero   Bueno, no es un (9) _____. Ellos te informan cuál es tu horario
para cada semana.

Manolo   Gracias por su ayuda, pero creo que por ahora voy a quedarme con *(keep)*
mi trabajo.

E. ¿Qué sabes hacer? Indicate whether you (or the people you know) know how to do the following things, using the verb **saber**. If you do not know anyone, use **nadie** (nobody).

jugar tenis	**esquiar**	**usar las computadoras**
patinar en línea (rollerblade)	**cocinar**	**hablar bien español**

> **Modelo**   Mis primos Mark y Jim saben patinar en línea.

1. _____
2. _____
3. _____
4. _____
5. _____
6. _____

F. ¿Qué quiere saber Wayne? Sofía and Wayne are talking on the phone. Judging from Sofía's answers, write down what Wayne asks her.

1. Wayne _____
   Sofía   Hago la tarea en la biblioteca.
2. Wayne _____
   Sofía   Los sábados salgo con Ana Mari y Ramón o con Manolo.
3. Wayne _____
   Sofía   No, no veo mucho la tele. Prefiero leer o usar Internet.
4. Wayne _____
   Sofía   Sí, me gusta mucho ver películas extranjeras.
5. Wayne _____
   Sofía   Pues, pongo atención en clase y por eso salgo bien.
6. Wayne _____
   Sofía   No, no sé cocinar, pero quiero aprender.

G. Justificaciones. Complete the sentences logically.

> **Modelo**   No sé tocar el piano porque **no tengo tiempo para aprender.**

1. No hago la tarea cuando _____.
2. A veces no pongo atención en clase porque _____.
3. Mis amigos y yo vemos películas en casa cuando _____.
4. Hago ejercicio porque _____.
5. Salgo con mis amigos cuando_____.
6. Voy a salir bien en esta clase porque_____.
7. No pongo mi ropa en el clóset cuando_____.
8. No sé jugar fútbol porque _____.

Gramática 2

Saying what people do for you
• The object pronouns <u>me</u> and <u>te</u>

H. Adriana está muy ocupada. Everybody wants Adriana's help today. Use the expressions to complete the questions her family asks her.

me lees	ayudarme	me llamas
me prestas	me cuentas	comprarme
pagarme	invitarme	me dejas

Viviana   Mami, ¿vas a (1) _____ con la tarea esta noche?

Santiago   Cariño, ¿vas a (2) _____ a salir esta noche?

Carlos   Mami, ¿(3) _____ usar tu coche esta noche?

Viviana   Mami, ¿(4) _____ la carta de tía Cristina?

Santiaguito   Mami, ¿(5) _____ veinte dólares?

Viviana   Mami, ¿vas a (6) _____ un uniforme nuevo?

I. Mi mejor amiga.

Parte 1. Ana Mari explains why Sofía is her best friend. Complete the description, using verbs and object pronouns from this episode.

>   Sofía es mi mejor amiga. Ella (1) _____ con mis problemas. Hay mucha confianza *(trust)* entre nosotras. Ella (2) _____ sus problemas y secretos también. Además, (3) _____ consejos cuando los necesito. Si mi coche no funciona, ella (4) _____ usar el suyo *(hers)*. Los fines de semana, (5) _____ a salir al cine o a cenar. A veces vamos a tomar café o a visitar a Adriana. Una amiga así *(like her)* no es fácil de encontrar.

Parte 2. Now write what *your* best friend does for you.

_____

_____

_____

_____

_____

_____

_____

J. Mi profesor(a) favorito/a. Answer the questions in a paragraph to describe your favorite teacher.

¿Quién es tu profesor(a) favorito/a? ¿Qué clase enseña? ¿Te da mucha tarea? ¿Te deja entregar *(turn in)* la tarea tarde? ¿Te ayuda cuando no entiendes? ¿Te deja salir temprano? ¿Te escucha cuando haces una pregunta? ¿Necesitas estudiar mucho?

_____

_____

_____

_____

_____

K. Las personas que (no) me ayudan. Make up true statements about the people who do/not do the following things for you.

mandarte flores   prestarte dinero   llamarte con frecuencia
dejarte usar su computadora   darte consejos   invitarte a salir

| Modelo | Mi hermano Rubén nunca me presta dinero. |

1. _____
2. _____
3. _____
4. _____
5. _____
6. _____

Para terminar

L. La curiosa de Ana Mari. Ana Mari wants to know more about Manolo, so she is asking Sofía many questions. How would Ana Mari ask the following?

1. Do you know where he works? _____

2. Do you know who lives with him? _____

3. Do you know which days he works? _____

4. Do you know how many classes he takes? _____

5. Does he know how to play volleyball? _____

6. Does he know how to cook? _____

7. Do you know if he has a girfriend? _____

8. Do you know if he is going to ask me out? _____

M. Gustos y aptitudes. Read and complete the following survey to find out if your chosen career suits your talents and interests. Do not spend time thinking about your responses; instead, select the first answer that comes to mind.

Parte 1. Ocupaciones y profesiones. Para cada ocupación, selecciona la posibilidad de hacer ese trabajo: **(S) Sí:** me gustaría; **(I) Indiferente:** ni me gusta ni me disgusta; **(N) No:** no me gustaría.

	S	I	N			S	I	N	
1.	☐	☐	☐	Abogado/a	13.	☐	☐	☐	Ingeniero/a
2.	☐	☐	☐	Director(a) de ventas	14.	☐	☐	☐	Contador(a)
3.	☐	☐	☐	Político/a	15.	☐	☐	☐	Gerente
4.	☐	☐	☐	Ejecutivo/a internacional	16.	☐	☐	☐	Analista de sistemas
5.	☐	☐	☐	Educador(a)	17.	☐	☐	☐	Guardia de seguridad[1]
6.	☐	☐	☐	Maestro/a	18.	☐	☐	☐	Mecánico/a
7.	☐	☐	☐	Líder religioso	19.	☐	☐	☐	Guardabosques[2]
8.	☐	☐	☐	Sicólogo/a	20.	☐	☐	☐	Ingeniero/a mecánico/a
9.	☐	☐	☐	Farmacéutico/a	21.	☐	☐	☐	Fotógrafo/a
10.	☐	☐	☐	Cirujano/a	22.	☐	☐	☐	Músico/a
11.	☐	☐	☐	Asistente dental	23.	☐	☐	☐	Dibujante o Diseñador(a)
12.	☐	☐	☐	Investigador(a) científico/a	24.	☐	☐	☐	Escritor(a) de libros para niños

Parte 2. Materias de la escuela. Para cada materia, selecciona la mejor opción, aunque nunca hayas estudiado esa materia. *(It does not matter if you have never taken a class in that subject.)* **(S) Sí:** me interesa; **(I) Indiferente:** ni me gusta ni me disgusta; **(N) No:** no me interesa.

	S	I	N			S	I	N	
1.	☐	☐	☐	Leyes	13.	☐	☐	☐	Ley de impuestos
2.	☐	☐	☐	Administración	14.	☐	☐	☐	Administración laboral
3.	☐	☐	☐	Ciencias políticas	15.	☐	☐	☐	Computación
4.	☐	☐	☐	Idiomas	16.	☐	☐	☐	Composición
5.	☐	☐	☐	Salud	17.	☐	☐	☐	Educación física
6.	☐	☐	☐	Sicología infantil	18.	☐	☐	☐	Geología
7.	☐	☐	☐	Pedagogía	19.	☐	☐	☐	Reparación automotriz
8.	☐	☐	☐	Sicología	20.	☐	☐	☐	Electricidad
9.	☐	☐	☐	Filosofía	21.	☐	☐	☐	Arte visual
10.	☐	☐	☐	Química	22.	☐	☐	☐	Historia de la música
11.	☐	☐	☐	Matemáticas	23.	☐	☐	☐	Diseño gráfico/dibujo
12.	☐	☐	☐	Estadística	24.	☐	☐	☐	Literatura

[1] *Security guard*   [2] *Park ranger*

Parte 3. Actividades. Selecciona las actividades que te gustan o te interesan.

S	I	N			S	I	N	
1. ☐	☐	☐	Hablar en público	13.	☐	☐	☐	Preparar tus propios impuestos
2. ☐	☐	☐	Entrevistar personas	14.	☐	☐	☐	Trabajar en la computadora
3. ☐	☐	☐	Discutir de política	15.	☐	☐	☐	Escribir tus gastos del mes
4. ☐	☐	☐	Ver las noticias de otros países	16.	☐	☐	☐	Organizar tus documentos
5. ☐	☐	☐	Ayudar a personas con problemas	17.	☐	☐	☐	Ir a exposiciones de armas
6. ☐	☐	☐	Cuidar niños	18.	☐	☐	☐	Ir de campamento
7. ☐	☐	☐	Ser voluntario en tu comunidad	19.	☐	☐	☐	Limpiar el motor de tu coche
8. ☐	☐	☐	Organizar actividades en grupo	20.	☐	☐	☐	Participar en actividades deportivas
9. ☐	☐	☐	Hablar del significado de la vida	21.	☐	☐	☐	Ir a conciertos/galerías de arte
10. ☐	☐	☐	Hacer experimentos químicos	22.	☐	☐	☐	Hacer trabajos manuales/dibujar
11. ☐	☐	☐	Ver una operación de corazón	23.	☐	☐	☐	Ir a desfiles de modas[1]
12. ☐	☐	☐	Leer artículos de medicina	24.	☐	☐	☐	Escribir historias

Parte 4. Tipo de personas. Piensa si te interesa socializar con personas con las siguientes características.

S	I	N			S	I	N	
1. ☐	☐	☐	Personas ricas	8.	☐	☐	☐	Personas estables y tranquilas
2. ☐	☐	☐	Personas de distintas culturas	9.	☐	☐	☐	Personas deportistas
3. ☐	☐	☐	Bebés/Ancianos	10.	☐	☐	☐	Personas a las que les gusta
4. ☐	☐	☐	Personas con problemas de salud					el peligro[2]
5. ☐	☐	☐	Científicos	11.	☐	☐	☐	Genios musicales
6. ☐	☐	☐	Personas famosas o importantes	12.	☐	☐	☐	Personas con talentos artísticos
7. ☐	☐	☐	Personas que tienen tus mismos intereses					

Parte 5. Tus características Selecciona las respuestas que describan el tipo (kind) de persona que eres. (S) Sí: me describe; (D) Depende: depende de la situación: a veces sí, a veces no; (N) No: no me describe.

S	D	N			S	D	N	
1. ☐	☐	☐	Puedes resolver problemas entre dos personas.	7.	☐	☐	☐	Prefieres trabajar horas regulares.
2. ☐	☐	☐	Te comunicas fácilmente con personas de otras culturas.	8.	☐	☐	☐	Prefieres trabajar solo/a que en comités.
3. ☐	☐	☐	Te gusta organizar actividades en tu grupo.	9.	☐	☐	☐	Tienes habilidades mecánicas.
4. ☐	☐	☐	Tienes paciencia para enseñar.	10.	☐	☐	☐	Prefieres estar al aire libre que en una oficina.
5. ☐	☐	☐	Te gusta aprender cosas nuevas.	11.	☐	☐	☐	Prefieres trabajar sin horario fijo.
6. ☐	☐	☐	Sabes escribir bien; de forma clara y concisa.	12.	☐	☐	☐	Te gusta crear cosas originales.

[1]*desfiles...fashion shows* [2]*danger*

Parte 6. Interpretación de resultados. Basado en el exámen *STRONG: Strong Interest Inventory* (publicado por *Consulting Psychologists Press, Inc.*), el inventario de preferencias, gustos e intereses puede dividirse en seis áreas principales:

Mecánica: construcción, reparación, trabajar al aire libre

Investigativa: investigación y análisis

Artística: crear y disfrutar el arte, drama, música, escribir

Social: ayudar, enseñar y cuidar a otros

Comercial: ventas, administración, persuasión

Tradicional: contabilidad, organizar, procesamiento de datos

Para saber en qué área están tus intereses, sigue los siguientes pasos:

1. Primero examina las **Partes 1**, **2** y **3** escribe el número total de veces en las que marcaste la columna **(Sí)** de las preguntas:

Preguntas	1–4	5–8	9–12	13–16	17–20	21–24
	____	____	____	____	____	____

2. Ahora determina el área de interés predominante. Por ejemplo, si en las preguntas 13–16 tienes el número más alto, entonces quiere decir que tus intereses están en el área tradicional. Busca arriba las carreras y profesiones del área tradicional.

Partes 1, 2 y 3

1–4: Comercial   13–16: Tradicional

5–8: Social   17–20: Mecánica

9–12: Investigativa   21–24: Artística

3. Ahora examina las **Partes 4** y **5** y haz lo mismo: escribe el número total de veces en las que marcaste la columna **(Sí)** de las preguntas.

Preguntas	1–2	3–4	5–6	7–8	9–10	11–12
	____	____	____	____	____	____

4. Ahora determina el área de interés predominante. Luego busca las carreras o profesiones de esa área.

Partes 4 y 5

1–2: Comercial   7–8: Tradicional

3–4: Social   9–10: Mecánica

5–6: Investigativa   11–12: Artística

Resultado final: Mi área de interés es _____ y las carreras que podría (*I could*) estudiar son: _____

¡A escuchar!

Episodio

11

Comprensión

Audio
CD-ROM

A. ¿Qué hacen por ti?

Parte 1. You are going to hear six questions about what people do for you. Answer the questions aloud using the written cues provided. Then repeat the correct answer after the speaker.

Modelo	You see:	**cien dólares**
	You hear:	**¿Cuánto te pagan por semana?**
	You say:	**Me pagan cien dólares.**

1. un regalo   2. un secreto   3. consejos   4. mi compañero   5. mi hermano   6. bien

Parte 2. A friend is telling you who does things for her, but you cannot hear her very well in the noisy cafeteria where you are having a cup of coffee together. Each time she finishes a sentence, you have to ask her about what she said. Formulate your questions, using the written cues provided and an indirect object pronoun. Then repeat the correct question after the speaker.

Modelo	You see:	**invitar al cine**
	You hear:	**Mi hermana me invita al cine.**
	You say:	**¿Quién te invita al cine?**

1. escuchar en clase   3. conocer bien   5. prometer cosas
2. ayudar en casa   4. escribir cartas   6. dar dinero

Audio
CD-ROM

B. El horario de Wayne. You are going to hear Wayne describe a normal Tuesday in his weekly schedule. Listen and write down his schedule on the daily planner. **¡Atención!** Remember to change the verbs to the **él** form. You will hear Wayne's description twice.

El martes			
Hora		**Hora**	
8:00	Hace ejercicio.	**1:00**	
9:00		**2:00**	
10:00		**3:00**	
11:00		**4:00**	
12:00		**5:00**	
		6:00	

Pronunciación

Audio
CD-ROM

La x. The letter **x (equis)** most often represents the combination of the English sounds *ks*. Repeat these words after the speaker.

explicar	examen	existir	taxi
excelente	mixta	expresar	sexto

Spoken with certain accents, the letter **x (equis)** sometimes represents the sound of the English *s*. Many native Mexican words and names have this sound. Repeat these words after the speaker.

exacto	exquisito	Taxco	Xochimilco

The letter **x** also sounds somewhat similar to English *h* and Spanish **j** in some native Mexican words and names. Repeat these words after the speaker.

México	Oaxaca	Xoco

Más escenas de la vida

Ramón, Ana Mari, Wayne, and Sofía are leaving the theater and going home. Listen to their conversation, and then complete activities **A** and **B**. You will hear the conversation twice.

Audio
CD-ROM

A. Emparejar. Match the following phrases with the correct responses, according to what you heard in the conversation.

_____ 1. ¿Llevas a Sofía a su casa?

_____ 2. ¿Te gusta vivir en el dormitorio?

_____ 3. Debe ser horrible vivir solo.

_____ 4. No sé cómo puedes vivir con tus padres.

_____ 5. No entiendo cómo tú puedes vivir sin tu familia.

a. Para nosotros la independencia es primero.

b. En mi casa tengo todo.

c. Claro.

d. Sí, mucho.

e. No, estoy contento.

Audio
CD-ROM

B. Responde. Write the answers to the following questions.

1. ¿Cómo está Wayne en el dormitorio? _____

2. ¿Quién está triste? ¿Qué hace ella? _____

3. ¿Por qué a Wayne le gusta vivir solo? _____

4. ¿Por qué le gusta a Sofía vivir con su familia? ¿Qué dice *(says)* de su mamá?

_____

5. ¿Qué dice *(says)* de su papá? _____

Objetivos comunicativos

In this episode, you will practice:

✓ discussing professional plans

✓ talking about people and places you know

✓ talking about salaries

✓ avoiding repetition when answering questions

Episodio 12

Escenas de la vida: Los planes profesionales

Video CD-ROM

A. ¡Mira cuánto puedes entender! Escucha a los personajes expresar sus planes para saber...

Audio CD-ROM

a. ¿Qué quiere ser Sofía?

contadora

arquitecta

Sofía dice que...

☐ quiere trabajar con números.

☐ quiere diseñar edificios modernos.

☐ conoce a un arquitecto que gana más de $80.000.

☐ conoce a un contador que gana más de $8.000.

b. ¿Qué quiere ser Wayne?

periodista

analista de sistemas

Wayne dice que...

☐ entiende mejor a las personas.

☐ entiende mejor las computadoras.

☐ va a empezar con un sueldo bajo.

☐ va a ganar $45.000.

c. ¿Qué quiere ser Ana Mari?

abogada

maestra

1. ¿A quién quiere ayudar?

_____

_____

2. ¿A quién admira, y por qué?

_____

_____

d. ¿Qué quiere ser Ramón?

oficial de prisión

hombre de negocios

1. ¿Qué quiere estudiar?

_____

2. ¿Qué necesitan los profesionales del siglo XXI?

_____

3. ¿Cuántos idiomas sabe hablar?

_____

e. ¿Qué debe ser Manolo?

artista

veterinario

1. ¿Qué quiere ser Manolo?

_____

2. ¿Qué cosas le gusta hacer?

_____
_____

3. ¿Qué debería (should he) estudiar?

_____
_____

Video
CD-ROM

Audio
CD-ROM

B. ¿Te diste cuenta? Escucha los comentarios otra vez para indicar si las oraciones son **ciertas** o **falsas**.

	Cierto	Falso
1. Sofía toma una clase de diseño de circuitos.	☐	☐
2. Ana Mari no va a defender criminales.	☐	☐
3. Ana Mari es idealista.	☐	☐
4. Muchos trabajos requieren comunicación en tres idiomas.	☐	☐
5. Manolo va a ser maestro de primaria.	☐	☐

Video
CD-ROM

Audio
CD-ROM

C. ¿Quién? Escucha para indicar a quién se refieren estos comentarios: Ana Mari (**AM**), Manolo (**M**), Ramón (**R**) o Wayne (**W**).

_____ 1. Habla japonés, pero no lo sabe escribir.

_____ 2. Va a empezar con 40.000 o 45.000 dólares de sueldo.

_____ 3. Dice que hay pocos abogados bilingües.

_____ 4. Tiene muchos talentos artísticos.

Práctica adicional

Cuaderno de tareas WB pp.311–312, A–C	Video CD-ROM Episodio 12

Cultura a lo vivo

In both Hispanic and Anglo cultures, most people are creative and productive; they take pride in their work and strive to support their families and improve their communities. Spanish speakers, however, do not generally define themselves by their work; they rather tend to place greater value on their relationships with family and friends. Spanish speakers do not find personal self-esteem in the amount of money they earn; far more important is the knowledge and level of education they acquire. Although in Latin America, for example, teachers do not earn a lot of money, they are greatly respected and appreciated by the community.

Para comunicarnos mejor

Vocabulario **1** Discussing professional plans
• Careers and professions

Carreras y ocupaciones con futuro

Agente de bienes raíces
Título: licencia
Sueldo promedio: variable

Bombero
Título: licencia
Sueldo promedio: $722
a la semana

Enfermero/a
Título: universitario
Sueldo promedio: $4.934
al mes

Carreras y profesiones

el/la abogado/a	*lawyer*	**el/la ingeniero/a en computación**	*computer engineer*
el/la administrador(a) de empresas	*business administrator*	**el/la investigador(a)**	*investigator*
el/la agente de bienes raíces	*real estate agent*	**el/la maestro/a**	*teacher*
el/la analista de sistemas	*systems analyst*	**el/la médico/a**	*physician*
el/la bombero	*firefighter*	**el/la oficial de prisión**	*prison guard/officer*
el/la contador(a)	*accountant*	**el/la periodista**	*journalist*
el/la diseñador(a) gráfico/a	*graphic designer*	**el/la policía**	*police officer*
el/la educador(a)	*educator*	**el/la profesor(a) de idiomas**	*language professor*
el/la enfermero(a)	*nurse*	**el/la programador(a)**	*computer programmer*
el/la fisioterapeuta	*physical therapist*	**el/la sicólogo/a**	*phychologist*
ganar	*to earn*		
el/la gerente de ventas y mercadeo	*sales and marketing manager*	**el/la técnico/a en computación**	*computer technician*
el/la higienista dental	*dental hygienist*	**el/la veterinario/a**	*veterinarian*

PRÁCTICA

A. Los profesionales. Empareja la descripción con la profesión.

_____ 1. Defiende a los criminales y a los inocentes.
_____ 2. Diseña casas o edificios.
_____ 3. Escribe artículos para periódicos.
_____ 4. Cuida a los pacientes.
_____ 5. Enseña en las escuelas.
_____ 6. Repara las computadoras.
_____ 7. Administra compañías y programas internacionales.
_____ 8. Protege a la comunidad.
_____ 9. Ayuda al veterinario.
_____ 10. Programa computadoras.

a. arquitecta
b. enfermero
c. maestro
d. programadora
e. periodista
f. técnico veterinario
g. policía
h. abogado
i. ejecutiva internacional
j. técnico en computación

B. Estereotipos sobre las profesiones. Completa las frases lógicamente. Algunas frases pueden tener varias respuestas.

1. Los _____ ganan mucho dinero.
2. Las _____ analizan a todas las personas con quienes hablan.
3. Las _____ son dulces y pacientes con los niños.
4. Los _____ saben hablar muchos idiomas.
5. Los _____ son estrictos y muy ordenados.

C. Adivina quién lo hace. Identifica la profesión que corresponde a cada descripción.

1. Este profesional le ayuda al dentista. También les limpia los dientes a los pacientes.

_____

2. Diseña sistemas de computación específicos a las necesidades de las compañías.

_____

3. Toma las decisiones importantes de una empresa. Diseña e implementa planes económicos y de trabajo.

_____

4. Representa a la organización; resuelve problemas entre personas y grupos.

_____

5. Vende casas, condominios y edificios.

_____

D. Aspectos personales. Contesta las preguntas y comparte la información con tu compañero/a para ver si tienen cosas en común.

1. ¿Qué ocupación o profesión tienen tus familiares y amigos?

_____

2. ¿Y tú, qué quieres ser?

_____

3. ¿Por qué quieres estudiar esa carrera *(major)*?

_____

4. ¿Cuáles son algunas ventajas de tu carrera?

_____

5. ¿Cuáles son algunas desventajas?

_____

6. ¿Cuántos años de preparación necesitas?

_____

7. ¿Dónde quieres trabajar?

_____

8. ¿Qué sueldo vas a ganar?

_____

9. ¿Qué prestaciones vas a tener?

_____

> **Práctica adicional**
>
> Cuaderno de tareas
> WB pp.312–313, D–E

Gramática 1   **Talking about people and places you know**
   • **The verb <u>conocer</u>**

Analizar y descubrir

Study the examples and answer the questions.

Conocer	
¿Quieres **conocer a** Wayne?	*Do you want to meet Wayne?*
Conozco a un arquitecto que gana mucho.	*I know an arquitect who earns a lot.*
¿Conoces Guadalajara?	*Do you know (Have you been to) Guadalajara?*
Ramón no **conoce a** mi abogado.	*Ramón doesn't know my lawyer.*
Mi hija y yo **conocemos a** una diseñadora excelente.	*My daughter and I know an excellent designer.*
¿Ustedes **conocen** Miami? **¿Conocéis** Miami? }	*Do you know (Have you been to) Miami?*
Ellos no **conocen a** Emilio.	*They don't know Emilio.*

1. What do you need to place after **conocer** when referring to a *specific* person?

_____

2. Do you do the same when you are talking about a place? _____

PRÁCTICA

E. Personas y lugares. Busca entre tus compañeros una persona que te pueda dar la siguiente información. Usa el verbo **conocer.**

> **Modelo** un buen dentista
> —¿Conoces un buen dentista?
> —Pues no. ¿Y tú?
> —Yo sí. Conozco a la doctora Villalba.

	Nombre	¿Dónde?
1. un buen dentista	Dra. Villalba	Chula Vista
2. una buena manicurista		
3. un buen restaurante chino		
4. un buen veterinario		
5. una buena discoteca		
6. un buen café		
7. un buen mecánico		

F. La familia de Sofía. La familia de Sofía viaja mucho y conoce muchos lugares famosos. Completa las frases para saber qué han visitado.

> **Modelo** Sofía _____ los Andes porque _____ Ecuador.
> **Sofía conoce los Andes porque visitó Ecuador.**

Banco de palabras

visité
I visited

visitaste
you visited

visitó
he/she visited

visitamos
we visited

visitaron
they/you visited

1. Mi hermano y yo _____ la Torre Eiffel porque _____ París el verano pasado.
2. Mis padres _____ las Pirámides de Chichen-Itzá porque _____ México en 1999.
3. Mis primos _____ la Estatua de la Libertad porque _____ Nueva York.
4. Mi abuelo _____ el Vaticano porque _____ Italia.
5. La profesora _____ Machu Picchu porque _____ Perú hace tres años (*three years ago*).
6. ¿Tú _____ Chicago?
7. Yo _____.

Práctica adicional

Cuaderno de tareas
WB pp.313–314, F–G

Vocabulario 2

Talking about salaries
• Numbers 101–100,000

When Wayne was thinking about his future career, he predicted that his entry-level salary would be between **cuarenta** and **cuarenta y cinco mil dólares.** Sofía said that she knows an architect who earns **más de ochenta mil dólares.** When talking about salaries, you will need to use numbers such as the following:

Más números			
101 **ciento uno**	120 **ciento veinte**	700 **setecientos**	20.000 **veinte mil**
102 **ciento dos**	200 **doscientos**	800 **ochocientos**	30.000 **treinta mil**
103 **ciento tres**	300 **trescientos**	900 **novecientos**	80.000 **ochenta mil**
104 **ciento cuatro**	400 **cuatrocientos**	1.000 **mil**	100.000 **cien mil**
105 **ciento cinco**	500 **quinientos**	2.000 **dos mil**	
110 **ciento diez**	600 **seiscientos**	10.000 **diez mil**	

1. The numbers from **doscientos** to **novecientos**, when followed by nouns, are adjectives and agree in gender with those nouns. Observe these masculine/feminine distinctions.

> Necesito quinient**os** pes**os**.
>
> Mi primo trabaja en Londres y gana seiscien**tas** lib**ras** *(pounds)* a la semana.

2. In some Latin American countries and in Spain, a period is used instead of a comma to indicate thousands, and a comma is used instead of a period to indicate decimals.

> En España: **2.367,00** euros En México: **2,367.00** pesos

PRÁCTICA

G. Los cheques de la señora Blasio. Ayuda a la abuela de Sofía a pagar sus cuentas. Escribe la cantidad que falta en cada cheque.

1.

> **Banco Santander Mexicano**
>
> Páguese por este cheque a:
> *Dr. Fernández*
>
> *8 de noviembre del 2003*
> Fecha
>
> $ *27.742,00*
> Moneda nacional
>
> La cantidad de _____
>
> Cuenta personal
> SARA BLASIO
>
> *Sara Blasio*
> Firma
>
> Cuenta   Cheque
> 7406-:11991715:(0011307993)-(0030) Santander S.A. Institución de Banca Múltiple
>
> 2810-2182-4-12-2000

2.

Banco Santander Mexicano

8 de noviembre del 2003
Fecha

Páguese por este cheque a:

Automotriz Salas

$ *97.845,00*
Moneda nacional

La cantidad de

Cuenta personal
SARA BLASIO

Sara Blasio

Firma

2810-2182-4-12-2000

Cuenta   Cheque
7406-:11991715:0011307993-0031   Santander S.A. Institución de Banca Múltiple

3.

Banco Santander Mexicano

8 de noviembre del 2003
Fecha

Páguese por este cheque a:

Palacio de Gobierno

$ *18.538,00*
Moneda nacional

La cantidad de

Cuenta personal
SARA BLASIO

Sara Blasio

Firma

2810-2182-4-12-2000

Cuenta   Cheque
7406-:11991715:0011307993-0032   Santander S.A. Institución de Banca Múltiple

4.

Banco Santander Mexicano

8 de noviembre del 2003
Fecha

Páguese por este cheque a:

Cablevisión

$ *15.269,00*
Moneda nacional

La cantidad de

Cuenta personal
SARA BLASIO

Sara Blasio

Firma

2810-2182-4-12-2000

Cuenta   Cheque
7406-:11991715:0011307993-0033   Santander S.A. Institución de Banca Múltiple

H. ¿Cuánto cuesta? You are helping an administrator with the budget for a new university classroom. Tell them the price of the items you have selected. Take turns with your partner.

> **Modelo** 10 calculadoras / $135.25
> **Diez calculadoras cuestan ciento treinta y cinco dólares con veinticinco centavos** *(cents)*.

1. 1 televisión /$326.64
2. 1 videocasetera / $213.00
3. 1 pizarrón / $111.99
4. 2 escritorios / $449.83
5. 2 sillas ergonómicas / $755.30

6. 6 programas de multimedia / $508.22
7. 15 diccionarios bilingües / $126.40
8. 1 computadora / $970.68
9. 1 cámara digital / $664.00
10. La Enciclopedia Hispánica / $843.10

I. Eventos históricos. Empareja las fechas con los eventos. Compara tus respuestas con las de tu compañero/a.

1. La conquista de México ocurre en _____.	a. 1492
2. El hombre va a la luna *(moon)* por primera vez en _____.	b. 1521
3. El muro de Berlín fue destruido en _____.	c. 1776
4. La Guerra Civil de Estados Unidos empieza en _____.	d. 1860
5. Estamos en el año de _____.	e. 1939
6. La Segunda Guerra Mundial empieza en _____.	f. 1969
7. La independencia de Estados Unidos es en _____.	g. 1989
8. Cristóbal Colón llega a América en _____.	h. _____

J. ¿Cuánto ganan estos profesionales? Cada dos años la Oficina de Estadística Laboral proyecta los sueldos promedio de las profesiones con más futuro. Escucha el informe *(report)* para completar la información.

Audio
CD-ROM

A la semana…
1. Un diseñador gana _____ a la semana.
2. Un doctor gana _____ a la semana.

Al mes *(month)*…
3. Un policía gana _____ al mes.
4. Un piloto gana _____ al mes.

Al año…
5. Un administrador de empresas gana _____ al año.
6. Un técnico en computación gana _____ al año.
7. Un fisioterapeuta gana _____ al año.
8. Un bombero gana _____ al año.

K. Los profesionales hablan. Escucha los comentarios que hacen José Martínez, un sicólogo, y Josefina López, una policía, sobre las ventajas y desventajas de sus trabajos. Después contesta las preguntas.

José Martínez

1. ¿Qué hace la compañía Electromex? _____

2. ¿Qué trabajo tiene José en esa compañía? _____
_____

3. ¿Cuáles son las ventajas de su trabajo? _____
_____

4. ¿Cuáles son las desventajas? _____
_____

5. ¿Cuánto gana? _____

6. ¿Crees que la carrera de José tiene futuro? _____

Josefina López

1. ¿Qué hace Josefina y quién es Daisy? _____

2. ¿Qué hacen antes de empezar su turno? _____

3. ¿Por qué le gusta su trabajo? _____
_____

4. ¿Cuáles son las desventajas de ser policía? _____

5. ¿Por qué quiere ser detective? _____

6. ¿Crees que la carrera de policía es buena? _____

L. Infórmate sobre tu carrera.

Parte 1. Busca información en Internet sobre tus planes profesionales y prepara un reporte escrito.

a. Prepara la información en español para compartir con tus compañeros.
b. Compara tus respuestas con las de la **Práctica D** en la página 291.

¡Fíjate!

Incluye la siguiente información: el sueldo, las prestaciones, el mercado de trabajo y los estudios necesarios.

Writing Strategy: Creating a simple plan

Planning to respond to a writing task in Spanish requires several steps:
1. First, you must be sure you understand what is being asked of you. To do this, you should read the task several times and make a brief outline of what is required. In this section, you are asked to use what you know about yourself—your interests, your abilities, the activities you enjoy—to explain why you have selected a certain career path. Perhaps you will focus on your personality as a key aspect of your choice.
2. Next, you need to determine the ideas you want to communicate. These must be simple enough to be communicated with the language you have learned: descriptive adjectives, verbs, and connecting words such as **por eso** and **porque.**
3. Finally, you need to organize your sentences in such a way that your meaning is clearly communicated. Use the outline you prepared to organize your writing.

Parte 2. En grupos de tres, hablen de sus planes profesionales, dónde hay trabajos en sus especialidades, qué sueldo van a ganar, qué prestaciones hay en sus campos *(fields)* y otra información interesante.

Práctica adicional

Cuaderno de tareas
WB p.314, H

Gramática 2

Avoiding repetition when answering questions
- **The direct object pronouns <u>lo</u>, <u>la</u>, <u>los</u>, and <u>las</u>**

Analizar y descubrir

In their remarks, the characters used the words **lo**, **la**, **los**, and **las** to avoid repeating words already mentioned. Study the following examples and answer the questions.

Voy a trabajar con computadoras.
    Las entiendo mucho mejor que a las personas.

Admiro mucho a Janet Reno.
    ¿**La** recuerdan?

También hablo japonés. Bueno, en realidad no **lo** hablo bien y no **lo** sé escribir.

Todos mis amigos ya saben qué quieren ser.
    Los envidio.

I'm going to work with computers.
    I understand them much better than people.

I admire Janet Reno a lot.
    Do you remember her?

I also speak Japanese. Well, actually I don't speak it well, and I don't know how to write it.

All my friends already know what they want to be. I envy them.

1. In the first example, what word does **las** replace? _____

2. In the second example, what words does **la** replace? _____

3. In the third example, what word does **lo** replace? _____

4. In the fourth example, what words does **los** replace? _____

5. Where, with respect to the verb, are **lo, la, los,** and **las** placed? _____

6. Which other pronouns that you know are also placed before the verb?

_____

7. In a construction with multiple verbs (**En poco tiempo voy a hablar*lo* bien. / En poco tiempo *lo* voy a hablar bien.**), where may the object pronoun be placed?

_____

In summary, direct object pronouns match in gender (masculine or feminine) and number (singular or plural) with the nouns they replace, and are placed in the same position as the object pronouns **me** and **te**—that is, before conjugated verbs or attached to infinitives.

PRÁCTICA

M. ¿Dónde está? Como ya sabes, el compañero de cuarto de Manolo es muy desordenado; él nunca sabe dónde están sus cosas. ¿Qué cosas busca ahora? Completa los diálogos con la(s) palabra(s) apropiada(s) de la lista.

¡Fíjate!

Remember that object pronouns match the nouns they replace in gender and in number.

discos compactos	**calculadora**	**diccionarios**
el cheque de la renta	**las fotografías**	**plumas**

1. —¿Tienes _____?

   —No, ¡tú lo tienes!

2. —¿Dónde está mi _____?

   —No sé. No la necesito para nada.

3. —¿Tienes mis _____?

   —No, no las tengo. Yo uso lápices.

4. —¿Dónde están mis _____?

   —No sé. Yo no los tengo. No escucho tu música.

5. —¿Tienes _____ de la fiesta?

   —No, Sofía las tiene.

6. —¿Tienes mis _____?

   —No, yo nunca los uso.

N. La comida. Contesta las preguntas acerca de lo que te gusta comer y beber.

> **Modelo** ¿Prefieres las hamburguesas con queso o sin queso?
> **Las prefiero sin queso.**

1. ¿Cómo sirven el pollo en tu casa, frito o asado? _____

2. ¿Cómo bebes el café, negro o con leche? _____

3. ¿Bebes la leche fría o caliente? _____

4. ¿Prefieres los huevos fritos o en *omelette*? _____

5. ¿Vas a pedir las quesadillas con jamón o sin jamón? _____

6. ¿Cómo sirven el espagueti, con carne o con mantequilla? _____

Ñ. ¡Cuánta repetición! The following comments are too repetitive. Use **lo, la, los,** and **las** to make the exchanges less repetitive. Then, practice the dialogue with a classmate.

> **Modelo** —¿Adónde va **tu novio**?
> —Va a San Francisco. Mañana tengo que llevar a **mi novio** al aeropuerto y no voy a ver a **mi novio** hasta el domingo.
>
> **Sin repetición**
> —Va a San Francisco. Mañana **lo** tengo que llevar al aeropuerto y no **lo** voy a ver hasta el domingo.
> or
> —Va a San Francisco. Mañana tengo que llevar**lo** al aeropuerto y no voy a ver**lo** hasta el domingo.

1. — ¡Qué bonita **pluma**!

   — Gracias. ¿Quieres **la pluma**? Tengo muchas.

   — ¿Puedo usar **la pluma?**

   — Sí, es tuya *(it's yours)*.

Sin repetición

   — ¡Qué bonita pluma!

   — _____

   — _____

   — _____

¡Fíjate!

Remember that object pronouns are placed before a conjugated verb or attached to an infinitive.

2. — ¿Ves **a tus padres** con frecuencia?

   — No mucho, veo **a mis padres** dos o tres veces al año.

   — ¿Tú visitas **a tus padres** en Miami o ellos te visitan aquí?

   — Yo visito **a mis padres**. Ellos no pueden viajar.

Sin repetición

   — ¿Ves a tus padres con frecuencia?

   — _____

   — _____

   — _____

3. — Mamá, **tu coche** siempre está limpio.

   — Por supuesto, lavo **mi coche** con mucha frecuencia. También pongo **mi coche**
      en el garaje. Además, cuido mucho **mi coche.**

Sin repetición

   — Mamá, tu coche siempre está limpio.

   — _____
      _____
      _____

Invitación a **Perú**

Del álbum de
Ana Marí

Perú es la tierra de los incas.
Su cultura, ropa, idioma,
comida y costumbres
continúan influenciando al
peruano moderno. Esta antigua
y avanzada cultura construyó
(built) increíbles ciudades
fortaleza en remotos lugares
de los Andes.

Práctica adicional

Website
vistahigher
learning.com

299

O. Preguntas personales. Usa las preguntas como guía para hablar con tu compañero/a; escribe sus respuestas. Usa **lo, la, los** y **las** para evitar la repetición cuando sea posible.

Modelo	— ¿Tienes muchos amigos? ¿Cuándo los ves? ¿Los visitas con frecuencia?
	— Me gusta tener amigos; por eso, tengo muchos. Los veo en la escuela todos los días, pero también los veo los fines de semana. Estudio con ellos con frecuencia. Casi nunca los visito porque ellos prefieren venir a mi casa.

¡Fíjate!

Be as creative as you can with your answers. Put all the Spanish you have acquired to work!

1. ¿Tienes muchos amigos? ¿Cuándo los ves? ¿Los visitas con frecuencia?

_____
_____
_____

2. ¿Qué computadora usas? ¿La usas con mucha frecuencia? ¿Dónde la tienes?

_____
_____
_____

3. ¿Siempre haces tu tarea? ¿A qué hora prefieres hacerla? ¿Dónde?

_____
_____
_____

4. ¿Tienes novio/a? ¿Cómo se llama? ¿Lo/La ves todos los días? ¿Tus padres lo/la conocen? ¿Qué piensan de él/ella?

_____
_____
_____

5. ¿Vives con tus padres? ¿Los ayudas en la casa? Si no vives con ellos, ¿los invitas a tu casa? ¿Los llamas por teléfono con frecuencia?

_____
_____
_____

Práctica adicional
Cuaderno de tareas
WB p.315, I–J
LM pp.317–318, A–B, Pron.
Audio CD-ROM Episodio 12

Actividades comunicativas

A. Larga distancia.

Instrucciones para **Estudiante 1**

Trabajas para la compañía de teléfonos más grande de Estados Unidos. Hay un problema con tu computadora y no puedes obtener el área telefónica de las siguientes regiones. Llama a tu compañero/a y pídele *(ask them for)* la información que necesitas. Él/Ella también te va a hacer preguntas; lee las respuestas como un solo número **(617 = seiscientos diecisiete)**.

Modelo
—¿Me puedes dar el área telefónica de Illinois?
—Es setecientos setenta y tres.

	Área
1. Juneau, Alaska	_____
2. Portland, Oregon	_____
3. Cheyenne, Wyoming	_____
4. Tucson, Arizona	_____
5. Fargo, North Dakota	_____
6. Little Rock, Arkansas	_____
7. Miami, Florida	_____
8. Portland, Maine	_____

A. Larga distancia.

Instrucciones para **Estudiante 2**

Trabajas para la compañía de teléfonos más grande de Estados Unidos. Hay un problema con tu computadora y no puedes obtener el área telefónica de las siguientes regiones. Tu compañero/a te llama para pedirte las áreas de teléfono que necesita. Dáselas *(give them to them)* y pídele *(ask them for)* la información que tú necesitas; lee las respuestas como un solo número **(617 = seiscientos diecisiete)**.

Modelo   —¿Me puedes dar el área telefónica de Illinois?
—Es setecientos setenta y tres.

	Área
1. Concord, New Hampshire	_____
2. Richmond, Virginia	_____
3. Omaha, Nebraska	_____
4. Sioux Falls, South Dakota	_____
5. Albuquerque, New Mexico	_____
6. Boise, Idaho	_____
7. Las Vegas, Nevada	_____
8. Washington, DC	_____

B. Crucigrama.

Instrucciones para **Estudiante 1**

Tu compañero/a y tú tienen el mismo crucigrama, pero tú tienes las respuestas que él/ella no tiene, y viceversa. Necesitas explicarle las palabras usando definiciones, sinónimos, antónimos o frases incompletas.

| Modelo | 11 vertical: | **Janet Reno es una...** |
| | 5 horizontal: | **Esta persona trabaja en una escuela y da clases.** |

B. Crucigrama.

Instrucciones para Estudiante 2

Tu compañero/a y tú tienen el mismo crucigrama, pero tú tienes las respuestas que él/ella no tiene, y viceversa. Necesitas explicarle las palabras usando definiciones, sinónimos, antónimos o frases incompletas.

Modelo	11 vertical:	**Janet Reno es una...**
	5 horizontal:	**Esta persona trabaja en una escuela y da clases.**

The crossword grid contains the following filled letters:

- 1 (vertical): S, I, C, Ó, L, O, G, O
- 2 (horizontal): I
- 3 (vertical): P, R, O, F, E, S, O, R, A
- 4 (vertical): A, G, E, N, T, E
- 5 (horizontal): E
- 6 (horizontal): E
- 7 (vertical): E, D, U, C, A, D, O, R, A
- 8 (vertical): E, N, F, E, R, M, E, R, A
- 9, 10 (vertical): T, É, C, N, I, C
- 11 (vertical): A, B, O, G, A, D, A
- 12 (horizontal)
- 13 (horizontal): O
- 14 (horizontal): C, O

C. La encuesta dice... Esta actividad es similar al programa *Family Feud*. En grupos de tres, escriban las cinco respuestas que ustedes creen que son las más comunes. Tu profesor(a) tiene las respuestas correctas.

1. ¿Qué hacen los estudiantes con el libro de español?

> **Modelo**   Lo compran en la librería.

a. _____
b. _____
c. _____
d. _____
e. _____

2. ¿Cómo debe comportarse *(should behave)* un buen hijo con su mamá?

> **Modelo**   Un buen hijo debe invitarla a comer o al cine.

Un buen hijo debe...

a. _____
b. _____
c. _____
d. _____
e. _____

3. ¿Qué hacen las personas con sus coches?

> **Modelo**   Las personas los manejan con cuidado.

a. _____
b. _____
c. _____
d. _____
e. _____

La correspondencia

El correo: Premio escolar "Espíritu de Superación". Acabas de recibir este artículo por correo. Lee las preguntas, y después lee el artículo para contestarlas.

1. ¿Quién otorga los premios? _____

2. ¿Cuántos estudiantes solicitaron *(applied for)* este premio? _____

3. ¿Cuál es el estado con mayor número de ganadores *(winners)*? _____

4. ¿Cuánto dinero van a recibir los estudiantes ganadores? _____

5. ¿A quién admira la ganadora Silvia Posada? _____

Cien estudiantes ganaron el premio
"Espíritu de Superación"

Cien estudiantes en su último año de estudios pre-universitarios ganaron el premio escolar "Espíritu de Superación," otorgado por el fabricante norteamericano de autos Ford. El objetivo del premio es apoyar y motivar a los estudiantes para continuar sus estudios universitarios y ayudarlos a alcanzar sus metas.

En colaboración con la cadena televisiva Univisión, un panel de jueces seleccionó a los cien mejores estudiantes de entre 35.000 participantes. Los requisitos eran: escribir una composición que hablara de la persona que más admiran y cómo esta persona se ha superado, estar en el último año de estudios secundarios y tener un promedio mínimo de 3,0. La selección de los ganadores se basó en la originalidad, creatividad, relevancia del tema y uso correcto del idioma.

Los ganadores van a recibir $1.200 cada uno y representan varios grupos étnicos de todas partes de la nación; el 88% de los ganadores son hispanos. El estado con mayor número de ganadores es California con un 38%; después vienen Texas con 16%, Nueva York y Nueva Jersey con 13%, Illinois con 11% y Florida con 6%.

"Para nosotros es un honor premiar a estudiantes que han demostrado esfuerzo y dedicación en sus estudios. Su espíritu de superación nos inspira," declaró Ross Roberts, Vicepresidente y Gerente General de la División Ford.

La ganadora Silvia Posada de Los Ángeles, California, escribe: "Yo admiro [a mi hermana] por todos sus logros en la escuela y por nunca dudar de sí misma. La seguridad y confianza que ella tiene en sus habilidades es la misma que tiene para mí y ése es el mejor regalo que me pueden ofrecer."

En papel: Mi futuro. Escribe una carta a la Ford, basándote en la lectura de **El correo**, en la que describas:

- tus estudios, tus notas y tus planes profesionales
- por qué necesitas $1.200 dólares y qué vas a hacer con el dinero

¡A ver de nuevo!

Video
CD-ROM

Audio
CD-ROM

Parte 1. Escucha la conversación de **Escenas de la vida** o mira el video para hacer un resumen de los planes profesionales de cada personaje.

Parte 2. Ahora trabaja con un(a) compañero/a para comparar la información y añadir lo que te haya faltado.

Práctica adicional		
Cuaderno de tareas WB p.316, K LM p.318, A–B	Audio CD-ROM Episodio 12	Website vistahigher learning.com

Vocabulario del Episodio 12

Objetivos comunicativos

You should now be able to do the following in Spanish:

✓ discuss professional plans

✓ talk about people and places you know

✓ talk about salaries

✓ avoid repetition when answering questions

Las profesiones y las ocupaciones

el/la abogado/a	*lawyer*
el/la administrador(a) de empresas	*business administrator*
el/la agente de bienes raíces	*real estate agent*
el/la analista de sistemas	*systems analyst*
el/la bombero	*firefighter*
el/la contador(a)	*accountant*
el/la diseñador(a) gráfico/a	*graphic designer*
el/la educador(a)	*educator*
el/la enfermero/a	*nurse*
el/la fisioterapeuta	*physical therapist*
el/la gerente de ventas y mercadeo	*sales and marketing manager*
el/la higienista dental	*dental hygienist*
el/la ingeniero/a en computación	*computer engineer*
el/la investigador(a)	*investigator*
el/la maestro/a	*teacher*
el/la médico/a	*physician*
el/la oficial de prisión	*prison guard/officer*
el/la periodista	*journalist*
el/la policía	*police officer*
el/la profesor(a) de idiomas	*language professor*
el/la programador(a)	*computer programmer*
el/la sicólogo/a	*psychologist*
el/la técnico/a en computación	*computer technician*
el/la veterinario/a	*veterinarian*

Verbos

conocer	*to know; to meet someone*
ganar	*to earn (money); to win*

Pronombres de complemento directo

¿Me ayudas?	*Will you help **me**?*
Sí, te ayudo.	*Yes, I'll help **you**.*
Lo sé.	*I know **it**.*
La veo, Lo veo.	*I see **her**, I see **him**.*
Los conozco.	*I know **them**. (m)*
Las ayudo.	*I help **them**. (f)*

Más números

101	**ciento uno**	600	**seiscientos**
102	**ciento dos**	700	**setecientos**
103	**ciento tres**	800	**ochocientos**
104	**ciento cuatro**	900	**novecientos**
105	**ciento cinco**	1.000	**mil**
110	**ciento diez**	2.000	**dos mil**
120	**ciento veinte**	10.000	**diez mil**
200	**doscientos**	20.000	**veinte mil**
300	**trescientos**	30.000	**treinta mil**
400	**cuatrocientos**	80.000	**ochenta mil**
500	**quinientos**	100.000	**cien mil**

Vocabulario personal

In this section, write the words you want to know in Spanish so you can talk about your professional plans.

¡A escribir!

Episodio

12

Escenas de la vida: Los planes profesionales

Video CD-ROM

A. ¡A ver cuánto entendiste! See how much of the **Escena** you understood by matching the Spanish sentences with their English equivalents. Then identify the speakers.

_____ 1. Conozco a un arquitecto que gana más de ochenta mil dólares al año.

_____ 2. Si no me electrocuto antes de terminar la clase de diseño de circuitos.

_____ 3. Los envidio.

_____ 4. Tengo que ganarme la vida.

_____ 5. Me gusta cuidar a los animales.

_____ 6. Las entiendo mucho mejor que a las personas.

_____ 7. Me gustaría diseñar edificios modernos.

a. I like to take care of animals.

b. I understand them much better than people.

c. I envy them.

d. I have to earn a living.

e. If I don't electrocute myself before I finish my circuit design class.

f. I would like to design modern buildings.

g. I know an architect that earns more than eighty thousand dollars a year.

Video CD-ROM

B. Los planes profesionales de Sofía y Wayne. Use the words from the list to complete the monologues.

casa	arquitecta	diseñar	sueldo	computadoras
suerte	las	ochenta mil	abogada	edificios

Sofía Quiero ser (1) _____ porque me gusta diseñar

(2) _____ modernos. Algún día voy a

(3) _____ mi propia (4) _____.

Conozco a un arquitecto que gana más de (5) _____ dólares al año.

Wayne Voy a trabajar con (6) _____. (7) _____

entiendo mucho mejor que a las personas. Sé que voy a empezar con

(8) _____ bueno, y con un poco de suerte...

Video
CD-ROM

C. Los planes profesionales de Ana Mari y Ramón. Answer the questions.

1. ¿Qué quiere ser Ana Mari? ¿A quién quiere ayudar? ¿A quién admira, por qué? ¿A quién nunca va a defender?

_____

_____

_____

2. ¿Por qué estudia Ramón negocios internacionales? ¿Qué dice (says) el artículo de periódico? ¿Qué idiomas habla? ¿Qué pasa con el japonés? ¿Cuándo lo va a hablar perfectamente?

_____

_____

_____

Vocabulario 1

Discussing professional plans
- **Careers and professions**

D. ¿Qué profesión tienen? Match the definitions with the illustrations; then, write the correct profession.

a   b   c   d   e

f   g   h   i   j

_____ 1. La persona que escribe para los periódicos. También hace entrevistas. _____

_____ 2. Una persona que trabaja en hospitales. Ayuda a los doctores. _____

_____ 3. Una persona que protege a la sociedad y busca a los criminales. _____

_____ 4. Esta persona diseña casas y edificios. _____

_____ 5. Esta persona vende casas y edificios. _____

_____ 6. Las personas que nos ayudan y protegen de los incendios. _____

_____ 7. Una persona que diseña sistemas de computación para empresas. _____

_____ 8. Estas personas enseñan a leer a los niños. _____

_____ 9. Una persona que crea esculturas y pinturas. _____

_____ 10. Las personas que llevan la contabilidad de una empresa. _____

E. Ventajas y desventajas. Based on what you know about the following professions, list the advantages, disadvantages, and rate the salary.

Carrera	Ventajas	Desventajas	Sueldo
policía	• prestaciones buenas • poder ayudar a las personas	• muchas horas de trabajo • horario de noche • peligroso	• bajo al empezar • buen sueldo con los años
gerente de ventas y mercadeo			
niñero/a			
escritor(a) de novelas (como Stephen King)			
sicólogo			

Gramática **1**	Talking about people and places you know • The verb <u>conocer</u>

F. Las grandes ciudades norteamericanas. You are talking to Sofía, who is interested in traveling in the United States. Tell her about cities you know.

> **Modelo** ¿Conoces la ciudad de Chicago?
> **No, no la conozco, pero sé que es muy grande, interesante y que hay muchos mexicanos.**

¿Conoces la ciudad de...

1. Nueva York? _____
_____

2. Miami? _____
_____

3. San Francisco? _____
_____

4. Atlanta? _____
_____

5. Seattle? _____
_____

6. Washington, DC? _____

_____

7. San Antonio? _____

_____

G. ¿A quién conocemos? Complete Manolo and Ana Mari's conversation using **conocer**.

Ana Mari — Manolo, ¿tú (1) _____ a alguien famoso?

Manolo — Pues no, pero mi hermana que vive en Miami (2) _____ al hermano de Julio Iglesias.

Ana Mari — Huy, ¡qué interesante! Yo tampoco (3) _____ a nadie famoso, pero mis papás (4) _____ a varios actores mexicanos.

Manolo — Wayne y yo (5) _____ la casa de alguien famoso.

Ana Mari — ¿De veras? ¿De quién?

Manolo — El castillo de Hurst.

Ana Mari — ¿El castillo de Hurst? ¡Ay Manolo, pero si eso es un museo!

Manolo — Bueno, pero era su casa, ¿no?

Vocabulario 2

Talking about salaries
• Numbers 101–100,000

H. ¿Cuánto?

Parte 1. Match each number with its written equivalent.

_____ 1. 54.641   a. cincuenta y cuatro mil setecientos cuarenta y uno

_____ 2. 183.835   b. dieciséis mil cuatrocientos noventa y seis

_____ 3. 16.496   c. veinte mil trescientos sesenta y tres

_____ 4. 54.741   d. cincuenta y cuatro mil seiscientos cuarenta y uno

_____ 5. 20.363   e. ciento ochenta y tres mil ochocientos treinta y cinco

Parte 2. Fill in the missing parts of the numbers.

1. 92.517   _____ y dos _____ _____ diecisiete

2. 75.409   _____ y cinco mil _____ nueve

3. 39.212   treinta y _____ mil_____ doce

4. 116.578   _____ dieciséis _____ _____

            _____ y ocho

5. 48.024   cuarenta _____ ocho mil _____

Nombre _____ Fecha _____

Gramática 2 — Avoiding repetition when answering questions
• The direct object pronouns <u>lo</u>, <u>la</u>, <u>los</u>, and <u>las</u>

I. El primer día de clases. Ana Mari's little brothers are preparing for their first day of school. Answer their questions using direct object pronouns.

> **Modelo** ¿Tengo que llevar la calculadora?
> No, **no la tienes que llevar./no tienes que llevarla.**

1. ¿Necesito el papel?

   Sí, _____.

2. ¿Podemos llevar al perro a la escuela?

   No, _____.

3. ¿Voy a usar mis lápices de colores?

   No, _____.

4. ¿Tengo que llevar las plumas?

   Sí, _____.

5. ¿Necesitamos los libros de texto?

   Sí, _____.

J. ¡Qué ocupados! Answer the questions about the characters, using direct object pronouns. You may make up some answers.

> **Modelo**
> ¿Con quién hace Sofía la tarea?
> **La hace con Adriana y Manolo.**

 ¡Fíjate!
Remember to place the direct object pronoun before the verb (**la hace**) and to match gender and number with the object it replaces (**la** because **tarea** is feminine).

1. 2. 3. 4. **1:00 pm** 5. **Los sábados**

1. ¿Con quién mira Sofía la tele? _____

2. ¿Qué va a hacer con la ropa? _____

3. ¿Adónde va a llevar a Manolo? _____

4. ¿A qué hora va a hacer Adriana el flan? _____

5. ¿Visitan a los abuelos entre semana? _____

Para terminar

K. La CIA: Agencia Central de Inteligencia. Read the article on the CIA, taken from *Hispanic Business* magazine. Then answer the questions.

1. ¿Qué características personales necesita tener un agente de la CIA?

_____

2. ¿Qué preparación académica necesitas para hacer una carrera en la CIA?

_____

3. ¿Qué tipo de experiencia o habilidades especiales son deseables?

_____

4. ¿Te parece interesante trabajar para la CIA? ¿Por qué sí o por qué no?

_____

Lo máximo en carreras internacionales

Para el individuo que quiere más que un simple trabajo, ésta es una carrera única; un estilo de vida que prueba[1] los límites de la inteligencia, la autosuficiencia[2] y la responsabilidad. Requiere un espíritu aventurero, una personalidad bien definida, una habilidad intelectual superior, fuerza[3] mental y un alto grado de integridad. Se necesitan habilidades especiales y disciplina profesional para producir resultados. Usted debe resolver situaciones volátiles, ambiguas y poco estructuradas que prueban al máximo su ingenio[4].

El Programa de Entrenamiento de la CIA es la puerta de entrada a una carrera internacional. Para calificar, usted debe poseer calificaciones de primera: título universitario con excelente historial académico, sólidas habilidades interpersonales, la habilidad de escribir clara y precisamente, y un inagotable interés en asuntos internacionales.

Las personas con estudios de posgrado, viajes al extranjero, que hablen otros idiomas, que hayan vivido en otros países, o con experiencia militar tienen ya cierta ventaja.

El sueldo va de $31.459 a $48.222 dependiendo de la experiencia y preparación. Los solicitantes deben someterse a un riguroso examen psicológico y médico, una entrevista poligráfica y una investigación extensa de antecedentes. La edad máxima para ingresar a la agencia es de 35 años, se requiere la ciudadanía[5] norteamericana para usted y su pareja. La CIA busca hombres y mujeres de todas las razas y de todos los sectores culturales de la población. La CIA representa a Estados Unidos y el personal debe ser representativo de la diversidad cultural del país. Para solicitar empleo, mande su currículum[6] (incluya promedio académico) y una carta que explique sus destrezas[7] y habilidades. En treinta días nos pondremos en contacto con los solicitantes mejor calificados.

---

[1]*tests* [2]*self-sufficiency* [3]*strength* [4] **prueban...** *test your resourcefulness to the limit* [5]*citizenship* [6]*résumé* [7]*skills*

Episodio 12

¡A escuchar!

Comprensión

Audio
CD-ROM

A. ¿Cuántos hay? Imagine that you and a classmate are working in a bookstore taking inventory. You are going to hear your co-worker call out eight items and ask how many there are. Consult the inventory list and report the quantities aloud. Your co-worker will then repeat the number to make sure she heard correctly. Repeat the number after her.

Modelo	You hear:	**¿Cuántas plumas hay?**
	You see:	**2.759 plumas**
	You say:	**Hay dos mil setecientas cincuenta y nueve plumas.**

Inventario

2.759	plumas	**987**	discos compactos
343	borradores	**2.525**	discos para la computadora
438	libros de consulta	**1.896**	lápices
662	cuadernos de composición	**520**	paquetes de papel
114	diccionarios		

Audio
CD-ROM

B. Las personas y sus trabajos. You are going to hear five people describe their careers and professions. Listen and select the correct job title of each person.

1. Carmen es...
   a. ingeniera   b. enfermera   c. profesora

2. Enrique es...
   a. mesero   b. arquitecto   c. científico

3. Marta es...
   a. abogada   b. periodista   c. maestra

4. Jesús es...
   a. sicólogo   b. escritor   c. policía

5. Miguel es...
   a. programador   b. veterinario   c. médico

Pronunciación

El enlace. In Spanish, in natural speech, words are linked together without regard to word boundaries, producing a smooth flow of articulation. This linking is called **enlace**. Repeat these questions and statements after the speaker.

Audio CD-ROM

¿Qué puedes hacer?	[ke-pue-de-sa-ser]
¿Me das una invitación?	[me-da-su-nain-bi-ta-sion]
Viven en la ciudad de Miami.	[bi-be-nen-la-siu-da-de-mia-mi]
¡Vamos a un restaurante italiano!	[ba-mo-saun-res-tau-ran-tei-ta-lia-no]

Más escenas de la vida

Adriana and Santiago are talking about Santiago's job. Listen to their conversation and then complete activities **A** and **B**. You will hear the conversation twice.

Adriana

Santiago

Audio CD-ROM

A. Emparejar. Match up these phrases based on what you heard in the conversation.

_____ 1. ¿Crees que no es suficiente?   a. Ay, Santiago, contigo no se puede hablar.

_____ 2. ¿Ahora eres sicóloga también?   b. A veces me preocupo mucho por ti.

_____ 3. ¿Ves por qué discutimos?   c. No es por el sueldo.

_____ 4. Sé que ganas bien pero...   d. Como tú ahora vas a la escuela…

Audio CD-ROM

B. Responde. Write the answers to the following questions.

1. ¿Por qué se preocupa Adriana por Santiago?

_____

2. ¿Por qué Adriana quiere que Santiago sea detective?

_____

3. ¿Santiago quiere seguir estudiando *(keep studying)*?

_____

4. ¿Por qué no quiere seguir estudiando?

_____

Episodio 13

Escenas de la vida: Las vacaciones

Video
CD-ROM

A. ¡Mira cuánto puedes entender! Escucha la conversación o mira el video para seleccionar la información correcta.

Audio
CD-ROM

Necesitamos pasaporte y visa para ir a México.

Ya tenemos las reservaciones de avión.

El boleto de ida y vuelta cuesta $390.00.

Hace calor durante el día.

Llueve mucho en el invierno.

Hace frío por la noche.

Manolo va a ayudar a Sofía con sus maletas.

Cultura a lo vivo

In both Hispanic and Anglo cultures, the climate, the weather, and the formality of the occasion determine the appropriateness of a particular outfit. Although it varies from country to country, in general, Spanish speakers dress more formally than people in the U.S.

Spanish speakers tend to dress formally for parties and social events. Depending on the country, Spanish speakers may not wear shorts or sandals unless they are at the beach. Even in the most informal situations, they do not go barefoot or shirtless.

Video
CD-ROM

Audio
CD-ROM

B. ¿Te diste cuenta? Escucha la conversación otra vez para indicar si las oraciones son **ciertas** o **falsas**.

	Cierto	Falso
1. Los chicos no necesitan pasaporte para ir a México.	☐	☐
2. Ana Mari conoce Guadalajara.	☐	☐
3. Manolo paga su boleto con tarjeta de crédito.	☐	☐
4. En Guadalajara siempre hace calor.	☐	☐
5. Los chicos quieren ir a la playa.	☐	☐

Video
CD-ROM

Audio
CD-ROM

C. No es cierto. Escucha la conversación de nuevo para seleccionar la respuesta falsa.

1. Los chicos…
   a. salen el 18 de diciembre para Guadalajara y regresan el primero de enero.
   b. dicen que en Guadalajara nieva en invierno.
   c. tienen que pagar los boletos antes del 10 de diciembre.

2. Manolo…
   a. ya tiene un pasaporte nuevo.
   b. no tiene dinero para pagar el boleto.
   c. va a ayudar a Sofía con sus maletas.

3. Sofía…
   a. va a llevar un traje de baño a Puerto Vallarta.
   b. le va a cobrar a Manolo el 50% de interés.
   c. va a pagar el boleto de Manolo.

4. Manolo dice…
   a. si tú me pagas mi boleto, yo te ayudo con tus maletas.
   b. ¿me puedes pagar mi boleto con tu tarjeta?
   c. no tengo ganas de ir a Puerto Vallarta.

Invitación a **Costa Rica**

Del álbum de
Sofía

Costa Rica es un paraíso para los amantes (*lovers*) de la naturaleza y del turismo de aventura. Los numerosos parques ecológicos del país ofrecen actividades para todos los gustos: desde caminatas en las selvas (*jungles*), exploración de volcanes (activos e inactivos), 'canopy' y surfeo, hasta paseos en balsas (*rafts*) por rápidos.

Práctica adicional		
Cuaderno de tareas	Video CD-ROM	Website
WB p.337, A–B	Episodio 13	vistahigher learning.com

Learning Strategy: Looking for similarities and differences in language structure

Noticing similarities and differences between English and Spanish word order will help you understand and learn Spanish. For instance, look at the placement of adverbs in the following examples:

¡Tú **nunca** vas al gimnasio!	You **never** go to the gym!
Yo hago ejercicio **todos los días**.	I exercise **every day**.

Notice that the placement of *never* (**nunca**) and *every day* (**todos los días**) is the same in English and in Spanish. You do not have to learn a different word order when using these words.

Differences in word order however, should be learned. These include:

- the placement of the direct object pronouns **me, te, lo, la, los,** and **las.**

Te doy un cheque la próxima semana.	I'll give **you** a check next week.

In Spanish, these pronouns are placed before a conjugated verb, whereas in English, they are placed after the verb.

- the placement of descriptive adjectives

Lleva ropa **ligera** para el día...	Take **light** clothing for daytime...

In Spanish, most descriptive adjectives are placed after the noun, whereas in English, they come before the noun.

When you study, concentrate on the differences and just make a mental note of the similarities.

Para comunicarnos mejor

 Vocabulario 1

Talking about dates and the weather
• Seasons, months, and the weather

In the conversation, you heard the following statements.

Salimos **el 18 de diciembre.**	*We're leaving on the 18th of December.*
Regresamos **el primero de enero.**	*We're returning on the first of January.*
Durante el día **hace calor...**	*During the day it's hot...*
Por la noche... **hace** bastante **frío.**	*At night... it's rather cold.*
Llueve durante el verano.	*It rains during the summer.*

1. Use **el** + [*number*] + **de** + [*month*] to talk about dates.
2. Use **el primero** to say *the first of* [*month*].
3. Notice that months are not capitalized in Spanish.

• Seasons, months, and the weather

	¿Qué tiempo hace?	La temperatura	Los meses
	el invierno		
	Hace frío.	-15° – 10°	diciembre
	Llueve o nieva.		enero
	Hace mal tiempo.		febrero
	la primavera		
	Hace fresco.	10° – 18°	marzo
	Llueve.		abril
	Hace viento.		mayo
	el verano		
	Hace calor.	20° – 30°	junio
	Hace sol.		julio
	Hace buen tiempo.		agosto
	el otoño		
	Hace viento.	10° – 22°	septiembre
	Está nublado.		octubre
	Hace fresco.		noviembre

PRÁCTICA

A. ¿Cuándo se celebra? Escribe la fecha de estas celebraciones.

> **Modelo** El Día de los Muertos es **el dos de noviembre.**

1. El Día de San Valentín es _____.
2. El Día de la Independencia de Estados Unidos es _____.
3. La Navidad es _____.
4. El Día de los Inocentes *(April Fool's Day)* es _____.
5. El Día de Año Nuevo es _____.
6. El día de mi cumpleaños es _____.

B. Fechas importantes. Escribe cinco fechas importantes para ti. Incluye dos cumpleaños, un aniversario y dos días festivos *(holidays)*. Después comparte con tu compañero/a las actividades que haces en esos días.

> **Modelo** **El 9 de octubre es importante para mí porque es el cumpleaños de mi mamá. Mi familia y yo salimos a cenar con ella. Generalmente vamos a un restaurante elegante.**

1. _____
_____
2. _____
_____
3. _____
_____
4. _____
_____
5. _____
_____

C. ¿Dónde? Indica en qué ciudades de Estados Unidos existen estas condiciones climatológicas.

| Tampa | Seattle | Chicago | Buffalo |

1. En esta ciudad llueve todo el año. Hace fresco. La temperatura promedio durante la primavera es de 60°F. _____
2. En esta ciudad hace mucho frío durante el invierno. Nieva mucho. La temperatura promedio es de 5°F bajo cero. _____
3. En esta ciudad el clima es húmedo y hace mucho calor en el verano. _____
4. En esta ciudad hace viento. El clima es extremo: hace calor en el verano y hace frío en el invierno. _____

D. El mes de enero. Escucha la narración acerca del clima de Guayaquil, en Ecuador, y de Madrid, en España. Indica el clima de cada lugar.

Clima en enero	Guayaquil, Ecuador	Madrid, España
1. Hace frío.		
2. Hace calor.		
3. Hace buen tiempo.		
4. Hace sol.		
5. Llueve.		
6. Nieva.		
7. Está nublado.		

Práctica adicional

Cuaderno de tareas
WB pp.338–339, C–F

Vocabulario 2

Planning your wardrobe
• **Clothing and colors**

La ropa que Sofía quiere llevar a Guadalajara

el abrigo

la blusa morada

las botas

los zapatos de tacón

la falda roja

el vestido negro

la camiseta azul

las sandalias verdes

los pantalones anaranjados

La ropa que Manolo va a llevar a Guadalajara

los lentes de sol

el paraguas

la camisa gris

los tenis

el traje de baño

la corbata

los pantalones
cortos

los jeans

También se dice...

la chaqueta ⟶ la chamarra, el saco

color café ⟶ marrón, pardo

la falda ⟶ la pollera

la maleta ⟶ la valija, la petaca, el veliz

los jeans ⟶ los pantalones de mezclilla, los bluejeans, los mahones, los vaqueros

---

Más ropa

la bolsa	*bag*	**los guantes**	*gloves*	**el sombrero**	*hat*
la bufanda	*scarf*	**llevar/usar**	*to wear*	**la maleta**	*suitcase*
los calcetines	*socks*				

La maleta de Ana Mari

la blusa blanca

la chaqueta azul

el bikini

el suéter café

el impermeable gris

el/la pijama

el traje

la minifalda amarilla

PRÁCTICA

E. ¿Qué ropa llevan? Describe la ropa que los chicos piensan llevar a una fiesta.

1. Manolo piensa llevar _____

_____ .

2. Sofía quiere llevar _____

_____ .

¡Fíjate!

Remember to use **un, una, unos,** and **unas** when talking about the clothes people wear.

3. Ana Mari va a llevar _____

_____ .

4. Ramón quiere llevar _____

_____ .

 F. ¿Qué llevan? Comenta con un(a) compañero/a la ropa que llevan los chicos para salir en Guadalajara.

G. Las estaciones. Describe la ropa que usas en las siguientes situaciones; menciona colores cuando sea posible. Después de contestar las preguntas, comparte tus respuestas con tu compañero/a.

1. En el invierno para ir a la universidad, uso _____.

2. En la primavera para ir al trabajo, llevo _____.

3. Cuando la temperatura es de 80°F, uso _____.

4. Cuando la temperatura es de -10°F, llevo _____.

5. Cuando voy a la playa, llevo _____.

6. Cuando voy al supermercado, uso _____.

7. Cuando voy a una fiesta elegante, llevo _____.

8. Para ir a una entrevista de trabajo, uso _____.

H. ¿Qué tiempo hace? Tú eres un(a) agente de viajes y tu trabajo es informar a tus clientes qué clima hay en diferentes ciudades de Latinoamérica. Mira el mapa para saber la información necesaria. Túrnate con un(a) compañero/a.

$$F= (C \times 1.8) + 32$$

Práctica adicional

Cuaderno de tareas
WB pp.339–341, G–J
LM pp.345–346, A–B, Pron.

Audio
CD-ROM
Episodio 13

1. ¿Qué tiempo hace en Bariloche en junio? ¿Qué estación del año es? ¿Qué ropa necesita llevar?

2. ¿Qué tiempo hace en Viña del Mar en enero? ¿Qué estación del año es? ¿Qué ropa necesita llevar?

3. ¿Qué tiempo hace en Cuzco en marzo? ¿Qué estación del año es? ¿Qué ropa necesita llevar?

4. ¿Qué tiempo hace en Quito en septiembre? ¿Qué estación del año es? ¿Qué ropa necesita llevar?

Actividades comunicativas

A. Un viaje a México.

Instrucciones para **Estudiante 1**

You want to go to Mexico on vacation. Call your travel agent to plan your trip. Look at the map and ask about places that interest you. Your requirements: a destination that is hot and sunny, and a price of $600 or less. You want to leave on Monday, July 20, and return on Friday, July 25, at night.

> **Modelo** —¿Qué tiempo hace en... ?
> —¿Cuánto cuesta el viaje *(the trip)* a... ?

A. Un viaje a México.

Instrucciones para **Estudiante 2**

You are a travel agent. Your job is to help your client plan a vacation. Answer your client's questions about the weather conditions of the place they would like to visit, and give prices. Once you know where your client wants to go, fill in the card.

VIAJES MAJESTIC

Acapulco $450   Tijuana $520   Cancún $870   Tampico $640

Mazatlán $465   La Paz $500   Oaxaca $395

Cliente _____ Teléfono _____

Viaja a _____

Quiere salir el _____

Quiere regresar el _____

Viajan _____ personas

Precio _____

¡Cinco días en México!

B. Diferencias.

Instrucciones para Estudiante 1

Aquí tienes un dibujo de Sofía y sus amigos en la playa de Puerto Vallarta. Hay varias diferencias entre tu dibujo y el de tu compañero/a. Para encontrarlas, describe el clima, las actividades y la ropa. Escribe siete diferencias que encontraste.

> **Modelo** Manolo duerme en la hamaca. Lleva unos pantalones azules cortos, ¿no?

B. Diferencias.

Instrucciones para **Estudiante 2**

Aquí tienes un dibujo de Sofía y sus amigos en la playa de Puerto Vallarta. Hay varias diferencias entre tu dibujo y el de tu compañero/a. Para encontrarlas, describe el clima, las actividades y la ropa. Escribe siete diferencias que encontraste.

> **Modelo**   Manolo lleva unos pantalones cortos azules, ¿no? Lee el periódico.

C. De vacaciones. Talk to your partner about a place you like to go to when you are on vacation. Describe the season, month or date you like to go, the weather, the clothing you usually take with you, who you go with, and what you do there.

Banco de palabras			
la bahía *bay*	**los lagos** *lakes*	**el parque de atracciones** *amusement park*	**remar** *to row*
esquiar *to ski*	**las montañas** *mountains*	**el planetario** *planetarium*	**el zoológico** *zoo*

La correspondencia

El correo: Aprenda español en Costa Rica. Lee la información acerca de los programas para aprender español en Costa Rica. Después contesta las preguntas.

Instituto Forester

El Forester Instituto Internacional, en San José, Costa Rica, ofrece varios programas de instrucción en español. El instituto está localizado en una zona exclusiva de la ciudad, a sólo veinte minutos del centro.

Nuestros estudiantes. El Instituto recibe estudiantes de diversos países, diferentes edades y necesidades de aprendizaje:
- personas que buscan unas vacaciones diferentes y productivas
- ejecutivos de corporaciones e instituciones
- estudiantes de preparatorias y universidades
- diplomáticos
- doctores y enfermeros
- personas jubiladas[1] que desean mantenerse activas
- empleados de la líneas aéreas

Nuestros profesores. La lengua materna de todo el profesorado es el español. Además, tienen títulos universitarios y amplia experiencia en enseñar el español como segunda lengua.

Las familias anfitrionas[2]. El Instituto selecciona cuidadosamente a las familias anfitrionas. Son muy amables y abiertas, les gusta relacionarse con personas de otros países y tienen interés en ayudar a los estudiantes extranjeros. El estudiante tendrá cuarto privado, desayuno y cena. Todas las familias viven a menos de veinte minutos del Instituto, y es fácil llegar en autobús o a pie[3].

Días festivos. El Instituto está cerrado durante algunos días festivos nacionales que se celebran en Costa Rica: el primero de enero, el Jueves Santo y el Viernes Santo[4], el primero de mayo (Día del Trabajo), el 15 de agosto (la Asunción y Día de las Madres), el 15 de septiembre (Día de la Independencia) y el 25 de diciembre.

Clima. La temperatura varía muy poco durante el año. Obviamente, hace más frío en las montañas que en la costa (San José está a 4.000 pies de altura). La temporada de lluvias es de mayo a noviembre, y generalmente hace sol por las mañanas y llueve por las tardes. La temporada seca[5] es de diciembre a abril.

---

[1]*retired* [2]*host* [3]*on foot* [4]*Holy Thursday and Good Friday* [5]*dry season*

Sugerencias para la ropa. Los costarricenses usan ropa informal. Es una buena idea llevar ropa ligera y una chaqueta o un suéter. Es recomendable llevar un paraguas o un impermeable si va a visitar el país durante la temporada de lluvias. Durante la temporada seca, las noches pueden ser bastantes frías. Mujeres: jeans, camisetas, pantalones y blusas, un suéter y/o una chaqueta. Uno o dos vestidos para ocasiones especiales. Hombres: jeans, camisetas, pantalones y camisas. Se recomienda llevar un saco y una corbata para eventos especiales. Tanto las mujeres como los hombres deben llevar zapatos cómodos, tenis o sandalias. Y por supuesto, ¡los trajes de baño son indispensables!

1. ¿A qué van personas de diferentes profesiones y edades a Costa Rica?

_____

2. ¿Por qué es importante aprender un segundo idioma? ¿Qué ventajas tiene?

_____

_____

3. ¿Qué características tienen las familias anfitrionas?

_____

_____

4. ¿Qué fiestas nacionales se celebran en Costa Rica?

_____

_____

5. ¿Qué clima tiene San José? ¿Qué ropa recomiendan para viajar en Costa Rica?

_____

_____

6. ¿Te gustaría participar en un programa así? ¿Por qué sí o por qué no?

_____

_____

En papel: ¡Ven, visita mi ciudad! Muchos costarricences tienen interés en visitar Estados Unidos. Escribe un artículo sobre tu ciudad para una revista de turismo en Costa Rica. Incluye la siguiente información:

- el clima en las diferentes estaciones
- la ropa que uno debe llevar
- atracciones y lugares de interés
- actividades interesantes

¡Fíjate!
Create a simple outline of the information you want to include before you begin to write.

Banco de palabras		
el zoológico	**el planetario**	**las montañas**
zoo	*planetarium*	*mountains*
los lagos	**el parque de atracciones**	**la bahía**
lakes	*amusement park*	*bay*

333

Video
CD-ROM

¡A ver de nuevo!

Parte 1. Con tus propias palabras, haz un resumen del episodio.

Audio
CD-ROM

Parte 2. Ahora trabaja con un(a) compañero/a para comparar la información y añadir lo que te haya faltado.

Práctica adicional		
Cuaderno de tareas WB pp.342–344, K–L LM pp.346, A–B	Audio CD-ROM Episodio 13	Website vistahigher learning.com

Vocabulario del Episodio 13

Los meses *The months*

enero	*January*
febrero	*February*
marzo	*March*
abril	*April*
mayo	*May*
junio	*June*
julio	*July*
agosto	*August*
septiembre	*September*
octubre	*October*
noviembre	*November*
diciembre	*December*

Las estaciones *The seasons*

la primavera	*spring*
el verano	*summer*
el otoño	*fall*
el invierno	*winter*

¿Qué tiempo hace? *What's the weather like?*

Hace buen/mal tiempo.	*The weather is nice/bad.*
Hace (mucho) calor.	*It's (very) hot.*
Hace fresco.	*It's cool.*
Hace frío.	*It's cold.*
Hace sol.	*It's sunny.*
Hace viento.	*It's windy.*
Está nublado.	*It's cloudy.*
llover (o ⟶ ue)	*to rain*
nevar (e ⟶ ie)	*to snow*

La ropa *Clothes*

el abrigo	*coat*
el bikini	*bikini*
la blusa	*blouse*
la bolsa	*bag*
las botas	*boots*
la bufanda	*scarf*
los calcetines	*socks*
la camisa	*shirt*
la camiseta	*T-shirt*
la chaqueta	*jacket*
la corbata	*tie*
los guantes	*gloves*
el impermeable	*raincoat*
los jeans	*jeans*
los lentes de sol	*sunglasses*
llevar	*to wear*
la maleta	*suitcase*
la minifalda	*mini-skirt*

Los colores *Colors*

amarillo/a	*yellow*
anaranjado/a	*orange*
azul	*blue*
blanco/a	*white*
café	*brown*
gris	*gray*
morado/a	*purple*
negro/a	*black*
rojo/a	*red*
verde	*green*

Más vocabulario

los pantalones	*pants*
los pantalones cortos	*shorts*
el paraguas	*umbrella*
el/la pijama	*pajamas*
las sandalias	*sandals*
el sombrero	*hat*
el suéter	*sweater*
el traje	*suit*
el traje de baño	*bathing suit*
usar	*to wear*
el vestido	*dress*
los zapatos (de tacón)	*(high-heeled) shoes*
los (zapatos) tenis	*tennis shoes*

Vocabulario personal

Write all the words you need to know in Spanish so that you can better talk about the clothes you like to wear, the weather in your city, and important dates in your family.

¡A escribir!

Episodio 13

Escenas de la vida: Las vacaciones

Video
CD-ROM

A. ¡A ver cuánto entendiste! Match the Spanish sentences with their English equivalents.

_____ 1. Te doy un cheque la próxima semana.

_____ 2. Tienes que pagarlo antes de diciembre.

_____ 3. Salimos el 18 de diciembre.

_____ 4. Cuesta trescientos noventa dólares.

_____ 5. Ya tenemos las reservaciones de avión.

_____ 6. No te voy a ayudar con las maletas.

_____ 7. ¿Cuánto cuesta el boleto?

_____ 8. Todavía no me pagan.

_____ 9. Mi pasaporte está vencido.

a. We're leaving on the 18th of December.

b. We already have the plane reservations.

c. My passport has expired.

d. I'll give you a check next week.

e. You have to pay it before December.

f. They haven't paid me yet.

g. I'm not going to help you with your suitcases.

h. It costs three hundred and ninety dollars.

i. How much does a ticket cost?

Video
CD-ROM

B. Las vacaciones. Choose the correct answer.

1. El boleto cuesta…
   a. cincuenta dólares.
   b. quinientos treinta dólares.
   c. trescientos noventa dólares.

2. Para ir a México los chicos necesitan…
   a. permiso de turista.
   b. pasaporte y visa.
   c. visa.

3. ¿Puedes pagar mi boleto…
   a. con dinero?
   b. con mi tarjeta de crédito?
   c. con tu tarjeta de crédito?

4. En invierno en Guadalajara…
   a. hace frío y nieva.
   b. hace calor durante el día.
   c. hace calor por la noche.

5. Los chicos salen…
   a. el 10 de diciembre.
   b. el primero de enero.
   c. el 18 de diciembre.

6. Para usar durante el día, los chicos deben llevar…
   a. un impermeable.
   b. un abrigo.
   c. ropa ligera.

Vocabulario 1

Talking about dates and the weather
• Seasons, months, and the weather

C. Algunas fechas importantes en Hispanoamérica. Write the following dates in Spanish. Do you know what holidays they are?

1. January 6 _____ 4. March 21 _____
2. February 14 _____ 5. July 4 _____
3. May 1 _____ 6. October 12 _____

D. ¿Qué tiempo hace? Indicate the weather conditions and the temperature in the following places for the month in question, based on the temperature and the illustration. Remember, to convert from Celsius to Fahrenheit: **F = (C x 1.8) + 32.**

> **Modelo**
>
> Ciudad de México / /17°C /septiembre
>
> **En la Ciudad de México generalmente llueve en el mes de septiembre.**
> **Hace fresco, la temperatura promedio es de sesenta y tres grados Fahrenheit.**

1. Managua, Nicaragua / / 30°C/ enero

_____

_____

2. San Juan Bautista, Paraguay / / 37°C / febrero

_____

_____

3. Bariloche, Argentina / / 10°C / julio

_____

_____

4. Barcelona, España/ abril / 27°C /

_____

_____

5. La Habana, Cuba / diciembre / / 32°C

_____

_____

E. El hemisferio sur. Indicate the seasons in which these holidays take place in the Southern Hemisphere. Remember that it is not the same as in the United States.

1. En Argentina las vacaciones de diciembre son en _____

2. En Uruguay, en las vacaciones de julio es _____

3. En Paraguay, el 21 de marzo es el primer día de _____

4. En Perú, el 21 de septiembre es el primer día de _____

F. Odette quiere saber. Answer Odette's questions about weather in the United States.

1. ¿Qué tiempo hace en Nueva York en invierno?

_____

2. ¿Qué tiempo hace en Las Vegas en verano?

_____

3. ¿Qué tiempo hace en San Francisco en primavera?

_____

4. ¿Qué tiempo hace en Minneapolis en otoño?

_____

Vocabulario **2**	**Planning your wardrobe** • **Clothing and colors**

G. La ropa para Guadalajara. Write the names of the items the characters are bringing to Guadalajara.

a. La ropa de Sofía

1. _____
2. _____
3. _____
4. _____
5. _____
6. _____
7. _____

b. La ropa de Manolo

1. _____
2. _____
3. _____
4. _____
5. _____
6. _____
7. _____
8. _____

c. La ropa de Ana Mari

1. _____
2. _____
3. _____
4. _____
5. _____
6. _____
7. _____
8. _____

H. ¿Qué color? What color do you associate with the following foods?

1. el arroz _____
2. las uvas _____
3. el plátano _____
4. la naranja _____
5. la lechuga _____
6. el tomate _____
7. los frijoles _____
8. el chocolate _____

I. ¿Qué no le queda? *(What doesn't match?)* Indicate the item that does not match. Then explain your choice.

> **Modelo**   Hoy Lynn va a la playa; por eso, lleva: un traje de baño, unas sandalias blancas, un sombrero, un suéter amarillo y unos lentes de sol.
> **En la playa hace calor, no necesita llevar un suéter.**

1. Hoy hace frío, Nancy lleva: un abrigo largo, unos pantalones cortos, un suéter verde, unos zapatos verdes y un sombrero.

_____

2. Esta noche Joe va a una fiesta; por eso, lleva: una corbata roja, un traje negro, una camisa blanca y unos lentes de sol.

_____

3. Es verano. Para trabajar Carlos lleva: unos zapatos de tacón, unos pantalones cortos y una camisa ligera.

_____

4. Hoy llueve; por eso, Larry lleva: un impermeable gris, una blusa anaranjada, una chaqueta azul, pantalones grises y una camisa azul.

_____

5. Es otoño en Nueva York. Valerie lleva: una blusa morada, una falda negra, un traje de baño y unos tenis morados.

_____

6. Hoy hace sol y buen tiempo, para ir con sus amigos al parque, Joe lleva una camiseta blanca, unos jeans, unos tenis y un paraguas café.

_____

J. ¿Qué me pongo? Imagine this is the city where you live. For each illustration, describe the weather, the season, and the clothes you wear during each season.

a

_____
_____
_____
_____
_____
_____

b

_____
_____
_____
_____
_____
_____

c

_____
_____
_____
_____
_____
_____

Para terminar

K. Cruceros Festival. Read the brochure about a boat tour in Mexico and answer the questions.

Reading Strategy: Looking for specific information

As you become a proficient reader in Spanish, you will learn not to be disturbed by "noise"—language you do not yet understand. Instead, you will be aware of your purpose for reading a text and will only need to use a dictionary if understanding the details is important to your purpose. Most often, you will use your background knowledge—what you know about the world—and the context of the words to guess the meaning.

You are about to read a travel brochure. The information you most likely will find in a travel brochure is activities to do, interesting places to see, special events, and information about weather, costs, currency, passport, visas, and vaccinations. Your purpose in reading is to gather details about the Mexican cruise in order to answer the following questions.

---

1. ¿Qué día llega el barco a Cabo San Lucas? ¿Cuántas horas se queda ahí?

   _____

2. ¿A qué hora se va el barco de Puerto Vallarta?

   _____

3. ¿Dónde está Cabo San Lucas?

   _____

4. ¿Qué lugares interesantes puedes visitar ahí?

   _____

5. ¿Cómo es Mazatlán?

   _____

6. ¿En qué mes hace más calor? ¿Cuál es la temperatura durante el invierno?

   _____

7. ¿Qué actividades puedes hacer en Mazatlán?

   _____

8. ¿Qué característica especial tiene Puerto Vallarta?

   _____

9. ¿Qué es Yelapa y cómo puedes llegar allí?

   _____

10. ¿Conoces alguna de estas ciudades? ¿Cuál(es)? ¿Cuál te gustaría *(would like)* conocer? ¿Por qué?

    _____

    _____

    _____

¡Descubra los tesoros[1] de México!

Ud. descubrirá tesoros: en sus playas y ciudades, en sus atardeceres[2] dorados, en la sonrisa de la gente, en la comida y en la famosa artesanía mexicana.

Itinerario

Día	Puerto	Llegada	Salida
domingo	San Diego		16:00
lunes	Travesía del Mar		
martes	Cabo San Lucas	07:00	22:00
miércoles	Mazatlán	07:00	24:00
jueves	Puerto Vallarta	07:00	23:00
viernes	San Diego	22:00	

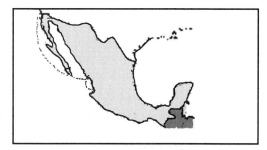

El primer tesoro: Cabo San Lucas

Cabo San Lucas está en el extremo sur de la península de Baja California, que se extiende 1.500 kilómetros al sur de la frontera con Estados Unidos. Esta pequeña ciudad, bañada por el sol los 365 días del año, tiene docenas de playas vírgenes y de aguas templadas, de arena blanca y las doradas montañas del desierto a la distancia. Cabo San Lucas es famoso por sus enormes rocas en forma de arco, donde se bañan al sol las focas[3] y los leones marinos; y donde las ballenas grises de Alaska pasan el invierno.

El segundo tesoro: Mazatlán

Mazatlán, en el estado de Sinaloa, es el puerto con la mayor flota camaronera[4] del país. Es muy popular entre los turistas mexicanos, estadounidenses y canadienses por la pesca y el veleo[5]. Esta ciudad relativamente nueva y moderna tiene playas magníficas. También hay hoteles de la mejor calidad, y la Zona Dorada, en el centro de la ciudad, tiene una gran variedad de tiendas. Pero principalmente, Mazatlán ofrece una excelente vida nocturna: restaurantes, terrazas, bares y discotecas. Es fácil y barato transportarse del puerto al centro en las famosas "pulmonías".

Temperaturas

mes	alta	baja
ene.	73	63
feb.	73	63
mar.	73	63
abr.	77	66
may.	81	72
jun.	84	77
jul.	91	79
ago.	88	79
sep.	86	77
oct.	80	76
nov.	81	70
dic.	73	64

El tercer tesoro: Puerto Vallarta

Puerto Vallarta es una pequeña ciudad de la Riviera mexicana que conserva su aire tradicional de pequeño pueblo mexicano. Tiene estrechas calles empedradas[6], una linda plaza a la orilla del mar, donde se hacen representaciones de pastorelas[7] durante la época de Navidad y donde tocan bandas musicales el resto del año. Tiene que visitar la catedral de Nuestra Señora de Guadalupe y caminar por la zona central de la ciudad. También hay pequeñas tiendas de artesanías, artículos de piel[8], cerámica y joyerías. Tiene que visitar Yelapa. Debe tomar un pequeño barco local que visita la Isla de las Rocas y la playa de Mismaloya antes de llegar a la playa de Yelapa. Ahí Ud. debe nadar hasta la playa (está muy cerca) e ir a caballo hasta el nacimiento del río.

[1]*treasures* [2]*sunsets* [3]*seals* [4]*shrimp population* [5]**pesca...** *fishing and sailing* [6]*cobblestone* [7]*humorous popular plays representing the struggle between good and evil* [8]*leather*

L. Un lugar bonito que tú conoces. Write a description of a vacation place you have visited. Talk about the weather in the season you usually go, the activities you usually do, etc.

Writing Strategy: Using simple language to express your ideas

You may feel frustrated when you cannot communicate your ideas in written Spanish as well as you can in English. For this reason, you may make the mistake of using a dictionary and creating sentences that Spanish speakers would not be able to understand. A much more effective strategy is to limit your messages to what you are able to communicate.

You have just read a tourist brochure in Spanish. By using the illustrations, your background knowledge, and context, you were probably able to understand most of the text. But you are probably not yet able to use that level of language to communicate your own ideas. For example, in the brochure you read this about Cabo San Lucas: **Esta pequeña ciudad, bañada por el sol los 365 días del año, tiene docenas de playas vírgenes...** Although you cannot yet write a similar description, you can write something like: **Cabo San Lucas es una ciudad pequeña. Siempre hace sol y calor, y hay muchas playas bonitas,** which any Spanish speaker would understand. Using simple language enables you to express yourself effectively while you build your writing communication skills.

_____

_____

_____

_____

_____

_____

_____

_____

_____

_____

_____

_____

_____

_____

_____

_____

_____

_____

_____

¡A escuchar!

Episodio

13

Comprensión

Audio
CD-ROM

A. De compras con Sofía y Ana Mari. Sofía and Ana Mari are shopping for clothing that they will need in Guadalajara. Listen to their conversation and list the articles they buy, how many they buy, and the color of each article. You will hear the conversation twice.

	cantidad	artículo	color
Sofía			
Ana Mari			

Audio
CD-ROM

B. ¡Gran liquidación en el Almacén Franco! You are going to listen to a radio advertisement for a clothing store. Listen and select the best completion for each sentence. You will hear the advertisement twice.

Banco de palabras			
almacén	liquidación	descuento	rebajado/a
(department) store	sale	discount	reduced

1. En el Almacén Franco, se vende...
   a. ropa para hombres.   b. ropa para niños.   c. ropa para mujeres.
2. La liquidación es de ropa...
   a. de verano.   b. para la playa.   c. de invierno.
3. Hay un descuento de 50% (por ciento) en...
   a. las camisas.   b. los suéteres.   c. los pantalones.
4. Hay liquidación...
   a. el 4 y el 5 de enero.   b. por una semana.   c. por dos días.
5. Las corbatas tienen el precio de...
   a. 20% de descuento.   b. dos por una.   c. $25.
6. Por solamente $38 se puede comprar...
   a. una chaqueta.   b. una corbata.   c. un suéter.
7. Hay pantalones...
   a. de muchos colores.   b. rebajados.   c. por $20.

Pronunciación

Audio
CD-ROM

Entonación. Intonation (**entonación**) is the way in which the speaker conveys meaning by emphasizing words, pausing, and using the voice to rise and fall in pitch. The more closely you imitate a native speaker's intonation, the closer you will come to native pronunciation. Ordinary statements generally have an even pitch, dropping off on the last syllable, while *yes/no* questions rise in pitch on the last syllable. Repeat these sets of statements and questions after the speaker.

Las chicas van de compras.	**¿Las chicas van de compras?**
No saben cuánto cuestan las blusas.	**¿No saben cuánto cuestan las blusas?**

While *yes/no* questions rise in pitch on the last syllable, information questions drop in pitch on the last syllable, and the interrogative word is emphasized.

¿Dónde está el teléfono? **¿Quién es esa chica?** **¿Por qué no vas conmigo?**
¿Qué es eso? **¿Cuánto cuesta la bolsa?** **¿Cuándo vamos a la playa?**

In *either/or* questions, the pitch rises at the end of the first choice and drops at the end of the second. Repeat these questions after the speaker.

¿Quieres comprar la blusa ... o la chaqueta? ¿Comemos en un restaurante ... o en casa?

Más escenas de la vida

Ana Mari is chatting with Sofía, who is packing. Listen to the conversation and then complete activities **A** and **B**. You will hear the conversation twice.

Audio
CD-ROM

A. ¿Qué ropa llevo? Indicate the clothes that Sofía says she is taking on the trip.

— 1. un vestido elegante   — 4. zapatos para caminar   — 7. un pijama
— 2. tres o cinco pantalones   — 5. dos o tres suéteres   — 8. un par de faldas
— 3. un abrigo   — 6. zapatos de tacón

Audio
CD-ROM

B. Responde. Write the answers to the following questions.

1. ¿Por qué Sofía no quiere llevar mucha ropa? _____

2. ¿Qué consejo da la madre de Ana Mari? _____

_____

3. ¿Cuánto tiempo van a estar en Guadalajara? _____

4. ¿Por qué Sofía no necesita diez blusas? _____

5. ¿Qué tiempo hace en Guadalajara? _____

6. ¿Quién puede prestarle ropa a Sofía si necesita? _____

7. ¿Sofía y Wayne, son novios? _____

Objetivos comunicativos

In this episode, you will practice:

✓ talking about your daily routine

✓ comparing what you do when you are in school and when you are on vacation

✓ talking about special celebrations

Escenas de la vida: ¡Estás muy americanizada!

Video
CD-ROM

A. ¡Mira cuánto puedes entender! Sofía y Odette hablan de sus rutinas diarias. Escucha la conversación o mira el video para indicar las actividades que mencionan.

Audio
CD-ROM

Sofía se pone pantalones de mezclilla para ir a la universidad.

Odette se pone ropa elegante sólo para salir.

Odette no sale de casa sin pintarse.

Odette sale con sus amigos entre semana.

Sofía se queda en casa entre semana.

Sofía siempre se pinta.

Odette se acuesta tarde y se levanta temprano.

Sofía y Odette se van a divertir en el teatro esta noche.

Sofía prefiere bañarse por la noche.

B. ¿Quién lo dijo? Escucha la conversación o mira el video para indicar quién hizo los siguientes comentarios: Odette (**O**) o Sofía (**S**).

_____ 1. ¿Adónde vas tan elegante?

_____ 2. No salgo de mi casa sin pintarme.

_____ 3. En Estados Unidos hay más oportunidades profesionales para las mujeres.

_____ 4. Para mí, es muy importante tener vida social.

_____ 5. Casi todos salen del trabajo, van a casa, ven la tele y se acuestan.

C. ¿Te diste cuenta? Escucha la conversación o mira el video otra vez para completar las frases.

1. No _____ elegante; es mi _____ normal.

2. Sofía está muy _____ .

3. ¿Te gusta _____ ?

4. El problema es que yo ya no _____ eso.

5. Odette piensa que en Estados Unidos la vida es muy _____ porque las personas no salen entre semana.

Cultura a lo vivo

In Spanish-speaking countries, people are used to going out regularly on weekday evenings. For Hispanics, is very important to keep in touch with their family and friends, so informal get-togethers are a constant. It's very common between Spanish speakers to improvise parties or gatherings for the pleasure of seeing each other again, regardless of the day of the week or time of day.

Práctica adicional

Cuaderno de tareas	Video CD-ROM
WB p.361, A–B	Episodio 14

Para comunicarnos mejor

Gramática 1

Describing your daily routine
• Reflexive pronouns

Analizar y descubrir

In the conversation, you heard the following:

Sólo **me pongo** camisetas…	_I only wear T-shirts..._
¿Y **te pintas**?	_And do you wear makeup?_
La gente **se acuesta** temprano.	_People go to bed early._
Nos levantamos temprano.	_We get up early._

1. The verb forms **me pongo**, **te pintas**, **se acuesta**, and **nos levantamos** each include a reflexive pronoun. You will know that a verb is conjugated with a reflexive pronoun when **se** appears in the infinitive form: **ponerse**, **pintarse**, **acostarse**, **levantarse**. Reflexive verbs have the same endings as other **-ar**, **-er**, and **-ir** verbs.

Study the following examples and answer the questions.

Verbos con pronombres reflexivos

Los sábados **me levanto** tarde.	*On Saturdays I get up late.*
¿A qué hora **te levantas**?	*What time do you get up?*
Usted nunca **se acuesta** temprano, ¿verdad?	*You never go to bed early, do you?*
Sofía **se quita** los lentes de contacto para dormir.	*Sofía takes off her contact lenses to sleep.*
Nosotros **nos bañamos** por la mañana.	*We take a shower/bathe in the morning.*
¿Ustedes **se divierten** en la clase ¿no? ¿Vosotros **os divertís** en la clase ¿no? }	*You have fun in class, right?*
Los niños no **se lavan** las manos antes de comer.	*The kids do not wash their hands before eating.*

2. Which reflexive pronoun is used...

    a. with the **yo** form of the verb? _____   e. with the **nosotros/as** form? _____

    b. with the **tú** form? _____   f. with the **ustedes** form? _____

    c. with the **usted** form? _____   g. with the **ellos/as** form? _____

    d. with the **él/ella** form? _____

3. Spanish uses the definite article (**el, la, los, las**) when reflexive verbs are used with parts of the body and clothing. English uses a possessive adjective (*my, your, her*). Identify the statements above that illustrate this rule.

    a. _____

    b. _____

4. Reflexive pronouns, like direct object pronouns, may be placed before a conjugated verb or attached to the infinitive.

        Tengo que **levantarme** temprano porque hoy voy a trabajar.

    or   **Me** tengo que **levantar** temprano porque hoy voy a trabajar.

5. Reflexive pronouns are not optional. Verbs used reflexively have different meanings than those used without reflexive pronouns; for example, while **ir** means *to go*, **irse** means *to leave*.

Para hablar de tu rutina diaria

acostarse tarde (o ⟶ ue)	*to go to bed late*	**levantarse temprano**	*to get up early*
bañarse por la noche	*to take a bath/shower at night*	**pintarse**	*to put on makeup*
divertirse (e ⟶ ie)	*to have fun*	**ponerse la ropa**	*to put on/wear clothing*
irse (a)	*to leave*	**quedarse en casa**	*to stay home*
irse de vacaciones	*to go on vacation*	**quitarse los zapatos**	*to take off one's shoes*
juntarse	*to get together*		
lavarse las manos	*to wash one's hands*		
los dientes	*to brush one's teeth*		

También se dice...

pintarse ——► maquillarse

lavarse los dientes ——► cepillarse los dientes

Some people make a distinction between **bañarse** (*to take a bath*) and **ducharse** (*to shower*).

Learning Strategy: Quiet rehearsal

Your instructor will frequently ask students to respond before, during, or after participating in various activities. Think of how you would respond, even if you do not have a chance to speak aloud. Compare your answer with the one given by someone else. This strategy is a great way to practice and learn without being put on the spot!

PRÁCTICA

A. ¿Qué hacen? Empareja las ilustraciones con las descripciones.

a

b

c

d

e

f

_____ 1. Sofía se levanta tarde los sábados.

_____ 2. ¿Te pintas todos los días?

_____ 3. Me baño por la noche cuando hace frío.

_____ 4. Todos se divierten cuando se juntan para salir.

_____ 5. Nosotros nos quedamos en casa esta noche.

_____ 6. Me pongo pantalones para ir a la universidad.

B. La rutina diaria. Ordena las frases del uno al diez en una secuencia lógica.

_____ a. Y me acuesto porque ya es tarde.

_____ b. Luego me voy a la universidad.

_____ c. Luego me pongo el pijama.

_____ d. Después me baño.

_____ e. Voy a mi cuarto a ponerme la ropa.

_____ f. Me lavo los dientes antes de acostarme.

_____ g. Me quedo en la universidad todo el día.

_____ h. Me levanto temprano porque es lunes.

_____ i. Me voy a casa porque ya estoy cansado.

_____ j. Me divierto un rato mirando mi programa cómico favorito.

C. Lotería.

Parte 1. Encuentra un(a) compañero/a que haga las siguientes cosas. Escribe su nombre en el cuadro indicado. La persona que llene todas las líneas sin repetir nombres gana el juego.

> **Modelo** _____ prefiere bañarse por la noche.
> —¿Te bañas por la noche?
> —No, por la mañana. ¿Y tú?

_____ se acuesta antes de las once de la noche.	_____ sabe jugar golf.	_____ se levanta tarde los domingos.	_____ no se pone pijama para dormir.
_____ se divierte en su trabajo.	_____ no conoce a los padres de su novio/a.	_____ se queda en casa los sábados por la tarde.	_____ no se pinta todos los días.
_____ prefiere bañarse por la noche.	_____ se va de vacaciones todos los años.	_____ se junta con la familia el día de su cumpleaños.	_____ ayuda a su mamá en la casa.
_____ se quita los zapatos cuando llega a casa.	_____ se lava los dientes con *Aquafresh*.	_____ nunca pide postre en los restaurantes.	_____ usa lentes de contacto.

> **¡Fíjate!**
> Remember to use reflexive pronouns only with reflexive verbs!

Parte 2. Comparte *(share)* la información con la clase.

> **Modelo** Estudiante 1: **Rick se va de vacaciones todos los años.**
> Estudiante 2: **¿Adónde vas?**
> Rick: **Generalmente vamos a Utah a esquiar.**

D. En casa de Ramón y Ana Mari.

Parte 1. Ana Mari describe la rutina diaria de su familia. Conjuga los verbos para formar frases completas y haz los cambios necesarios.

En mi casa:

1. mis padres / levantarse / antes que todos

_____

2. a mí / me / gustar / acostarse temprano

_____

3. por eso / (yo) bañarse / por la noche

_____

4. mis hermanos / preferir / bañarse / por la mañana

_____

5. mi mamá / pintarse / mientras que mi papá / preparar / el desayuno

_____

6. a las ocho / todos (nosotros) / desayunar / juntos

_____

7. luego / todos irse / al trabajo o a la escuela

_____

Parte 2. Ahora contesta las preguntas.

1. ¿Quién se levanta primero en casa de Ramón y Ana Mari? ¿Y en tu casa?

_____

2. ¿Quién se baña por la noche? Y tú, ¿cuándo te bañas?

_____

3. ¿Quién prepara el desayuno? ¿Y en tu casa?

_____

E. ¿Cómo cambia tu rutina cuando estás de vacaciones?

Parte 1. Adriana describe cómo cambia (*changes*) su rutina cuando está de vacaciones. Lee la descripción en la siguiente página y contesta las preguntas.

1. ¿Cuáles son las diferencias principales en sus actividades?

_____

_____

2. ¿Por qué se levanta temprano durante las vacaciones?

_____

_____

3. ¿Adónde se va de vacaciones generalmente? ¿Por qué va allí? ¿Qué hacen?

_____

_____

Cuando estoy de vacaciones mi rutina de las mañanas no cambia[1] mucho. Generalmente me levanto temprano porque mi esposo siempre se levanta temprano, vacaciones o no.

La ropa que me pongo sí es diferente: para ir a trabajar me pongo vestidos, faldas o pantalones más formales. En cambio[2], cuando estoy de vacaciones me pongo jeans, camisetas y ropa muy informal. No me pinto todos los días, si no tengo que trabajar o ir a la universidad.

La diferencia más importante son las actividades que hago después de trabajar: en las vacaciones me divierto mucho más porque hago lo que yo quiero. No tengo tantas obligaciones y me puedo quedar tranquila en casa o juntarme con amigos si tengo ganas. Cuando estoy en clases siempre estudio y hago la tarea antes de acostarme.

En invierno, generalmente me voy de vacaciones a Puerto Rico a ver a mi hermana. Allá, nos acostamos muy tarde porque nos gusta mucho salir o juntarnos con la familia para hablar, cantar y bailar hasta la madrugada[3].

¡Fíjate!

Notice that verbs are not conjugated after prepositions: **para hablar, cantar...,** **después de** trabajar, **antes de** acostarme.

[1]*doesn't change* [2]*on the other hand* [3]*dawn*

Parte 2. Usa la descripción de Adriana como modelo para escribir cómo cambia tu rutina cuando estás de vacaciones.

Audio
CD-ROM

F. ¡Qué divertido! Listen to the story Ana Mari's younger brothers tell about about when they visited their grandmother. Indicate whether their behaviors are good or bad. Share your answers with a partner.

	bueno	malo			bueno	malo
1.	☐	☐		5.	☐	☐
2.	☐	☐		6.	☐	☐
3.	☐	☐		7.	☐	☐
4.	☐	☐		8.	☐	☐

G. ¡A hablar! En grupos de cuatro, hablen de sus rutinas por la mañana y por la noche, para encontrar quién en el grupo es el/la madrugador(a) (*earlybird*), quién es el/la más elegante, quién se acuesta más temprano y quién es el/la parrandero/a (*night owl*).

Modelo	Rosario es la madrugadora porque todos los días se levanta a las cinco y media.

Práctica adicional

Cuaderno de tareas WB pp.362–366, C–H LM pp.369–370, A–B, Pron.	Audio CD-ROM Episodio 14

Actividades comunicativas

 A. Submarino. First, draw a submarine in five of the boxes on your grid. Then, take turns asking your partner yes/no questions, matching an action pictured at the top of the grid with one of the people on the side. Depending on your partner's answer, write **sí** or **no** in that box. The first person to locate all five submarines wins.

> **Modelo**   — ¿Adriana se pinta para ir a la universidad?
>   — **Sí, se pinta.** *(If there is a submarine in that box)*
>   or   — **No, no se pinta.** *(If there is not a submarine there)*

Tú				
Tus primos				
Adriana				
Ustedes				

Invitación a **Nicaragua**

Del álbum de
Wayne

Nicaragua es un poco más pequeño que el estado de Nueva York y tiene 5 millones de habitantes. Se le conoce como el país de los lagos (*lakes*) y los volcanes. Los volcanes Concepción y Madera están en el Lago Managua. Una erupción formó más de 300 islas volcánicas en el enorme lago, cerca de la ciudad de Granada.

Práctica adicional

Website
vistahigher
learning.com

B. Sopa de palabras.

Instrucciones para **Estudiante 1**

Primero escribe oraciones lógicas usando todas las palabras. La primera y la última palabra ya están en su lugar. Después léele tus oraciones a tu compañero/a para verificar las respuestas. Si tiene errores, ayúdalo/la a encontrarlos, pero no le des *(don't give them)* la respuesta correcta inmediatamente. Deja que trate *(let them try)* de solucionar los problemas. Túrnense.

Modelo

Sofía pinta los se solamente **sábados**.
Sofía se pinta solamente los sábados.

Los fines de semana

1. **Los** tarde, mis esposo acuestan se pero sábados, acuesta se mi hijos **temprano**.

_____

2. **Me** llego cuando quitarme los a zapatos gusta **casa**.

_____

3. ¿**Te** para los todos ir solamente No, pintas las pinto a días? me **fiestas**.

_____

4. **Es** con importante con la muy familia juntarse **frecuencia**.

_____

5. **Los** vestido pongo me domingos mi **favorito**.

_____

Las respuestas de tu compañero/a:

1. Los lunes me levanto temprano, pero los sábados prefiero levantarme tarde.
2. Mis hijos se divierten mucho en la clase de karate.
3. No me gusta quedarme en casa los sábados; prefiero salir.
4. Mi esposo se acuesta muy tarde; yo necesito acostarme antes de las diez.
5. Siempre nos bañamos por la noche/mañana porque por la mañana/noche no tenemos tiempo.

B. Sopa de palabras.

Instrucciones para Estudiante 2

Primero escribe oraciones lógicas usando todas las palabras. La primera y la última palabra ya están en su lugar. Después léele tus oraciones a tu compañero/a para verificar las respuestas. Si tiene errores, ayúdalo/la a encontrarlos, pero no le des (*don't give them*) la respuesta correcta inmediatamente. Deja que trate (*let them try*) de solucionar los problemas. Túrnense.

> **Modelo**
> **Wayne** la camiseta ejercicio en se la pone hacer para **parque.**
> **Wayne** se pone la camiseta para hacer ejercicio en el parque.

Las actividades en casa

1. **Los** me temprano, lunes prefiero levanto sábados levantarme pero los **tarde.**

   _____

2. **Mis** divierten clase en la mucho se de hijos **karate.**

   _____

3. **No** me quedarme prefiero los sábados; casa gusta en **salir.**

   _____

4. **Mi** muy esposo tarde; se yo las acostarme antes acuesta necesito de **diez.**

   _____

5. **Siempre** bañamos mañana noche nos por la tenemos no porque por la **tiempo.**

   _____

Las respuestas de tu compañero/a:

1. Los sábados, mis hijos se acuestan tarde, pero mi esposo se acuesta temprano.
2. Me gusta quitarme los zapatos cuando llego a casa.
3. ¿Te pintas todos los días? No, me pinto solamente para ir a las fiestas.
4. Es muy importante juntarse con la familia con frecuencia.
5. Los domingos me pongo mi vestido favorito.

C. La fotonovela. En grupos de cuatro personas, seleccionen cinco de las siguientes actividades para escribir una descripción de lo que hacen Sofía y sus amigos los fines de semana. Después tu grupo va a leer la descripción a la clase y tus compañeros van a adivinar *(guess)* las letras de las actividades que usaron en la descripción.

Empiecen su fotonovela así: **El viernes por la tarde, generalmente Sofía…**

La correspondencia

El correo: La gritería nicaragüense. Lee el artículo del periódico *(paper)* del Club Latino acerca de *(about)* la más famosa celebración nicaragüense. Después contesta las preguntas.

1. ¿Qué es la gritería? ¿Qué y cuándo se celebra?

_____

2. ¿Qué hacen las personas durante la gritería?

_____

3. ¿Qué hacen ese día por la mañana? ¿A qué hora se levantan? ¿Por qué?

_____

_____

4. ¿Qué hacen ese día por la tarde?

_____

_____

La gritería, celebración nacional nicaragüense

Por Wayne Reilly

Hace dos años, visité Managua, la capital de Nicaragua. Una de mis mejores experiencias fue participar en "la gritería." La gritería es una fiesta dedicada a la Virgen María que se celebra el 7 de diciembre. Las personas van de casa en casa cantando y alabando[1] el nombre de la Virgen. Cuando un grupo llega a una casa, pregunta, "¿Qué causa tanta alegría?", y las personas de la casa contestan, "¡La concepción de María!".

En la casa de mi familia adoptiva, los preparativos empezaron muy temprano. Nos levantamos a las siete de la mañana, limpiamos toda la casa (tiene que estar todo muy limpio para los visitantes) y preparamos las canastas[2] de dulces para regalar. A las cinco de la tarde, salimos a la calle y fuimos a la casa de varios vecinos. Cantamos, disparamos cohetes,[3] vimos los fuegos artificiales,[4] comimos caña de azúcar, gofios (dulces hechos de masa de maíz) y dulces de leche. Después volvimos a la casa para esperar a que llegaran otras personas del barrio. Fue una noche fabulosa; cantamos, bailamos y conversamos. Yo me acosté a las tres de la mañana y mi familia se acostó todavía más tarde.

Los nicaragüenses me dijeron que la gritería es la celebración más esperada del año. Algunos años se celebra aun[5] en medio de situaciones violentas. La gente olvida la violencia y los conflictos políticos por un día y se dedica a celebrar con alegría.

Reading Strategy:
Looking for specific information

As you become a proficient reader in Spanish, you will learn not to be disturbed by "noise"—language you do not yet understand. Instead, you will be aware of your purpose for reading a text and will only need to use a dictionary if understanding the details is important to your purpose. Most often, you will use your background knowledge—what you know about the world—and the context of the words to guess the meaning.

Read the questions first in order to determine the specific information you will be looking for.

[1]*praising* [2]*baskets* [3]*firecrackers* [4]*fireworks* [5]*even*

En papel: Una celebración importante en mi país. Usa el artículo de Wayne como modelo para escribir sobre alguna celebración importante en la que tú participas con frecuencia. Recuerda que necesitas hacer un bosquejo *(outline)* primero con la información que quieres escribir.

Cultura a lo vivo

En muchas ciudades de Latinoamérica se celebran carnavales que marcan el inicio de la Cuaresma[1]. El carnaval es una fiesta popular de tradición católica que celebra con alegría y excesos el período antes de la Cuaresma. El carnaval de La Habana, Cuba, es famoso en todo el mundo. Dura varios días. Incluye un desfile donde toman parte grupos de baile y música, llamados *comparsas*. El público se divierte siguiendo la música y los pasos de los grupos; bailan, beben y comen al ritmo de tambores[2], trompetas y otros instrumentos típicos de la rica tradición musical afrocubana.

[1]Lent [2]drums

¡Fíjate!

Before you write your own description, re-read the article on the previous page. Pay attention to the way Wayne orders his thoughts, his use of transition words, and how he goes from general information in the first paragraph, to specific information in the second.

¡A ver de nuevo! Escucha la conversación de **Escenas de la vida** o mira el video otra vez para escribir un resumen contestando las siguientes preguntas.

Video
CD-ROM

Audio
CD-ROM

- ¿De qué hablan Odette y Sofía?
- ¿Qué diferencias notan entre México y Estados Unidos?
- ¿Por qué dice Sofía que está americanizada?
- ¿Estás de acuerdo con el último *(last)* comentario de Odette? Explica.

Sofía   **Odette**

Práctica adicional

Cuaderno de tareas
WB pp.366–368, I–J
LM p.370, A–B

Audio
CD-ROM
Episodio 14

Website
vistahigher
learning.com

Vocabulario del Episodio 14

Para hablar de tu rutina diaria

acostarse tarde (o ⟶ ue)	*to go to bed late*
bañarse por la noche	*to take a bath / shower at night*
divertirse (e ⟶ ie)	*to have fun*
irse (a)	*to leave*
irse de vacaciones	*to go on vacation*
juntarse	*to get together*
lavarse las manos	*to wash one's hands*
los dientes	*to brush one's teeth*
levantarse temprano	*to get up early*
pintarse	*to put on makeup*
ponerse la ropa	*to put on/wear clothing*
quedarse en casa	*to stay home*
quitarse los zapatos	*to take off one's shoes*

Vocabulario personal

Write the words you need to know to talk about your daily routine and important celebrations in your family.

¡A escribir!

Episodio

14

Escenas de la vida: ¡Estás muy americanizada!

Video CD-ROM

A. ¡A ver cuánto entendiste! See how much of the **Escena** you understood by matching the Spanish sentences with their English equivalents. At the end, identify the speaker.

1. ¿Quién lo dijo (Who said it)?

_____ 1. Sólo salen los fines de semana.

_____ 2. Yo estoy tan americanizada.

_____ 3. Me pinto cuando voy a salir.

_____ 4. Sólo me pongo camisetas.

_____ 5. Entre semana la gente se acuesta temprano.

a. I'm so Americanized.

b. I only wear T-shirts.

c. I put makeup on when I go out.

d. They only go out on weekends.

e. During the week, people go to bed early.

_____ **lo dijo.**

2. ¿Quién lo dijo?

_____ 1. Es mi ropa normal.

_____ 2. Pareces viejita.

_____ 3. Aquí la gente sale casi todos los días.

_____ 4. No necesitas levantarte todavía.

_____ 5. Aquí nos acostamos tarde.

a. Here people go out almost every day.

b. You're like an old woman.

c. You don't need to get up yet.

d. Here we go to bed late.

e. These are my normal clothes.

_____ **lo dijo.**

Video CD-ROM

B. Ponlo en orden, por favor. Review the **Escena** again and put the following statements in chronological order.

_____ a. ¿Te gusta vivir en Estados Unidos?

_____ b. No estoy elegante; es mi ropa normal.

_____ c. Para ir a la universidad, no. Me pinto cuando voy a salir.

_____ d. ¿Y te pintas?

_____ e. ¿Adónde vas tan elegante?

_____ f. Sí, me gusta porque hay más oportunidades profesionales para las mujeres.

_____ g. Pero la vida es aburrida, ¿no?

Gramática 1 Describing your daily routine
• Reflexive pronouns

C. ¿En qué secuencia? Sequence the following activities in the order in which the people indicated do them. Use **primero**, **después**, and **por último**.

Modelo	(yo)/ ponerse el pijama, acostarse, mirar la tele
	Primero miro la tele, después me pongo el pijama y por último me acuesto.

1. (Sofía)/ bañarse, ponerse la ropa, levantarse

_____

_____

2. (mi esposo y yo)/lavarse los dientes, acostarse, quitarse la ropa

_____

_____

3. (yo)/ irse de vacaciones, comprar ropa, pagar mis cuentas *(bills)*

_____

_____

4. (los niños)/ponerse el pijama, cenar, dormirse

_____

_____

5. (las mujeres)/peinarse, levantarse, pintarse

_____

_____

¡Fíjate!

Notice the difference between transition words like **después** and prepositions like **después de**.
  a. Odette se pinta **después de** <u>ponerse</u> la ropa.
  b. Odette se pinta, **después se** <u>pone</u> la ropa.
In **a**, Odette first puts her clothes on; in **b**, Odette first puts makeup on. Also notice that the verb is not conjugated after the preposition **de**.

Verbs are not conjugated after prepositions: e.g., **para, antes de**, and **después de**.
Verbs are conjugated after transition words: e.g., **cuando**, and **por eso, después, antes**.

D. ¿Qué hacen? Join the actions depicted below using a preposition and a conjunction (**por eso**, **para**, **cuando**, **antes de** and **después de**) to express the order in which you do the following activities. Review the **¡Fíjate!** on conjugating verbs on the previous page.

Modelo

Primero me lavo los dientes, después me acuesto.

1. _____

2. _____

_____

_____

3. _____

4. _____

_____

_____

_____

_____

E. La rutina de Manolo.

Parte 1. Manolo is spending a week back home with his parents. As he talks about his routine, complete the description with the appropriate forms of the verbs. Then answer the questions that follow.

Ahora estoy de vacaciones en casa de mis papás. Mi rutina aquí es un poco diferente que en mi casa. Siempre (1) _____ (bañarse) por las noches, pero en la Florida hace muchísimo calor. Por eso prefiero (2)_____ (bañarse) por las mañanas. Aquí todos (3) _____ (levantarse) temprano. Mis papás

(4) _____ (levantarse) temprano porque trabajan, y yo también

(5) _____ (levantarse) porque voy a surfear con mis primos.

Durante mi semestre regular, generalmente (6) _____ (acostarse) temprano porque tengo una clase de cálculo a las siete de la mañana. En casa de mis papás,

(7) _____ (acostarse) tardísimo porque hay muchísimas cosas que hacer.

Bueno, por las noches vienen mis primos y tíos de visita (¡viven en la casa de al lado!). Jugamos cartas o Monopolio. Mis primos y yo (8) _____ (quitarse) los zapatos, (9) _____ (ponerse) cómodos y (10) _____ (quedarse) en casa toda la tarde y parte de la noche. A la una o una y media, mis primos y tíos (11) _____ (irse) a su casa. La verdad es que yo (12) _____ (divertirse) con ellos.

Parte 2. Answer the following questions.

1. ¿Qué cosas hace Manolo diferentes en la casa de sus papás?

_____

2. ¿Por qué se acuesta tarde?

_____

3. ¿Por qué todos se levantan temprano?

_____

4. ¿Qué hacen Manolo y sus primos por las tardes?

_____

5. ¿A qué hora se van los tíos?

_____

F. Mi rutina de las vacaciones. Use Manolo's description as a model to write a description of your routine when you are on vacation.

_____

_____

_____

_____

_____

_____

G. ¡Pobre Carlos! In a letter to her sister in Puerto Rico, Adriana describes Carlos' life in the military. Write the appropriate forms of the verbs from the list to complete her letter. Then answer the questions.

1. ¿Por qué está contenta Adriana? _____

2. ¿Cómo es la rutina de Carlos? ¿Te gusta? ¿Por qué sí o por qué no? _____

_____

_____

3. ¿Por qué crees que se duerme inmediatamente? _____

4. ¿Por qué es buena la Fuerza Aérea para Carlos? _____

| acostarse | bañarse | dormir | irse | ponerse |
| ser | divertirse | hacer | levantarse | verte |

...por otra parte, también estoy un poco preocupada por Carlos. ¿Recuerdas que te dije que está en un entrenamiento[1] especial con la Fuerza Aérea? Pues, hoy recibí una tarjeta de él y me cuenta que está contento, pero que él y todos sus compañeros están cansados, con hambre y con sueño.

Los pobres chicos (1) _____ a las cuatro de la mañana y (2) _____ con agua fría. Después (3) _____ la ropa, y (4) _____ sus camas en menos de quince minutos, pues a las cuatro y cuarto deben reportarse con el sargento en el patio. Empiezan a hacer ejercicios físicos y prácticas militares; ¡todo esto antes de desayunar! Después, toda la mañana toman clases de aviación. Por la tarde hacen sus prácticas de vuelo. Tienen que (5) _____ a las ocho de la noche.

Me dice que en cuanto se acuesta, se (6) _____ inmediatamente. ¡Pobre de mi hijito, con lo dormilón que es! Me dice que también ha bajado de peso[2] pobrecito, con esa rutina. Lo bueno es que va a aprender a tener disciplina y a (7) _____ ordenado.

Bueno, Cristina, escríbeme pronto y cuéntame cómo va todo por allá. ¿Cuándo vas a venir? Tengo muchas ganas de (8) _____ .

Recibe un fuerte abrazo de tu hermana que te quiere,

Adriana

[1]*training* [2]*has lost weight*

H. Un poco de lógica. The verbs you are learning in this section use a reflexive pronoun. However, many of these same verbs may also be used without a reflexive pronoun. Compare the following models and then complete the sentences. Decide whether the reflexive pronoun is necessary or not.

Modelo

Laura lava los platos.

Laura se lava las manos.

Sofía/bañar

1. _____

Carlos/bañar

2. _____

Sofía/poner/lavadora

3. _____

Odette/poner

4. _____

Para terminar

I. Venezuela: Los diablos danzantes de Yare. Read about **Los diablos danzantes de Yare**. Then answer the questions. You may answer in English or in Spanish.

1. Before you read, look at the picture of **Los diablos**. What do you think **diablos** mean? What kind of celebration might it be?

_____

_____

2. When and where does this celebration take place?

_____

_____

3. What do participants do on the first day?

_____

_____

4. What do they wear on the second day?

_____

_____

5. What do they do after mass on the second day?

_____

_____

6. What do they do after the ceremony?

_____

_____

Los diablos danzantes de Yare

Una tradición medieval española que llega en 1619 a varias ciudades de Venezuela es la de los diablos danzantes[1]. Estos diablos celebran el Corpus Christi con ceremonias simbólicas de cómo la cruz (la religión católica) derrota el mal y los pecados[2] de la humanidad. El pueblo de San Francisco de Yare es famoso por su celebración de los diablos danzantes.

La celebración empieza el miércoles de Semana Santa[3]. Los participantes bailan por las calles del pueblo, y por la noche van al Calvario[4]. Al día siguiente, por la mañana, se ponen sus trajes rojos de diablo y van al cementerio a visitar a algunos diablos anteriores. Después van a misa. Al terminar la misa, cada diablo se acerca bailando al sacerdote[5] y le dice qué sacrificios va a hacer o no hacer. El sacerdote le pregunta cuál es el motivo del ofrecimiento y la duración de la promesa.

Al finalizar esta ceremonia, todos los diablos salen a bailar otra vez por las calles del pueblo. Este ritual combina elementos indígenas y africanos con la tradición católica romana.

Los diablos danzantes bailan por las calles de San Francisco de Yare, en Venezuela.

Los músicos, vestidos de rojo, acompañan a los diablos danzantes.

[1]*dancing devils* [2]*defeats evil and the sins* [3]*Holy Week* [4]*Calvary (symbolic of the place where Jesus was crucified)* [5]*priest*

J. Una miniprueba. Complete the following tasks in Spanish; write your answers below.

1. Ask Sofía
    a. when she gets up on Sundays
    b. if she goes to bed later on weekends
    c. what she wears to go to the gym

Sofía

2. Ask Adriana
    d. how often she gets together with her sister
    e. if she is going to go on vacation this winter
       or if she is going to stay home
    f. what the weather is like where she lives

Adriana

a. _____
   _____

b. _____
   _____

c. _____
   _____

d. _____
   _____

e. _____
   _____

f. _____
   _____

¡A escuchar!

Episodio **14**

Comprensión

Audio CD-ROM

A. La rutina diaria. Describe the daily routines of the people mentioned, using the three verbs provided for each item. Then, repeat the correct answer after the speaker.

Modelo	You hear:	**tú**
	You see:	**lavarse las manos, peinarse y afeitarse** (*to shave*)
	You say:	**Te lavas las manos, te peinas y te afeitas.**

Por la mañana…

1. levantarse, bañarse y ponerse la ropa
2. bañarse, lavarse los dientes y afeitarse
3. peinarse, pintarse y ponerse ropa elegante

Por la noche en Guadalajara…

4. salir, divertirse y acostarse tarde

A las ocho de la noche…

5. quitarse la ropa, bañarse y acostarse

Audio CD-ROM

B. Una mañana en casa de Odette. Listen to Odette as she describes the events of a morning in Guadalajara. Indicate whether the statements are **cierto** or **falso** and then correct any false statements. You will hear Odette's description twice.

	Cierto	Falso
1. Odette se levanta a las siete. _____	☐	☐
2. Sofía se baña y se peina antes que Odette. _____	☐	☐
3. Sofía y Odette escuchan la radio mientras Odette se pinta. _____	☐	☐
4. Odette prepara el desayuno para todos los amigos. _____	☐	☐
5. Sofía come mucho. _____	☐	☐
6. Los amigos comen huevos con jamón. _____	☐	☐
7. A los amigos les gusta el desayuno. _____	☐	☐

Pronunciación

Audio
CD-ROM

Acentuación: Parte 1. Every syllable in Spanish has at least one vowel, which you may think of as the nucleus of the syllable. One-syllable words do not usually carry a written accent mark. Exceptions will be presented in **Acentuación: Parte 2** in **Episodio 15**. Repeat these one-syllable words:

mi   su   por   sed   sin   con   seis   pues   diez

In each word of multiple syllables, one syllable carries a spoken stress. These words do not require an accent if the stress falls on the next to the last syllable in words ending in **-n, -s,** or a vowel.

taco   gustan   amigos   muchacha   chica   hablas

Words also do not require a written accent when the stress falls on the last syllable of words ending in any consonant other than **-n** and **-s.** Repeat these words after the speaker:

ciudad   arroz   trabajar   usted   azul   universidad

Más escenas de la vida

Manolo, Ramón, Odette, Sofía and Ana Mari are planning a trip. Listen to their conversation, and then complete activities **A** and **B**. You will hear the conversation twice.

Audio
CD-ROM

A. Unscramble. Put the words in these scrambled sentences in the correct order. The first and last words of each sentence have been put in their correct place for you.

1. Mi nos a papá llevar de estación la puede autobuses.

Mi _____ autobuses.

2. Sale ahí media las siete y a estar tenemos hora que antes.

Sale _____ antes.

3. Mejor al no y vamos de la dormimos nos posada autobús.

Mejor _____ autobús.

4. Yo el dormir necesito de y antes tomar bañarme autobús.

Yo _____ autobús.

5. Ana Mari la nos entonces que de la a tenemos posada ir una.

Ana Mari, _____ una.

Audio
CD-ROM

B. Responde. Write the answers to the following questions.

1. ¿A dónde se van el domingo los chicos? _____

2. ¿Por qué Sofía va a acostarse temprano el sábado? _____

3. ¿Qué prefiere hacer Manolo el sábado? _____

4. ¿Qué van a hacer en Puerto Vallarta? _____

5. ¿Dónde se queda a dormir Ana Mari? _____

Episodio

15

Escenas de la vida: La posada

Video
CD-ROM

Audio
CD-ROM

A. ¡Mira cuánto puedes entender! Indica en qué secuencia ocurrieron las actividades de la posada, según la **Escena.**

Ana Mari está feliz porque todos quieren bailar con ella.

La mitad de los invitados están en el jardín.

Manolo tocó la guitarra.

Empezó a llover y los mayores corrieron a la casa.

Sofía está en su cuarto.

Los niños se quedaron afuera. Están ocupados recogiendo dulces.

Todos cantaron los versos tradicionales.

Ramón está molesto con Ana Mari.

Sofía está enferma porque comió demasiado pozole.

B. ¿Te diste cuenta? Indica si los comentarios son **ciertos** o **falsos,** según ocurre en la **Escena**.

Video
CD-ROM

Audio
CD-ROM

	Cierto	Falso
1. Los niños no recogen los dulces de la piñata.	☐	☐
2. Todos los invitados llegaron a la casa de Odette.	☐	☐
3. Empezó a llover, pero los niños corrieron por sus dulces.	☐	☐
4. Las personas de afuera se quedan afuera toda la noche.	☐	☐
5. Al pedir posada, hay personas dentro y fuera de la casa.	☐	☐
6. Hay comida, bebidas y música toda la noche.	☐	☐

C. ¿Quién? Indica quién se siente (*feels*) así en la posada: Sofía (**S**), Ana Mari (**AM**), Manolo (**M**), Ramón (**R**), Odette (**O**) o los niños (**LN**).

Video
CD-ROM

Audio
CD-ROM

Sofía **Ana Mari** **Manolo** **Ramón** **Odette**

_____ 1. Están emocionados de comer dulces y jugar en la lluvia.

_____ 2. Está muy contenta porque todo va muy bien.

_____ 3. Está feliz porque está de vacaciones.

_____ 4. Está enojado.

_____ 5. Está emocionado porque es la primera vez que va a México.

_____ 6. Está en cama y solamente escucha la música y la risa (*laughter*) de los invitados.

Cultura a lo vivo

Even though Spanish speakers and English speakers, like all cultural groups, get together to enjoy each other's company, their parties differ in substantial ways. For most Spanish speakers, a party is only a **fiesta** if there is music, dancing, food, and drinks. Gatherings without dancing are called **reuniones** in Mexico and **tertulias** in Spain.

A **posada** is a special **fiesta** that takes place between December 17 and 23. Family and friends of all ages reenact the biblical story of Mary and Joseph's search for shelter before the birth of Jesus.

En esta fiesta, los niños están emocionados porque ya es hora de romper la piñata. Todos están listos con sus bolsitas para poner los dulces que van a recoger.

Práctica adicional

Cuaderno de tareas
WB p.389, A–C

Video
CD-ROM
Episodio 15

Para comunicarnos mejor

Gramática 1

Saying how you feel and where you are
• **Estar** + [*adjective*], **estar** + [*location*]

In the **Escena**, you heard these statements:

Ahora **estoy enferma**.	*Now I'm sick.*
Odette **está** muy **contenta**.	*Odette is very happy.*
Estoy feliz; estoy de vacaciones.	*I'm happy; I'm on vacation.*
Ramón **está molesto** conmigo...	*Ramón is upset with me...*
Los niños **están emocionados** de comer dulces.	*The kids are excited about eating candies.*

1. You have used the verb **estar** to find out how someone is (**¿Cómo estás?**) and to tell where someone is (**Estoy en mi casa**). **Estar** is also used to express how you are feeling at a particular time.

2. **Enferma, contenta, molesto,** and **emocionados** are adjectives and match the gender (masculine or feminine) and number (singular or plural) of the nouns they describe.

3. Adjectives ending in **-e** or **-z**, such as **feliz,** match with nouns only in number.

Para describir cómo estás (*To describe how you feel*)

A veces estoy...	Sometimes I am...		
aburrido/a	*bored*	**libre**	*free*
borracho/a	*drunk*	**listo/a**	*ready*
cansado/a	*tired*	**molesto/a**	*upset*
contento/a	*happy*	**nervioso/a**	*nervous*
desilusionado/a	*disappointed*	**ocupado/a**	*busy*
emocionado/a	*excited*	**preocupado/a**	*worried*
enfermo/a	*sick*	**tranquilo/a**	*calm*
enojado/a	*angry*	**triste**	*sad*

4. Here are some expressions of location that are used with **estar.**

Estar + [*location*]

¿Dónde están los personajes?	*Where are the characters?*
Están de vacaciones.	*They are on vacation.*
Odette está adentro.	*Odette is inside.*
Ramón está afuera, en el jardín.	*Ramón is outside, in the garden.*
Yo estoy en cama.	*I am in bed.*
Y tú estás en la clase de español, ¿verdad?	*And you are in Spanish class, right?*

5. Use **dentro de** and **fuera de** followed by a place; use **adentro** and **afuera** when no location follows.

—¿Quién dejó la leche **fuera del** refrigerador? —Ay, perdón, yo la dejé **afuera.**

PRÁCTICA

A. Los opuestos. Completa las descripciones de las personas en la posada.

1. Odette no está triste; está _____.

2. Ramón no está contento; está _____.

3. Sofía no está sana *(healthy)*; está _____.

4. Los niños no están desilusionados; están _____.

5. Manolo no está preocupado; está _____.

B. Causas. Con un(a) compañero/a empareja cada columna para formar frases lógicas en voz alta *(out loud)*. Usa **porque** or **por eso** para unir las ideas.

> **Modelo**   Odette está emocionada porque su amiga Sofía va a estar en su casa dos semanas.

1. Odette está preocupada
2. Ramón y Ana Mari están libres
3. Los niños están enojados
4. Wayne está muy ocupado
5. Manolo está un poco nervioso
6. Los amigos de Odette están desilusionados

por eso
porque

a. van a ir a Guadalajara de vacaciones.
b. llueve y no pueden salir a jugar.
c. Sofía está enferma.
d. Ana Mari no quiere bailar con ellos.
e. no puede ir a Guadalajara con Ramón.
f. no le gusta tocar la guitarra en público.

C. ¿Cómo estás? Usa expresiones con **estar** para describir cómo estás en las siguientes situaciones.

1. Mañana tengo un examen muy difícil; por eso, _____.

2. Los martes tengo cuatro clases y trabajo seis horas; por eso, _____.

3. Mi pareja admira a otras/os chicas/os, _____.

4. Mis padres me dan dinero, _____.

5. Mis amigos no me llaman, _____.

6. Quiero ir al parque y empieza a llover, _____.

7. Hace muchísimo calor, _____.

8. Es hora de estar en clase y no estoy listo/a, _____.

Práctica adicional

Cuaderno de tareas
WB pp.390–391, D–G

Gramática 2 Talking about past activities
• Introduction to the preterit tense

Analizar y descubrir

In the **Escena**, you heard these statements:

Manolo **tocó** la guitarra y **cantó...**   *Manolo played the guitar and sang...*
Comí demasiado pozole.   *I ate too much **pozole**.*
...los mayores **corrieron** a la casa.   *...the grown-ups ran into the house.*

1. **Tocó, cantó, comí,** and **corrieron** are preterit (past tense) forms of the verbs **tocar, cantar, comer,** and **correr.**

Study the examples and answer the questions.

Bailar	
Yo **bailé** toda la noche.	*I danced all night.*
Y tú, ¿**bailaste** con Manolo?	*And you, did you dance with Manolo?*
Manolo no **bailó** con Ana Mari.	*Manolo didn't dance with Ana Mari.*
Nosotras **bailamos** con Ramón.	*We danced with Ramón.*
¿Ustedes **bailaron** hasta tarde? ¿Vosotros **bailasteis** hasta tarde? }	*Did you dance until late?*
Los niños también **bailaron**.	*The kids also danced.*

2. In the preterit, the endings of **-er** verbs and **-ir** verbs are identical.

Comer	
Yo **comí** mucho.	*I ate a lot.*
Y tú, ¿**comiste** tamales?	*And you, did you eat tamales?*
Sofía **comió** demasiado pozole.	*Sofía ate too much pozole.*
Nosotros no **comimos** dulces.	*We didn't eat candy.*
¿Ustedes **comieron** pastel? ¿Vosotros **comisteis** pastel? }	*Did you eat cake?*
¡Los niños **comieron** muchos dulces!	*The kids ate a lot of candy!*

3. Now complete the conjugations of **hablar, beber,** and **escribir.**

El pretérito de los verbos regulares			
	-ar **hablar**	**-er** **beber**	**-ir** **escribir**
yo	_____	_____	_____
tú	_____	_____	_____
usted/él/ella	_____	_____	_____
nosotros/as	_____	_____	_____
ustedes/ellos/as	_____	_____	_____

a. What are the preterit endings for regular verbs in the **yo** form? _____

b. What are the endings for the **tú** form? _____

c. What are the endings for the **él, ella,** and **usted** form? _____

d. What are the endings for regular verbs in the **nosotros/as** form? _____

e. How are the **-ar nosotros/as** forms different from the present tense endings?
_____

f. What are the preterit endings for the **ellos, ellas,** and **ustedes** form? _____

4. The following are three common irregular verbs.

El pretérito de **ir, hacer** y **tener**	
ir	fui, fuiste, fue, fuimos, fueron
hacer	hice, hiciste, hizo, hicimos, hicieron
tener	tuve, tuviste, tuvo, tuvimos, tuvieron

—¿Adónde **fue** Adriana durante las vacaciones? — *Where did Adriana go during her vacation?*

—No **fue** a ninguna parte porque **tuvo** que trabajar. — *She didn't go anywhere because she had to work.*

—Y tú, ¿qué **hiciste**? — *What did you do?*

—**Fui** a Guadalajara. — *I went to Guadalajara.*

5. Verbs ending in **-ar** and **-er** that have stem changes (e ⟶ ie, o ⟶ ue) in the present tense will not have those changes in the preterit tense. Compare the two tenses:

present   preterit
Ramón **juega** fútbol, pero durante las vacaciones no **jugó**.

present   preterit
El partido nunca **empieza** a tiempo, y ayer tampoco **empezó** a tiempo.

6. Verbs ending in **-gar (llegar, pagar)**, **-car (sacar, tocar)**, and **-zar (empezar, organizar)** have spelling changes in the **yo** form.

El semestre pasado lle**gué** a tiempo a todas mis clases. Pa**gué** todas mis deudas *(debts)*. También to**qué** la guitarra en la banda de la escuela. Y lo mejor es que sa**qué** buenas notas porque empe**cé** a trabajar menos y a estudiar más; hasta organi**cé** un grupo de estudio con mis compañeros.

7. The following are some of the expressions used with the preterit tense to indicate past time.

Algunas expresiones para hablar del pasado			
ayer	*yesterday*	hace dos semanas	*two weeks ago*
anoche	*last night*	hace tres meses	*three months ago*
la semana pasada	*last week*	hace cuatro años	*four years ago*
el mes pasado	*last month*	esta mañana	*this morning*
el año pasado	*last year*	durante cinco años	*for five years*

PRÁCTICA

D. ¿Por qué estás así? Une las columnas con una línea para crear oraciones lógicas usando la palabra **porque.**

> **Modelo** Estoy contenta porque saqué A en mi examen de inglés.

1. Estoy nerviosa porque
2. Mi hija está triste
3. Estoy enfermo
4. Los niños están felices
5. Manolo y yo estamos cansados
6. Ramón está enojado

porque

a. recibieron mucho dinero para su cumpleaños.
b. comí demasiados mariscos.
c. jugamos fútbol toda la mañana.
d. tuvo que comprar muchos libros este semestre.
e. no encontró su bolsa.
f. no estudié para el examen que voy a tomar hoy.

E. ¿Qué hiciste ayer?

Parte 1. Indica si hiciste estas actividades la semana pasada. Después entrevista a tu compañero/a para ver si hicieron las mismas cosas.

	Sí	No
1. Me bañé muy temprano.	☐	☐
2. Lavé la ropa.	☐	☐
3. Limpié mi cuarto.	☐	☐
4. Comí en un restaurante elegante.	☐	☐
5. Visité a mis abuelos/papás.	☐	☐
6. Me quedé en casa toda la tarde.	☐	☐
7. Fui a un lugar divertido.	☐	☐
8. Tuve que trabajar.	☐	☐
9. Hice toda mi tarea.	☐	☐
10. Me acosté a las diez de la noche.	☐	☐

Parte 2. Cambia las oraciones a preguntas para entrevistar a tu compañero/a. Después escribe acerca de lo que hizo tu compañero/a.

> **Modelo** —Jim, ¿lavaste la ropa la semana pasada?
> —Sí, la lavé. ¿Y tú?
> —Yo también.   o   —Yo no.

¡Fíjate!

Use **lo, la, los,** and **las** when you have a direct object. Remember, not all verbs take a direct object.

F. ¿Adónde fuiste?

Parte 1. Indica a qué lugares fueron las personas según lo que hicieron.

> **Modelo** Ayer hice mucho ejercicio.
> **Fuiste al gimnasio.**

1. La semana pasada compré una blusa nueva.

   _____

2. Ana Mari y Ramón vieron una película muy interesante.

   _____

3. Ayer jugué a las cartas con Manolo.

   _____

4. Anoche Adriana estudió con sus compañeros.

   _____

5. Hace tres días comí comida china.

   _____

6. El domingo pasado hicimos un picnic para Wayne.

   _____

7. El verano pasado tomé el sol y nadé.

   _____

8. El sábado pasado Ana Mari bailó toda la noche.

   _____

 Parte 2. Ahora habla con un(a) compañero/a sobre tres cosas que hiciste la semana pasada.

G. Ana Mari escribe a casa.
Escribe el pretérito de los verbos entre paréntesis para completar la carta de Ana Mari.

Queridos papá y mamá:

Ayer Ramón y yo (1) _____ (ir) a casa de Odette porque ella
(2) _____ (hacer) una posada fantástica.
Yo (3) _____ (bailar) toda la noche y (4) _____
(comer) de todo: tamales, pozole, taquitos, etc.
También (5) _____ (cantar; nosotros) las canciones típicas
navideñas y de posada. ¡Hacía mucho que no me divertía tanto! A la
hora de romper la piñata (6) _____ (empezar) a llover y todos
(7) _____ (correr) a la casa. Los niños (8) _____
(comer) muchos dulces y (9) _____ (jugar) en la lluvia. Pobre
Sofía (10) _____ (comer) tanto pozole el día anterior que se
enfermó y no (11) _____ (ir) a la posada. ¡Pobrecita!

H. ¿Qué hicieron? Usa las fotos para escribir qué hicieron Sofía y Wayne el domingo. Ordena los eventos lógicamente. Usa **por la mañana, después, a las … de la noche,** etc.

_____

_____

_____

_____

_____

_____

I. ¡A hablar! En grupos de tres personas, hablen de sus actividades de un fin de semana divertido. Por lo menos, tienen que mencionar cinco actividades.

| Modelo | Hace un mes fui a un juego de vóleibol. Después, mis compañeros y yo fuimos a comer. Por la noche, salí con unas amigas; vimos una película muy buena. |

Audio
CD-ROM

J. Todos a bordo. Escucha el mensaje que hay en tu correo de voz _(voicemail)_ para contestar las preguntas.

1. ¿Qué ganaste? _____

2. ¿En qué fecha lo tienes que tomar? _____

3. ¿Qué tiempo hace en invierno? _____

4. ¿Cuáles son las actividades del barco? _____

   _____

5. ¿Qué actividades se pueden hacer en cada puerto? _____

   _____

6. ¿Qué necesitas hacer para aceptar el premio? _____

   _____

Práctica adicional

Cuaderno de tareas
WB pp.391–394, H–N
LM pp.397–398, A–B, Pron.

Audio
CD-ROM
Episodio 15

Actividades comunicativas

A. Un día en la guardería "El Porvenir".

Instrucciones para **Estudiante 1**

Tú eres el/la supervisor(a) en la guardería "El Porvenir". Hoy hablas con un(a) empleado/a nuevo/a. Dile cómo se llaman los niños con quienes va a trabajar. También dile lo que sabes de cada niño. Tu compañero/a empieza con una pregunta.

Modelo	La niña que lleva la blusa rosa se llama Eliana. Está contenta porque es su cumpleaños y recibió muchos regalos.

Eliana
Today is her birthday and she got many presents.

Noni and Laura
They are going on vacation tomorrow.

Juan
He does not like the music.

Maggie
Mario did not play with her all day.

Iván and Rubén
They do not know anybody because it's their first day.

Concetta
She has new shoes.

Mario
He went to bed at midnight.

Tommy
He ate Maggie's crayons (**crayolas**).

Brandon
Noni and Laura do not want to talk to him.

A. Un día en la guardería "El Porvenir".

Instrucciones para **Estudiante 2**

Hoy es tu primer día de trabajo en la guardería "El Porvenir". Pregúntale a tu supervisor(a) cómo se llaman los niños con quienes vas a trabajar. También tienes que preguntar por qué están contentos, tristes, preocupados, enojados, etc. Escribe la información de cada niño. Tú empiezas.

Modelo —¿Cómo se llama la niña que lleva una blusa rosa?
—¿Por qué está contenta?

B. La historia va así.

Audio
CD-ROM

Parte 1. Escucha lo que hizo Sofía la semana pasada y mira las ilustraciones. Identifica el orden, del uno al ocho, en que ocurrieron los eventos. Escucha una vez más para verificar tus respuestas.

___ a

___ b

___ c

___ d

___ e

___ f

___ g

___ h

Parte 2. Ahora en grupos escriban una historia diferente.

_____

_____

_____

_____

_____

_____

C. Las actividades de mis compañeros.

Parte 1. En la columna **B**, escribe **yo** junto a las actividades que sí hiciste la semana pasada. Después entrevista a tus compañeros para llenar *(to fill)* todos los espacios en las dos columnas con sus nombres.

La semana pasada…	A	B
1. ¿Compraste ropa nueva?	_____	_____
2. ¿Tuviste que trabajar?	_____	_____
3. ¿Hiciste ejercicio?	_____	_____
4. ¿Almorzaste en la cafetería?	_____	_____
5. ¿Fuiste a una fiesta?	_____	_____
6. ¿Comiste comida italiana?	_____	_____
7. ¿Jugaste ráquetbol?	_____	_____
8. ¿Saliste con tus amigos?	_____	_____
9. ¿Te acostaste temprano todas las noches?	_____	_____
10. ¿Te levantaste tarde más de dos días?	_____	_____

Parte 2. Escribe un informe con la información que tienes. Incluye por lo menos seis oraciones. Necesitas estar preparado/a para compartir la información con la clase.

> **Modelo**
> **Ana y yo compramos ropa nueva.**
> **Tom y Alex tuvieron que trabajar.**
> **Sharon almorzó en la cafetería.**

Invitación a **México**

Del álbum de
Sofía

Muchos de los elementos de la cultura mexicana conocidos en todo el mundo provienen del estado de Jalisco, cuya capital es Guadalajara. De ahí vienen los mariachis, los charros y charreadas: fiestas en rodeos donde se combinan las habilidades artísticas con el colorido y belleza de la ropa, las técnicas en el manejo del caballo y la elegancia del jinete *(rider)*; los palenques (ferias donde hay cantantes y peleas de gallos) y mucha de la "comida mexicana" es originaria de Jalisco. También, grandes escritores mexicanos como Juan Rulfo y Mariano Azuela son jaliscienses.

Práctica adicional

Website
vistahigher
learning.com

La correspondencia

 El correo: Manolo escribe desde Guadalajara. Manolo les escribe a sus padres una carta desde Guadalajara comentándoles su visita a México. Léela y contesta las preguntas.

1. ¿Qué es una posada? ¿Qué hacen los invitados en una posada? _____
_____

2. ¿Dónde está Manolo? ¿Qué tiempo hace allí? _____
_____

3. ¿Adónde van Manolo y sus amigos por las noches? _____
_____

4. ¿Adónde fueron? ¿Qué lugares conocieron? _____
_____

Queridos papás: Guadalajara, 26 de diciembre

Espero que estén bien. Yo nunca he pasado[1] mejores vacaciones. Odette y su familia son muy amables. Anteayer hicieron una posada fabulosa aquí en la casa de Odette. Comí muchos platos típicos mexicanos que no conocía. Me estoy divirtiendo como no tienen idea.

Guadalajara es una ciudad realmente bonita. Tiene zonas supermodernas y zonas coloniales; tiene árboles y flores por todas partes, pues el clima es ideal para las plantas (llueve bastante y hace calor, pero no tiene clima tropical). El lunes pasado fuimos al Museo Regional de Guadalajara, donde hay una colección de artículos de la revolución y de la independencia mexicana. También hay unas pinturas fabulosas de los mejores artistas regionales y nacionales.

Otro día visitamos el mercado de Tlaquepaque donde venden artesanía, comida típica y todo lo que se puedan imaginar. Yo no sabía que la artesanía mexicana era tan bonita y fina. Hacen una cosas de plata, cobre, latón, barro y vidrio[2], que son unas obras de arte. Compré muchas cosas y no pagué mucho.

Por las noches hay mil cosas que hacer. Una noche cantamos y bailamos en la Plaza del Mariachi, donde se pueden escuchar varios grupos de mariachis, y no se paga nada a menos que uno pida que canten algo. También fuimos a escuchar al grupo de rock Maná, unos muchachos jóvenes con mucho talento, que son de Guadalajara.

Otra noche fuimos al Teatro Degollado a ver el ballet folclórico de la Universidad de Guadalajara. Compré un video del ballet para ustedes. Les va a gustar mucho el vestuario, la música, los bailes, la alegría… ¡tienen que verlo!

En el Hospicio Cabañas están los famosos murales de Orozco. Hay unos frescos enormes, llenos de color y, lo más importante, con contenido social.

Bueno, ya tengo que irme a dormir porque mañana tenemos que madrugar[3]; salimos para Puerto Vallarta. Les mando un beso y los llamo cuando regrese a Estados Unidos.

Su hijo que los quiere,
Manolo

[1]*have spent* [2]**plata,...** *silver, copper, brass, clay, and glass* [3]*get up early (at dawn)*

En papel: Una celebración familiar. Escríbele una carta a Odette sobre un evento o una fiesta que celebraste con tu familia.

Incluye la siguiente información:

- dónde fue
- cuándo fue
- qué celebraron
- qué actividades hicieron
- quiénes fueron
- qué ropa llevaste
- qué comiste

Writing Strategy: Using simple language to express your ideas

You may feel frustrated when you cannot communicate your ideas in written Spanish as well as you can in English. For this reason, you may make the mistake of using a dictionary and creating sentences that Spanish speakers would not be able to understand. A much more effective strategy is to limit your messages to what you are able to communicate.

You have just read Manolo's letter. By using your background knowledge, and context, you were probably able to understand most of the text. But you are probably not yet able to use that level of language to communicate your own ideas.

For example, in the letter you read this about Guadalajara: **En el Hospicio Cabañas están los famosos murales de Orozco. Hay unos frescos enormes, llenos de color y … contenido social…** Although you cannot yet write a similar description, you can write something like: **En el Hospicio Cabañas hay unos murales muy bonitos e interesantes,** which any Spanish speaker would understand. Using simple language enables you to express yourself effectively while you build your writing communication skills.

¡Fíjate!

Remember to create an outline in simple Spanish. Write a first draft with your ideas. Then use connectors to join your sentences. In the final draft, check vocabulary and grammar.

Video
CD-ROM

Audio
CD-ROM

¡A ver de nuevo!

Parte 1. Escucha la narración de **Escenas de la vida** o mira el video para hacer un resumen que conteste todas las preguntas.

1. ¿Qué hacen las personas a la hora de pedir posada?
2. ¿Por qué está contenta Odette?
3. ¿Por qué está feliz Ana Mari?
4. ¿Qué hizo Manolo en la posada?
5. ¿Qué pasó con Sofía? ¿Por qué no fue a la posada?

Parte 2. Ahora trabaja con un(a) compañero/a para añadir lo que te haya faltado.

Práctica adicional		
Cuaderno de tareas WB pp.394–395, Ñ LM p. 398, A–B	Audio CD-ROM Episodio 15	Website vistahigher learning.com

Vocabulario del Episodio 15

Para describir cómo estás

A veces estoy...	Sometimes I am...
aburrido/a	bored
borracho/a	drunk
cansado/a	tired
contento/a	happy
desilusionado/a	disappointed
emocionado/a	excited
enfermo/a	sick
enojado/a	angry
libre	free
listo/a	ready
molesto/a	upset
nervioso/a	nervous
ocupado/a	busy
preocupado/a	worried
tranquilo/a	quiet, calm
triste	sad

Estar + [*location*]

estar...	to be...
adentro/dentro de	inside
afuera/fuera de	outside
en cama	in bed
en clase	in class
de vacaciones	on vacation

Algunas expresiones para hablar del pasado

ayer	yesterday	hace dos semanas	two weeks ago
anoche	last night	hace tres meses	three months ago
la semana pasada	last week	hace cuatro años	four years ago
el mes pasado	last month	esta mañana	this morning
el año pasado	last year	durante cinco años	for five years

Vocabulario personal

In this section, write all the words you need to know in order to better talk about your own activities.

¡A escribir!

Episodio

15

Escenas de la vida: La posada

A. ¡A ver cuánto entendiste! Match the sentences with their translations.

Video
CD-ROM

_____ 1. La otra mitad se queda dentro de la casa.

_____ 2. Ya es hora de pedir posada.

_____ 3. Los niños decidieron recoger los dulces y juguetes.

_____ 4. Están emocionados de romper la piñata.

_____ 5. Empezó a llover.

_____ 6. Todos tienen una vela y los versos tradicionales.

a. They're excited about breaking the piñata.

b. It began to rain.

c. It's time to ask for shelter.

d. Everyone has a candle and the traditional verses.

e. The kids decided to pick up the candies and toys.

f. The other half stays in the house.

B. ¿Quién se siente así? *(Who feels that way?)* Indicate who the following statements describe: Sofía (**S**), Manolo (**M**), Ramón (**R**), Ana Mari (**AM**), or Odette (**O**).

Video
CD-ROM

_____ 1. Está desilusionada porque Manolo no bailó con ella.

_____ 2. No puede usar su vestido elegante ni sus zapatos de tacón.

_____ 3. Está molesto porque llegaron tarde a la posada.

_____ 4. Está feliz porque está de vacaciones.

_____ 5. Está emocionado porque es la primera vez que va a México.

_____ 6. Está muy contenta porque su posada va muy bien.

C. La posada. Use the words to complete the description.

Video
CD-ROM

pozole	organizó	enferma	bailar
cuidar	cama	tocó	cantó

Todos los invitados se divierten mucho en la posada que Odette (1) _____ .

Todos los muchachos quieren (2) _____ con Ana Mari. Ramón está molesto.

Cree que todavía tiene que (3) _____ a su hermana. Manolo (4) _____

la guitarra y (5) _____ . Sofía está en la (6) _____ . Está (7) _____ .

Comió demasiado (8) _____ .

Gramática 1 Saying how you feel and where you are
•**Estar** + [*adjective*], **estar** + [*location*]

D. Usa la lógica. Combine elements from the three columns to make logical sentences.

1. estoy aburrido/a
2. estamos cansados/as
3. estoy listo/a
4. mi novio/a está molesto/a
5. mi papá está tranquilo
6. los chicos están preocupados
7. tú estás enfermo/a

porque
por eso

podemos irnos en este momento
vamos a descansar y dormir un rato
comiste muchos tacos de pescado
todos están en casa
sacaron F en el examen
mis amigos están ocupados y no
    pueden salir conmigo
no la/o llamé por teléfono anoche

1. _____
2. _____
3. _____
4. _____
5. _____
6. _____
7. _____

E. ¿Por qué estás así? Complete the following statements in a logical manner.

> **Modelo** Estoy triste porque mis amigos no me invitan a sus fiestas.

1. Estoy aburrido/a porque _____.

2. Estoy cansado/a porque _____.

3. Mi mamá está enojada conmigo porque _____.

4. Estoy molesto/a porque _____.

5. Estoy tranquilo/a porque _____.

6. Estoy contento/a porque _____.

7. Estoy triste porque _____.

8. Mis padres están preocupados porque _____.

F. Un día muy interesante. Describe how people in the images feel, where they are, and the reason they feel that way using any expression with **estar.**

_____
_____
_____
_____
_____
_____

G. ¿Dónde está Migdalia? Describe where Manolo's cat, Migdalia, is, using **en, dentro del,** and **afuera.**

1. Migdalia, la gata de Manolo, a veces está _____.

2. Otras veces está _____ la cama de Manolo.

3. Pero cuando Manolo no está, a la gata le gusta estar _____ cajón
   (drawer) de los suéteres.

Gramática 2

Talking about past activities
• Introduction to the preterit tense

H. ¡Dime más! When Manolo mentions the things he did last week, Ramón follows every statement with a question. What does Ramón ask?

Modelo	Manolo	**Hablé por teléfono con mis padres.**
	Ramón	**¿Y cómo están?**

Manolo	**Ramón**
_____ 1. Salí con Ana Mari.	a. ¿Para quién?
_____ 2. Fui a un concierto.	b. ¿Adónde fueron?
_____ 3. Vi una buena película.	c. ¿A qué grupo escuchaste?

_____ 4. Aprendí una canción nueva
en la guitarra.

_____ 5. Almorcé comida cubana.

_____ 6. Llegué tarde a clase.

_____ 7. Trabajé hasta las tres de la mañana.

_____ 8. Escribí un poema.

d. ¿Y tienes que trabajar hoy también?

e. ¿Tuviste que practicar mucho?

f. ¿Qué comiste?

g. ¿Ah sí, cuál?

h. ¿Hablaste con la profesora?

I. Explicaciones. Complete the statements logically using verbs in the preterit.

> **Modelo**   Estoy cansada porque **ayer trabajé mucho.**

1. Estoy enfermo/a porque _____.
2. Estoy desilusionado/a porque _____.
3. Estoy molesto/a porque _____.
4. Estoy nervioso/a porque _____.
5. Estoy libre porque _____.
6. Estoy emocionado/a porque _____.

J. ¿Qué hicieron en la playa? Use the illustration to complete Sofía's description with the following verbs: **jugar, hacer, hablar, comer, ir, beber,** and **descansar.**

Ayer, (1) _____ a la playa con todos mis amigos. Por suerte (2) _____ muy buen tiempo: calor y sol. Ana Mari y yo (3) _____ vóleibol un par de horas. Manolo no (4) _____ con nosotras; leyó el periódico y (5) _____ en una hamaca. Odette (6) _____ mucho con Ramón. Ellos (7) _____ camarones y (8) _____ refrescos.

K. Los problemas de Adriana. Describe what happened in Adriana's house last weekend. Use the illustrations to describe what she did.

El sábado por la mañana Adriana (1) _____ a Viviana a su clase de baile. Luego regresó a casa. Primero (2) _____ los platos y luego (3) _____ un trabajo en la computadora para su clase de composición. También (4) _____ con Santiago un par de horas. Llegó a casa muy cansada así que (5) _____ un rato en el sofá de la sala. Por la noche Adriana y su amiga (6) _____. Vieron una película de misterio. El domingo en la mañana todos (7) _____ a los abuelos. Cuando llegaron a casa, ella (8) _____ con Santiago otra vez; por eso, se fue a la biblioteca de la universidad a estudiar y no (9) _____ hasta las diez de la noche.

L. Ahora te toca a ti. Tell what you did last weekend. Write at least six sentences.

_____
_____
_____
_____
_____
_____

M. ¿Cuándo fue la última vez? Use the expressions to tell when you last did the following activities. Include direct object pronouns when possible.

ayer	**anoche**	**la semana pasada**
hace tres meses	**el mes pasado**	**hace un año**

> **Modelo**   ¿Cuándo hiciste la tarea?
> **La hice ayer por la mañana.**

1. ¿Cuándo lavaste tu coche?

_____

2. ¿Cuándo fuiste al supermercado?

_____

3. ¿Cuándo viste a tus padres?

_____

4. ¿Cuándo limpiaste tu cuarto?

_____

5. ¿Cuándo almorzaste con toda tu familia?

_____

N. El fin de semana pasado. Answer the questions with as much detail as you can.

1. ¿Adónde fuiste el fin de semana pasado? ¿Con quién? ¿Qué hicieron ahí?

_____

_____

_____

_____

2. ¿Tuviste que trabajar? ¿Qué otras cosas tuviste que hacer?

_____

_____

_____

3. ¿Te levantaste tarde o temprano? ¿Te bañaste por la mañana o por la noche?

_____

_____

_____

_____

4. ¿Comiste en un restaurante? ¿Qué comiste?

_____

_____

_____

_____

5. ¿Hiciste tarea o estudiaste? ¿Para qué clase? ¿Dónde?

_____

_____

_____

_____

Para terminar

Ñ. Cuba: El carnaval de La Habana. Read about the celebration of **Carnaval** in Havana, Cuba, and then answer the questions.

1. ¿Qué es un carnaval?

_____

_____

2. ¿Qué temas *(themes)* representan las comparsas en el desfile *(parade)*?

_____

_____

3. ¿Por dónde pasa el desfile?

_____

_____

4. ¿Qué comida se vende durante estas fiestas?

_____

_____

5. En Estados Unidos, ¿hay celebraciones similares a los carnavales? ¿En dónde? ¿Cuáles son? ¿Cuándo?

_____

_____

_____

_____

_____

_____

6. ¿Asistes a esas celebraciones? ¿Las ves en la televisión? ¿Qué hacen las personas que participan?

_____

_____

_____

_____

_____

_____

_____

En muchas ciudades de Latinoamérica se celebran carnavales que marcan el inicio de la Cuaresma[1]. El carnaval es una fiesta popular de tradición católica que celebra con alegría y excesos el período antes de la Cuaresma. El carnaval de La Habana es famoso en todo el mundo y dura varios días. Incluye un desfile donde toman parte grupos de baile y música, llamados *comparsas*. Estos grupos practican todo el año para presentar al público su habilidad e imaginación artística. Cada grupo se pone extravagantes trajes y adornos en la cabeza. Además llevan un estandarte[2] que identifica el barrio de procedencia y el tema de la coreografía (temas históricos, folclóricos o literarios relacionados con Cuba o de carácter universal).

La participación de las comparsas alterna con el desfile de numerosas e impresionantes carrozas[3] alegóricas. El desfile pasa por las calles principales

de la ciudad hasta llegar al palco presidencial donde hay un jurado[4] que determina el mejor grupo de danza y la mejor carroza. El público se divierte siguiendo la música y los pasos de los grupos; bailan, beben y comen al ritmo de tambores[5], trompetas y otros instrumentos típicos de la rica tradición musical afrocubana. A lo largo del malecón[6], la venta de yuca, congrí (arroz con frijoles negros), cerveza, malta, refrescos y ron deleita al público cubano y extranjero.

El carnaval ha estado varias veces en peligro[7] de desaparecer por motivos políticos y económicos. Fue suprimido en 1970 y a principios de los años 90. Afortunadamente y como resultado del descontento popular y el aumento del turismo, se vuelve a celebrar por las calles de la vieja ciudad el carnaval lleno de música y de esperanza para el porvenir[8].

[1]*Lent* [2]*banner* [3]*floats* [4]*(panel of) judges* [5]*drums* [6]*avenue closest to the ocean* [7]*danger*
[8]**esperanza...** *hope for the future*

¡A escuchar!

Comprensión

Audio
CD-ROM

A. Un día especial en Tlaquepaque. You are going to hear Sofía and Ana Mari discuss Ana Mari's trip to Tlaquepaque, a Mexican city famous for its typical arts and crafts **(artesanías)**. Listen and then select the answers to the questions. **¡Atención!** Each question has more than one correct answer. You will hear the conversation twice.

Banco de palabras			
barro	**fábrica**	**latón**	**vajilla**
clay	factory	brass	set of table ware
camión	**lámpara**	**lluvia**	
bus (in Mexico)	lamp	rain	

1. ¿Quiénes fueron a Tlaquepaque?

  a. Sofía   b. Ana Mari   c. Manolo   d. Ramón   e. Odette

2. ¿Qué tiempo hizo?

  a. Hizo calor.   b. Empezó a llover.   c. Hizo mal tiempo.   e. Hizo buen tiempo.

3. ¿Qué hicieron en Tlaquepaque?

  a. Bailaron.   c. Se sentaron en la plaza.   e. Escucharon a los mariachis.

  b. Comieron.   d. Bebieron aguas frescas.   f. Se perdieron.

4. ¿Qué compraron Ana Mari y Manolo?

  a. una bolsa y una chaqueta   c. una pintura   e. una vajilla de barro

  b. camisas típicas   d. una lámpara   f. unos libros

Audio
CD-ROM

B. La respuesta más lógica. You will hear brief descriptions of six situations in the form of questions or statements. Choose the most logical response to each situation.

1. a. Compró un vestido muy bonito.   b. No encuentra su pasaporte.   c. Fue a la fiesta con sus amigos.

2. a. Está afuera.   b. Está enferma.   c. Está cansada.

3. a. Hace calor.   b. Hace sol.   c. Hace frío.

4. a. Voy a quitarme la ropa.   b. Necesito un impermeable.   c. Necesito un traje.

5. a. Van a una fiesta.   b. Llueve y no pueden salir a jugar.   c. Tienen una piñata con dulces y frutas.

6. a. Saliste con Ramón.   b. Voy a una fiesta.   c. Bailé toda la noche.

Pronunciación

Acentuación: Parte 2. The written accent mark in Spanish is used for two different purposes. Accents are used for grammatical distinctions. Here are some examples of how they are used to distinguish between different parts of speech.

a. unstressed possessive article **mi** and stressed prepositional pronoun **mí**

¿Quieres usar **mi** lápiz?　　　　Esta carta es para **mí**.

b. unstressed pronoun **te** and stressed noun **té**

Te levantas temprano.　　　　¿Quieres una taza de **té?**

c. unstressed conjunctions and stressed interrogative words

Estudio **cuando** hay examen.　　　　**¿Cuándo** es el examen?

Es un chico **que** conozco.　　　　**¿Qué** tiempo hace?

Accents also denote spoken stress in pronunciation. When a word ending in **–n, -s,** or a vowel is not stressed on the next-to-last syllable, an accent mark is placed on the vowel of the stressed syllable to indicate where the stress falls.

ca**fé**　　auto**bús**　　**nú**mero　　pe**lí**cula　　es**tás**　　des**pués**

When a word ending in any consonant other than **–n** or **-s** is not stressed on the last syllable, the stressed syllable is likewise indicated by an accent mark.

suéter　　di**fí**cil　　**ár**bol　　**fá**cil

When a stressed **i** or **u** fall next to a vowel, an accent mark is used to indicate the stress.

día　　poli**cí**a　　So**fí**a　　**leí**a　　libre**rí**a　　gra**dú**a

Más escenas de la vida

Ana Mari, Sofía, and Manolo chat at the beach in Puerto Vallarta. Listen to their conversation, and then complete activities **A** and **B**. You will hear the conversation twice.

A. ¿Quién lo dijo? Indicate who made each of the following statements in the conversation: Manolo **(M)**, Ana Mari **(AM)**, or Sofía **(S).**

_____ 1. Me impresionó la pintura de Orozco.　　_____ 4. ¿Y se casó o tuvo hijos?

_____ 2. Sus murales sólo reflejan injusticias sociales.　　_____ 5. ¿Qué hicieron el viernes?

_____ 3. Vivió en Estados Unidos varios años.

B. Responde. Write the answers to the following questions.

1. ¿Qué lugares de Estados Unidos visitó Orozco? _____

2. ¿A quiénes invitó la abuela a su casa? _____

3. ¿Después adónde los llevaron? ¿Qué hicieron ahí? _____

_____

4. ¿Adónde fueron Sofía y Manolo? ¿Qué hicieron ahí? _____

Glossary of Grammatical Terms

ADJECTIVE A word that modifies or describes a noun or pronoun.

muchos libros
many books

un hombre **rico**
*a **rich** man*

las mujeres **altas**
*the **tall** women*

Demonstrative adjective An adjective that points out a specific noun.

esta fiesta
this party

ese chico
that boy

aquellas flores
those flowers

Possessive adjective An adjective that indicates ownership or possession.

mi mejor vestido
my best dress

Éste es **mi** hermano.
*This is **my** brother*

Stressed possessive adjective A possessive adjective that emphasizes the owner or possessor.

Es un libro **mío**.
*It's **my book**./It's a book **of mine**.*

Es amiga **tuya**; yo no la conozco.
*She's a friend **of yours**; I don't know her.*

ADVERB A word that modifies or describes a verb, adjective, or another adverb.

Pancho escribe **rápidamente**.
*Pancho writes **quickly**.*

Este cuadro es **muy** bonito.
*This picture is **very** pretty.*

ARTICLE A word that points out either a specific (definite) noun or a non-specific (indefinite) noun.

Definite article An article that points out a specific noun.

el libro
the book

la maleta
the suitcase

los diccionarios
the dictionaries

las palabras
the words

Indefinite article An article that points out a noun in a general, non-specific way.

un lápiz
a pencil

una computadora
a computer

unos pájaros
some birds

unas escuelas
some schools

CLAUSE A group of words that contains both a conjugated verb and a subject, either expressed or implied.

Main (or Independent) clause A clause that can stand alone as a complete sentence.

Pienso ir a cenar pronto.
I plan to go to dinner soon.

Subordinate (or Dependent) clause A clause that does not express a complete thought and therefore cannot stand alone as a sentence.

Trabajo en la cafetería **porque necesito dinero para la escuela**.
*I work in the cafeteria **because I need money for school.***

COMPARATIVE A word or construction used with an adjective or adverb to express a comparison between two people, places, or things.

Este programa es **más interesante que** el otro.
*This program is **more interesting than** the other one.*

Tomás no es **tan alto como** Alberto.
*Tomás is not **as tall as** Alberto.*

CONJUGATION A set of the forms of a verb for a specific tense or mood or the process by which these verb forms are presented.

Preterit conjugation of **cantar**

cant**é**	cant**amos**
cant**aste**	cant**asteis**
cant**ó**	cant**aron**

CONJUNCTION A word or phrase used to connect words, clauses, or phrases.

Susana es de Cuba **y** Pedro es de España.
*Susana is from Cuba **and** Pedro is from Spain.*

No quiero estudiar, **pero** tengo que hacerlo.
*I don't want to study, **but** I have to do it.*

CONTRACTION The joining of two words into one. The only contractions in Spanish are **al** and **del**.

Mi hermano fue **al** concierto ayer.
*My brother went **to the** concert yesterday.*

Saqué dinero **del** banco.
*I took money **from the** bank.*

DIRECT OBJECT A noun or pronoun that directly receives the action of the verb.

Tomás lee **el libro**.
*Tomás reads **the book**.*

La pagó ayer.
*She paid **it** yesterday.*

GENDER The grammatical categorizing of certain kinds of words, such as nouns and pronouns, as masculine, feminine, or neuter.

Masculine
articles **el**, un**o**
pronouns **él**, **lo**, mí**o**, ést**e**, és**e**, aquell**o**
adjective simpátic**o**

Feminine
articles **la**, un**a**
pronouns **ella**, **la**, mí**a**, ést**a**, és**a**, aquéll**a**
adjective simpátic**a**

GERUND See Present Participle, p. 402.

IMPERSONAL EXPRESSION A third-person pl. and sing. expression with no expressed or specific subject.

Es muy importante.
*It's **very important**.*

Llueve mucho.
*It's **raining** hard.*

Aquí **se habla** español.
*Spanish **is spoken** here.*

Sirven lasaña.
They serve lasagna.

INDIRECT OBJECT A noun or pronoun that receives the action of the verb indirectly; the object, often a living being, to or for whom an action is performed.

Eduardo **le** dio un libro **a Linda**.
*Eduardo gave a book **to Linda**.*

La profesora **me** dio una C en el examen.
*The professor gave **me** a C on the test.*

INFINITIVE The basic form of a verb. Infinitives in Spanish end in **-ar**, **-er**, or **-ir**.

hablar
to speak

correr
to run

abrir
to open

INTERROGATIVE An adjective or pronoun used to ask a question.

¿**Quién** habla?
Who is speaking?

¿**Cuántos** compraste?
How many did you buy?

¿**Qué** piensas hacer hoy?
What do you plan to do today?

INVERSION Changing the word order of a sentence, often to form a question.

Statement: Tu mamá vive en Boston.

Inversion: ¿(A)dónde vive tu mamá?

MOOD A grammatical distinction of verbs that indicates whether the verb is intended to make a statement or command, or to express a doubt, emotion, or condition contrary to fact.

imperative mood Verb forms used to make commands.

Diga la verdad.
Tell the truth.

Caminen Uds. conmigo.
Walk with me.

¡**Comamos ahora!**
Let's eat now!

Indicative mood Verb forms used to state facts, actions, and states considered to be real.

Sé que **tienes** el dinero.
I know that you have the money.

Subjunctive mood Verb forms used principally in subordinate (or dependent) clauses to express wishes, desires, emotions, doubts, and certain conditions, such as contrary-to-fact situations.

Prefieren que **hables** en español.
*They prefer that **you speak** in Spanish.*

Dudo que Luis **tenga** el dinero necesario.
*I doubt that Luis **has** the necessary money.*

NOUN A word that identifies people, animals, places, things, and ideas.

hombre
man

gato
cat

México
Mexico

casa
house

libertad
freedom

NUMBER A grammatical term that refers to singular or plural. Nouns in Spanish and English have number. Other parts of a sentence, such as adjectives, articles, and verbs, can also have number.

Singular	Plural
una cosa	**unas** cosas
a thing	*some things*
el profesor	**los** profesor**es**
the professor	*the professors*

NUMBERS Words that represent amounts.

Cardinal numbers Words that show specific amounts.

cinco minutos
five minutes

el año **dos mil dos**
the year 2002

Ordinal numbers Words that indicate the order of a noun in a series.

el **cuarto** jugador   la **décima** hora
the fourth player   *the tenth hour*

PAST PARTICIPLE A past form of the verb used in compound tenses. The past participle may also be used as an adjective, but it must then agree in number and gender with the word it modifies.

Han **buscado** por todas partes.
They have searched everywhere.

Yo no había **estudiado** para el examen.
I hadn't studied for the exam.

Hay una **ventana rota** en la sala.
There is a broken window in the living room.

PERSON The form of the verb or pronoun that indicates the speaker, the one spoken to, or the one spoken about. In Spanish, as in English, there are three persons: first, second, and third.

Person	Singular		Plural	
1st	**yo**	*I*	**nosotros/as**	*we*
2nd	**tú, Ud.**	*you*	**vosotros/as, Uds.**	*you*
3rd	**él, ella**	*he/she*	**ellos, ellas**	*they*

PREPOSITION A word that describes the relationship, most often in time or space, between two words.

Anita es **de** California.
Anita is from California.

La chaqueta está **en** el carro.
The jacket is in the car.

¿Quieres hablar **con** ella?
Do you want to speak to her?

PRESENT PARTICIPLE In English, a verb form that ends in *-ing*. In Spanish, the present participle ends in **–ndo**, and is often used with **estar** to form a progressive tense.

Mi hermana está **hablando** por teléfono ahora mismo.
My sister is talking on the phone right now.

PRONOUN A word that takes the place of a noun or nouns.

Demonstrative pronoun A pronoun that takes the place of a specific noun.

Quiero **ésta**.
I want this one.

¿Vas a comprar **ése**?
Are you going to buy that one?

Juan prefirió **aquéllos**.
Juan preferred those (over there).

Object pronoun A pronoun that functions as a direct or indirect object of the verb. Object pronouns may be placed before conjugated verbs or attached to an infinitive or present participle.

Te digo la verdad.
I'm telling you the truth.

Me lo trajo Juan.
Juan brought it to me.

Lo voy a llevar a la escuela.
Voy a **llevarlo** a la escuela.
I'm going to bring him to school.

Me estaba llamando por teléfono.
Estaba **llamándome** por teléfono.
She was calling me on the phone.

Reflexive pronoun A pronoun that indicates that the action of a verb is performed by the subject on itself. These pronouns are often expressed in English with *-self: myself, yourself,* etc.

Yo **me bañé** antes de salir.
I bathed (myself) before going out.

Elena **se acostó** a las once y media.
Elena went to bed at eleven-thirty.

Relative pronoun A pronoun that connects a subordinate clause to a main clause.

El chico **que** nos escribió viene a visitarnos mañana.
The boy who wrote to us is coming to visit us tomorrow.

Ya sé **lo que** tenemos que hacer.
I already know what we have to do.

Subject pronoun A pronoun that replaces the name or title of a person or thing and acts as the subject of a verb.

Tú debes estudiar más.
You should study more.

Él llegó primero.
He arrived first.

SUBJECT A noun or pronoun that performs the action of a verb and is often implied by the verb.

María va al supermercado.
María goes to the supermarket.

(Ellos) Trabajan mucho.
They work hard.

Esos **libros** son muy caros.
Those books are very expensive.

SUPERLATIVE A word or construction used with an adjective or adverb to express the highest or lowest degree of a specific quality among three or more people, places, or things.

Entre todas mis clases, ésta es la **más interesante**.
Among all my classes, this is the most interesting.

Raúl es el **menos simpático** de los chicos.
Raúl is the least pleasant of the boys.

TENSE A set of verb forms that indicates the time of an action or state: past, present, or future.

Compound tense A two-word tense made up of an auxiliary verb and a present or past participle. In Spanish, there are two auxiliary verbs: **estar** and **haber**.

En este momento, **estoy estudiando**.
At this time, I am studying.

El paquete no **ha llegado** todavía.
The package has not arrived yet.

Simple tense A tense expressed by a single verb form.

María **estaba** mal anoche.
María was ill last night.

Juana **hablará** con su mamá mañana.
Juana will speak with her mom tomorrow.

VERB A word that expresses actions or states-of-being.

Auxiliary verb A verb used with a present or past participle to form a compound tense. **Haber** is the most commonly used auxiliary verb in Spanish.

Los chicos **han** visto los elefantes.
The children have seen the elephants.

Espero que **hayas** comido.
I hope you have eaten.

Reflexive verb A verb that describes an action performed by the subject on itself and is always used with a reflexive pronoun.

Me compré un carro nuevo.
I bought myself *a new car.*

Pedro y Adela **se levantan** muy temprano.
Pedro and Adela get (themselves) up very early.

Spelling change verb A verb that undergoes a predictable change in spelling in order to reflect its actual pronunciation in the various conjugations.

practicar	c ➤ qu	practico	practi**qué**
dirigir	g ➤ j	diri**j**o	dirig**í**
almorzar	z ➤ c	almor**z**ó	almor**cé**

Stem-changing verb A verb whose stem vowel undergoes one or more predictable changes in the various conjugations.

entender (i ➤ ie)	ent**ie**ndo
pedir (e ➤ i)	p**i**den
dormir (o ➤ ue, u)	d**ue**rmo, d**u**rmieron

Verb conjugation tables

The verb lists

The list of verbs below and the model-verb tables that start on page 406 show you how to conjugate every verb taught in **INVITACIONES**. Each verb in the list is followed by a model verb conjugated according to the same pattern. The number in parentheses indicates where in the tables you can find the conjugated forms of the model verb. If you want to find out how to conjugate **divertirse**, for example, look up number 29, **sentir**, the model for verbs that follow the **i** ➤ **ie** stem-change pattern.

How to use the verb tables

In the tables you will find the infinitive, past and present participles, and all the simple forms of each model verb. The formation of the compound tenses of any verb can be inferred from the table of compound tenses, pages 406–407, either by combining the past participle of the verb with a conjugated form of **haber** or combining the present participle with a conjugated form of **estar**.

abrir like vivir (3) *except* past participle is abierto
acabar de like hablar (1)
aceptar like hablar (1)
aconsejar like hablar (1)
acostarse (o ➤ ue) like contar (21)
afeitarse like hablar (1)
ahorrar like hablar (1)
almorzar (o ➤ ue) like contar (21) *except* (z ➤ c)
alquilar like hablar (1)
andar like hablar (1) *except* preterit stem is anduv-
aprender like comer (2)
armar like hablar (1)
ayudar(se) like hablar (1)

bailar like hablar (1)
bañarse like hablar (1)
barrer like comer (2)
beber like comer (2)
besar(se) like hablar (1)
bucear like hablar (1)
buscar (c ➤ qu) like tocar (35)

cambiar like hablar (1)
cantar like hablar (1)
casarse like hablar (1)
castigar like hablar (1)
cenar like hablar (1)

chocar (c ➤ qu) like tocar (35)
colorear like hablar (1)
comer (2)
compartir like vivir (3)
comprar like hablar (1)
conocer (c ➤ zc) (30)
contar (o ➤ ue) (21)
correr like comer (2)
cortar like hablar (1)
costar (o ➤ ue) like contar (21)
creer (y) (31)
cruzar (z ➤ c) (32)
cuidar(se) like hablar (1)

dar(se) (4)
deber like comer (2)
decidir like vivir (3)
decir (e ➤ i) (5)
dejar like hablar (1)
desayunar like hablar (1)
descansar like hablar (1)
descomponerse like poner(se) (12)
dibujar like hablar (1)
discutir like vivir (3)
disfrazar(se) like hablar (1)
divertirse (e ➤ ie) like sentir (29)
divorciarse like hablar (1)
dormir(se) (o ➤ ue) (22)
ducharse like hablar (1)
dudar like hablar (1)

embarazar(se) like hablar (1)
empezar (e ➤ ie) (z ➤ c) (23)
empujar like hablar (1)
enamorarse like hablar (1)
encantar like hablar (1)
encontrar(se) (o ➤ ue) like contar (21)
enfermarse like hablar (1)
enseñar like hablar (1)
entender (e ➤ ie) (24)
entrar like hablar (1)
entregar like hablar (1) *except* (g ➤ gu)
entrenarse like hablar (1)
escribir like vivir (3) *except* past participle is escrito
escuchar like hablar (1)
esperar like hablar (1)
esquiar (esquío) (33)
estacionar(se) like hablar (1)
estar (6)
estudiar like hablar (1)
explicar (c ➤ qu) like tocar (35)

fascinar like hablar (1)
frenar like hablar (1)
fumar like hablar (1)

ganar like hablar (1)
gastar like hablar (1)
gustar like hablar (1)

haber (hay) (7)
hablar (1)
hacer (8)

iluminar like hablar (1)
importar like hablar (1)
interesar like hablar (1)
invitar like hablar (1)
ir(se) (9)

jugar (u→ue) (g→gu) (25)
juntar(se) like hablar (1)

lastimarse like hablar (1)
lavar(se) like hablar (1)
leer (y) like creer (31)
levantar(se) like hablar (1)
limpiar like hablar (1)
llamar(se) like hablar (1)
llegar (g→gu) (34)
llenar like hablar (1)
llevar(se) like hablar (1)
mandar like hablar (1)
manejar like hablar (1)
mirar like hablar (1)
molestar like hablar (1)
montar like hablar (1)
morir (o→ue) like dormir (22)
  except past participle is muerto
mudarse like hablar (1)

necesitar like hablar (1)
nevar (e→ie) like pensar (27)

obedecer (c→zc) like conocer (30)
ofrecer (c→zc) like conocer (30)
oír (10)

pagar (g→gu) like llegar (34)
parar(se) like hablar (1)
pasar(se) like hablar (1)
pasear like hablar (1)
patinar like hablar (1)
pedir (e→i) (26)
pegar like hablar (1) *except* (g→gu)
pelearse like hablar (1)
pensar (e→ie) (27)
perder (e→ie) like entender (24)
pintar(se) like hablar (1)
planchar like hablar (1)
poder (o→ue) (11)
poner(se) (12)

ponchar(se) like hablar (1)
portar(se) like hablar (1)
practicar (c→qu) like tocar (35)
preferir (e→ie) like sentir (29)
prestar like hablar (1)
prometer like comer (2)

quedar(se) like hablar (1)
querer (e→ie) (13)
quitar(se) like hablar (1)

rasurar(se) like hablar (1)
recibir(se) like vivir (3)
recomendar (e→ie) like pensar (27)
recordar (o→ue) like contar (21)
regalar like hablar (1)
regañar like hablar (1)
romper(se) like comer (2) *except* past
  participle is roto

saber (14)
sacar (c→qu) like tocar (35)
salir(se) (15)
saltar like hablar (1)
seguir (e→i) (28)
sentir(se) (e→ie) (29)
separarse like hablar (1)
ser (16)
servir (e→i) like pedir (26)
solicitar like hablar (1)
subir(se) like vivir (3)

tener (e→ie) (17)
terminar like hablar (1)
tocar (c→qu) (35)
tomar like hablar (1)
trabajar like hablar (1)
traer (18)

usar like hablar (1)

vender like comer (2)
venir (e→ie) (19)
ver (20)
vestir(se) (e→i) (36)
viajar like hablar (1)
visitar like hablar (1)
vivir (3)

406

Regular verbs: simple tenses

Infinitive	INDICATIVE					SUBJUNCTIVE		IMPERATIVE
	Present	Imperfect	Preterit	Future	Conditional	Present	Past	
1 hablar	hablo	hablaba	hablé	hablaré	hablaría	hable	hablara	
	hablas	hablabas	hablaste	hablarás	hablarías	hables	hablaras	habla tú (no hables)
	habla	hablaba	habló	hablará	hablaría	hable	hablara	hable Ud.
Participles:	hablamos	hablábamos	hablamos	hablaremos	hablaríamos	hablemos	habláramos	hablemos
hablando	habláis	hablabais	hablasteis	hablaréis	hablaríais	habléis	hablarais	hablad (no habléis)
hablado	hablan	hablaban	hablaron	hablarán	hablarían	hablen	hablaran	hablen Uds.
2 comer	como	comía	comí	comeré	comería	coma	comiera	
	comes	comías	comiste	comerás	comerías	comas	comieras	come tú (no comas)
	come	comía	comió	comerá	comería	coma	comiera	coma Ud.
Participles:	comemos	comíamos	comimos	comeremos	comeríamos	comamos	comiéramos	comamos
comiendo	coméis	comíais	comisteis	comeréis	comeríais	comáis	comierais	comed (no comáis)
comido	comen	comían	comieron	comerán	comerían	coman	comieran	coman Uds.
3 vivir	vivo	vivía	viví	viviré	viviría	viva	viviera	
	vives	vivías	viviste	vivirás	vivirías	vivas	vivieras	vive tú (no vivas)
	vive	vivía	vivió	vivirá	viviría	viva	viviera	viva Ud.
Participles:	vivimos	vivíamos	vivimos	viviremos	viviríamos	vivamos	viviéramos	vivamos
viviendo	vivís	vivíais	vivisteis	viviréis	viviríais	viváis	vivierais	vivid (no viváis)
vivido	viven	vivían	vivieron	vivirán	vivirían	vivan	vivieran	vivan Uds.

All verbs: compound tenses

PERFECT TENSES

INDICATIVE

Present Perfect			Past Perfect			Future Perfect			Conditional Perfect		
he	hablado		había	hablado		habré	hablado		habría	hablado	
has	comido		habías	comido		habrás	comido		habrías	comido	
ha	vivido		había	vivido		habrá	vivido		habría	vivido	
hemos			habíamos			habremos			habríamos		
habéis			habíais			habréis			habríais		
han			habían			habrán			habrían		

SUBJUNCTIVE

Present Perfect			Past Perfect		
haya	hablado		hubiera	hablado	
hayas	comido		hubieras	comido	
haya	vivido		hubiera	vivido	
hayamos			hubiéramos		
hayáis			hubierais		
hayan			hubieran		

PROGRESSIVE TENSES

	INDICATIVE					SUBJUNCTIVE	
Present Progressive	**Past Progressive**		**Future Progressive**		**Conditional Progressive**	**Present Progressive**	**Past Progressive**
estoy	estaba		estaré		estaría	esté	estuviera
estás hablando	estabas	hablando	estarás	hablando	estarías	estés hablando	estuvieras
está comiendo	estaba	comiendo	estará	comiendo	estaría	esté comiendo	estuviera
estamos viviendo	estábamos	viviendo	estaremos	viviendo	estaríamos	estemos viviendo	estuviéramos
estáis	estabais		estaréis		estaríais	estéis	estuvierais
estan	estaban		estarán		estarían	estén	estuvieran

Irregular verbs

	INDICATIVE					SUBJUNCTIVE		IMPERATIVE
Infinitive	**Present**	**Imperfect**	**Preterit**	**Future**	**Conditional**	**Present**	**Past**	
4 dar	**doy**	daba	**di**	daré	daría	**dé**	**diera**	
	das	dabas	**diste**	darás	darías	**des**	**dieras**	da tú (no **des**)
Participles:	da	daba	**dio**	dará	daría	**dé**	**diera**	**dé** Ud.
dando	**damos**	dábamos	**dimos**	daremos	daríamos	**demos**	**diéramos**	**demos**
dado	dais	dabais	**disteis**	daréis	daríais	**deis**	**dierais**	dad (no **deis**)
	dan	daban	**dieron**	darán	darían	**den**	**dieran**	**den** Uds.
5 decir (e → i)	**digo**	decía	**dije**	**diré**	**diría**	**diga**	**dijera**	
	dices	decías	**dijiste**	**dirás**	**dirías**	**digas**	**dijeras**	**di** tú (no **digas**)
Participles:	**dice**	decía	**dijo**	**dirá**	**diría**	**diga**	**dijera**	**diga** Ud.
diciendo	decimos	decíamos	**dijimos**	**diremos**	**diríamos**	**digamos**	**dijéramos**	**digamos**
dicho	decís	decíais	**dijisteis**	**diréis**	**diríais**	**digáis**	**dijerais**	decid (no **digáis**)
	dicen	decían	**dijeron**	**dirán**	**dirían**	**digan**	**dijeran**	**digan** Uds.
6 estar	**estoy**	estaba	**estuve**	estaré	estaría	esté	**estuviera**	
	estás	estabas	**estuviste**	estarás	estarías	estés	**estuvieras**	está tú (no estés)
Participles:	está	estaba	**estuvo**	estará	estaría	esté	**estuviera**	esté Ud.
estando	estamos	estábamos	**estuvimos**	estaremos	estaríamos	estemos	**estuviéramos**	estemos
estado	estáis	estabais	**estuvisteis**	estaréis	estaríais	estéis	**estuvierais**	estad (no estéis)
	están	estaban	**estuvieron**	estarán	estarían	estén	**estuvieran**	estén Uds.

7. haber
Participles: habiendo, habido

	INDICATIVE					SUBJUNCTIVE		IMPERATIVE
	Present	Imperfect	Preterit	Future	Conditional	Present	Past	
	he	había	hube	habré	habría	haya	hubiera	
	has	habías	hubiste	habrás	habrías	hayas	hubieras	
	ha	había	hubo	habrá	habría	haya	hubiera	
	hemos	habíamos	hubimos	habremos	habríamos	hayamos	hubiéramos	
	habéis	habíais	hubisteis	habréis	habríais	hayáis	hubierais	
	han	habían	hubieron	habrán	habrían	hayan	hubieran	

8. hacer
Participles: haciendo, hecho

	INDICATIVE					SUBJUNCTIVE		IMPERATIVE
	Present	Imperfect	Preterit	Future	Conditional	Present	Past	
	hago	hacía	hice	haré	haría	haga	hiciera	
	haces	hacías	hiciste	harás	harías	hagas	hicieras	haz tú (no hagas)
	hace	hacía	hizo	hará	haría	haga	hiciera	haga Ud.
	hacemos	hacíamos	hicimos	haremos	haríamos	hagamos	hiciéramos	hagamos
	hacéis	hacíais	hicisteis	haréis	haríais	hagáis	hicierais	haced (no hagáis)
	hacen	hacían	hicieron	harán	harían	hagan	hicieran	hagan Uds.

9. ir
Participles: yendo, ido

	INDICATIVE					SUBJUNCTIVE		IMPERATIVE
	Present	Imperfect	Preterit	Future	Conditional	Present	Past	
	voy	iba	fui	iré	iría	vaya	fuera	
	vas	ibas	fuiste	irás	irías	vayas	fueras	ve tú (no vayas)
	va	iba	fue	irá	iría	vaya	fuera	vaya Ud.
	vamos	íbamos	fuimos	iremos	iríamos	vayamos	fuéramos	vamos
	vais	ibais	fuisteis	iréis	iríais	vayáis	fuerais	id (no vayáis)
	van	iban	fueron	irán	irían	vayan	fueran	vayan Uds.

10. oír (y)
Participles: oyendo, oído

	INDICATIVE					SUBJUNCTIVE		IMPERATIVE
	Present	Imperfect	Preterit	Future	Conditional	Present	Past	
	oigo	oía	oí	oiré	oiría	oiga	oyera	
	oyes	oías	oíste	oirás	oirías	oigas	oyeras	oye tú (no oigas)
	oye	oía	oyó	oirá	oiría	oiga	oyera	oiga Ud.
	oímos	oíamos	oímos	oiremos	oiríamos	oigamos	oyéramos	oigamos
	oís	oíais	oísteis	oiréis	oiríais	oigáis	oyerais	oíd (no oigáis)
	oyen	oían	oyeron	oirán	oirían	oigan	oyeran	oigan Uds.

11. poder (o→ue)
Participles: pudiendo, podido

	INDICATIVE					SUBJUNCTIVE		IMPERATIVE
	Present	Imperfect	Preterit	Future	Conditional	Present	Past	
	puedo	podía	pude	podré	podría	pueda	pudiera	
	puedes	podías	pudiste	podrás	podrías	puedas	pudieras	puede tú (no puedas)
	puede	podía	pudo	podrá	podría	pueda	pudiera	pueda Ud.
	podemos	podíamos	pudimos	podremos	podríamos	podamos	pudiéramos	podamos
	podéis	podíais	pudisteis	podréis	podríais	podáis	pudierais	poded (no podáis)
	pueden	podían	pudieron	podrán	podrían	puedan	pudieran	puedan Uds.

12. poner
Participles: poniendo, puesto

	INDICATIVE					SUBJUNCTIVE		IMPERATIVE
	Present	Imperfect	Preterit	Future	Conditional	Present	Past	
	pongo	ponía	puse	pondré	pondría	ponga	pusiera	
	pones	ponías	pusiste	pondrás	pondrías	pongas	pusieras	pon tú (no pongas)
	pone	ponía	puso	pondrá	pondría	ponga	pusiera	ponga Ud.
	ponemos	poníamos	pusimos	pondremos	pondríamos	pongamos	pusiéramos	pongamos
	ponéis	poníais	pusisteis	pondréis	pondríais	pongáis	pusierais	poned (no pongáis)
	ponen	ponían	pusieron	pondrán	pondrían	pongan	pusieran	pongan Uds.

13. querer (e→ie) — Participles: queriendo, querido

	INDICATIVE					SUBJUNCTIVE		IMPERATIVE
	Present	Imperfect	Preterit	Future	Conditional	Present	Past	
	quiero	quería	quise	querré	querría	quiera	quisiera	
	quieres	querías	quisiste	querrás	querrías	quieras	quisieras	quiere tú (no quieras)
	quiere	quería	quiso	querrá	querría	quiera	quisiera	quiera Ud.
	queremos	queríamos	quisimos	querremos	querríamos	queramos	quisiéramos	queramos
	queréis	queríais	quisisteis	querréis	querríais	queráis	quisierais	quered (no queráis)
	quieren	querían	quisieron	querrán	querrían	quieran	quisieran	quieran Uds.

14. saber — Participles: sabiendo, sabido

	INDICATIVE					SUBJUNCTIVE		IMPERATIVE
	Present	Imperfect	Preterit	Future	Conditional	Present	Past	
	sé	sabía	supe	sabré	sabría	sepa	supiera	
	sabes	sabías	supiste	sabrás	sabrías	sepas	supieras	sabe tú (no sepas)
	sabe	sabía	supo	sabrá	sabría	sepa	supiera	sepa Ud.
	sabemos	sabíamos	supimos	sabremos	sabríamos	sepamos	supiéramos	sepamos
	sabéis	sabíais	supisteis	sabréis	sabríais	sepáis	supierais	sabed (no sepáis)
	saben	sabían	supieron	sabrán	sabrían	sepan	supieran	sepan Uds.

15. salir — Participles: saliendo, salido

	INDICATIVE					SUBJUNCTIVE		IMPERATIVE
	Present	Imperfect	Preterit	Future	Conditional	Present	Past	
	salgo	salía	salí	saldré	saldría	salga	saliera	
	sales	salías	saliste	saldrás	saldrías	salgas	salieras	sal tú (no salgas)
	sale	salía	salió	saldrá	saldría	salga	saliera	salga Ud.
	salimos	salíamos	salimos	saldremos	saldríamos	salgamos	saliéramos	salgamos
	salís	salíais	salisteis	saldréis	saldríais	salgáis	salierais	salid (no salgáis)
	salen	salían	salieron	saldrán	saldrían	salgan	salieran	salgan Uds.

16. ser — Participles: siendo, sido

	INDICATIVE					SUBJUNCTIVE		IMPERATIVE
	Present	Imperfect	Preterit	Future	Conditional	Present	Past	
	soy	era	fui	seré	sería	sea	fuera	
	eres	eras	fuiste	serás	serías	seas	fueras	sé tú (no seas)
	es	era	fue	será	sería	sea	fuera	sea Ud.
	somos	éramos	fuimos	seremos	seríamos	seamos	fuéramos	seamos
	sois	erais	fuisteis	seréis	seríais	seáis	fuerais	sed (no seáis)
	son	eran	fueron	serán	serían	sean	fueran	sean Uds.

17. tener (e→ie) — Participles: teniendo, tenido

	INDICATIVE					SUBJUNCTIVE		IMPERATIVE
	Present	Imperfect	Preterit	Future	Conditional	Present	Past	
	tengo	tenía	tuve	tendré	tendría	tenga	tuviera	
	tienes	tenías	tuviste	tendrás	tendrías	tengas	tuvieras	ten tú (no tengas)
	tiene	tenía	tuvo	tendrá	tendría	tenga	tuviera	tenga Ud.
	tenemos	teníamos	tuvimos	tendremos	tendríamos	tengamos	tuviéramos	tengamos
	tenéis	teníais	tuvisteis	tendréis	tendríais	tengáis	tuvierais	tened (no tengáis)
	tienen	tenían	tuvieron	tendrán	tendrían	tengan	tuvieran	tengan Uds.

18. traer — Participles: trayendo, traído

	INDICATIVE					SUBJUNCTIVE		IMPERATIVE
	Present	Imperfect	Preterit	Future	Conditional	Present	Past	
	traigo	traía	traje	traeré	traería	traiga	trajera	
	traes	traías	trajiste	traerás	traerías	traigas	trajeras	trae tú (no traigas)
	trae	traía	trajo	traerá	traería	traiga	trajera	traiga Ud.
	traemos	traíamos	trajimos	traeremos	traeríamos	traigamos	trajéramos	traigamos
	traéis	traíais	trajisteis	traeréis	traeríais	traigáis	trajerais	traed (no traigáis)
	traen	traían	trajeron	traerán	traerían	traigan	trajeran	traigan Uds.

Infinitive	INDICATIVE					SUBJUNCTIVE		IMPERATIVE
	Present	Imperfect	Preterit	Future	Conditional	Present	Past	
19 venir (e→ie)	**vengo**	venía	**vine**	**vendré**	**vendría**	**venga**	**viniera**	
	vienes	venías	**viniste**	**vendrás**	**vendrías**	**vengas**	**vinieras**	**ven** tú (no **vengas**)
	viene	venía	**vino**	**vendrá**	**vendría**	**venga**	**viniera**	**venga** Ud.
Participles:	venimos	veníamos	**vinimos**	**vendremos**	**vendríamos**	**vengamos**	**viniéramos**	**vengamos**
viniendo	venís	veníais	**vinisteis**	**vendréis**	**vendríais**	**vengáis**	**vinierais**	venid (no **vengáis**)
venido	**vienen**	venían	**vinieron**	**vendrán**	**vendrían**	**vengan**	**vinieran**	**vengan** Uds.
20 ver	**veo**	veía	**vi**	veré	vería	**vea**	**viera**	
	ves	veías	**viste**	verás	verías	**veas**	**vieras**	ve tú (no **veas**)
	ve	veía	**vio**	verá	vería	**vea**	**viera**	**vea** Ud.
Participles:	vemos	veíamos	**vimos**	veremos	veríamos	**veamos**	**viéramos**	veamos
viendo	veis	veíais	**visteis**	veréis	veríais	**veáis**	**vierais**	ved (no **veáis**)
visto	ven	veían	**vieron**	verán	verían	**vean**	**vieran**	**vean** Uds.

Stem—changing verbs

Infinitive	INDICATIVE					SUBJUNCTIVE		IMPERATIVE
	Present	Imperfect	Preterit	Future	Conditional	Present	Past	
21 contar (o→ue)	**cuento**	contaba	conté	contaré	contaría	**cuente**	contara	
	cuentas	contabas	contaste	contarás	contarías	**cuentes**	contaras	**cuenta** tú (no **cuentes**)
	cuenta	contaba	contó	contará	contaría	**cuente**	contara	**cuente** Ud.
Participles:	contamos	contábamos	contamos	contaremos	contaríamos	contemos	contáramos	contemos
contando	contáis	contabais	contasteis	contaréis	contaríais	contéis	contarais	contad (no contéis)
contado	**cuentan**	contaban	contaron	contarán	contarían	**cuenten**	contaran	**cuenten** Uds.
22 dormir (o→ue)	**duermo**	dormía	dormí	dormiré	dormiría	**duerma**	**durmiera**	
	duermes	dormías	dormiste	dormirás	dormirías	**duermas**	**durmieras**	**duerme** tú (no **duermas**)
	duerme	dormía	**durmió**	dormirá	dormiría	**duerma**	**durmiera**	**duerma** Ud.
Participles:	dormimos	dormíamos	dormimos	dormiremos	dormiríamos	**durmamos**	**durmiéramos**	**durmamos**
durmiendo	dormís	dormíais	dormisteis	dormiréis	dormiríais	**durmáis**	**durmierais**	dormid (no **durmáis**)
dormido	**duermen**	dormían	**durmieron**	dormirán	dormirían	**duerman**	**durmieran**	**duerman** Uds.
23 empezar (e→ie) (c)	**empiezo**	empezaba	**empecé**	empezaré	empezaría	**empiece**	empezara	
	empiezas	empezabas	empezaste	empezarás	empezarías	**empieces**	empezaras	**empieza** tú (no **empieces**)
	empieza	empezaba	empezó	empezará	empezaría	**empiece**	empezara	**empiece** Ud.
Participles:	empezamos	empezábamos	empezamos	empezaremos	empezaríamos	**empecemos**	empezáramos	**empecemos**
empezando	empezáis	empezabais	empezasteis	empezaréis	empezaríais	**empecéis**	empezarais	empezad (no **empecéis**)
empezado	**empiezan**	empezaban	empezaron	empezarán	empezarían	**empiecen**	empezaran	**empiecen** Uds.

24 entender (e→ie)
Participles: entendiendo, entendido

	INDICATIVE					SUBJUNCTIVE		IMPERATIVE
	Present	Imperfect	Preterit	Future	Conditional	Present	Past	
	entiendo	entendía	entendí	entenderé	entendería	entienda	entendiera	
	entiendes	entendías	entendiste	entenderás	entenderías	entiendas	entendieras	entiende tú (no entiendas)
	entiende	entendía	entendió	entenderá	entendería	entienda	entendiera	entienda Ud.
	entendemos	entendíamos	entendimos	entenderemos	entenderíamos	entendamos	entendiéramos	entendamos
	entendéis	entendíais	entendisteis	entenderéis	entenderíais	entendáis	entendierais	entended (no entendáis)
	entienden	entendían	entendieron	entenderán	entenderían	entiendan	entendieran	entiendan Uds.

25 jugar (u→ue) (gu)
Participles: jugando, jugado

	INDICATIVE					SUBJUNCTIVE		IMPERATIVE
	Present	Imperfect	Preterit	Future	Conditional	Present	Past	
	juego	jugaba	jugué	jugaré	jugaría	juegue	jugara	
	juegas	jugabas	jugaste	jugarás	jugarías	juegues	jugaras	juega tú (no juegues)
	juega	jugaba	jugó	jugará	jugaría	juegue	jugara	juegue Ud.
	jugamos	jugábamos	jugamos	jugaremos	jugaríamos	juguemos	jugáramos	juguemos
	jugáis	jugabais	jugasteis	jugaréis	jugaríais	juguéis	jugarais	jugad (no juguéis)
	juegan	jugaban	jugaron	jugarán	jugarían	jueguen	jugaran	jueguen Uds.

26 pedir (e→i)
Participles: pidiendo, pedido

	INDICATIVE					SUBJUNCTIVE		IMPERATIVE
	Present	Imperfect	Preterit	Future	Conditional	Present	Past	
	pido	pedía	pedí	pediré	pediría	pida	pidiera	
	pides	pedías	pediste	pedirás	pedirías	pidas	pidieras	pide tú (no pidas)
	pide	pedía	pidió	pedirá	pediría	pida	pidiera	pida Ud.
	pedimos	pedíamos	pedimos	pediremos	pediríamos	pidamos	pidiéramos	pidamos
	pedís	pedíais	pedisteis	pediréis	pediríais	pidáis	pidierais	pedid (no pidáis)
	piden	pedían	pidieron	pedirán	pedirían	pidan	pidieran	pidan Uds.

27 pensar (e→ie)
Participles: pensando, pensado

	INDICATIVE					SUBJUNCTIVE		IMPERATIVE
	Present	Imperfect	Preterit	Future	Conditional	Present	Past	
	pienso	pensaba	pensé	pensaré	pensaría	piense	pensara	
	piensas	pensabas	pensaste	pensarás	pensarías	pienses	pensaras	piensa tú (no pienses)
	piensa	pensaba	pensó	pensará	pensaría	piense	pensara	piense Ud.
	pensamos	pensábamos	pensamos	pensaremos	pensaríamos	pensemos	pensáramos	pensemos
	pensáis	pensabais	pensasteis	pensaréis	pensaríais	penséis	pensarais	pensad (no penséis)
	piensan	pensaban	pensaron	pensarán	pensarían	piensen	pensaran	piensen Uds.

28 seguir (e→i) (gu)
Participles: siguiendo, seguido

	INDICATIVE					SUBJUNCTIVE		IMPERATIVE
	Present	Imperfect	Preterit	Future	Conditional	Present	Past	
	sigo	seguía	seguí	seguiré	seguiría	siga	siguiera	
	sigues	seguías	seguiste	seguirás	seguirías	sigas	siguieras	sigue tú (no sigas)
	sigue	seguía	siguió	seguirá	seguiría	siga	siguiera	siga Ud.
	seguimos	seguíamos	seguimos	seguiremos	seguiríamos	sigamos	siguiéramos	sigamos
	seguís	seguíais	seguisteis	seguiréis	seguiríais	sigáis	siguierais	seguid (no sigáis)
	siguen	seguían	siguieron	seguirán	seguirían	sigan	siguieran	sigan Uds.

29 sentir (e→ie)
Participles: sintiendo, sentido

	INDICATIVE					SUBJUNCTIVE		IMPERATIVE
	Present	Imperfect	Preterit	Future	Conditional	Present	Past	
	siento	sentía	sentí	sentiré	sentiría	sienta	sintiera	
	sientes	sentías	sentiste	sentirás	sentirías	sientas	sintieras	siente tú (no sientas)
	siente	sentía	sintió	sentirá	sentiría	sienta	sintiera	sienta Ud.
	sentimos	sentíamos	sentimos	sentiremos	sentiríamos	sintamos	sintiéramos	sintamos
	sentís	sentíais	sentisteis	sentiréis	sentiríais	sintáis	sintierais	sentid (no sintáis)
	sienten	sentían	sintieron	sentirán	sentirían	sientan	sintieran	sientan Uds.

Reflexive verbs and verbs with spelling changes

30 — conocer (c → zc) · Participles: conociendo, conocido

Infinitive	INDICATIVE					SUBJUNCTIVE		IMPERATIVE
	Present	Imperfect	Preterit	Future	Conditional	Present	Past	
conocer (c → zc)	**conozco**	conocía	conocí	conoceré	conocería	**conozca**	conociera	
	conoces	conocías	conociste	conocerás	conocerías	**conozcas**	conocieras	conoce tú (no **conozcas**)
	conoce	conocía	conoció	conocerá	conocería	**conozca**	conociera	**conozca** Ud.
Participles:	conocemos	conocíamos	conocimos	conoceremos	conoceríamos	**conozcamos**	conociéramos	**conozcamos**
conociendo	conocéis	conocíais	conocisteis	conoceréis	conoceríais	**conozcáis**	conocierais	conoced (no **conozcáis**)
conocido	conocen	conocían	conocieron	conocerán	conocerían	**conozcan**	conocieran	**conozcan** Uds.

31 — creer (y) · Participles: creyendo, creído

Infinitive	INDICATIVE					SUBJUNCTIVE		IMPERATIVE
	Present	Imperfect	Preterit	Future	Conditional	Present	Past	
creer (y)	creo	creía	creí	creeré	creería	crea	**creyera**	
	crees	creías	**creíste**	creerás	creerías	creas	**creyeras**	cree tú (no creas)
	cree	creía	**creyó**	creerá	creería	crea	**creyera**	crea Ud.
Participles:	creemos	creíamos	**creímos**	creeremos	creeríamos	creamos	**creyéramos**	creamos
creyendo	creéis	creíais	**creísteis**	creeréis	creeríais	creáis	**creyerais**	creed (no creáis)
creído	creen	creían	**creyeron**	creerán	creerían	crean	**creyeran**	crean Uds.

32 — cruzar (c) · Participles: cruzando, cruzado

Infinitive	INDICATIVE					SUBJUNCTIVE		IMPERATIVE
	Present	Imperfect	Preterit	Future	Conditional	Present	Past	
cruzar (c)	cruzo	cruzaba	**crucé**	cruzaré	cruzaría	**cruce**	cruzara	
	cruzas	cruzabas	cruzaste	cruzarás	cruzarías	**cruces**	cruzaras	cruza tú (no **cruces**)
	cruza	cruzaba	cruzó	cruzará	cruzaría	**cruce**	cruzara	**cruce** Ud.
Participles:	cruzamos	cruzábamos	cruzamos	cruzaremos	cruzaríamos	**crucemos**	cruzáramos	**crucemos**
cruzando	cruzáis	cruzabais	cruzasteis	cruzaréis	cruzaríais	**crucéis**	cruzarais	cruzad (no **crucéis**)
cruzado	cruzan	cruzaban	cruzaron	cruzarán	cruzarían	**crucen**	cruzaran	**crucen** Uds.

33 — esquiar (esquío) · Participles: esquiando, esquiado

Infinitive	INDICATIVE					SUBJUNCTIVE		IMPERATIVE
	Present	Imperfect	Preterit	Future	Conditional	Present	Past	
esquiar (esquío)	**esquío**	esquiaba	esquié	esquiaré	esquiaría	esquíe	esquiara	
	esquías	esquiabas	esquiaste	esquiarás	esquiarías	esquíes	esquiaras	**esquía** tú (no **esquíes**)
	esquía	esquiaba	esquió	esquiará	esquiaría	esquíe	esquiara	**esquíe** Ud.
Participles:	esquiamos	esquiábamos	esquiamos	esquiaremos	esquiaríamos	esquiemos	esquiáramos	esquiemos
esquiando	esquiáis	esquiabais	esquiasteis	esquiaréis	esquiaríais	esquiéis	esquiarais	esquiad (no esquiéis)
esquiado	**esquían**	esquiaban	esquiaron	esquiarán	esquiarían	esquíen	esquiaran	**esquíen** Uds.

34 — llegar (gu) · Participles: llegando, llegado

Infinitive	INDICATIVE					SUBJUNCTIVE		IMPERATIVE
	Present	Imperfect	Preterit	Future	Conditional	Present	Past	
llegar (gu)	llego	llegaba	**llegué**	llegaré	llegaría	**llegue**	llegara	
	llegas	llegabas	llegaste	llegarás	llegarías	**llegues**	llegaras	llega tú (no **llegues**)
	llega	llegaba	llegó	llegará	llegaría	**llegue**	llegara	**llegue** Ud.
Participles:	llegamos	llegábamos	llegamos	llegaremos	llegaríamos	**lleguemos**	llegáramos	**lleguemos**
llegando	llegáis	llegabais	llegasteis	llegaréis	llegaríais	**lleguéis**	llegarais	llegad (no **lleguéis**)
llegado	llegan	llegaban	llegaron	llegarán	llegarían	**lleguen**	llegaran	**lleguen** Uds.

	INDICATIVE					SUBJUNCTIVE		IMPERATIVE
Infinitive	**Present**	**Imperfect**	**Preterit**	**Future**	**Conditional**	**Present**	**Past**	
35 tocar (qu)	toco	tocaba	**toqué**	tocaré	tocaría	**toque**	tocara	
	tocas	tocabas	tocaste	tocará	tocarías	**toques**	tocaras	**toca** tú (no **toques**)
	toca	tocaba	tocó	tocarás	tocaría	**toque**	tocara	**toque** Ud.
Participles:	tocamos	tocábamos	tocamos	tocaremos	tocaríamos	**toquemos**	tocáramos	**toquemos**
tocando	tocáis	tocabais	tocasteis	tocaréis	tocaríais	**toquéis**	tocarais	tocad (no **toquéis**)
tocado	tocan	tocaban	tocaron	tocarán	tocarían	**toquen**	tocaran	**toquen** Uds.
36 vestir(se) (e→i)	**me visto**	me vestía	me vestí	me vestiré	me vestiría	**me vista**	**me vistiera**	
	te vistes	te vestías	te vestiste	te vestirás	te vestirías	**te vistas**	**te vistieras**	**vístete** tú
	se viste	se vestía	**se vistió**	se vestirá	se vestiría	**se vista**	**se vistiera**	**vístase** Ud.
Participles:	nos vestimos	nos vestíamos	nos vestimos	nos vestiremos	nos vestiríamos	**nos vistamos**	**nos vistiéramos**	**vistámonos**
vistiendo	os vestís	os vestíais	**os vestisteis**	os vestiréis	os vestiríais	**os vistáis**	**os vistierais**	vestíos (no os **vistáis**)
vestido	**se visten**	se vestían	**se vistieron**	se vestirán	se vestirían	**se vistan**	**se vistieran**	**vístanse** Uds.

Mar Caribe

Barranquilla
Maracaibo
Caracas ★
Venezuela
Puerto España
Trinidad y Tobago

Medellín
Colombia
Bogotá ★
Cali
R. Orinoco
Georgetown ★
Guyana
Paramaribo ★
Suriname
Cayena ★
Guayana Francesa

Pasto
R. Magdalena

★ Quito
Ecuador
Guayaquil
R. Negro
R. Amazonas
Belém
Manaus

• Iquitos
Perú
R. Madeira

Recife

Cordillera de los Andes
Lima ★
• Cuzco
Lago Titicaca

Brasil
★ Brasilia
Salvador

Arequipa
★ La Paz
Bolivia
Arica
Sucre ★
R. Paraguay
R. Paraná
Belo Horizonte

Iquique

Océano Pacífico

Antofagasta
São Paulo
Río de Janeiro
Santos

Salta
Paraguay
Asunción ★

Chile
R. Paraná
R. Uruguay
Porto Alegre

Córdoba
Valparaíso
Mendoza
Rosario
Uruguay
★ Santiago
Buenos Aires ★
★ Montevideo

Océano Atlántico

Concepción
Argentina
Bahía Blanca

Cordillera de los Andes

Puerto Montt

N
O ← → E
S

Estrecho de Magallanes
Islas Malvinas
Punta Arenas

Tierra del Fuego

América del Sur

Islas Galápagos
Océano Pacífico
Isla Pinta
Isla Marchena
Isla Genovesa
Isla Isabela
Línea Ecuatorial
Volcán Darwin
Isla Santiago (San Salvador)
ECUADOR
Isla Fernandina
Puerto Ayora
Isla San Cristóbal
Santo Tomás
Isla Santa Cruz
Puerto Barquerizo Moreno
Isla Santa María
Isla Española

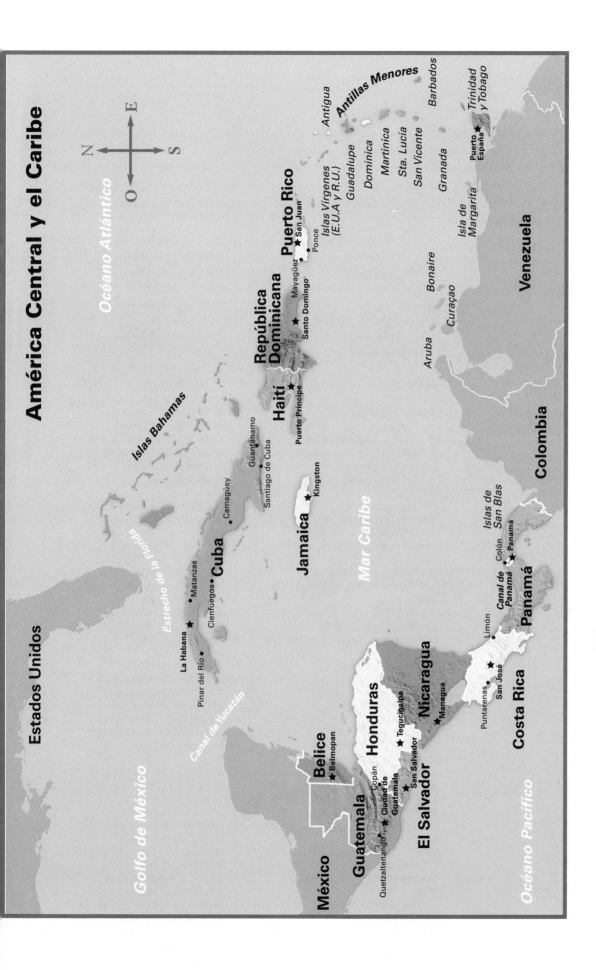

América Central y el Caribe

Estados Unidos

Golfo de México

Océano Atlántico

Islas Bahamas

Estrecho de la Florida

La Habana
Pinar del Río
Matanzas
Cienfuegos
Camagüey

Cuba

Santiago de Cuba

Guantánamo

Canal de Yucatán

Jamaica
Kingston

Mar Caribe

Haití
Puerto Príncipe

República Dominicana
Santo Domingo

Puerto Rico
San Juan
Mayagüez
Ponce

Islas Vírgenes
(E.U.A y R.U.)

Antillas Menores

Antigua
Guadalupe
Dominica
Martinica
Sta. Lucía
San Vicente
Granada
Barbados

Trinidad
y Tobago
Puerto
España

Isla de
Margarita

Aruba
Bonaire
Curaçao

Venezuela

Colombia

México

Belice
Belmopan

Guatemala
Copán
Ciudad de
Guatemala
Quetzaltenango

El Salvador
San Salvador

Honduras
Tegucigalpa

Nicaragua
Managua

Costa Rica
Puntarenas
San José

Limón

Panamá
Canal de
Panamá
Colón
Panamá

Islas de
San Blas

Océano Pacífico

N
E
O
S

Guide to Vocabulary

Note on alphabetization

Formerly, **ch**, **ll**, and **ñ** were considered separate letters in the Spanish alphabet, **ch** appearing after **c**, **ll** after **l**, and **ñ** after **n**. In current practice, for purposes of alphabetization, **ch** and **ll** are not treated as separate letters, but **ñ** still follows **n**. Therefore, in this glossary you will find that **añadir**, for example, appears after **anuncio**.

The numbers that follow the entries indicate the episode number where the words are taught; entries labelled 1–15 are found in **Primera Parte**, and entries marked 16–30 are found in **Segunda Parte**.

Abbreviations used in this glossary

adj.	adjective	*i.o.*	indirect object	*prep.*	preposition
adv.	adverb	*irr*	irregular	*pron.*	pronoun
conj.	conjunction	*m.*	masculine	*ref.*	reflexive
d.o.	direct object	*n.*	noun	*sing.*	singular
f.	feminine	*obj.*	object	*sub.*	subject
fam.	familiar	*p.p.*	past participle	*v.*	verb
form.	formal	*pl.*	plural		
interj.	interjection	*poss.*	possessive		

Spanish-English

A

a *prep.* to
abierto/a *adj.* open
abogado/a *n.* lawyer 12
abrazo *n., m* hug
abrigo *n., m* coat, jacket 13
abril *n.* April 13
abrir *v.* to open 8
abuelo/a *n.*
  grandfather/grandmother 4
abuelos *n., m* grandparents 4
aburrido/a *adj.* boring 6; bored 15
acabar de *v.* to have just 21
acampar *v.* to camp
aceite *n., m* oil
aceptar *v.* to accept 28
aconsejar *v.* to advise 27
acostarse (o→ue) *v.* to go to bed 14
activo/a *adj.* active 3
acuario *n., m* aquarium
acuático/a *adj.* aquatic
además *adv.* besides
(a)dentro *adv.* inside 15
adiós *interj.* good-bye 1
administración *n., f* management
administrador(a) de empresas *n.*
  business administrator 12
adolorido/a *adj.* sore 21
aeropuerto *n., m* airport 8
afeitarse *v.* to shave 23
aficionado/a *n.* fan
(a)fuera *adv.* outside 15
agente *n., mf* agent 12
agosto *n., m* August 13
agradable *adj.* nice 6
agregar *v.* to add
agua, (el) *n., f* water 9
aguacate *n., m* avocado
ahí *adv.* there
ahora *adv.* now 28

ahorrar dinero *v.* to save money 28
aire *n., m* air
ajeno/a *n.* stranger
ajo *n., m* garlic
alberca *n., f* swimming pool
alcanzar *v.* to reach; to achieve
alcoba *n., f* bedroom
alegrarse *v.* to be happy for
alfombra *n., f* carpet 18
algo *n.* something 18
alguien *n.* somebody 18
algún, alguna *adj.* some 18
alguna vez ever 28
allí/allá *adv.* there
almohada *n., f* pillow
almorzar (o→ue) *v.* to have lunch 10
almuerzo *n., m* lunch 9
alojamiento *n., m* lodging
alpinismo *n., m* mountain climbing
alquilar *v.* to rent
alrededor *adv.* around
alto *n., m* stop (sign)
alto/a *adj.* tall, high 11
alumno/a *n.* student
ama de casa, (el) *n., f* housewife, home-maker 11
amable *adj.* kind, nice, friendly 6
amante *n., mf* lover
amarillo/a *adj.* yellow 13
ambicioso/a *adj.* ambitious 3
amigo/a *n.* friend 4
amistad *n., f* friendship
amor *n., m* love
amueblar *v.* to furnish
analista *n., mf* analyst 12
anaranjado/a *adj.* orange 13
andar en bicicleta *v.* to ride bikes 18
anfitrión, anfitriona *n.* host
ángel *n., m* angel
anillo *n., m* ring 27
anoche *adv.* last night 15
anteayer *adv.* day before yesterday

antemano, (de) *adv.* beforehand
antes (de) que *adv.* before 30
antibiótico *n., m* antibiotic 21
antigüedad *n., f* antiquity; seniority
antipático/a *adj.* irritating, nasty 6
antropología *n., f* anthropology 1
anuncio *n., m* advertisement
añadir *v.* to add
año *n., m* year
Año Nuevo *n., m* New Year
aparcar *v.* to park
apartamento *n., m* apartment 18
apellido *n., m* last name
apenas *adv.* just, barely
apostar (o→ue) *v.* to bet
apoyar *v.* to support
aprender *v.* to learn 19
apretado/a *adj.* tight
apuesta *n., f* wager
apuntes *n., m* notes
araña *n., f* spider
árbol *n., m* tree 20
armar (un rompecabezas) *v.* to assemble (a puzzle) 22
armario *n., m* closet
arquitecto/a *n.* architect 12
arquitectura *n., f* architecture
arrancar *v.* to start
arrecife *n., m* reef
arreglado/a *adj.* tidy 18
arreglar *v.* to tidy up, to fix
arrestar *v.* to arrest
arriba *adv.* above
arrogante *adj.* arrogant 3
arroz *n., m* rice 9
artesanía *n., f* hand-made crafts
artista *n., mf* artist 12
asador *n., m* barbecue 18
asistir *v.* to attend
aspiradora *n., f* vacuum cleaner
aspirina *n., f* aspirin 21
astronomía *n., f* astronomy 1
asunto *n., m* matter, issue
asustado/a *adj.* scared

atender a los clientes *v.* to take care of clients **11**
atento/a *adj.* kind, attentive
atractivo/a *adj.* attractive **3**
atrás *adv.* behind **25**
atún *n., m* tuna **9**
auditorio *n., m* auditorium, theater **2**
aula *n., f* classroom
aunque *conj.* although
auto *n., m* car
autobús *n., m* bus **5**
autopista *n., f* freeway, expressway **26**
autorretrato *n., m* self-portrait
autosuficiencia *n., f* self-sufficiency
avenida *n., f* avenue **26**
aventar *v.* to throw
avión *n., m* airplane **20**
ayer *adv.* yesterday **15**
ayudar *v.* to help **11**
azul *adj.* blue **13**

B

bachillerato *n., m* high school
bailar *v.* to dance **5**
bajo/a *adj.* short, low **6**
balcón *n., m* balcony
banana *n., f* banana
banco *n., m* bank
bandera *n., f* flag **2**
bañarse *v.* to shower, to take a bath **14**
bañera *n., f* bathtub
baño *n., m* bathroom **2**
bar *n., m* bar
barato/a *adj.* cheap, inexpensive
barda *n., f* fence
barrer *v.* to sweep **18**
barrio *n., m* neighborhood
bastante *adv.* quite
basura *n., f* trash **18**
bebé *n., mf* baby **8**
beber *v.* to drink
bebida *n., f* beverage
beca *n., f* scholarship
béisbol *n., m* baseball
bello/a *adj.* beautiful
berrinche *n., m* tantrum **22**
besar *v.* to kiss **20**
beso *n., m* kiss **20**
biblioteca *n., f* library **2**
bien *adv.* well, good **1**
bienes raíces *n., m* real estate **12**
bikini *n., m* bikini **13**
billetera *n., f* wallet
biología *n., f* biology **1**
bistec *n., m* steak
blanco/a *adj.* white **13**
bluejeans *n., m* jeans
blusa *n., f* blouse **13**
boca *n., f* mouth **21**
bocacalle *n., f* intersection

boda *n., f* wedding
bolera *n., f* bowling
boleto *n., m* ticket
boliche *n., m* bowling **8**
bolígrafo *n., m* pen
bolos *n., m* bowling
bolsa *n., f* bag, purse
bolsillo *n., m* pocket, purse
bombero *n., m* firefighter **12**
bonito/a *adj.* pretty **6**
borracho/a *adj.* drunk
botánica *n., f* botany
bote de basura *n., m* trash can
brazalete *n., m* bracelet
brazo *n., m* arm **21**
brincar *v.* to jump
brócoli *n., m* broccoli **9**
bronca *n., f* problem, fight
bruja *n., f* witch
bucear *v.* to scuba dive **18**
buen *adj.* good (before the noun)
buenas noches good evening, good night **1**
buenas tardes good afternoon **1**
bueno/a *adj.* good (after the noun) **6**
buenos días good morning **1**
bufanda *n., f* scarf **13**
buró *n., m* night table
buscar *v.* to look for **5**
buzón *n., m* mail box

C

caballo *n., m* horse **18**
cabeza *n., f* head **21**
cacahuate *n., m* peanut
cada *adj.* each
café *n., m* coffee, coffee shop **5**
café *adj.* brown **13**
cafetería *n., f* cafeteria **2**
caja *n., f* box, cash register
calculadora *n., f* calculator **2**
caliente *adj.* hot
calificaciones *n., f* grades
calificado/a *adj.* qualified
calle *n., f* street **26**
calor *n., m* heat, hot **13**; **hace calor** it's hot
caloría *n., f* calorie
cama *n., f* bed **15**
cámara *n., f* camera
camarero/a *n.* waiter/waitress
camarón *n., m* shrimp **9**
cambiar *v.* to change **28**
cambiarse (de casa) *v.* to move
caminata *n., f* hike
camino *n., m* way
camión *n., m* truck
camisa *n., f* shirt **13**
camiseta *n., f* T-shirt **13**
campamento *n., m* camp
cancha *n., f* court, field **2**
canción *n., f* song

canica *n., f* marble
cansado/a *adj.* tired **15**
cantar *v.* to sing **20**
capacitación *n., f* training **28**
capaz *adj.* capable
carga *n., f* freight
caricatura *n., f* cartoon
cariñoso/a *adj.* affectionate **6**
carne *n., f* meat **9**
carne de res *n., f* beef **9**
carnet (de conducir) *n., m* driver's license
caro/a *adj.* expensive
carrera *n., f* major, field of study
carretera *n., f* highway **26**
carril *n., m* lane
carro *n., m* car
carta *n., f* letter
cartas *n., f* deck of cards
cartera *n., f* wallet, purse
casa *n., f* house **8**
casado/a *adj.* married **6**
casarse *v.* to get married **27**
casero/a *adj.* homemade
casi *adv.* almost **8**
caso *n., m* case
castaño/a *adj.* brunet(te)
castigar *v.* to punish **22**
castigo *n., m* punishment
casualidad, (por) *n., f* by chance
catarro *n., m* cold **21**
católico/a *adj.* Catholic **22**
celebrar *v.* to celebrate **28**
celos *n., m* jealousy
celoso/a *adj.* jealous
cena *n., f* dinner, supper **9**
cenar *v.* to dine **9**
centavo *n., m* cent
centro *n., m* downtown; middle, center
centro comercial *n., m* mall, shopping center **8**
cepillarse los dientes *v.* to brush one's teeth
cerca *n., f* fence
cerca (de) *adv.* close, near
cercano/a *adj.* close
cerdo *n., m* pork **9**
cereal *n., m* cereal **9**
cerrar (e → ie) *v.* to close
cerveza *n., f* beer **9**
césped *n., m* lawn
chamarra *n., f* jacket
chaqueta *n., f* jacket **13**
cheque *n., m* (personal) check
chico/a *n.* young person **4**
chilaquiles *n., m* Mexican dish with tortilla, salsa, and cheese
chillar *v.* to yell; to cry
chimenea *n., f* fire place
chiste *n., m* joke
chistoso/a *adj.* funny
chocar *v.* to dislike (**me choca**) **19**; *v.* to hit (a car) **26**
chocolate *n., m* chocolate

chofer *n., mf* driver **11**
choque *n., m* car accident (crash) **26**
cierto *adj.* true, certain
cine *n., m* movies, movie theater **8**
cinta *n., f* tape
cinturón (de seguridad) *n., m* seat belt **26**
cirujano/a *n.* surgeon
cita *n., f* date, appointment
ciudad *n., f* city
ciudadanía *n., f* citizenship
ciudadano/a *n.* citizen
claro *interj.* of course
clase *n., f* class **2**
claxon *n., m* horn
clima *n., m* weather
clóset *n., m* closet **18**
cobrar *v.* to charge, collect
cobre *n., m* copper
coche *n., m* car **5**
cochera *n., f* garage
cocina *n., f* kitchen **18**
cocinar *v.* to cook
colar (o➞ue) *v.* to strain
colegio *n., m* school **22**
colgar (o➞ue) *v.* to hang
colonia *n., f* neighborhood
color *n., m* color **13**
colorear *v.* to color **22**
comedor *n., m* dining room **18**
comer *v.* to eat **8**; *v.* to have lunch **9**
comida *n., f* food **5**
cómo *adv.* how (interrogative) **6**
como *prep.* as (comparison)
cómoda *n., f* dresser **18**
comodidad *n., f* comfort
cómodo/a *adj.* comfortable **20**
compañero/a *n.* mate **2**
compañía *n., f* company, business
compartir *v.* to share **22**
competente *adj.* competent **3**
completo/a *adj.* complete, full
comportamiento *n., m* behavior
comportarse *v.* to behave oneself
comprar *v.* to buy **5**
comprensión *n., f* understanding
compromiso *n., m* engagement **27**
computadora *n., f* computer **5**
común *adj.* common
con *prep.* with
con frecuencia *adv.* frequently
conducir (yo conduzco) *v.* to drive
conductor(a) *n.* driver **26**
confianza *n., f* trust
confundir *v.* to confuse
conmigo *prep. pron.* with me
conmoción *n., f* concussion
conocer *v.* to meet; *v.* to know **12**
conocimiento *n., m* knowledge
consejero/a *n.* advisor **2**
consejo *n., m* advice **11**
consentido/a *adj.* spoiled (person) **22**
consultorio *n., m* doctor's office

consumidor *n., m* consumer
contable *adj.* countable
contador(a) *n.* accountant **12**
contar (o➞ue) *v.* to tell **11**; *v.* to count
contento/a *adj.* happy **15**
contestar *v.* to answer
contigo *prep. pron.* with you
contra *prep.* against
contrario, (al) *prep.* on the contrary
conversación *n., f* conversation
conversar *v.* to talk, to chat
corbata *n., f* tie **13**
coro *n., m* choir
correo *n., m* post office, mail
correo electrónico *n., m* e-mail
correr *v.* to run, to jog **8**
cortar el pasto *v.* to mow the lawn **18**
cortarse *v.* to cut (oneself)
corto/a *adj.* short **13**
cosa *n., f* thing **2**
cosecha *n., f* crops
coser *v.* to sew
costar (o➞ue) *v.* to cost
crear *v.* to create
creativo/a *adj.* creative **3**
crecer (yo crezco) *v.* to grow
creer *v.* to believe, to think **17**
crema *n., f* cream
cruce *n., m* intersection; junction
crudo/a *adj.* raw
Cruz Roja *n., f* Red Cross
cruzadas *n., f* Crusades
cruzar *v.* to cross **26**
cuaderno *n., m* notebook **2**
cuadra *n., f* city block **26**
cuadro *n., m* picture; square
cuál *pron.* which, what (interrogative) **6**
cuando *prep., conj.* when
cuándo *adv.* when (interrogative) **6**
cuánto/a(s) *adj.* how much/many (interrogative) **6**
Cuaresma *n., f* Lent
cuarto *n., m* room **5**
cubrir *v.* to cover
cuchara *n., f* spoon
cucharita *n., f* teaspoon
cuchillo *n., m* knife
cuello *n., m* neck **21**
cuenta *n., f* bill **9**
cuerda *n., f* rope **22**
cuerpo *n., m* body **21**
cueva *n., f* cave
cuidado *n., m* care; caution
cuidar *v.* to take care of; **cuidarse** to take care of (oneself) **21**
culpa *n., f* fault **25**
culpar *v.* to blame
cumpleaños *n., m* birthday
cumplido *n., m* compliment
cuñado/a *n.* brother-in-law / sister-in-law **4**
cura *n., m* priest

curar *v.* to cure
curiosidades *n., f* curios
currículum *n., m* résumé **28**

D

damas chinas *n., f* checkers **22**
dar (yo doy) *v.* to give **11**; **dar de comer** *v.* to feed **18**; **dar gusto** *v.* to please; **dar un paseo** *v.* to go for a walk **18**; **dar vuelta** *v.* to turn **26**; **darse cuenta** *v.* to realize **25**; **darse vuelta** *v.* to turn **25**
de repente *adv.* suddenly, all of a sudden **25**
deber *v.* must, ought to
decir (yo digo) *v.* to tell **20**
dedicar *v.* to dedicate
defender (e➞ie) *v.* to defend
defensa *n., f* defense
dejar *v.* to allow; to leave; to drop off **11**
dejar de *v.* to stop (doing something)
delgado/a *adj.* thin **6**
demasiado/a *adj.,* too much
demonio *n., m* demon
departamento *n., m* apartment
deporte *n., m* sport
derecha *n., f* right **23**
derecho *n., m* law
derecho/a *adj.* straight **26**
desagradable *adj.* unpleasant
desarreglado/a *adj.* messy **18**
desastre *n., m* disaster
desayunar *v.* to have breakfast **9**
desayuno *n., m* breakfast **9**
descanso *n., m* rest **21**
descansar *v.* to rest **5**
descomponerse *v.* to break down
descubrimiento *n., m* discovery
descubrir *v.* to uncover; to discover
desde *prep.* since
desear *v.* to wish; to hope
desempeñar *v.* to perform
deseo *n., m* wish
desfile *n., m* parade
desierto *n., m* desert
deshonesto/a *adj.* dishonest **3**
desilusionado/a *adj.* disappointed **15**
desobedecer (yo desobedezco) *v.* to disobey **22**
despacho *n., m* office
despedir (e➞i) *v.* to fire, to lay off; **despedirse (e➞i)** *v.* to say good-bye
despertador *n., m* alarm clock
después *adv.* after, later
desventaja *n., f* disadvantage **11**
detalle *n., m* detail
devolver *v.* to return (merchandise) **27**

día *n., m* day

diario *n., m* newspaper; diary; journal

diario/a *adj.* daily

dibujar *v.* to draw 22

dibujo *n., m* drawing

dibujo animado *n., m* cartoon 22

diccionario *n., m* dictionary 2

diciembre *n., m* December 13

dieta *n., f* diet

diferente *adj.* different 6

difícil *adj.* hard, difficult 6

dinero *n., m* money 11

dirección *n., f* address

direcciones *n., f* directions, instructions

director(a) *n.* principal, director

disco compacto (CD) *n., m* compact disc

discoteca *n., f* disco 8

discreto/a *adj.* discrete 3

disculparse *v.* to apologize

discutir *v.* to argue; to discuss 8

diseñador(a) gráfico/a *n.* graphic designer 12

diseñar *v.* to design

disfrazarse de *v.* to wear a . . . costume 20

disfrutar *v.* to enjoy

dispuesto/a *adj.* willing

divertido/a *adj.* fun 6

divertirse (e ➞ ie) *v.* to have fun 14

divorciarse *v.* to get divorced 28

doblar *v.* to turn 26

doctor(a) *n.* doctor 1

doctorado *n., m* doctorate, Ph. D. 28

dólar *n., m* dollar

doler (o ➞ ue) *v.* to hurt

dolor *n., m* pain

domingo *n., m* Sunday 5

dona *n., f* donut 9

dónde *adv.* where (interrogative) 6

dormir (o ➞ ue) *v.* to sleep 10

dormirse *v.* to fall asleep

dormitorio *n., m* bedroom

drama *n., m* drama 1

ducha *n., f* shower 18

ducharse *v.* to shower

duda *n., f* doubt

dudar *v.* to doubt

dueño/a *n.* owner

dulce *n., m* candy

dulce *adj.* sweet 9

durante *prep.* during

E

economía *n., f* economics 1

edad *n., f* age

edificio *n., m* building 2

educación física *n., f* physical education 1

educador(a) *n.* educator 12

---

egoísta *adj.* selfish

ejecutivo/a *n., adj.* executive

ejercicio *n., m* exercise

ejército *n., m* army

ejotes *n., m* green beans

embarazarse *v.* to get pregnant

embarazo *n., m* pregnancy

emocionado/a *adj.* excited 15

empezar (e ➞ ie) *v.* to start, to begin 10

empleado/a *n.* employee 11

empresa *n., f* company, business 12

empujar *v.* to push 25

en cuanto *adv. conj.* as soon as 30

en vez de *prep.* instead of

enamorado/a *v.* to be in love

enamorarse *v.* to fall in love 28

encantado/a *interj.* delighted 1

encantar *v.* to enchant 19

encontrar (o ➞ ue) *v.* to find 10

enero *n., m* January 13

enfermarse *v.* to get sick 21

enfermería *n., f* health center 2

enfermero/a *n.* nurse 12

enfermo/a *adj.* sick 15

enfrente *prep.* across from, in front of 26

engordar *v.* to gain weight

enojado/a *adj.* upset, mad 15

enojarse *v.* to get upset

ensalada *n., f* salad 9

ensanchar *v.* to widen

enseñar *v.* to teach; to show 24

entender (e ➞ ie) *v.* to understand 10

entonces *adv.* then

entrada *n., f* entrance 26

entrar *v.* to enter 28

entre semana *adv.* on weekdays 5

entregar *v.* to deliver; to turn in 24

entrenamiento *n., m* training

entrenar *v.* to train

entrevista *n., f* interview 28

enviar *v.* to send

envolver (o ➞ ue) *v.* to wrap

equipo *n., m* equipment; team

escandalosa/o *adj.* scandalous

escoger *v.* choose

esconderse *v.* to hide

escondidillas *n., f* hide-and-seek 22

escondite *n., m* hiding place

escondite (al) *n., m* hide-and-seek 22

escribir *v.* to write 8

escribir a máquina *v.* to type

escritor(a) *n.* writer

escritorio *n., m* desk 2

escuchar *v.* to listen 5

escuela *n., f* school 8

escuela pública *n., f* public school 22

escuela de niñas/os *n., f* all-girls/boys school 22

escultor(a) *n.* sculptor

ese/a *adj.* that 6

---

esencial *adj.* essential

esfuerzo *n., m* effort

esos/as *adj.* those 6

espagueti *n., m* spaghetti 9

espalda *n., f* back 21

español *n., m* Spanish 1; **español(a)** *adj.* Spaniard

espantoso/a *adj.* horrendous

espejo *n., m* mirror 18

esperanza *n., f* hope

esperar *v.* to wait; *v.* to hope, to expect 27

esponja *n., f* sponge

esposo/a *n.* husband/wife 4

esquiar (yo esquío) *v.* to ski 18

esquina *n., f* corner 26

esta noche *n.* tonight

estable *adj.* stable

estación *n., f* season 13

estacionamiento *n., m* parking 2

estacionar(se) *v.* to park 26

estadio *n., m* stadium 2

estancia *n., f* stay, visit

estandarte *n., m* banner

estar (yo estoy) *v.* to be 15

estar en *v.* to be at/in/on

estar listo/a *v.* to be ready 15

estar seguro *v.* to be sure

este *n., m* east 26

este/a *adj.* this 6

éste/a *n.* this one

estómago *n., m* stomach 21

estos/as *adj.* these 6

estrecho/a *adj.* narrow, close

estricto/a *adj.* strict

estudiante *n., mf* student 2

estudiar *v.* to study 5

estudios *n., m* studies

estudioso/a *adj.* studious 3

estufa *n., f* stove 18

estupendo/a *adj.* great

etapa *n., f* stage

evitar *v.* to avoid

examen *n., m* exam, test

excelente *adj.* excellent 3

exceso *n., m* excess

exhibición de arte *n., f* art exhibition 8

exigente *adj.* demanding

exigir (g ➞ j) *v.* to demand

éxito *n., m* success

experto/a *n.* expert

explicar *v.* to explain 24

extrañar *v.* to miss

extranjero/a *adj.* foreign; **extranjero/a** *n.* foreigner

extraño/a *adj.* strange

extrovertido/a *adj.* extroverted 3

F

fácil *adj.* easy 6

falda *n., f* skirt 13

faltar *v.* to be missing, to lack

familia *n., f* family
familiares *n., m* relatives 4
farmaceuta *n., mf* pharmacist
fascinar *v.* to love; to be fascinated by 19
febrero *n., m* February 13
fecha *n., f* date (calendar)
felicidad *n., f* happiness
feliz *adj.* happy 20
feo/a *adj.* ugly 6
fibra *n., f* fiber
fiebre *n., f* fever 21
fiesta *n., f* party
fijarse *v.* to pay attention
fijo/a *adj.* fixed, steady 11
filosofía *n., f* philosophy 1
fin de semana *n., m* weekend 5
final *adj.* final
final *n., m* end
fino/a *adj.* fine, high quality
firma *n., f* signature
firmar *v.* to sign
flaco/a *adj.* thin
flan *n., m* flan, custard 9
flexible *adj.* flexible 3
flojo/a *adj.* lazy, loose
flor *n., f* flower
folleto *n., m* brochure
formal *adj.* formal 20
fortaleza *n., f* fort
fosforescente *adj.* fluorescent
fotografía *n., f* picture
fractura *n., f* fracture
francés *n., m* French; **francés, francesa** *adj.* French
frecuencia *adv.* often, frequently
fregadero *n., m* kitchen sink 18
frenar *v.* to break 26
freno *n., m* brake
frente *n., f* forehead
frente a *prep.* in front of
fresco/a *adj.* fresh, cool 13; **hace fresco** it's cool 13
frijoles *n., m* beans 9
frío/a *adj.* cold 13; **hace frío** it's cold 13
frito/a *adj.* fried
frontera *n., f* border
fruta *n., f* fruit 9
fuente *n., f* fountain
fuerte *adj.* strong
fuerza *n., f* force
fumar *v.* to smoke 19
funcionar *v.* to work, to function
fútbol *n., m* soccer 8

G

galleta *n., f* cookie 9
ganar *v.* to win 12
ganarse *v.* to earn
garaje *n., m* garage 18
garganta *n., f* throat 21
gaseosa *n., f* soda

gasolina *n., f* gas 26
gasolinera *n., f* gas station
gastar *v.* to spend 19
gato/a *n.* cat 4
generoso/a *adj.* generous 3
gente *n., f* people
geografía *n., f* geography 1
gerente *n., mf* manager 12
gimnasio *n., m* gym 2
gobierno *n., m* government 28
golpe *n., m* hit 25
goma *n., f* tire
gordo/a *adj.* fat 6
grabado *n., m* print, carving
grabadora *n., f* tape recorder
gracias *interj.* thank you 1
gracioso/a *adj.* funny 6
grado *n., m* degree (temperature)
graduación *n., f* graduation 28
graduarse *v.* to graduate 28
grama *n., f* grass
grande *adj.* big, large 6
grasa *n., f* fat
gratis *adj.* free (of charge)
grave *adj.* serious
gripe *n., f* flu
gris *adj.* gray 13
gritar *v.* to shout, to yell
grosero/a *adj.* impolite, rough, rude 6
guapo/a *adj.* handsome, good-looking 6
guantes *n., m* gloves 13
guardabosques *n., mf* park ranger
guayaba *n., f* guava
güero/a *adj.* blond(e)
guerra *n., f* war
guía *n., mf* tour guide (person)
guía *n., f* guide book, pamphlet
guineo *n., m* banana
guitarra *n., f* guitar 5
gustar (me gusta) *v.* to like 3

H

habilidad *n., f* ability
habitación *n., f* bedroom, room
hábito *n., m* habits
hablar *v.* to speak, to talk 5
hacer (yo hago) *v.* to do, to make 8; **hacer berrinches** *v.* to throw tantrums 22; **hacer ejercicio** *v.* to exercise 8; **hacer las maletas** *v.* to pack 20; **hacer travesuras** *v.* to get into trouble 22; **hacer un picnic** *v.* to have a picnic 18; **hacer un viaje** *v.* to take a trip 18; **hacer una fiesta** *v.* to throw a party 18; **hacer una maestría** *v.* to pursue a Master's degree 28; **hacerse daño** *v.* to hurt oneself
hambre, (el) *n., f* hunger
hamburguesa *n., f* hamburger 9
hasta (que) *prep.* until 28; **hasta**

ahora until now 28; **hasta luego** see you later 1; **hasta mañana** see you tomorrow 1
hay *v.* there is/are
hecho, (de) *n., m* in fact
helado *n., m* ice cream 9
herida *n., f* wound
hermano/a *n.* brother, sister 4
hielo *n., m* ice
hierba *n., f* grass, herb
hierro *n., m* iron
higienista dental *n., mf* dental hygienist 12
hijo/a *n.* son, daughter 4
hijo/a único/a *n.* only child 6
historia *n., f* history; story 1
hola *interj.* hello, hi 1
hombre *n., m* man
honesto/a *adj.* honest 3
hora *n., f* hour, time (of day)
horario *n., m* schedule 11; **horario fijo** fixed schedule 11; **horario flexible** flexible schedule 11
horno *n., m* oven 18
horno, (al) *adj.* baked
horrible *adj.* horrible
hoy *n.* today
huarache *n., m* sandal
huevo *n., m* egg 9
huir *v.* to flee
húmedo/a *adj.* humid
hundirse *v.* to sink

I

idealista *n., mf* idealist 3
idioma *n., m* language 12
iglesia *n., f* church 8
igual *adj.* same, equal 21
igualmente *adv.* likewise 1
iluminar *v.* to color
imaginar *v.* to imagine
imaginativo/a *adj.* imaginative
impaciente *adj.* impatient 3
impermeable *n., m* raincoat 13
importante *adj.* important 27
impuesto *n., m* tax
inagotable *adj.* inexhaustible
incendio *n., m* fire
incluir *v.* to include
increíble *adj.* incredible 3
indiscreto/a *adj.* indiscreet
infección *n., f* infection 21
información *n., f* information 5
informal *adj.* casual 20
ingeniero/a en computación *n.* computer engineer 12
inglés *n., m* English; **inglés, inglesa** *adj.* English
inscripción *n., f* registration
inseguro/a *adj.* uncertain, insecure
insoportable *adj.* unbearable
inteligente *adj.* intelligent
interesante *adj.* interesting 3

interesar (me interesa) *v.* to interest 19

intersección *n., f* intersection 26

inundación *n., f* flood

investigación *n., f* research

investigador(a) *n.* investigator 12

invierno *n., m* winter 13

invitado/a *n.* guest

invitar *v.* to invite 10

inyección *n., f* shot, injection

ir (irr.) *v.* to go 20; **ir (a exceso de velocidad)** *v.* to speed 26; **ir de campamento** *v.* to go camping 18; **ir de compras** *v.* to go shopping; **ir de excursión** *v.* to hike 18; **irse** to leave 14; **irse de vacaciones** to go on vacation 14

irreconocible *adj.* unrecognizable

irresponsable *adj.* irresponsible 3

izquierda *n., f* left 26

izquierdo/a *adj* left 23

J

jamón *n., m* ham 9

jarabe para la tos *n., m* cough syrup 21

jardín *n., m* backyard, garden 18

jeans *n. m* jeans 13

jefe/a *n.* boss

¡jolines! *interj.* Wow!

joven *n., mf* young man, woman 6

joyería *n., f* jewelry store 27

jubilado/a *adj.* retired

judío/a *adj.* Jewish; **judío/a** *n.* Jew

juego *n., m* game

jueves *n., m* Thursday 5

jugador(a) *n.* player

jugar (u➜ue) *v.* to play (sports, games) 10

jugo *n., m* juice 9

juguete *n., m* toy 22

julio *n., m* July 13

junio *n., m* June 13

junta *n., f* meeting

juntarse *v.* to get together 14

junto/a *adj.* together

jurado *n., m* jury (panel of judges)

L

lado *n., m* side 23

lado, (al) *prep.* next to

ladrón, ladrona *n.* thief

lago *n., m* lake

lámpara *n., f* lamp 18

langosta *n., f* lobster 9

lápiz *n., m* pencil 2

largo/a *adj.* long

lastimarse *v.* to get hurt 21

latón *n., m* brass

lavabo *n., m* bathroom sink 18

lavar *v.* to wash 5

lavar los platos *v.* to do (wash) the dishes 18

lavarse *v.* to wash (oneself)

lavarse las manos *v.* to wash one's hands 14

lavarse los dientes *v.* to brush one's teeth 14

lección *n., f* lesson

leche *n., f* milk 9

lechón *n., m* suckling pig

lechuga *n., f* lettuce 9

leer *v.* to read 8

lejos *adv.* far

lengua *n., f* tongue; language

lentes de sol *n., m* sun glasses 13

levantar pesas *v.* to lift weights 18

levantarse *v.* to get up 14

ley *n., f* law

libre *adj.* free 15

librería *n., f* bookstore 2

libro *n., m* book 2

licencia de manejar *n., f* driver's license 26

licenciatura *n., f* bachelor's degree

liceo *n., m* high school

ligero/a *adj.* light 13

límite *n., m* limit

limonada *n., f* lemonade 9

limpiar *v.* to clean 5

limpio/a *adj.* clean 18

línea *n., f* line

lío *n., m* problem

líquidos *n., m* liquids 21

listo/a (ser) *adj.* smart 6

literatura *n., f* literature 1

llamar *v.* to call 11

llanta *n., f* tire 26

llegada *n., f* arrival

llegar *v.* to arrive 5

llenar *v.* to fill 28

llevar *v.* to take someone somewhere 24; to wear 13; **llevarse bien/mal** *v.* to get along well/poorly 22

llorar *v.* to cry

llorón, llorona *adj.* crybaby 22

llover (o➜ue) *v.* to rain 13

lluvia *n., f* rain

loco/a *adj.* crazy, mad

logro *n., m* accomplishment, achievement

lucha *n., f* struggle

luego *adv.* later

lugar *n., m* place 11

lujo *n., m* luxury

lunes *n., m* Monday 5

luz *n., f* light

M

madre *n., f* mother 4

madrugar *v.* to get up early

maduro/a *adj.* mature 3

maestría *n., f* Master's 28

maestro/a *n.* teacher

mágico/a *adj.* magical

magisterio *n., m* teaching

mahones *n., m* jeans

majo/a *adj.* nice, cute

mal *adv.* bad, ill 21

malecón *n., m* seawall

maleducar *v.* to spoil

malentendido *n., m* misunderstanding

maleta *n., f* suitcase 13

malo/a *adj.* bad 6

malta *n., f* malt

mamá *n., f* mom

mandar *v.* to send 11

mandar un fax *v.* to fax

mandón, mandona *adj.* bossy

manejar *v.* to drive 26

manera *n., f* way

mango *n., m* mango

maní *n., m* peanut

mano *n., f* hand 14

mantequilla *n., f* butter

manzana *n., f* apple 9; city block

mañana *n., f* morning 11

mañana *adv.* tomorrow

mañanitas *n., f* birthday song 20

mapa *n., m* map 2

maquillarse *v.* to apply makeup

máquina *n., f* machine

máquina de escribir *n., f* typewriter

mareado/a *adj.* dizzy 21

mariscos *n., m* seafood 9

marrón *adj.* brown

martes *n., m* Tuesday 5

marzo *n., m* March 13

más *adv.* more; **más o menos** so-so 1; **más... que** more... than 17

masaje *n., m* massage

mascota *n., f* pet

matatena *n., f* jacks

matemáticas *n., f* math 1

materia *n., f* subject

materialista *adj.* materialistic 3

materno/a *adj.* maternal

matrimonio *n., m* marriage

mayo *n., m* May 13

mayor *adj.* older 6

mayor, (el/la) *n.* the oldest 6

mayoría *n., f* majority

mecánica *n., f* mechanics

mecánico/a *adj.* mechanic

médico/a *n.* doctor 12

medio/a *n., adj.* half, medium

mediodía *n., m* noon

mejor que *adj.* better than 17

menor *adj.* younger 6

menor, (el/la) *n.* the youngest 6

menos que, (a) *conj.* unless 30

menos... que *adv.* less... than 17

mensaje *n., m* message

mentira *n., f* lie 24

menú *n., m* menu

mercadeo *n., m* marketing

mercadotécnia *n., f* marketing 12

mermelada *n., f* marmalade
mes *n., m* month 13
mesa *n., f* table 18; **mesa de noche**
  n., f night table 18
mesero/a *n.* waiter, waitress 9
meta *n., f* goal
meterse *v.* to get involved
metro *n., m* subway; meter
  (measurement)
mezclilla *n., f* denim
microondas, (el) *n., f* microwave
  (oven) 18
miedo *n., m* fear
mientras *adv.* while
miércoles *n., m* Wednesday 5
mil *adj.* thousand
milla *n., f* mile
minifalda *n., f* mini-skirt 13
mirar *v.* to see, to watch 5
misa *n., f* mass; religious service
mismo/a *n., adj.* same; self
mochila *n., f* backpack 2
moderno/a *adj.* modern 20
moler (o ➜ ue) *v.* to grind
molestar *v.* to bother 19
molesto/a *adj.* upset 15
momento *n., m* moment 28
moneda *n., f* coin
montaña *n., f* mountain
montar *v.* to ride 18
morado/a *adj.* purple 13
moreno/a *adj.* dark-skinned,
  tanned 6
morir (o ➜ ue) *v.* to die 28
mostrar (o ➜ ue) *v.* to show
mover (o ➜ ue) *v.* to move
mozo/a *n.* waiter, waitress
muchacho/a *n.* young person
mucho/a *adv.* a lot 5; **mucho gusto**
  nice to meet you 1
muchos/as *adj.* many
mudarse *v.* to move 28
mueble *n., m* furniture 18
mujer *n., f* woman
mujeriego *n., m* womanizer
multa *n., f* fine, ticket 26
muñeco/a *n.* doll 22
muro *n., m* wall (outside)
museo *n., m* museum 8
música *n., f* music 1; **poner la**
  música muy alta *v.* to play loud
  music 23
muy *adv.* very; **muy bien** very well
  1

N

nada *n.* nothing, anything 18
nadar *v.* to swim
nadie *n.* anybody, nobody, no one
  18
naranja *n., f* orange 9
nariz *n., f* nose 21
Navidad *n., f* Christmas

necesario/a *adj.* necessary
necesitar *v.* to need 5
negarse (e ➜ ie) *v.* to refuse
negocio *n., m* business
negro/a *adj.* black 13
nervioso/a *adj.* nervous 3
neumático *n., m* tire
nevar (e ➜ ie) *v.* to snow 13
ni *conj.* neither, nor; **ni siquiera** *adv.*
  not even
nieto/a *n.* grandson/daughter 4
ningún, ninguna *adj.* not any 18;
  ninguna parte, (a) nowhere 8
niñero/a *n.* baby-sitter 11
niñez *n., f* childhood
niño/a *n.* child, kid 4
nivel *n., m* level
noche *n., f* evening, night 11
nombre *n., m* name
normalista *n., mf* elementary
  teacher
norte *n., m* north 26
nota *n., f* grades; note 5
notar *v.* to notice
noticias *n., f* news
novela *n., f* novel
noviazgo *n., m* engagement
noviembre *n., m* November 13
novio/a *n.* boy/girlfriend 4
nublado/a *adj.* cloudy 13; **está**
  nublado it's cloudy 13
nudo *n., m* knot
nuera *n., f* daughter-in-law
nuevo/a *adj.* new 6
número *n., m* number 1
nunca *adv.* never 8

O

obedecer (yo obedezco) *v.* to obey
  22
obediente *adj.* obedient
obligación *n., f* duty
obra de arte *n., f* work of art
octubre *n., m* October 13
ocupación *n., f* occupation
ocupado/a *adj.* busy 15
odiar *v.* to hate
oeste *n., m* west 26
oficial de prisión *n., mf* prison
  guard 12
oficina *n., f* office 2
ofrecer (yo ofrezco) *v.* to offer 24
oído *n., m* (inner) ear 20
oír (yo oigo) *v.* to hear 17
ojalá que... *interj.* hopefully 27
ojo *n., m* eye 21
olvidar *v.* to forget
onda *n., f* wave
oportunidad *n., f* opportunity
optimista *adj.* optimistic 3
ordenado/a *adj.* tidy
ordenador *n., m* computer
organizar *v.* to organize

orgullo *n., m* pride
orgulloso/a *adj.* proud
origen *n., m* origin
ostión *n., m* oyster
otoño *n., m* fall 13
otra vez again
otro/a *adj.* another

P

paciencia *n., f* patience
paciente *n., mf* patient 3
padre *n., m* father; priest 4
padres *n., m* parents 4
paella *n., f* Spanish rice dish
pagar *v.* to pay 11
país *n., m* country
pájaro *n., m* bird 4
palabra *n., f* word
pan tostado *n., m* toast 9
pantalones *n., m* pants 13;
  pantalones de mezclilla *n., m*
  jeans; **pantalones cortos** *n., m*
  shorts 13
papa *n., f* potato 9; **papas fritas** *n., f*
  french fries 9
papá *n., m* dad
papás *n., m* parents
papel *n., m* paper; role 2
papelería *n., f* office supply store
par *n., m* pair, couple; even
para *prep.* for
para que *conj.* so that 30
parabrisas *n., m* windshield
paraguas *n., m* umbrella 13
pararse *v.* to stop 26
parcial *adj.* part-time; partial
pardo *adj.* brown
parecer (yo parezco) *v.* to seem; to
  look like
pared *n., f* wall
pareja *n., f* couple
parientes *n., m* relatives
parque (de atracciones) *n., m*
  (amusement) park 8
parte *n., f* part
particular *adj.* private 22
partido *n., m* match, game 8
partir *v.* to cut; to depart
pasado/a *adj.* last (year,...), past 15
pasar *v.* to pass 26
pasar la aspiradora *v.* to vacuum 18
pasarse (el alto/el semáforo en rojo)
  v. to run a red light 26
pasear *v.* to walk, to stroll
paseo *n., m* walk, stroll
pastel *n., m* cake 9
pastilla *n., f* pill 21
pasto *n., m* lawn, grass 18
patata *n., f* potato
paterno/a *adj.* paternal
patinar en línea, en hielo *v.* to skate;
  to rollerblade; to ice skate 18
patio *n., m* patio 18

pavo *n., m* turkey **9**
pedazo *n., m* piece
pedida *n., f* marriage proposal
pedir (e → i) *v.* to ask, to request **9**
pedir cosas prestadas *v.* to borrow things **11**
pedir la mano *v.* to propose (marriage)
pegar *v.* to hit, to glue **25**; **pegarse** *v.* to stick; to hit yourself
peinarse *v.* to comb one's hair
pelar *v.* to peel
pelearse *v.* to fight **22**
película *n., f* film
peligro *n., m* danger
peligroso/a *adj.* dangerous
pelirrojo/a *adj.* red-haired
pelota *n., f* ball
pena *n., f* pity, sorrow
pensar (e → ie) *v.* to think **10**; **pensar + [verb]** *v.* to plan
peor que *adv.* worse than **17**
pequeño/a *adj.* small **6**
pera *n., f* pear **9**
perder (e → ie) *v.* to lose; to miss **17**
perdón *interj.* sorry
perdonar *v.* to forgive; to excuse
perezoso/a *adj.* lazy **6**
perico/a *n.* parakeet
periódico *n., m* newspaper
periodista *n., mf* journalist **12**
perro/a *n.* dog **4**
persona *n., f* person
personaje *n., m* character (movie, book)
personal *n., m* personnel
pesado/a *adj.* heavy
pesar, (a) *conj.* despite
pescado *n., m* fish (food) **9**
pesimista *adj.* pessimistic **3**
peso *n., m* weight, currency
petaca *n., f* suitcase
pez *n., m* fish (live) **4**
pie *n., m* foot **21**
piel *n., f* leather; skin
pierna *n., f* leg **21**
pieza *n., f* bedroom
pijama *n., m, n., f* pajamas **13**
pincharse (una llanta) *v.* to have a flat tire
pintar *v.* to paint
pintarse *v.* to put on makeup **14**
pintor(a) *n.* painter
pintura *n., f* painting
piñata *n., f* container filled with candies **22**
pirámide *n., f* pyramid
piscina *n., f* swimming pool **2**
piso *n., m* apartment
pista *n., f* track, runway
pizarra *n., f* blackboard
pizarrón *n., m* blackboard **2**
placar *n., m* closet
plan *n., m* plan

planchar *v.* to iron **18**
plata *n., f* silver
plátano *n., m* banana **9**
platicar *v.* to chat
platillo *n., m* dish **9**
plato *n., m* dish, plate **9**
playa *n., f* beach **8**
pleito *n., m* fight
pluma *n., f* pen **2**
pobre *adj.* poor **6**
pobrecito/a *n.* poor thing
pobreza *n., f* poverty
poco/a *adj.* a little **5**
poder *n., m* power **10**
poder (o → ue) *v.* to be able to, can **20**
poema *n., m* poem
policía *n., m, n., f* police officer **12**
policía *n., f* the police force **23**
pollera *n., f* skirt
pollo *n., m* chicken **9**
poncharse (una llanta) *v.* to have a flat tire **26**
poner (yo pongo) *v.* to put, to place **11**; **poner el árbol** *v.* to decorate the tree **20**; **poner la mesa** *v.* to set the table **18**; **ponerse (irr. yo)** *v.* to wear, to put on, to become **14**
por *prep.* for, because of; **por cierto** *interj.* by the way; **por favor** please; **por lo menos** at least; **por qué** why **6**; **por supuesto** of course
porque *conj.* because
portarse bien/mal *v.* to behave, misbehave **22**
posada *n., f* shelter; a traditional Mexican pre-Christmas party
posgrado *n., m* graduate school
posible *adj.* possible
pozole *n., m* corn and meat soup
precio *n., m* price
preferir (e → ie) *v.* to prefer **10**
preguntar *v.* to ask (questions)
preocupado/a *adj.* worried **15**
preparatoria *n., f* high school **22**
prestación *n., f* fringe benefits **11**
prestar *v.* to lend **11**
pretexto *n., m* excuse, pretext
primaria *n., f* grammar school **22**
primavera *n., f* spring **13**
primero/a *adj.* first **26**
primeros auxilios *n., m* first aid
primo/a *n.* cousin **4**
principiante *n.* beginner
principio *n., m* beginning, principle
prisa *n., f* hurry
probar *v.* to taste, to try
problema *n., m* problem **11**
profesión *n., f* profession
profesor(a) *n.* professor **1**
programa *n., m* program **28**
programador(a) *n.* computer programmer **12**

promedio *n., m* average
prometer *v.* to promise **24**
propina *n., f* tip
propio *adj.* own, self
proteger *v.* to protect
protestante *n., mf* Protestant
próximo/a *adj.* next, close
prueba *n., f* test **2**
público/a *adj.* public
público *n., m* public
pueblo *n., m* town
puerta *n., f* door **2**
puesto *n., m* position, job **11**
pupitre *n., m* student desk **2**

Q

que *conj. pron.* that **27**
qué *adv. pron.* what **6**
quedar embarazada *v.* to get pregnant **28**
quedarse *v.* to stay, to remain **14**
quehacer *n., m* chore **18**
queja *n., f* complaint
quejarse *v.* to complain
quemados *n., m* dodge ball **22**
querer (e → ie) *v.* to love (a person) **10**; to want **27**
queso *n., m* cheese **9**
quién *n.* who **6**
química *n., f* chemistry **1**
quitarse *v.* to take off (clothes) **14**
quizá *adv.* maybe

R

radiador *n., m* radiator
rallar *v.* to grate
raro/a *adj.* strange
rasurarse *v.* to shave
ratito *n., m* little while
rato *n., m* while (short time)
reaccionar *v.* to react
reata *n., f* rope
rebanada *n., f* slice
rebelde *adj.* rebellious **22**
recámara *n., f* bedroom
receta *n., f* recipe
recibir *v.* to get, to receive **8**
recibirse *v.* to graduate **28**
recoger (g → j) *v.* to pick up **18**
recoger la mesa *v.* to clear the table **18**
recomendar (e → ie) *v.* to recommend **27**
recordar (o → ue) *v.* to remember **10**
recuerdo *n., m* memory
recuperación *n., f* recovery
refresco *n., m* soda **9**
refrigerador *n., m* refrigerator **18**
refrito/a *adj.* fried
regalar *v.* to give a gift **20**

regalo *n., m* gift, present **11**
regañar *v.* to scold, to reprimand **22**
regresar *v.* to come back, to return, to get back
reloj *n., m* watch, clock
remedio *n., m* remedy
reparar *v.* to repair, to mend
repartir *v.* to deliver
requisito *n., m* requirement
reservado/a *adj.* reserved **3**
resfriado *n., m* cold
residencia *n., f* residence
residencia estudiantil *n., f* dormitory **2**
resolver (o→ue) *v.* to solve **28**
respetuoso/a *adj.* respectful
respirar *v.* to breathe
responsable *adj.* responsible **3**
restaurante *n., m* restaurant **8**
revisar *v.* to check
revista *n., f* magazine
revuelto/a *adj.* scrambled
Reyes Magos *n., m* the Magi (of Catholic tradition)
rico/a *adj.* rich; tasty **6**
risa *n., f* laughter
rojo/a *adj.* red **13**
romántico/a *adj.* romantic **3**
rompecabezas *n., m* jigsaw puzzle **22**
romper *v.* to break **22**; **romperse** to break (a hand, an arm) **21**
ropa *n., f* clothes **5**
ropero *n., m* closet
rubio/a *adj.* blond(e) **6**
ruido *n., m* noise
ruta *n., f* route
rutina *n., f* routine

S

sábado *n., m* Saturday **5**
saber (yo sé) *v.* to know **11**
sacar *v.* to take (out) **18**; **sacar buenas notas** to get good grades **5**; **sacar al perro a pasear** to take out (walk) the dog **18**
saco *n., m* jacket
sala *n., f* living room **18**; classroom
salida *n., f* exit
salir (yo salgo) *v.* to go out, to date **8**
salirse (en) *v.* to get off (at) **26**
salón *n., m* classroom **2**; living room; **salón de belleza** *n., m* beauty salon
saltar *v.* to jump **22**
salud *n., f* health **21**
saludable *adj.* healthy
salvar *v.* to save (a life)
sandalias *n., f* sandals **13**
sándwich *n., m* sandwich **9**
sano/a *adj.* healthy

seco/a *adj.* dry
secundaria, (escuela) *n., f* high school **22**
sed *n., f* thirst; **tener sed** to be thirsty **9**
seguir (e→i) *v.* to continue, to follow **26**
según *prep.* according to
segundo *n., m* second **26**
segundo/a *adj.* second (2nd)

seguridad *n., f* safety
seguro *n., m* insurance, safe **26**
selva *n., f* jungle
semáforo *n., m* street light **25**
semana *n., f* week **15**
sentarse (e→ie) *v.* to sit
sentido contrario *n.* wrong way
sentimental *adj.* sentimental **3**
sentimiento *n., m* feeling
sentir (e→ie) *v.* to feel (sorry); **sentirse** *v.* to feel **21**
señor(a) *n.* mister, missus **1**
señorita *n., f* miss **1**
separarse *v.* to separate **28**
septiembre *n., m* September **13**
ser (irr.) *v.* to be **4**
serio/a *adj.* serious **3**
servir (e→i) *v.* to serve **9**
sicología *n., f* psychology **1**
sicólogo/a *n.* psychologist **12**
siempre *adv.* always **8**
siguiente *adj.* next, following
silla *n., f* chair **18**
sillón *n., m* armchair **18**
similar *adj.* similar **6**
simpático/a *adj.* funny
sin *prep.* without **26**
sin embargo *conj.* nevertheless
sino *conj.* but
sistema *n., m* system **12**
sobrino/a *n.* nephew, niece **4**
sociable *adj.* sociable **3**
sofá *n., m* sofa **18**
sol *n., m* sun; **hace sol** it's sunny **13**
solamente *adv.* only
solicitar empleo *v.* to request, to apply for a job **28**
solicitud *n., f* application **28**
sólo *adv.* only
solo/a *adj.* alone
soltero/a *adj.* single (unmarried) **6**
sombrero *n., m* hat **13**
sonar (o→ue) *v.* to ring (bells); to sound
sopa *n., f* soup **9**
subirse a los árboles *v.* to climb trees **22**; **subirse a los columpios** to go on the swings **22**; **subirse a los juego** to go on rides **20**
sucio/a *adj.* dirty **18**
sudor *n., m* sweat
suegro/a *n.* father/mother-in-law **4**
sueldo *n., m* salary, wage **11**
suelo *n., m* floor **18**

sueño *n., m* dream
suerte *n., f* luck
suéter *n., m* sweater **13**
suficiente *adj.* enough, sufficient
sugerir (e→ie) *v.* to suggest
superarse *v.* to better oneself
superficie *n., f* surface
supermercado *n., m* market **8**
suponer (yo supongo) *v.* to suppose
sur *n., m* south **26**
surfear *v.* to surf
susto *n., m* scare, fright

T

tacón *n., m* heel
tal vez *adv.* maybe, perhaps
tamaño *n., m* size
también *adv.* also **18**
tambor *n., m* drum
tampoco *adv.* neither **18**
tan *adj.* as; **tan [adjective] como** as [adjective] as **17**
tanque *n., m* tank
tanto *adv.* so much; **tanto/a [noun] como** as [noun] as **17**
tapas *n., f* snacks
tardar(se) *v.* to take long
tarde *adv.* late **5**
tarde *n., f* afternoon
tarea *n., f* homework
tarjeta *n., f* (credit) card
té *n., m* tea **9**
teatro *n., m* theater
técnico/a en computación *n.* computer technician **12**
telaraña *n., f* cobweb
televisión *n., f* TV **2**
televisor *n., m* TV
teléfono *n., m* telephone **5**
tema *n., m* theme
temprano *adv.* early **5**
tenedor *n., m* fork
tener (yo tengo, e→ie) *v.* to have **4**; **tener calor** to be hot; **tener dolor de...** to have a(n) ...ache **21**; **tener frío** to be cold; **tener ganas de** to feel like **7**; **tener hambre** to be hungry **9**; **tener miedo** to be afraid; **tener prisa** to be in a hurry; **tener que** to have to **20**; **tener razón** to be right; **tener sed** to be thirsty **9**; **tener sueño** to be sleepy; **tener suerte** to be lucky
tenis *n., m* tennis (sport) **2**; tennis sneakers **13**
terapeuta *n., mf* therapist
tercero/a *adj.* third
terminar *v.* to finish, to end **28**
terremoto *n., m* earthquake
terrible *adj.* terrible **3**
tiempo *n., m* time, weather; occasion **13**; **tiempo, (a)**; on time **5**; **tiempo, (hace buen/mal)** the

weather is nice/bad 13; **tiempo completo/parcial** full-time, part-time 11; **tiempo libre** spare time 11

tienda *n., f* store 8; **tienda de campaña** *n., f* tent

tierra *n., f* earth, soil

tímido/a *adj.* shy 3

tina *n., f* bathtub 18

tío/a *n.* uncle, aunt 4

tipo *n., m* type, kind

tira cómica *n., f* comic strip

tirar *v.* to throw; to pull

título *n., m* degree, title

toalla *n., f* towel 18

tocar *v.* to play (instrument); to touch 5

tocino *n., m* bacon

todavía *adv.* already, yet 28

todo/a *adj.* all, everything; **todos los días** every day 5

tomar *v.* to take, to drink 5

tomate *n., m* tomato 9

tonto/a *adj.* dumb, silly 6

tortilla *n., f* tortilla

tos *n., f* cough 21

trabajador(a) *adj.* hard-working 6

trabajar *v.* to work 5

trabajo *n., m* work, job 8

traductor(a) *n.* translator

traer (yo traigo) *v.* to bring, to take 20

tráfico *n., m* traffic

traje *n., m* suit 13

traje de baño *n., m* swimming suit 13

tranquilo/a *adj.* calm, quiet 3

tranvía *n., m* trolley

trapear *v.* to mop

trapo *n., m* cloth

trastes *n., m* dishes

travesura *n., f* mischief 22

través, (a) *prep.* through

travieso/a *adj.* mischievous 22

tren *n., m* train

triste *adj.* sad 15

turno *n., m* shift, turn 11

U

últimamente *adv.* lately 28

último/a *adj.* last

único/a *adj.* unique, only

universidad *n., f* university

usar *v.* to use 5; to wear 13

útil *adj.* useful

uva *n., f* grape 9

V

vacaciones *n., f* vacation 11

vacaciones, (de) on vacation 13

vacunar *v.* to vaccinate

vajilla *n., f* dishes

valija *n., f* suitcase

vaqueros *n., m* jeans

varios/as *adj.* several

vaso *n., m* glass

veces, (a) *adv.* sometimes 8

vecino/a *adj.* neighbor 23

veliz *n., m* suitcase

velocidad *n., f* speed

veloz *adv.* quick

vencido/a *adj.* expired, defeated

vendedor(a) *n.* salesperson

vender *v.* to sell 8

venir (yo vengo, e ➤ ie) *v.* to come 20

ventaja *n., f* advantage 11

ventana *n., f* window 2

ver (yo veo) *v.* to see, to watch 8

verano *n., m* summer 13

verdad *n., f* truth

verde *adj.* green 13

verdura *n., f* vegetable

vergüenza *n., f* shame, embarrassment

verificar *v.* to verify

vestido *n., m* dress 13

vestirse (e ➤ i) *v.* to get dressed

veterinario *n., mf* veterinarian 12

vez *n., m* time

viajar *v.* to travel

viaje *n., m* trip 18

vida *n., f* life

videocasetera *n., f* VCR 2

vidrio *n., m* glass (crystal)

viejo/a *adj.* old 6

viento *n., m* wind; **hace viento** it's windy 13

viernes *n., m* Friday 5

villancicos *n., m* carols 20

vino *n., m* wine 9

violín *n., m* violin

virar *v.* to turn

visitar *v.* to visit 5

vivir *v.* to live 8

volante *n., m* steering wheel

vóleibol *n., m* volleyball 2

volver (o ➤ ue) *v.* to return; to come back 28; **volverse** to become

vuelo *n., m* flight

vuelta *n., f* turn 25

Y

y *conj.* and

ya *adv.* already, still 28

yate *n., m* yacht

yerno *n., m* son-in-law

yo *pron.* I

yogur *n., m* yogurt 9

yuca *n., f* yucca

Z

zanahoria *n., f* carrot 9

zapato *n., m* shoe 13

zoológico *n., m* zoo

English-Spanish

A

able *adj.* capaz; **to be able** poder
　　(o→ue)
aboard *adv.* a bordo
above *adv.* arriba
abroad *adv.* en el extranjero
according (to) *prep.* según
account *n., f* cuenta
accountant *n.* contador(a) 12
across from *prep.* enfrente 26
active *adj.* activo/a 3
actor *n., m* actor
actress *n., f* actriz
advertisment *n., m* anuncio
address *n., f* dirección
adult *n., m* adulto
advantage *n., f* ventaja 11
advice *n., m* consejo 11
advise *v.* aconsejar 27
advisor *n.* consejero/a 2
affectionate *adj.* cariñoso/a 6
after *prep.* después
afternoon *n., f* tarde
again *adv.* otra vez
against *prep.* contra
age *n., f* edad
agent *n., mf* agente 12
agree *v.* aceptar, estar de acuerdo
agreement *n., m* acuerdo
AIDS *n., m* SIDA
air *n., m* aire
airplane *n., m* avión 20
airport *n., m* aeropuerto 8
all *adj.* todo/a
all-boys/girls school *n., f* escuela de
　　niños/as 22
allow *v.* dejar, permitir 11
almost *adv.* casi 8
alone *adj.* solo/a
already *adv.* ya 28
also *adv.* también 18
although *conj.* aunque
always *adv.* siempre 8
a.m. de la mañana
ambitious *adj.* ambicioso/a 3
ambulance *n., f* ambulancia
amusement park *n., m* parque de
　　atracciones 8
analyst *n., mf* analista 12
antiquity *n., f* antigüedad
angel *n., m* ángel
another *n.* otro/a
answer *v.* contestar
anthropology *n., f* antropología 1
antibiotic *n., m* antibiótico 21
anybody *n.* alguien
apartment *n., m* apartamento 18
apologize *v.* disculparse
apple *n., f* manzana 9
application *n., f* solicitud 28
apply for a job *v.* solicitar empleo 28

April *n., m* abril 13
aquatic *adj.* acuático/a
architect *n.* arquitecto/a 13
architecture *n., f* arquitectura
argue *v.* discutir 8
arm *n., m* brazo 21
armchair *n., m* sillón 21
around *prep.* alrededor
arrest *v.* arrestar
arrival *n., f* llegada
arrive *v.* llegar 5
arrogant *adj.* arrogante 3
art exhibition *n., f* exhibición de
　　arte 8
artist *n., mf* artista 12
as soon as *adv.* en cuanto 30
as [adjective] as *adv.* tan [adjective]
　　como 17
as [noun] as *adv.* tanto/a [noun]
　　como 17
ask (questions) *v.* preguntar; **ask
　　(to request)** pedir (e→i) 9
aspirin *n., f* aspirina 21
assemble (a puzzle) *v.* armar (un
　　rompecabezas) 22
astronomy *n., f* astronomía 1
attend *v.* asistir
attractive *adj.* atractivo/a 3
auditorium *n., m* auditorio 2
August *n., m* agosto 13
aunt *n., f* tía 4
avenue *n., f* avenida 26
average *n., m* promedio
avocado *n., m* aguacate

B

baby *n., mf* bebé
baby-sitter *n.* niñero/a 11
bachelor's *n., f* licenciatura
back *n., f* espalda 21
backpack *n., f* mochila 2
backyard *n., m* jardín 18
bacon *n., m* tocino
bad *adj.* malo/a, mal 6
bag *n., f* bolsa
baked *adj.* al horno
balcony *n., m* balcón
ball *n., f* pelota 22
banana *n., m* plátano, *f* banana, *m*
　　guineo 9
bank *n., m* banco
bar *n., m* bar
barbecue *n., m* asador 18
baseball *n., m* béisbol
bathtub *n., f,* bañera, tina 18
bathe *v.* bañarse 14
bathroom *n., m* baño 2
bathroom sink *n., m* lavabo 18
be *v.* estar (yo estoy) 15; **be** ser
　　(irr.) 4; **be able to** poder
　　(o→ue) 20; **be afraid** tener
　　miedo; **be at/in/on** estar en; **be
　　cold (person)** tener frío; **be cold**

(thing) estar frío/a; **be cold
　　(place)** hacer frío 13; **be happy
　　for** alegrarse; **be hot (person)**
　　tener calor; **be hot (thing)** estar
　　caliente; **be hot (place)** hacer
　　calor 13; **be hungry** tener hambre
　　9; **be in a hurry** tener prisa; **be
　　interested** interesar 19; **be lucky**
　　tener suerte; **be ready** estar listo
　　15; **be right** tener razón; **be
　　sleepy** tener sueño; **be sure** estar
　　seguro; **be thirsty** tener sed 9
beach *n., f* playa 8
beans *n., m* frijoles 9
beautiful *adj.* bello/a
beauty salon *n., m* salón de belleza
because *conj.* porque
become *v.* ponerse (yo me pongo)
　　20
bed *n., f* cama 15
bedroom *n., f* cuarto 18
beef *n., f* carne de res 9
beer *n., f* cerveza 9
before *prep.* antes (de) que 30
begin *v.* empezar (e→ie),
　　comenzar (e→ie) 10
beginner *n., mf* principiante
behave *v.* portarse bien 22; **behave
　　oneself** comportarse
behavior *n., m* comportamiento
behind *prep.* atrás 25
believe *v.* creer 17
belt *n., m* cinturón 26
benefits *n., f* prestaciones 11
bet *v.* apostar (o→ue)
better than *adj.* mejor que 17
better (oneself) *v.* mejorar,
　　superarse
beverage *n., f* bebida 8
big *adj.* grande 6
bikini *n., m* bikini 13
bill *n., f* cuenta 9
biology *n., f* biología 1
bird *n., m* pájaro 4
birthday *n., m* cumpleaños; **birthday
　　song** *n. f* mañanitas 20
black *adj.* negro/a 13
blackboard *n., m* pizarrón, *f* pizarra
　　2
blame *v.* culpar
blond(e) *adj.* rubio/a 6
blouse *n., f* blusa 13
blue *adj.* azul 13
body *n., m* cuerpo 21
book *n., m* libro 2
bookstore *n., f* librería 2
bored *adj.* aburrido/a 15
boring *adj.* aburrido/a 6
borrow things *v.* pedir cosas
　　prestadas 11
boss *n.* jefe/a
bossy *adj.* mandón, mandona
botany *n., f* botánica
bother *v.* molestar 19
bowling *n., m* boliche 8

boy *n., m* niño 4
boyfriend *n., m* novio 4
brake *n., m* freno; *v.* frenar
break *v.* romper; **break (a hand, an arm)** romperse (la mano, el brazo) 21; **break down** descomponerse
breakfast *n., m* desayuno 9
bring *v.* traer (yo traigo) 20
broccoli *n., m* brócoli 9
brother *n., m* hermano 4
brother-in-law *n., m* cuñado 4
brown *adj.* café (color) 13
brunet(te) *adj.* castaño/a
brush (oneself) *v.* cepillarse; **brush one's teeth** lavarse los dientes 14
building *n., m* edificio 2
bus *n., m* autobús 5
business *n., m* negocio, *f* empresa 12
business administrador *n.* administrador(a) de empresas 12
busy *adj.* ocupado/a 15
but *conj.* pero
butter *n., f* mantequilla
buy *v.* comprar 5

C

cafeteria *n., f* cafetería 2
cake *n., m* pastel 9
calculator *n., f* calculadora 2
call *v.* llamar 11
calorie *n., f* caloría
camp *v.* acampar; *n., m* campamento
can *v.* poder (o→ue) 22
candy *n., m* dulce 9
capable *adj.* capaz
car *n., m* coche 5
car accident (crash) *n., m* choque 26
cards *n., f* cartas
care *n., m* cuidado
carols *n., m* villancicos 20
carpet *n., f* alfombra 18
cartoon *n., m* dibujo animado 22
case *n., m* caso
cash register *n., f* caja
casual *adj.* informal 20
cat *n.* gato/a 4
Catholic *adj.* católico/a 22
caution *n., m* cuidado
cave *n., f* cueva
celebrate *v.* celebrar 28
cent *n., m* centavo
cereal *n., m* cereal 9
chair *n., f* silla 18
chance, (by) *n., f* por/de casualidad
change *v.* cambiar 28
character (in book) *n., m* personaje; **character (personality)** *n., m* carácter

charge *v.* cobrar
chat *v.* platicar
cheap *adj.* barato/a
check (personal) *n., m* cheque; **check (bill)** *n., f* cuenta; **check** *v.* revisar
checkers *n., f* damas chinas 22
cheese *n., m* queso 9
chemistry *n., f* química 1
chicken *n., m* pollo 9
child *n.* niño/a 4
childhood *n., f* niñez
chocolate *n., m* chocolate
choir *n., m* coro
chore *n., m* quehacer 18
chose *v.* escoger
Christmas *n., f* Navidad
church *n., f* iglesia 8
citizen *n.* ciudadano/a
citizenship *n., f* ciudadanía
city *n., f* ciudad; **city block** *n., f* cuadra, *f* manzana 26
class clase *n., f* 2
classroom *n., m* salón de clase, *f* sala 2
clean *v.* limpiar; *adj.* limpio/a 5
clear the table *v.* recoger la mesa 18
climb trees *v.* subirse a los árboles 22
close *adj.* cerca
close *v.* cerrar (e→ie)
closet *n., m* clóset 18
clothes *n., f, sing.* ropa 5
cloudy, (it's) *adj.* (está) nublado 13
coat *n., m* abrigo 13
cookie *n., f* galleta 9
coffee *n., m* café 5
cold catarro *n., m*, resfriado 21; **it's cold** *adj.* hace frío 13
color *n., m* color; *v.* colorear 13
comb one's hair *v.* peinarse
come *v.* venir (yo vengo, e→ie) 20; **come back** regresar, volver (o→ue) 28
comfortable *adj.* cómodo/a 20
comic strip *n., f* tira cómica
common *adj.* común
company *n., f* compañía
competent *adj.* competente 3
complain *v.* quejarse
complaint *n., f* queja
complete *adj.* completo/a
compliment *n., m* cumplido
computer *n., f* computadora 5; **computer engineer** *n.* ingeniero/a en computación 12; **computer programmer** *n.* programador(a) 12; **computer technician** *n.* técnico/a en computación 12
concussion *n., f* conmoción
confuse *v.* confundir
consumer *n., m* consumidor
continue *v.* seguir (e→i)
conversation *n., f* conversación
cook *v.* cocinar

cool *adj.* fresco/a 13; **it's cool** hace fresco 13
corner *n., f* esquina 26
cost *v.* costar (o→ue)
cough *n., f* tos 21
cough syrup *n., m* jarabe para la tos 21
count *v.* contar (o→ue)
country *n., m* país
couple *n., f* pareja
court (sports) *n., f* cancha 2
cousin *n.* primo/a 4
cover *v.* cubrir
crash *v.* chocar
crazy *adj.* loco/a
cream *n., f* crema
create *v.* crear
creative *adj.* creativo/a 3
credit card *n., f* tarjeta
cross *v.* cruzar 26
cry *v.* llorar
cry baby *n.* llorón, llorona 22
cure *v.* curar
curios *n., f* curiosidades
custard *n., m* flan
cut *v.* cortar, partir (un pastel) 18; **cut (oneself)** cortarse

D

dad *n., m* papá
daily *adj.* diario/a
dance *v.* bailar 5
dangerous *adj.* peligroso/a
dark-skinned *adj.* moreno/a 6
date *v.* salir (con) (yo salgo); **date (appointment)** *n., f* cita 8; **date (calendar)** *n., f* fecha
daughter-in-law *n., f* nuera
day *n., m* día
December *n., m* diciembre 13
decorate the tree *v.* poner el árbol 20
dedicate *v.* dedicar
defend *v.* defender (e→ie)
defense *n., f* defensa
degree *n., m* título
degree (temperature) *n., m* grado
delighted *adj.* encantado/a 1
demand *v.* exigir (g→j)
demanding *adj.* exigente
demon *n., m* demonio
denim *n., f* mezclilla
dental hygienist *n., mf* higienista 12
depart *v.* salir (yo salgo)
design *v.* diseñar
designer *n.* diseñador(a) 12
desk *n., m* escritorio 2
detail *n., m* detalle
dictionary *n., m* diccionario 2
die *v.* morir (o→ue) 28
diet *n., f* dieta
different *adj.* diferente 6
dine *v.* cenar 9

dining room *n., m* comedor 18
dinner *n., f* cena 9
dirty *adj.* sucio/a 18
disadvantage *n., f* desventaja 11
disappointed *adj.* desilusionado/a 15
disaster *n., m* desastre
disco *n., f* discoteca 8
discover *v.* descubrir
discovery *n., m* descubrimiento
discrete *adj.* discreto/a 3
dish *n., m* plato, platillo 9
dishonest *adj.* deshonesto/a 3
dislike *v.* chocar 19
disobey *v.* desobedecer (yo desobedezco) 22
divorce *v.* divorciarse 28
dizzy *adj.* mareado/a 21
do *v.* hacer (yo hago) 8; **do the dishes** lavar los platos 18
doctor *n.* doctor(a), médico/a 1; **doctor's degree** *n., m* doctorado 28; **doctor's office** *n., m* consultorio
dodge ball *n., m* quemados 22
dog *n.* perro/a 4
doll *n.* muñeco/a 22
dollar *n., m* dólar
donut *n., f* dona 9
door *n., f* puerta 2
dormitory *n., f* residencia estudiantil 2
doubt *v.* dudar
downtown *n., m* centro
drama *n., m* drama 1
draw *v.* dibujar 22
drawing *n., m* dibujo
dream *n., m* sueño
dress *n., m* vestido 13
dresser *n., f* cómoda 18
drink *v.* beber, tomar 8
drive *v.* manejar 26, conducir (yo conduzco)
driver *n.* conductor(a) 26
driver's license *n., f* licencia de manejar 26, *n., m* carnet de conducir
drunk *adj.* borracho/a
dry *adj.* seco/a
dumb *adj.* tonto/a 6
during *adv.* durante
duty *n., f* obligación

E

each *adj.* cada
ear (inner) *n., m* oído 20
early *adv.* temprano 5
earn *v.* ganarse
easy *adj.* fácil 6
eat *v.* comer 8
economics *n., f* economía 1
educator *n.* educador(a) 12
egg *n., m* huevo 9

e-mail *n., m* correo electrónico
embarrassment *n., f* vergüenza
employee *n.* empleado/a 11
end *v.* terminar 28
engagement *n., m* compromiso, noviazgo 27
engineer *n.* ingeniero/a 12
English *n., m* inglés 1; **English** *adj.* inglés, inglesa
enter *v.* entrar 28
enjoy *v.* disfrutar
essential *adj.* esencial
evening *n., f* noche 11
ever *adv.* alguna vez 28
every day *n.* todos los días 5
everything *n.* todo
exam *n., m* examen
excellent *adj.* excelente 3
excess *n., m* exceso
excited *adj.* emocionado/a 15
executive *adj.* ejecutivo/a
exercise *v.* hacer ejercicio 8
exercise *n., m* ejercicio
expect *v.* esperar 27
expensive *adj.* caro/a
expired *adj.* vencido/a
explain *v.* explicar
expressway *n., f* autopista 26
extroverted *adj.* extrovertido/a 3
eye *n., m* ojo 21

F

fascinate *v.* fascinar 19
fall (season) *n., m* otoño 13
fall *v.* caerse; **fall asleep** dormirse (o→ue); **fall in love** enamorarse 28
family *n., f* familia
fan *n.* aficionado/a
far *adv.* lejos
fat *adj.* gordo/a 6
fat (in food) *n., f* grasa
father *n., m* padre 4
father-in-law *n., m* suegro 4
fault *n., f* culpa 25
February *n., m* febrero 13
feed *v.* dar de comer 18
feel *v.* sentir(se) (e→ie) 21; **feel like** tener ganas de
fence *n., f* barda, cerca
fever *n., f* fiebre 21
few *adj.* poco/a
fiber *n., f* fibra
fight *v.* pelear 22
fill *v.* llenar 28
film *n., f* película 8
final *adj.* final
find *v.* encontrar (o→ue) 10
fine *adv.* bien 1
fine (high quality) *adj.* fino/a
finish *v.* terminar 28
fire (from work) *v.* despedir (e→i)
fireplace *n., f* chimenea

firefighter *n., m* bombero 12
first *adj.* primero/a 26
first aid *n., m* primeros auxilios
fish (live) pez *n., m* 4; **fish (food)** pescado 9
fix *v.* arreglar, componer
fixed schedule *n., m* horario fijo 11
flag *n., f* bandera 2
flat *adj.* desinflada/o
flexible *adj.* flexible 3
flexible schedule *n., m* horario flexible 11
flight *n., m* vuelo
floor *n., m* suelo 18
flu *n., f* gripe
follow *v.* seguir (e→i), continuar 26
food *n., f* comida 5
foot *n., m* pie 21
forehead *n., f* frente
foreign *adj.* extranjero/a
foreigner *n.* extranjero/a
forget *v.* olvidar
forgive *v.* perdonar
fork *n., m* tenedor
formal *adj.* formal 20
fracture *n., f* fractura
free *adj.* libre 15; **free (of charge)** gratis
freeway *n., f* autopista 26
freight *n., f* carga
French *n., m* francés; **French** *adj.* francés, francesa
french fries *n., f* papas fritas 9
frequently *adv.* con frecuencia
Friday *n., m* viernes 5
fried *adj.* frito/a
friend *adj.* amigo/a 4
friendship *n., f* amistad
front *prep.* frente a
fruit *n., f* fruta 9
full *adj.* lleno/a
full-time tiempo completo 11
fun *adj.* divertido/a 6
funny *adj.* gracioso/a 6
furnish *v.* amueblar
furniture *n., m* muebles 18

G

gain weight *v.* engordar
gamble *v.* apostar (o→ue)
game *n., m* juego
game (match) *n., m* partido 8
garage *n., m* garaje 18
garden *n., m* jardín 18
garlic *n., m* ajo
gas *n., f* gasolina 26
gas station *n., f* gasolinera
generous *adj.* generoso/a 3
geography *n., f* geografía 1
get (obtain) *v.* recibir 18; **get along** llevarse bien/mal 22; **get divorced** divorciarse 28; **get**

dressed vestirse (e➤i); **get good grades** sacar buenas notas 5; **get hurt** lastimarse 21; **get into trouble** hacer travesuras 22; **get involved** meterse; **get married** casarse 27; **get off (at)** salirse (en) 26; **get off (leave) early/late** salir temprano/tarde 11; **get pregnant** quedar embarazada 28; **get sick** enfermarse 21; **get together** juntarse 14; **get up** levantarse 14; **get up early** madrugar; **get upset** enojarse
gift *n., m* regalo 11
girl *n., f* niña 4
girlfriend *n., f* novia 4
give *v.* dar (yo doy) 11
glass *n., m* vaso
gloves *n., m* guantes 13
go *v.* ir (irr.) 20; **go for a walk** dar un paseo 18; **go on rides** subirse a los juegos 20; **go on the swings** subirse a los columpios 22; **go on vacation** ir de vacaciones 14; **go out** salir (yo salgo) 8; **go to bed** acostarse (o➤ue) 14
goal *n., f* meta
good *adj.* bueno/a, buen 6; **good afternoon** buenas tardes 1; **good evening (night)** buenas noches 1; **good morning** buenos días 1
good-bye *interj.* adiós 1
government *n., m* gobierno 28
grade (temperature) *n., m* grado
grades *n., f* calificación, nota
graduate *v.* recibirse, graduarse 28
graduate school *n., m* posgrado
graduation *n., f* graduación 28
grammar school *n., f* primaria 22
grandfather *n., m* abuelo 4
granddaughter *n., f* nieta 4
grandmother *n., f* abuela 4
grandparents *n., m* abuelos 4
grandson *n., m* nieto 4
grape *n., f* uva 9
graphic designer *n.* diseñador(a) gráfico/a 12
gray *adj.* gris 13
green *adj.* verde 13
green beans *n., m* ejotes
grind *v.* moler (o➤ue)
grow (up) *v.* crecer (yo crezco)
guava *n., f* guayaba
guest *adj.* invitado/a
guide book *n., f* guía
guitar *n., f* guitarra 5
gym *n., m* gimnasio 2

H

habits *n., m* hábito
half *adj.* medio/a
ham *n., m* jamón 9
hamburger *n., f* hamburguesa 9

hand *n., f* mano 14
hand-made crafts *n., f* artesanía
handsome *adj.* guapo/a 6
hang *v.* colgar (o➤ue)
happiness *n., f* felicidad
happy *adj.* contento/a, feliz 15
hard (difficult) *adj.* difícil 6
hard-working *adj.* trabajador(a) 6
hat *n., m* sombrero 13
hate *v.* odiar
have *v.* tener (yo tengo, e➤ie) 4; **have a(n) ...ache** tener dolor de... 21; **have a picnic** hacer un picnic 18; **have a flat tire** poncharse una llanta 26, pincharse; **have breakfast** desayunar 9; **have fun** divertirse (e➤ie) 14; **have just** acabar de 21; **have lunch** comer 9; almorzar (o➤ue) 10; **have to** tener que 20
head *n., f* cabeza 21
health *n., f* salud 21
health center *n., f* enfermería 2
healthy *adj.* sano/a, saludable
hear *v.* oír (yo oigo) 17
heat *n., m* calor 13
heavy *adj.* pesado/a
heel *n., m* tacón
hello *interj.* hola 1
help *v.* ayudar 11
hi *interj.* hola 1
hide-and-seek *n., f* escondidillas, al escondite 22
hiding place *n., m* escondite
high *adj.* alto/a 11
high school *n., f* escuela secundaria, preparatoria 22
highway *n., f* carretera 26
hike *v.* ir de excursión 18
history *n., f* historia 1
hit *n.,m* golpe 25
hit *v.* pegar 25; **hit (oneself)** pegarse
homemade *adj.* casero/a
homework *n., f* tarea
honest *adj.* honesto/a 3
hope *v.* desear, esperar 27
hopefully *interj.* ojalá que... 27
horn *n., m* claxon
horrible *adj.* horrible
horse *n., m* caballo 18
host(ess) *n.* anfitrión, anfitriona
hot *adj.* caliente **it's hot** *adj.* hace calor 13
hour *n., f* hora
house *n., f* casa 8
housewife *n., f* (el) ama de casa 11
how *adv.* cómo 6
how much (many) *adv.* cuánto/a(s) 6
hug *n., m* abrazo
humid *adj.* húmedo/a
hunger *n., m* hambre
hurry *n., f* prisa
hurt *v.* doler (o➤ue)
husband *n., m* esposo 4

I

idealist *n., mf* idealista 3
ice *n., m* hielo
ice cream *n., m* helado 9
imaginative *adj.* imaginativo/a
impatient *adj.* impaciente 3
impolite *adj.* grosero/a 6
important *adj.* importante 27
in *prep.* en, dentro de; **in fact** de hecho; **in front of** enfrente de 26
incredible *adj.* increíble
indiscreet *adj.* indiscreto/a
inexpensive *adj.* barato/a
infection *n., f* infección 21
information *n., f* información 5
injection *n., f* inyección
inside *adv.* (a)dentro 15
instead of *prep.* en vez de
instructions *n., f* direcciones, instrucciones
insurance *n., m* seguro 26
intelligent *adj.* inteligente
interesting *adj.* interesante 3
intersection *n., f* intersección 26, bocacalle, *m* cruce
interview *n., f* entrevista 28
investigador *n.* investigador(a) 12
invite *v.* invitar 10
iron *v.* planchar 18
irresponsible *adj.* irresponsable 3
irritating *adj.* antipático/a 6
issue *n., m* asunto

J

jacket *n., m* chaqueta, *n., m* saco 13
jacks (to play) *n., f* matatena
jam *n., f* mermelada
January *n., m* enero 13
jealous *adj.* celoso/a
jealousy *n., m* celos
jeans *n., m* jeans 13, pantalones de mezclilla
jewelry store *n., f* joyería 27
Jewish *adj.* judío/a
jigsaw puzzle *n., m* rompecabezas 22
job *n., m* trabajo 8
jog *v.* correr 8
joke *n., m* chiste
journalist *n., mf* periodista 12
juice *n., m* jugo 9
July *n., m* julio 13
jump *v.* brincar, saltar 22
June *n., m* junio 13
just (barely) *adv.* apenas

K

kind *adj.* atento/a
kiss *v.* besar; *n., m* beso 20
kitchen *n., f* cocina 18

kitchen sink *n., m* fregadero **18**
knife *n., m* cuchillo
know (a person, a place) *v.* conocer **12**; **know (about, how)** saber (yo sé) **12**
knowledge *n., m* conocimiento

L

lake *n., m* lago
lamp *n., f* lámpara **18**
lane *n., m* carril
language *n., m* idioma **12**
large *adj.* grande **6**
last *adj.* último/a
last (year,...) *adj.* (año,...) pasado/a **15**
last name *n., m* apellido
last night *adv.* anoche **15**
late *adv.* tarde **5**
lately *adv.* últimamente **28**
later *adv.* después, luego
law (academic field) *n., m* derecho
law *n., f* ley
lawn *n., m* pasto **18**
lawyer *n.* abogado/a **12**
lazy *adj.* perezoso/a, flojo/a **6**
learn *v.* aprender **19**
leave *v.* irse (irr.)**14**
left *n., f* izquierda **23**
leg *n., f* pierna **21**
lemonade *n., f* limonada **9**
lend *v.* prestar **11**
less... than *adv.* menos... que **17**
lesson *n., f* lección
letter *n., f* carta
lettuce *n., f* lechuga **9**
level *n., m* nivel
library *n., f* biblioteca **2**
license *n., f* licencia **26**
lie *n., f* mentira **24**
life *n., f* vida
lift weights *v.* levantar pesas **18**
light *n., f* ligero/a, luz **13**
like *v.* gustar **19**
likewise *adv.* igualmente **1**
limit *n., m* límite
liquids *n., m* líquidos **21**
listen *v.* escuchar **5**
literature *n., f* literatura **1**
little, (a) *adj.* (un) poco **5**
live *v.* vivir **8**
living room *n., f* sala **18**
lobster *n., f* langosta **9**
lodging *n., m* alojamiento
long *adj.* largo/a
look *v.* mirar, ver (yo veo)
look for *v.* buscar **5**
lose *v.* perder (e➜ie) **17**
lot, (a) *adj.* mucho **5**
love (a person) *v.* querer **10**; **love (something)** *v.* encantar **19**
lover *n., mf* amante
luck *n., f* suerte
lunch *n., m* almuerzo **9**
luxury *n., m* lujo

M

machine *n., f* máquina
mad *adj.* enojado/a **15**
magazine *n., f* revista
Magi *n., m* Reyes Magos
mail box *n., m* buzón
major (field of study) *n., f* carrera
majority *n., f* mayoría
make *v.* hacer (yo hago) **8**; **make a decision** tomar una decisión
makeup *n., m* maquillaje
mall *n., m* centro comercial **8**
man *n., m* hombre
management *n., f* administración
manager *n., mf* gerente **12**
many *adj.* muchos/as
map *n., m* mapa **2**
marbles *n., f* canicas
March *n., m* marzo **13**
market *n., m* supermercado **8**
marketing *n., f* mercadotécnia, *n., m* mercadeo **12**
marriage *n., m* matrimonio
married *adj.* casado/a **6**
marry *v.* casarse
mass *n., f* misa
Master's degree *n., f* maestría **28**
mate *n.* compañero/a **2**
materialistic *adj.* materialista **3**
maternal *adj.* materno/a
math *n., f* matemáticas **1**
mature *adj.* maduro/a **3**
May *n., m* mayo **13**
maybe *adv.* tal vez
meat *n., f* carne **9**
mechanic *adj* mecánico/a
mechanics *n., f* mecánica
memory *n., m* recuerdo
menu *n., m* menú
messy *adj.* desarreglado/a **18**
microwave (oven) *n., m* microondas **18**
middle school *n., f* secundaria **22**
mile *n., f* milla
milk *n., f* leche **9**
mini-skirt *n., f* minifalda **13**
mirror *n., m* espejo **18**
misbehave *v.* portarse mal **22**
mischief *n., f* travesura **22**
mischievous *adj.* travieso/a **22**
miss *n., f* señorita **1**
miss (a person) *v.* extrañar; **miss (a flight)** perder (e➜ie); **miss (lacking)** faltar
mister señor **1**
misunderstanding *n., m* malentendido
modern *adj.* moderno/a **20**
mom *n., f* mamá **4**
moment *n., m* momento **28**
Monday *n., m* lunes **5**
money *n., m* dinero **11**
month *n., m* mes **13**
mop *v.* trapear

more *adj.* más **17**; **more... than** más... que **17**
morning *n., f* mañana **11**
mother *n., f* madre **4**
mother-in-law *n., f* suegra **4**
mountain *n., f* montaña
mountain climbing *n., m* alpinismo
mouth *n., f* boca **21**
move (change residence) *v.* mudarse **28**, cambiarse de casa; **move (objects)** mover (o➜ue)
movies *n., m* cine
mow (the lawn) *v.* cortar (el pasto) **18**
museum *n., m* museo **8**
music *n., f* música **1**
music, (to play loud music) *v.* poner la música muy alta **23**
must *v.* deber

N

name *n., m* nombre
narrow *adj.* estrecho/a
near *prep.* cerca (de)
necessary *adj.* necesario/a
neck *n., m* cuello **21**
need *v.* necesitar **5**
neighbor *n.* vecino/a **23**
neighborhood *n., f* colonia, *n., m* barrio
neither *conj.* tampoco **18**
nephew *n., m* sobrino **4**
nervous *adj.* nervioso/a **3**
never *adv.* nunca **8**
new *adj.* nuevo/a **6**
New Year *n., m* Año Nuevo
news *n., f* noticias
newspaper *n., m* periódico
next (to) *prep.* al lado; **next (close)** *adj.* próximo, cerca de; **next (following)** siguiente
nice *adj.* agradable **6**; **nice (friendly)** amable **6**; **nice to meet you** mucho gusto **1**
niece *n., f* sobrina **4**
night table *n., m* mesa de noche **18**
not even *adj.* ni siquiera
nobody *n.* nadie **18**
noon *n., m* mediodía
north *n., m* norte **26**
nose *n., f* nariz **21**
not any *adj.* ningún, ninguna **18**
notebook *n., m* cuaderno **2**
notes *n., m* apuntes
nothing *n.* nada **18**
notice *v.* notar
novel *n., f* novela
November *n., m* noviembre **13**
now *adv.* ahora **28**
nowhere *adv.* a ninguna parte **8**
number *n., m* número
nurse *n.* enfermero/a **12**

O

obedient *adj.* obediente
obey *v.* obedecer (yo obedezco) **22**
occupation *n., f* ocupación
October *n., m* octubre **13**
of course claro
offer *v.* ofrecer (yo ofrezco) **24**
office *n., f* oficina **2**
office supply store *n., f* papelería
often *adv.* con frecuencia
oil *n., m* aceite
old *adj.* viejo/a **6**
oldest *n.* (el/la) mayor **6**
only *adv.* solamente, sólo
only child *n.* hijo/a único/a **6**
open *v.* abrir **8**
optimistic *adj.* optimista **3**
orange (color) *adj.* anaranjado/a
   13; **orange (fruit)** *n., f* naranja **9**
organize *v.* organizar
origin *n., m* origen
outside *adv.* (a)fuera **15**
oven *n., m* horno **18**
oyster *n., m* ostión

P

pack *v.* hacer las maletas **20**
pain *n., m* dolor
paint *v.* pintar
painter *n.* pintor(a)
painting *n., f* pintura
pajamas *n., mf* pijama **13**
pants *n., m* pantalones **13**
paper *n., m* papel **2**
parakeet *n.* perico/a
parents *n., m* padres **4**
park *v.* estacionar(se) **26**
park ranger *n., mf* guardabosques
parking *n., m* estacionamiento **2**
part *n., f* parte
part-time *adj.* tiempo parcial **11**
party *n., f* fiesta
pass *v.* pasar **26**
paternal *adj.* paterno/a
patience *n., f* paciencia
patient *n., mf* paciente **3**
patio *n., m* patio **18**
pay *v.* pagar **11**; **pay attention**
   fijarse
peanut *n., m* maní, cacahuate
pear *n., f* pera **9**
pen *n., f* pluma **2**
pencil *n., m* lápiz **2**
people *n., f* gente
perform *v.* desempeñar
perhaps *adv.* tal vez, quizás
person *n., f* persona
personnel *n., m* personal
pessimistic *adj.* pesimista **3**
pet *n., f* mascota
pharmacist *n., mf* farmaceuta
philosophy *n., f* filosofía **1**

physical education *n., f* educación
   física **1**
pick up *v.* recoger (g→j) **18**
picture *n., f* fotografía
picture (painting) *n., m* cuadro
pill *n., f* pastilla **21**
pillow *n., f* almohada
pity *n., f* pena
place *n., m* lugar **11**
place *v.* poner (yo pongo) **11**
plan *n., m* plan
plan *v.* pensar + [*verb*]
plate *n., m* plato **9**
play (instrument) *v.* tocar **5**; **play**
   (sports, games) jugar (u→ue)
   10
player *n.* jugador(a)
please por favor
pocket *n., m* bolsillo
poem *n., m* poema
police force *n., f* policía **23**
police (officer) *n., mf* policía **12**
poor *adj.* pobre **6**
pork *n., m* cerdo **9**
position (job) *n., m* puesto **11**
possible *adj.* posible
post office *n., m* correo
potato *n., f* papa **9**
prefer *v.* preferir (e→ie) **10**
pregnancy *n., m* embarazo
present *n., m* regalo **11**
pretty *adj.* bonito/a **6**
price *n., m* precio
principal *n.* director(a)
prison guard *n., mf* oficial de
   prisión **12**
private *adj.* particular **22**
problem *n., m* problema **11**
profession *n., f* profesión
professor *n.* profesor(a) **1**
program *n., m* programa **28**
promise *v.* prometer **24**
propose (marriage) *v.* pedir la
   mano
protect *v.* proteger
Protestant *adj.* protestante
proud *adj.* orgulloso/a
psychologist *n.* sicólogo/a **12**
psychology *n., f* sicología **1**
public *adj.* público
public school *n.* escuela pública **22**
pull *v.* jalar, tirar, halar
punish *v.* castigar **22**
punishment *n., m* castigo
purple *adj.* morado/a **13**
purse *n., f* bolsa
pursue a master's degree hacer una
   maestría **28**
push *v.* empujar **25**
put *v.* poner (yo pongo) **11**; **put on**
   makeup pintarse **14**; **put on**
   (wear) ponerse **14**

Q

qualified *adj.* calificado/a
quick *adj.* rápido/a
quiet *adj.* tranquilo/a **3**
quit (a job) *v.* renunciar
quit (a habit, action) *v.* dejar de
quite *adv.* muy, bastante

R

radiator *n., m* radiador
rain *n., f* lluvia
rain *v.* llover (o→ue) **13**
raincoat *n., m* impermeable **13**
raw *adj.* crudo/a
react *v.* reaccionar
read *v.* leer **8**
ready *adj.* (estar) listo/a **15**
real estate *n., m* bienes raíces **12**
realize *v.* darse cuenta **25**
rebellious *adj.* rebelde **22**
receive *v.* recibir **8**
recipe *n., f* receta
recommend *v.* recomendar (e→
   ie) **27**
recovery *n., f* recuperación
red *adj.* rojo **13**
Red Cross *n., f* Cruz Roja
red-haired *adj.* pelirrojo/a
reef *n., m* arrecife
refrigerator *n., m* refrigerador **18**
refuse *v.* negarse (e→ie)
registration *n., f* inscripción
relatives *n., m* familiares, parientes
   4
remain *v.* quedarse
remedy *n., m* remedio
remember *v.* recordar (o→ue) **10**
rent *v.* alquilar
repair *v.* reparar, arreglar
reprimand *v.* regañar **22**
request *v.* solicitar **28**, pedir
requirement *n., m* requisito
reserved *adj.* reservado/a **3**
residence *n., f* residencia
respectful *adj.* respetuoso/a
responsible *adj.* responsable **3**
rest *v.* descansar; *n., m* descanso **5**
restaurant *n., m* restaurante **8**
résumé *n., m* currículum (vitae) **28**
return *v.* regresar, volver (o→ue)
   28; **return (merchandise)**
   devolver **27**
rice *n., m* arroz **9**
rich *adj.* rico/a **6**
ride (bikes) *v.* andar en bicicleta **18**
right *n., f* derecha **23**
ring (engagement) *n., m* anillo (de
   compromiso) **27**
rollerblade *v.* patinar en línea **18**
romantic *adj.* romántico/a **3**
room *n., m* cuarto, *n., f* habitación **5**
rope *n., f* cuerda **22**

routine *n., f* rutina
rude *adj.* grosero/a, maleducado/a 6
run *v.* correr 8; **run a red light** pasarse el alto/el semáforo en rojo 26

S

sad *adj.* triste 15
safety *n., f* seguridad
salad *n., f* ensalada 9
salary *n., m* sueldo 11
salesperson *n.* vendedor(a)
same *adj.* igual 21; mismo/a
sandals *n., f* sandalias 13
Saturday *n., m* sábado 5
save money *v.* ahorrar dinero 28
say good-bye *v.* despedirse (e→i)
scandalous *adj.* escandaloso/a
scare *n., m* susto
scared *adj.* asustado/a
scarf *n., f* bufanda 13
schedule *n., m* horario 11
scholarship *n., f* beca
school *n., f* escuela 8
scold *v.* regañar 22
scrambled *adj.* revuelto/a
scuba dive *v.* bucear 18
sculptor *n.* escultor(a)
seafood *n., m* mariscos 9
season *n., f* estación 13
seat belt *n., m* cinturón de seguridad 26
second *adj.* segundo/a 26
second *n., m* segundo
see *v.* mirar 5; **see you later** hasta luego 1; **see you tomorrow** hasta mañana 1
self propio
selfish *adj.* egoísta
sell *v.* vender 8
send *v.* mandar, enviar 11
sentimental *adj.* sentimental 3
separate *v.* separarse 28
September *n., m* septiembre 13
serious *adj.* serio/a 3
serve *v.* servir (e→i) 9
set the table *v.* poner la mesa 18
several *adj.* varios/as
sew *v.* coser
share *v.* compartir 22
shave *v.* afeitarse 23, rasurarse
shift (turn) *n., m* turno 11
shirt *n., f* camisa 13
shoe *n., m* zapato 13
short (length) *adj.* corto/a 13; **short (height)** bajo/a 6
shorts *n., m* pantalones cortos 13
show *v.* mostrar (o→ue)
shower *v.* bañarse, ducharse 14; **shower** *n., f* ducha 18
shrimp *n., m* camarón 9
shy *adj.* tímido/a 3

sick *adj.* enfermo/a 15
side *n., m* lado 23
sight *n., f* vista
sign *v.* firmar
signature *n., f* firma
silverware *n., m* cubierto
similar *adj.* similar 6
since *conj.* desde
sing *v.* cantar 20
single (unmarried) *adj.* soltero/a 6; **single room** *n., f* habitación sencilla
sister *n., f* hermana 4
sister-in-law *n., f* cuñada 4
sit *v.* sentarse (e→ie)
size *n., m* tamaño
skate *v.* patinar 18
ski *v.* esquiar 18
skirt *n., f* falda 13
sleep *v.* dormir (o→ue) 10
small *adj.* pequeño/a 6
smart *adj.* (ser) listo/a 6
snacks *n., f* tapas
snow *v.* nevar (e→ie) 13
so much tanto
so-so más o menos 1
so that para que 30
soccer *n., m* fútbol 8
sociable *adj.* sociable 3
soda *n., m* refresco 9
sofa *n., m* sofá 18
solve *v.* resolver (o→ue) 28
some *pron.* algún, alguna 18
somebody *n.* alguien 18
something *n.* algo 18
sometimes *adv.* a veces 8
son *n., m* hijo 4
son-in-law *n., m* yerno
song *n., f* canción
sore *adj.* adolorido/a 21
sorry (to apologize) perdón; **to be sorry** *v.* sentirlo
soup *n., f* sopa 9
south *n., m* sur 26
spaghetti *n., m* espagueti 9
Spanish *n., m* español 1; **Spanish** *adj.* español/a
spare (part) *n., m* repuesto, *n., f* refacción
spare time *n., m* tiempo libre 11
speak *v.* hablar 5
speed *v.* ir a exceso de velocidad 26
speed limit *n., f* velocidad máxima
spend *v.* gastar 19
spider *n., f* araña
spoil *v.* maleducar
spoiled *adj.* consentido/a 22
spoon *n., f* cuchara
sports *n., m* deportes
spring *n., f* primavera 13
stadium *n., m* estadio 2
stage *n., f* etapa
start *v.* empezar (e→ie) 10
start (a car) *v.* arrancar

stay *v.* quedarse 14
steak *n., m* bistec
stomach *n., m* estómago 21
stop *v.* pararse 26
stop (sign) *n., m* alto 26
store *n., f* tienda 8
story *n., f* historia, *n., m* cuento
stove *n., f* estufa 18
straight *adj.* derecho/a 26
strain *v.* colar (o→ue)
street *n., f* calle 26
street light *n., m* semáforo 25
strict *adj.* estricto/a
stroll *n., m* paseo
student *n., mf* estudiante 2; **student desk** *n., m* pupitre 2
studies *n., m* estudios
studious *adj.* estudioso/a 3
study *v.* estudiar 5
subject *n., f* materia
subway *n., m* metro
suddenly *adv.* de repente 25
suggest *v.* sugerir (e→ie)
suit *n., m* traje 13
suitcase *n., f* maleta 13
summer *n., m* verano 13
sun *n., m* sol
sun glasses *n., m* lentes de sol 13
Sunday *n., m* domingo 5
sunny, (it's) hace sol 13
support *v.* apoyar
suppose *v.* suponer (yo supongo)
surf *v.* surfear
surgeon *n.* cirujano/a
sweater *n., m* suéter 13
sweep *v.* barrer 18
sweet *n., f* dulce 9
swim *v.* nadar
swimming pool *n., f* piscina, alberca 2
swimming suit *n., m* traje de baño 13
system *n., m* sistema 12

T

T-shirt *n., f* camiseta 13
table *n., f* mesa 18
take *v.* tomar 5; **take (out)** sacar 18; **take a trip** hacer un viaje 18; **take care of** cuidar 11; **take care of (oneself)** cuidarse 21; **take care of clients** atender a los clientes 11; **take long** tardarse; **take off (clothes)** quitarse 14; **take out (walk) the dog** sacar al perro a pasear 18; **take someone somewhere** llevar 24
talk *v.* hablar 5
tall *adj.* alto/a 11
tank *n., m* tanque
tantrum *n., m* berrinche 22
tape *n., f* cinta
tea *n., m* té 9

teach *v.* enseñar 24
teacher *n.* maestro/a 12
　teaching (profession) *n., m*
　magisterio
team *n., m* equipo
teaspoon *n., f* cucharita
telephone *n., m* teléfono 5
tell *v.* decir (yo digo), contar 20
tennis (sport) *n., m* tenis 2; **tennis
　(sneakers)** tenis 13
tent *n., f* tienda de campaña
terrible *adj.* terrible 3
test *n., f* prueba 2
thank you *interj.* gracias 1
that *adj.* ese/a 6
theater *n., m* teatro
theme *n., m* tema
then *adv.* entonces
therapist *n., mf* terapeuta
there *adj.* ahí, allí, allá
there is/are hay
these *adj.* estos/as 6
thin *adj.* delgado/a 6
thing *n., f* cosa 2
think *v.* pensar (e→ie) 10
third *adj.* tercero/a
thirst *n., f* sed; **to be thirsty** tener
　sed
this (object) *adj.* este, esta 6
those *adj.* esos/as 6
thousand *n.* mil
throat *n., f* garganta 21
through *prep.* a través
throw *v.* aventar, tirar; **throw a
　party** hacer una fiesta 18; **throw
　tantrums** hacer berrinches 22
Thursday *n., m* jueves 5
ticket (plane) *n., m* boleto (de
　avión); **ticket (fine)** *n., f* multa 26
tidy *adj.* ordenado/a 18
tidy up *v.* arreglar
tie *n., f* corbata 13
tight *adj.* apretado/a
time *n., m* tiempo; *n., f* vez
time, (on) *adv.* a tiempo 5
tip *n., f* propina
tire *n., f* llanta 26, goma, *n., m*
　neumático
tired *adj.* cansado/a 15
title *n., m* título
toast *n., m* pan tostado 9
today *adv.* hoy
together *adj.* junto/a
tomato *n., m* tomate 18
tomorrow *n., m* mañana 22
tonight *adv.* esta noche
towel *n., f* toalla 18
toy *n., m* juguete 22
track *n., f* pista
traffic *n., m* tráfico
train *v.* entrenar; *n., m* tren
training *n., f* capacitación, *n., m*
　entrenamiento 28
translator *n.* traductor(a)
trash *n., f* basura 18

trash can *n., m* bote de basura
travel *v.* viajar
tree *n., m* árbol 20
trip *n., m* viaje 18
truck *n., m* camión
true (certain) *adj.* cierto
trust *n., f* confianza
truth *n., f* verdad
Tuesday *n., m* martes 5
tuna *n., m* atún 9
turkey *n., m* pavo 9
turn *v.* dar vuelta, doblar 25, virar
TV *n., f* televisión 2
type *v.* escribir a máquina

U

ugly *adj.* feo/a 6
umbrella *n., m* paraguas 13
unbearable *adj.* insoportable
uncle *n., m* tío 4
understand *v.* entender (e→ie) 10
understanding *n., f* comprensión
university *n., f* universidad
unless *conj.* a menos que 30
unpleasant *adj.* desagradable
until *conj.* hasta (que) 28
upset *adj.* molesto/a 15, enojado/a
use *v.* usar 5

V

vacation *n., f* vacaciones 11; **on
　vacation** de vacaciones 13
vacuum *v.* pasar la aspiradora 18
vacuum cleaner *n., f* aspiradora
VCR *n., f* videocasetera 2
vegetable *n., f* verdura 9
very *adv.* muy
very well *adv.* muy bien 1
veterinarian *n.* veterinario/a 12
violin *n., m* violín
visit *v.* visitar 5
volleyball *n., m* vóleibol 2

W

wager *n., f* apuesta
wait *v.* esperar 27
waiter *n., m* mesero, camarero 9
waitress *n., f* mesera, camarera 9
wall *n., f* pared
wallet *n., f* billetera, cartera
want *v.* querer (e→ie) 27
war *n., f* guerra
wash *v.* lavar 5; **wash (oneself)**
　lavarse 14; **wash one's hands**
　lavarse las manos 14
watch *v.* ver (yo veo) 8
watch *n., m* reloj 2
water *n., f* (el) agua 9
water ski *n., m* esquí acuático
watercolor *n., f* acuarela

way *n., m* camino
way *n., f* manera
wear *v.* ponerse (yo me pongo) 14;
　wear a costume disfrazarse 20
weather *n., m* clima; **the weather is
　nice/bad** hace buen/mal tiempo
　13
Wednesday *n., m* miércoles 5
week *n., f* semana 15
weekdays, (on) *adv.* entre semana 5
weekend *n., m* fin de semana 5
weight *n., m* peso
well *adv.* bien 1
west *n., m* oeste 26
what *pron.* qué 6
when *adv.* cuándo 6
when *conj.* cuando 30
where *adv.* dónde 6
which *adv.* cuál 6
while *conj.* mientras
white *adj.* blanco/a 13
who *pron.* quién 6
why *adv.* por qué 6
wife *n., f* esposa 4
win *v.* ganar 12
wind *n., m* viento
windy, (it's) *n.* hace viento 13
window *n., f* ventana 2
windshield *n., m* parabrisas
wine *n., m* vino 9
winter *n., m* invierno 13
wish *v.* desear; *n., m* deseo
witch *n., f* bruja
with *prep.* con; **with me** conmigo;
　with you contigo
without *prep.* sin 26
woman *n., f* mujer
word *n., f* palabra
work *v.* trabajar 5
work (job) *n., m* trabajo 8
worried *adj.* preocupado/a 15
worse than *adj.* peor que 17
wound *n., f* herida
write *v.* escribir 8
writer *n.* escritor(a)

Y

year *n., m* año
yellow *adj.* amarillo 13
yesterday *adv.* ayer 15
yet *adv.* todavía 28
yogurt *n., m* yogur 9
young man/woman *n., mf* joven 6
young person *n.* chico/a 4
younger *adj.* menor 6
youngest *n.* (el/la) menor 6
yucca *n., f* yuca

Z

zero *n., m* cero
zip code *n., m* código postal
zoo *n., m* zoológico

Each entry is followed by a citation, **(1)** or **(2)**. All entries followed by a **(1)** are found on the corresponding page in **INVITACIONES: Primera parte**; entries followed by a **(2)** are found on the page noted in **INVITACIONES: Segunda parte**.

Photo Credits: Primera parte

Corbis Images: 2 (tr) © Graham Neden, (bl) © James Marshall, (br) © Darrell Jones. **3** (tl) © Pablo Corral V, (tr) © Francesco Venturi. **15** © Morton Beebe. **48** © Tony Arruza. **66** © Tizziana and Gianni Baldizzone. **119** © Buddy Mays. **142** © Shaul Schwarz. **193** © Nik Wheeler. **216** (l) © Miki Kratsman, (r) © Owen Franken. **239** © Hans Georg Roth. **273** © Wolfgang Kaehler. **320** © Amos Nachoum. **354** © Nik Wheeler. **367** (l) © Michael Freeman. **383** © Doug Wilson. **391** © Rob Lewine. **396** (b) © Reuters NewMedia Inc./Rafael Perez.

CyberSpain: 3 (bl) permission to reproduce J. Carballo.

Randy Krauss: 3 (br)

Latin Focus: 151 © Jimmy Dorantes. **152** © Jimmy Dorantes.

Courtesy Mabis Robledo: 2 (tl)

Photo Credits: Segunda parte

Art Explosion: 330

Cantomedia: 251 © Frank Cantor 2003.

Alex Cauldwell: 127

Corbis Images: 20 © Jacques Pavlovsky. **49** (l) © Charles & Josette Lenars, (r) © Jeremy Horner. **50** © Barnabas Bosshart. **78** (tl) © Adam Woolfitt, (tr) © Paul Hardy, (b) Tony Savino. **104** © Tom Bean. **128** © Jeremy Horner. **145** © Bettmann. **154** © Macduff Everton. **173** © Reuters NewMedia Inc./Andrees Latif. **207** © Tom Brakefield. **230** © Joyce Naltchayan. **232** © Charles & Josette Lenars. **278** © Dave G. Houser. **308** © AFP/Daniel Garcia. **359** © Pablo Corral. **359** © Jeremy Horner. **372** (l) © Brooks Kraft, (m) © Bill Gentile, (r) © Reuters NewMedia Inc./Enrique Shore.

Randy Krauss: 49 (m). **335**

Lucky S. R. L.: 375 Gunter Dittmar.

Courtesy Mabis Robledo: 11

Margorie Stitson: 150

Text and Realia Credits: Primera parte

Pages 6 and 37: "*Catálogo de carreras*" adapted and reprinted with permission from Único – Universidad de la Comunidad, Universidad Autónoma de Guadalajara.
Page 307: "Premio escolar espíritu de superación." Adapted and reprinted with permission from Zubi Advertising.
Page 83: "¡Vivir bien con poca grasa!" ad adapted and reprinted with permission from Rodale Press International.
Page 223: "Estancia Santa Gertrudis." Ad adapted and reprinted with permission from Darío Saráchaga.
Page 316: "The Ultimate Oversees Career," 1997. Translated and adapted with permission from *Hispanic Magazine*.
Page 332: "Instituto Forrester." Ad adapted and reprinted with permission from Instituto Forrester, S.A.

Text and Realia Credits: Segunda parte

Page 495 "Grandes mujeres humildes," 1998. Reprinted with permission from *Revista La Pandilla*.

About the Authors

Deana Alonso-Lyrintzis was born and raised in Mexico City. After graduating from High School and studying for a year at the *Universidad Nacional Autónoma de México* (UNAM) her family moved to the United States. She earned a Bachelor of Arts Degree in Mathematics and a Master's Degree in Spanish from San Diego State University. She also holds a Master's Degree in Teaching English to Speakers of Other Languages from California State University, Los Angeles. She served for four years as consultant and teacher leader at the Los Angeles Area Site of the California Foreign Language Project. In addition, Deana co-authored several texts for McGraw-Hill, Prentice Hall and National Textbook Company. She taught Spanish for five years at Citrus College and she is presently a Professor of Spanish at Southwestern College. She has traveled extensively throughout Europe and Latin America.

Esther Alonso was born and raised in Mexico City. After graduating from High School and studying for two years at the *Universidad Internacional de Turismo,* her family moved to the United States. She earned a Bachelor's Degree in Linguistics and a Master's Degree in Spanish and English Sociolinguistics from San Diego State University. Esther was a consultant and teacher leader for the Los Angeles Area Site of the California Foreign Language Project for a year. She has published her research on language assessment in professional journals. She taught Spanish for five years at California State University, San Marcos where she currently is the Language Proficiency Assessor. She is presently an Associate Professor of Spanish at Southwestern College. She has traveled extensively through Europe and Latin America.

Brandon Zaslow was born and educated in the United States. He holds graduate degrees in Spanish and Education from the University of California, Los Angeles, where he was a University Distinguished Scholar and from California State University, Los Angeles. From 1990 to 1995, he held a teaching position in UCLA's Graduate School of Education where he taught Methods of Foreign Language Instruction and Primary and English Language Development. Since 1995, he serves as Director of the Los Angeles Area Site of the California Foreign Language Project, which is funded by the legislature through the Office of the President of the University of California to improve K–16 foreign, second and heritage language programs. In addition to serving on a team that authored a program for heritage speakers of Spanish, Brandon worked to develop California's Classroom Oral Competency Interview (COCI), Classroom Writing Competency Assessment (CWCA), and Classroom Receptive Competency Matrix (CRCM) and was contributor and consultant to the 2001 Foreign Language Framework for California Public Schools. Recently, Brandon was honored by his colleagues being named California Language Teacher of the Year.